The Social Amplification c

The management of and communication about risks has become a major question of public policy and intellectual debate in the modern world. The social amplification of risk framework describes how both social and individual factors act to amplify or dampen perceptions of risk and through this create secondary effects such as stigmatization of technologies, economic losses, or regulatory impacts. This volume, edited by three of the world's leading analysts of risk and its communication, brings together contributions from a group of international experts working in the field of risk perception and risk communication. Key conceptual issues are discussed as well as a range of recent case studies (spanning BSE and food safety, AIDS/HIV, nuclear power, child protection, Y2K, electromagnetic fields, and waste incineration) that take forward the state-of-the-art in risk amplification theory. The volume also draws attention to lessons for public policy, risk management, and risk communication practice.

Nick Pidgeon is Professor of Environmental Sciences at the University of East Anglia, and Director of the Centre for Environmental Risk. He has written extensively on risk communication and perception issues, including a major contribution to the UK Royal Society Report on Risk (1992), as well as on causes of organizational accidents. He is the author of *Man-Made Disasters* (with B. A. Turner, 1997).

Roger E. Kasperson is Director of the Stockholm Environment Institute. He has been one of the leading geographers in the field of risk and risk communication for the last thirty years. His publications include *Global Environmental Risks* (with J. X. Kasperson, 2001), *Communicating Risks to the Public* (with J. Stallen, 1991), *Nuclear Risk Analysis in Comparative Perspective* (1987), *Acceptable Evidence: Science and Values in Hazard Management* (with J. X. Kasperson, 1991), and *Regions at Risk* (with J. X. Kasperson and B. L. Turner, 1995).

Paul Slovic is President of Decision Research and Professor of Psychology at the University of Oregon. He has been one of the leading psychologists in the field of risk perception and behavioral decision making for the past thirty years. His publications include *Acceptable Risk* (with B. Fischhoff, S. Lichtenstein, R. Keeney, and P. Derby, Cambridge, 1981), *Judgement Under Uncertainty* (with D. Kahneman and A. Tversky, Cambridge, 1982), *The Perception of Risk* (2000), and *Risk, Media and Stigma* (with J. Flynn and H. Kunreuther 2001).

The Social Amplification of Risk

Edited by

Nick Pidgeon
University of East Anglia

Roger E. Kasperson
Stockholm Environment Institute

and

Paul Slovic
Decision Research and University of Oregon

CAMBRIDGE
UNIVERSITY PRESS

PUBLISHED BY THE PRESS SYNDICATE OF THE UNIVERSITY OF CAMBRIDGE
The Pitt Building, Trumpington Street, Cambridge CB2 1RP, United Kingdom

CAMBRIDGE UNIVERSITY PRESS
The Edinburgh Building, Cambridge, CB2 2RU, UK
40 West 20th Street, New York, NY 10011–4211, USA
477 Williamstown Road, Port Melbourne, VIC 3207, Australia
Ruiz de Alarcón 13, 28014 Madrid, Spain
Dock House, The Waterfront, Cape Town 8001, South Africa

http://www.cambridge.org

First published 2003

Printed in the United Kingdom at the University Press, Cambridge

Typeface Plantin 10/12 pt.   *System* LATEX 2_ε [TB]

A catalogue record for this book is available from the British Library

ISBN 0 521 81728 5 hardback
ISBN 0 521 52044 4 paperback

Dedicated to the memory of Jeanne X. Kasperson

Contents

Part V Policy and management

Figures

Tables

Contributors

JULIE BARNETT Department of Psychology, University of Surrey, Guildford, UK

GLYNIS M. BREAKWELL University of Bath, Bath, UK

MARTIN CLAUBERG Research Centre Jülich, Germany

JOHN ELDRIDGE Department of Sociology, University of Glasgow, Glasgow, UK

JAMES FLYNN Decision Research, Eugene, Oregon, USA

WILLIAM R. FREUDENBURG Environmental Studies Program, University of California-Santa Barbara, Santa Barbara, USA

LYNN J. FREWER Department of Marketing and Consumer Behavior, University of Wageningen, The Netherlands

M. V. RAJEEV GOWDA Economics and Social Sciences, Indian Institute of Management – Bangalore, Bangalore, India

TOM HORLICK-JONES School of Social Sciences, University of Wales Cardiff, Cardiff, UK

JEANNE X. KASPERSON Stockholm Environment Institute, Stockholm, Sweden

ROGER E. KASPERSON Stockholm Environment Institute, Stockholm, Sweden

WILLIAM LEISS Faculty of Management, University of Calgary, Calgary, Canada

DONALD G. MACGREGOR Decision Research, Eugene, Oregon, USA

CLAIRE MAYS Institut Symlog, Cachan, France

GRAHAM MURDOCK Department of Social Sciences, Loughborough University, Loughborough, UK

JUDITH PETTS   School of Geography and Environmental Sciences, The University of Birmingham, Birmingham, UK

NICK PIDGEON   School of Environmental Sciences, University of East Anglia, Norwich, UK

MARC POUMADÈRE   Ecole Normale Supérieure, Cachan, France

JACQUIE REILLY   Department of Sociology, University of Glasgow, Glasgow, UK

ORTWIN RENN   Center of Technology Assessment, Stuttgart, Germany

EUGENE A. ROSA   Department of Sociology, Washington State University, Pullman, Washington, USA

HOLGER SCHÜTZ   Research Centre Jülich, Germany

JONATHAN SIME   University of Utah, Salt Lake City, Utah, USA, and Jonathan Sime Associates, Godalming, UK

PAUL SLOVIC   Decision Research and University of Oregon, Eugene, Oregon, USA

ARVIND SUSARLA   School of Geography, Clark University, Worcester, Massachusetts, USA

PETER M. WIEDEMANN   Research Centre Jülich, Germany

Acknowledgments

This book and the work it describes are part of a set of research projects funded by the United Kingdom Cabinet Office, Civil Aviation Authority, Economic and Social Research Council, Environment Agency, Food Standards Agency, Department of Health, Health and Safety Executive and the Health and Safety Executive for Northern Ireland. The editors wish to thank the programme steering committee, drawn from various of these sponsoring Departments, and in particular Jean Le Guen and David Rickwood of HSE's Risk Policy Unit, for their consistent help and encouragement throughout the project. We would also like to thank the staff of the St. Catharine's Foundation at Cumberland Lodge for generating such an unique workshop environment, and Dr. Jörg Niewöhner for assisting during the workshop. Above all, the book project would not have been completed without the considerable efforts of Sarah Pearce and Aleks Lopata, who expertly brought the whole manuscript up to a publishable standard, and of Natalia Jones who consolidated the bibliography. We also thank Faye Auty, Nicola Baker, Susan Beer, Peter Bennett, Colleen Bowen, Sarah Caro, David Coles, Gillian Dadd, Neil de Cort, Claire Marris, Jim McQuaid, Adrian Sayce, Peter Simmons, Caroline Tahourdin, Claire Twigger-Ross, and Brian Wynne. The final stages of editing were supported in part by the Leverhulme Trust through the programme grant on Understanding Risk to the University of East Anglia. Individual contributors' acknowledgments appear as footnotes at the beginning of the chapters. Of course, the opinions in this book remain those of the authors alone, and do not represent the views of any government department.

Introduction

Nick Pidgeon, Roger E. Kasperson, and Paul Slovic

The past twenty-five years have seen considerable social science research on the risks of technologies and economic activities, and an even lengthier legacy of studies on natural hazards. This work has generated a substantial knowledge base from which to interpret such issues as the sources and causes of changing risks and the ways in which various groups and different societies assess, view, and cope with those risks. In particular, risk perception researchers have investigated in depth how judgments about perceived risks and their acceptability arise, and how such judgments are related to risk "heuristics" (e.g. the memorability, representativeness, and affective qualities of risk events) and the qualitative characteristics of risk (e.g. voluntariness or catastrophic potential). Patterns of risk perception have also been found to relate to both group and cultural affiliations. Meanwhile, dramatic events such as the Chernobyl disaster, the BSE ("mad cow") and the genetically modified crops controversies in Europe, the September 11th attacks in the United States, and the prospect of global climate change have driven home to responsible authorities and corporate managers the extensive intertwining of technical risk with social considerations and processes. As Kai Erikson (1994) succinctly puts it, modern disasters present us with a "new species of trouble."

These events and the growing knowledge base are changing the ways in which societies assess, respond to, and communicate about risks. In the United Kingdom in the early 1990s, the Royal Society Study Group on Risk had as a specific mandate the task of bridging the gap between scientific knowledge and "the way in which public opinion gauges risk and makes decisions" (Royal Society 1992, p. 1). More recently in the United States, the National Research Council, in a dramatic break with its earlier "red book" on risk assessment and management (National Research Council 1983), reconceived risk analysis and characterization as an "analytic and deliberative process," whose task is "to describe a potentially hazardous situation in as accurate, thorough, and decision relevant a manner as possible, addressing the significant concerns of the interested and affected parties, and to make this information understandable and accessible to public officials and the parties" (Stern and Fineberg 1996, p. 2). The United Kingdom Interdepartmental Liaison Group on Risk Assessment (1998a; see also United Kingdom Cabinet Office, 2002) similarly called for major revisions and significant broadening in the conduct of risk assessment, with greater attention to social issues, risk communication, and public involvement. In short, the institutional climate is changing substantially, enlarging the prospect of broad-based social research on risk attracting more interested users and greater institutional embrace.

But social research on risk, despite substantial progress, is still quite handicapped in seizing the opportunity. In theoretical terms, the risk perception and risk communication literatures remain seriously fragmented: between the psychometric paradigm and cultural theories of risk perception; between postmodernist and discourse-centered approaches and behavioral studies of risk; between economic/utility-maximization and economic-justice approaches; and between communications and empowerment strategies for risk communication. Meanwhile, a professional and cultural divide continues to separate the natural-hazards and risk-analysis schools of inquiry, despite the obvious and considerable convergence of interests. Clearly, a more comprehensive and systematic understanding of the social experiences of risk is crying out for overarching, integrative approaches.

To this end, researchers from Clark University (Kasperson, Kasperson, Renn, and colleagues) and Decision Research (Slovic and colleagues) created the social amplification of risk framework (SARF) in 1988. The framework (outlined in detail in Kasperson et al. this volume chapter 1) aims to examine broadly, and in social and historical context, how risk and risk events interact with psychological, social, institutional, and cultural processes in ways that amplify or attenuate risk perceptions and concerns, and thereby shape risk behavior, influence institutional processes, and affect risk consequences.

The present book aims to evaluate the current state of our knowledge about amplification theory and processes, illustrated through a wide range of contemporary case studies and examples. We wish also to examine where the amplification framework holds important lessons for contemporary risk policy and risk communication practice. The germ for such a project started when over thirty academics and policy makers, drawn primarily from North America and Europe, met to debate these issues in September 1999 in the delightful setting of the St. Catharine's Foundation conference centre, Cumberland Lodge, in the Windsor Great Park, England. Participants at the workshop included both the originators of the framework and other leading international researchers of risk perception and communication issues. We were fortunate in gaining sponsorship for this workshop from a group of United Kingdom Government Departments (under the auspices of ILGRA and the United Kingdom Health and Safety Executive). Written papers were prepared by authors in advance of the workshop, stimulating an extensive set of debates. Following the Cumberland Lodge workshop all of the papers were subject to peer review, and revised (in most cases substantially) on the basis of the reviews and workshop discussions.

The book itself is organized into five thematic parts, although most chapters inevitably touch upon several of the themes (for example, all of the authors were asked wherever possible to conclude their contributions with lessons learned for risk communication and policy). Part I addresses the Conceptual Foundations of the social amplification framework (SARF), and in chapter 1, Jeanne and Roger Kasperson, together with Nick Pidgeon and Paul Slovic, describe the basic framework, at the same time reviewing fifteen years of research. They include the empirical record and its relation to the domains of communication and the media, stigma and effects, trust in institutions, and organizational risk processing. The authors also debate a number of the critiques of SARF which have been advanced over the past fifteen years. In chapter 2, Eugene Rosa critically evaluates the key philosophical foundation of SARF – the ontological status of risk. Steering a course between social constructivist and realist representations, Rosa develops the framework in relation to sociologist Luhmann's distinction between risk and danger, and to lay ontologies of hazards. Glynis Breakwell and Julie Barnett in chapter 3 draw upon the observation that amplification and attenuation processes are complex dynamic social phenomena which almost always involve several levels (or layers) of social process, and accordingly of potential evidence. They describe a new approach – the layering method – that can be used to further develop and test the empirical claims of SARF, and hence to increase the predictive power of models designed to understand risk amplification. Its use is illustrated with data collected in relation to BSE and AIDS/HIV. Finally, in chapter 4, William Freudenburg turns attention to the important question of organizational processing of risk issues. He argues that extending the social amplification framework to incorporate organizational issues will require greater attention to be given to two issues. First, the ways in which "real risks" are created, amplified and/or dampened by the very persons and organizations that are expected to control or manage them. These "human" and "organizational factors" can be important or even dominant contributors to the overall risks from complex sociotechnical systems. Second, the issue of understanding what kinds of risks are most and least likely to receive intensified attention from the mass media and the broader public. His suggestion is that intensified attention is likely in cases where an incident suggests the potential presence of organizational *recreancy*, or institutional failure.

From a policy perspective, the conceptual chapters in part I illustrate the point (which also recurs in other parts of the book) that SARF does not itself address the basic political, sociological, or psychological processes which might underlie amplification or attenuation of risk signals and perceptions in any *specific* context. What is needed is an understanding of which other theoretical models might then be used in conjunction with SARF, such that conceptual explication and specific predictions can be advanced. For risk communication policy this implies, above all, a need to explore the context (and the history) of events, trying to understand the key actors or issues (media, historical stigma, trans-national politics, blame and mis-management, interest group behaviors, legislative or political cultures etc.) *in the particular case at hand*. The appropriate social science models can then be drawn upon to guide understanding of that case.

Following on from the above, the links between risk controversies and the prior behavior of agencies and risk managers is a key policy theme. As Freudenburg (chapter 4) notes, rather than responding to the substance of citizen concerns, policy makers of the past have sometimes employed "diversionary reframing" – attempts to divert attention *away* from citizens' real concerns by "reframing" the debate as being "about" something else, and that such efforts have often failed to counteract credibility problems, often backfiring. For the future, according to Freudenburg, there would appear to be significant potential benefit in exploring an entirely different approach – not of trying to divert policy attention *away* from citizen concerns, but instead taking them seriously as one part of the risk assessment and management process. Not only have a growing number of analysts come to focus on the problems associated with what Barry Turner (1978) originally called "organizational exclusivity," or the "disregard of non-members," but some have also come to suggest that increased "institutional permeability" may deserve much greater attention as an antidote to the blind-spots created or reinforced by such forms of insularity. Agencies in particular might do well to examine their *own* recent history, roles, assumptions, and frames of reference for understanding risk, and the extent to which risk management will fail if critical assumptions are subsequently proved wrong.

In part II of the book we turn to the important issue of Risk Signals and the Mass Media. Media analysis provides an important route for empirical tests of the core idea that important social sites exist, of which the media are but one, where messages about risk are constructed, communicated, and transformed. In chapter 5, Lynn Frewer introduces social psychological theory on trust and attitudes, which might prove fruitful in understanding how the dynamics of attitude change and media reporting of risk issues are related. She illustrates her argument with data on media coverage and public attitudes in Europe in relation to Chernobyl and, ten years later, the BSE crisis. In chapter 6, John Eldridge and Jacquie Reilly draw upon an extensive sociological programme of research, conducted by the Glasgow Media Group over the past ten years, looking at media, risk discourses, and political responses to the BSE crisis. On the basis of this case study they question whether a generalized notion of "climate of risk," as advanced by social theorists Giddens (1991) and Beck (1995b) amongst others, can fully explain the complex relationship that exists between scientific experts, policy makers, and the media. They conclude that SARF does indeed help to describe certain aspects of the dynamics of the BSE affair, but that further development of the framework, in particular stressing conceptual issues drawn from symbolic interaction theory (Blumer 1969), might prove fruitful. Related conceptual arguments are advanced by Graham Murdock, Judith Petts, and Tom Horlick-Jones in chapter 7. Their chapter presents results from empirical work in the United Kingdom across a range of risk issues, noting also that media analysis for risk research purposes might usefully draw upon the wealth of existing experience and theorizing in the area of mainstream media studies. They highlight the very different risk representations adopted by the national press in the United Kingdom (e.g. tabloid vs. broadsheet newspapers), as well as the balance between mediated and lay understandings in public perceptions of these issues. Drawing upon Pierre Bourdieu's work (e.g. 1998) on "fields of action" they argue that the media are both highly differentiated in their reporting of risk, and a key political site for the social framing of such issues. In chapter 8, Arvind Susarla addresses the concept of blame – previously identified as an important contribution to risk controversy and amplification processes (Burns et al. 1993). In a comparative study, he investigates blame signals in the local press reporting of two risk events in India, one of which was ultimately highly amplified (discovery of bacterium *Yersinia Pestis* in the city of Surat) and the other attenuated (arsenic contamination in West Bengal). Susarla finds different, and complex, patterns of blaming adopted in the two cases.

Issues of trust and blame are likely to be the key to both amplification and attenuation effects. However, in keeping with other recent commentators on this issue we conclude here that trust is not a simple "uni-dimensional" construct that can be simply "lost" or "replaced." Like amplification effects themselves, trust is a highly contextual, multi-dimensional concept – involving such things as knowledge/ expertise, implied public duty, a match between stated roles and corporate "body language," independence of a risk regulator, and the ability or resources to act upon intentions. A lesson then from a number of the chapters is that risk managers should *not* take a naive view of "trust." Hence, Murdock et al. stress the need for a design-based approach to risk communication, incorporating, presumably, attention to structural factors which might be influential on trust.

Part III presents a range of case studies involving Public Perceptions and Social Controversy. In chapter 9, Marc Poumadère and Claire Mays recount their research into an intriguing set of events during 1995–96 in the small town of Moirans, in the Jura Mountains of France. More than a dozen "spontaneous" house fires occurred here, with two deaths. As the cause remained unknown, media, politicians, and a range of local and national technical experts became increasingly involved in the search for the origin of the fires (with one hypothesis focusing upon underground electricity cables). The events, whose cause was finally tracked down to an arsonist, are analyzed theoretically using the social amplification framework, with focus upon the complex social and institutional dynamics surrounding the case. In an extension to the basic framework Poumadère and Mays suggest that risk discourse processes can themselves feed the dynamic construction of new signals about "risk events". Chapter 10 by Donald MacGregor reports data from his empirical study of public perception of responses to Y2K in North America during 1999. He argues that many of the manifest hazards created by Y2K arose from behaviors individuals adopted as part of risk *mitigation* (e.g. carrying large amounts of cash increasing crime risks). Thus the Y2K phenomenon (and its risks) may, in large part, have been a self-fulfilling prophecy exacerbated by social amplification processes. MacGregor also addresses possible reasons for the different public response to Y2K in the United States, in comparison to that in Europe. In chapter 11, Tom Horlick-Jones, Jonathan Sime, and Nick Pidgeon draw upon the tradition of qualitative risk research, investigating the underlying sensemaking activities entailed in communities living close to major sites of industrial activity. The analysis examines how the interaction of "local" experiences, politics, and symbolic linkages raises key conceptual issues for the original social amplification framework. In particular, "audiences" are not merely passive receivers of risk information, but have the capacity and inclination to engage actively in interrogation of risk communications and other related risk information.

In chapter 12, Peter Wiedemann, Martin Clauberg, and Holger Schütz develop a typology of lay narratives (or "risk stories") which might be implicated in the process of intensification of risk perceptions. Drawing upon the case of electromagnetic fields they describe the different ways in which "expert" and "lay" people might appraise such risks. As pointed out by Fischhoff (1995) risk communication efforts have often foundered on the misplaced ideal that "all we need to do is tell people the numbers." While an understandable view, as seen from the perspective of technical risk assessment, it misses the fundamental point about risk perceptions derived from decades of research – that anxieties, fears, and responses are sometimes based upon factors other than "objective" risk itself. Accordingly, the work of both Murdock et al. (chapter 7) and Wiedemann et al. (chapter 12) moves us in an important new direction. The former by asking what risk "narratives" are used in the media, and the latter by analyzing how the incompatibility of expert and lay narratives of risk might lead to amplification effects. Narrative (a coherent "story") can be a very powerful means of framing risk messages. The issue of using narrative for risk communication seems a fruitful area for further development in relation to social amplification of risk.

An important proposition of the social amplification framework was that amplification or attenuation of perceptions might feed into secondary "ripple" economic, social, or symbolic (e.g. stigma) consequences. Pidgeon (1997) has noted that it is often very difficult to obtain clear empirical evidence of the links between stage I processes of SARF (signal transformation and risk perception) and stage II effects (behavioral, economic, and symbolic impacts). In part IV we consider Ripple and Stigma Effects in greater detail. Chapter 13, by M. V. Rajeev Gowda, builds upon SARF to explain the proliferation in the USA of community "right-to-know" legislation in relation to the release of former sex-offenders (so-called "Megan's Laws"), contrasting this also with similar pressures in the United Kingdom. The analysis draws upon Kingdon's (1984) agenda-setting model to discuss the critical role played by the availability of viable policy solutions in the political stream (demonstrating, once more, how stepping out of the traditional risk communications and perception domain can productively build upon the framework which SARF provides). In the United States right-to-know is politically hard to oppose because it is supposed to empower people's risk management efforts, and seems innocuous in terms of its potential impacts and administrative burden. Gowda analyzes the unintended social consequences (e.g. uncontrolled vigilante action) of such laws in terms of secondary amplification "ripple" effects. By contrast the contemporary word "risk" applies to nuclear power first and foremost, and many early studies of risk perceptions were focused upon public concerns about this issue. Chapter 14 by James Flynn uses SARF to chart the historical and contextual reasons for the gradual stigmatization in the United States of nuclear weapon and energy technologies. Past organizational failures and undue secrecy, only now coming to light, are seen as crucial contextual drivers of such stigmatization. The fact that organizations themselves are a risk factor is almost never examined in formal risk assessments, and this chapter (also Freudenburg chapter 4) argues that they should be. More generally, as our knowledge of such "secondary" consequences increases, it becomes feasible that risk assessments for new technologies might explicitly incorporate them as a legitimate part of the consequence analysis during risk assessment.

In part V we conclude with two chapters which explicitly address social amplification in the context of Risk Policy and Management (although, as noted above, policy is a theme that weaves through all of the contributions to this book). Chapter 15, by William Leiss, asks whether SARF can help government agencies better meet their responsibilities. Public sector bodies with risk management responsibilities are ideal test beds for exploring the potential practical efficiency of the risk amplification concept, because they must take responsibility for both doing risk assessments and "responsible risk issue management." Responsible risk issue management is seen as primarily an exercise in good risk communication practice: specifically taking responsibility for the creation and maintenance of a "fair risk dialogue." Using wireless telecommunications as a case example, Leiss develops the possibilities of improved managerial competence. Inviting the public to be a part of the decision making process in risk analysis and its management has, of course, been a major recent objective in European and North American risk policy arenas. As a consequence, deliberative and participatory mechanisms have become increasingly important in the risk communication arena, and look set to be so for the foreseeable future. They can be seen as vehicles for appropriate two-way risk communication between policy makers and public, as discursive devices that empower communities, or sometimes as both (Pidgeon, Hood, Jones et al. 1992). However, the current popularity of such concepts obscures the challenge of how to put these worthwhile objectives into practice. Ortwin Renn addresses this considerable challenge in chapter 16. He reports work drawn from the extensive experience of the Center of Technology Assessment at Baden-Württemburg in participatory processes in Germany. In particular, Renn argues that people can experience both amplification and attenuation of risk perceptions in participatory settings. His argument draws upon material from two case studies: first, that of solid waste incinerator siting, and second of noise reduction. Renn draws the important inference that risk amplification and attenuation can be made a *deliberate* subject of discursive activities within participatory risk management procedures. Such discourse helps people to realize that it is normal, but also detrimental to prudent judgment, if one selects and transmits only those pieces of information that one likes, if one amplifies signals that support one's own view and attenuates those that do not. This holds out hope that greater understanding (if not necessarily consensus over) competing positions can be arrived at in conflicted risk debates.

Reflecting on the chapters as a whole, a range of broader issues can be discerned. A critique of the original 1988 formulation of SARF was of its rather static conception of communication. Unfortunately, as Horlick-Jones, Sime, and Pidgeon (chapter 11) point out, it is precisely those aspects of SARF that seem most problematic from an academic perspective which make the framework attractive to policy makers! However, in our view the work represented in this book *does* begin to demonstrate that the framework – used in a nuanced way – can help us to understand some of the complexities, constructedness, and messiness of real world risk communication contexts, and in this way both aid policy makers as well as map out a future research agenda.

To illustrate just some of the complexities, for policy makers one desired goal might be some form of simple *screening device* against which emerging or nascent risk issues can be evaluated. In discussing this Leiss raises the normative status of amplification effects, and points out that while clear-cut examples of good and bad attenuation and amplification can always be cited, in reality risk regulators are often faced with a basket of issues which are far less clear cut; that is they fall into a "holding" category where the implications of the issue are ambiguous or uncertain. Similarly, the contextually embedded nature of risk controversies, and *simultaneous* layering of amplification and attenuation effects across different stakeholders or publics in society (e.g. chapters by Breakwell and Barnett; Poumadère and Mays; Renn) makes screening for any particular "effect" more problematic. However, the chapters in this book illustrate that we probably *do* know enough about the key drivers, of risk intensification at least, to begin to map out research to develop such screening devices for policy.

The chapters probably say less about the cross-cultural transferability of SARF (originally developed primarily in the North American social context), than we would have liked. Some of the authors (e.g. Gowda's work on Megan's Laws; MacGregor's on Y2K) do touch upon interesting United States / Europe contrasts, and the possible reasons for this. Other chapters (Susarla; Poumadère and Mays; Renn) document amplification effects in rather different cultural contexts from that of North America. However, well-founded cross-cultural analysis would ideally require detailed *comparative* empirical work, which we do not currently have. On the other hand, detailed case studies (e.g. Poumadère and Mays; Flynn) can be used to highlight specific cultural issues which might be driving issues in specific contexts. Ultimately, the existence of such differences is an empirical question, and this cautions against simple transfer of findings (on perception of a new technology, say) from one cultural context to another without at least some such empirical work of one form or another.

Taken as a whole we do believe that the chapters in this book represent a significant step forward in our knowledge and thinking about the social amplification of risk framework, as well as its relationship to risk policy and risk communication practice. As editors we are deeply indebted to each of the individual authors and reviewers for helping us to achieve this goal.

Part I

Conceptual foundations

1 The social amplification of risk: assessing fifteen years of research and theory

Jeanne X. Kasperson, Roger E. Kasperson, Nick Pidgeon, and Paul Slovic

The social amplification of risk framework in brief

More than a decade has elapsed since the introduction in 1988 of the social amplification of risk framework (SARF) by researchers from Clark University (Kasperson, Kasperson, Renn, and colleagues) and Decision Research (Slovic and colleagues). During that time various researchers have enlisted the framework to complete a substantial number of empirical studies. All the while, the emergence of a much larger body of relevant knowledge has spawned a lively debate on aspects of the framework. In this chapter we consider these developments, inquiring into refinements, critiques, and extensions of the approach, the emergence of new issues, and the findings and hypotheses growing out of fifteen years of empirical research.

The theoretical foundations of SARF are developed in five principal publications (Kasperson, Renn, Slovic et al. 1988; Renn 1991a; Kasperson 1992; Burns et al. 1993; Kasperson and Kasperson 1996). The idea arose out of an attempt to overcome the fragmented nature of risk perception and risk communication research by developing an integrative theoretical framework capable of accounting for findings from a wide range of studies, including: from media research; from the psychometric and cultural schools of risk perception research; and from studies of organizational responses to risk. The framework also serves, more narrowly, to describe the various *dynamic* social processes underlying risk perception and response. In particular, those processes by which certain hazards and events that experts assess as relatively low in risk can become a particular focus of concern and sociopolitical activity within a society (risk amplification), while other hazards that experts judge more serious receive comparatively less attention from society (risk attenuation). Examples of significant hazards subject to social attenuation of risk perceptions might include naturally occurring radon gas, automobile accidents, or smoking. On the other hand, social amplification of risk perceptions appears to have been one result of events such as the King's Cross and

13

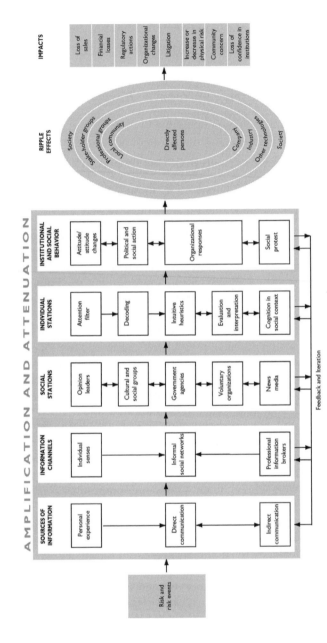

Figure 1.1 The social amplification of risk framework.

Lockerbie tragedies in the United Kingdom, the Bhopal (Wilkins 1987), Chernobyl (Otway et al. 1988), and Three Mile Island accidents, as well as the recent concerns precipitated by "mad cow" disease (Phillips et al. 2000) and by the future of genetically modified food in Europe (Anand 1997; Marris, Wynne, Simmons et al. 2001).

The theoretical starting-point is the assumption that "risk events," which might include actual or hypothesized accidents and incidents (or even new reports on existing risks), will be largely irrelevant or localized in their impact unless human beings observe and communicate them to others (Luhmann 1979). SARF holds that, as a key part of that communication process, risk, risk events, and the characteristics of both become portrayed through various risk signals (images, signs, and symbols), which in turn interact with a wide range of psychological, social, institutional, or cultural processes in ways that intensify or attenuate perceptions of risk and its manageability (see figure 1.1). The experience of risk therefore is not only an experience of *physical* harm but the result of processes by which groups and individuals learn to acquire or create *interpretations of risk*. These interpretations provide rules of how to select, order, and explain signals emanating from the physical world (Renn, Burns, Kasperson et al. 1992, p. 140). With this framework, risk experience can be properly assessed only through the interaction among the physical harms attached to a risk event and the social and cultural processes that shape interpretations of that event, secondary and tertiary consequences that emerge, and the actions taken by managers and publics.

The authors adopt the metaphor of amplification from classical communications theory and use it to analyze the ways in which various social agents generate, receive, interpret, and pass on risk signals. Kasperson et al. (1988) argue that such signals are subject to predictable transformations as they filter through various social and individual *amplification stations*. Such transformations can increase or decrease the volume of information about an event, heighten the salience of certain aspects of a message, or reinterpret and elaborate the available symbols and images, thereby leading to particular interpretations and responses by other participants in the social system. Amplification stations can include individuals, social groups, and institutions, for example, scientists or scientific institutions, reporters and the mass media, politicians and government agencies, or other social groups and their members.

For *social stations of amplification*, the likes of institutional structure, functions, and culture influence the amplification or attenuation of risk signals. Even the individuals in institutions do not simply pursue their personal values and social interpretations; they also perceive the risks, those who manage the risks, and the risk "problem" according to cultural biases and the values of their organization or group (Johnson and Covello 1987; Dake 1991; Rayner 1992; Peters and Slovic 1996; Marris, Langford, and O'Riordan 1998).

Individual stations of amplification are affected by such considerations, well documented in the psychometric tradition, as risk heuristics, qualitative aspects of the risks, prior attitudes, blame, and trust. These same individuals are also members of cultural groups (e.g. Vaughan 1995; Palmer, Carlstrom, and Woodward 2001) and other social units that codetermine the dynamics and social processing of risk.

In a second stage of the framework, directed primarily at risk-intensification processes, Kasperson et al. (1988) argue that social amplification can also account for the observation that some events will produce "ripples" of secondary and tertiary consequences that may spread far beyond the initial impact of the event and may even eventually impinge upon previously unrelated technologies or institutions. Such secondary impacts include market impacts (perhaps through consumer avoidance of a product or related products), demands for regulatory constraints, litigation, community opposition, loss of credibility and trust, stigmatization of a product, facility, or community, and investor flight. The terrorist attacks of September 11th 2001 in the United States, and their ensuing consequences (spanning a range of behavioral, economic, and social impacts) provide perhaps the most dramatic recent example of such secondary social amplification effects (Slovic 2002).

The analogy of dropping a stone into a pond (see figure 1.1) is apt here as it illustrates the spread of these higher-order impacts associated with the social amplification of risk. The ripples spread outward, first encompassing the directly affected victims or the first group to be notified, then touching the next higher institutional level (a company or an agency), and, in more extreme cases, reaching other parts of the industry or other social arenas with similar problems. This rippling of impacts is an important element of risk amplification since it suggests that the processes can extend (in risk amplification) or constrain (in risk attenuation) the temporal, sectoral, and geographical scales of impacts. It also points up that each order of impact, or ripple, may not only allocate social and political effects but also trigger (in risk amplification) or hinder (in risk attenuation) managerial interventions for risk reduction.

The record of empirical research

Since SARF is by design inclusive and integrative, the literature of relevant empirical work accomplished over the past fifteen years is potentially very large indeed. We begin by addressing the studies that apply the

Table 1.1 *Risk events with potentially high signal value*

Events	Messages
Report that chlorofluorocarbon releases are depleting the ozone layer	A new and possibly catastrophic risk has emerged
Resignation of regulators or corporate officials in "conscience"	The managers are concealing the risks: they cannot be trusted
News report of off-site migration at a hazardous waste site	The risk managers are not in control of the hazard
Scientific dispute over the validity of an epidemiological study	The experts do not understand the risks
Statement by regulators that the levels of a particular contaminant in the water supply involve only very low risks as compared with other risks	The managers do not care about the people who will be harmed; they do not understand long-term cumulative effects of chemicals

Source: Kasperson et al. 1988, p. 186.

general framework or core ideas and then proceed to more specialized applications and extensions of the framework.

The concept of "signal"

Slovic, Lichtenstein, and Fischhoff (1984; also Slovic 1987, 1992) first proposed that hazardous events might hold a "signal value." They reported that risks in the upper right-hand sector of the classic dread/knowledge psychometric factor space have high signal value in terms of serving as a warning signal for society, providing new information about the probability that similar or even more destructive mishaps might occur with this type of activity. They also suggest that high signal value might be linked to the potential for second-order effects, and hence may provide a rationale in specific cases for stricter regulation of such risks. The 1988 article suggested risk events that could have high signal value (table 1.1).

Building upon Slovic's work on risk signals, the research group at Clark University has developed a detailed methodology for identifying, classifying, and assessing risk signals in the print media pertaining to the proposed nuclear waste repository at Yucca Mountain in the United States (Kasperson, Kasperson, Perkins et al. 1992). Risk signals were defined as "messages about a hazard or hazard event that affect people's perceptions about the seriousness or manageability of the risk." They analyzed the "signal stream" as it appeared in the *Las Vegas Review Journal* between 1985 and 1989, including the symbols, metaphors, and images in news headlines, editorials, letters to the editor, and cartoons. The results reveal a dramatic shift in the discourse, symbols, and imagery, in which risk-related matters recede in importance in the face of a growing depiction of victimization, distrust, unfairness, and villainy.

In an individual difference analysis based upon the psychometric work of Slovic and colleagues, Trumbo (1996) uses people's judgments along the dread/knowledge dimensions to categorize individuals into risk "amplifiers" and "attenuators." He concludes that perceived individual risk (for amplifiers) and satisfaction in institutional response (for attenuators) are the important differences between the two groups in their interpretation of risk signals (cf. also Vlek and Stallen 1981). Interestingly, he also finds that, among amplifiers, concern over risk is driven more by interpersonal communication than by mediated communication (as in the mass media).

The 128-hazard-events study

This collaborative study between Clark University and Decision Research involved a large comparative statistical analysis of 128 hazard events, including biocidal hazards, persistent/delayed hazards, rare catastrophes, deaths from common causes, global diffuse hazards, and natural-hazard events that had occurred in the United States. Researchers used the News file of the Nexis data base to collect data on the actual volume of media coverage that each event received and then related the data to judgments made by experts and student panels of the physical consequences, risk perceptions, public response, potential for social group mobilization, and the potential for second-order societal impacts of each event. Findings indicated particularly that social amplification processes are as important as direct physical consequences in determining the full array of potential risk consequences. Hence, a risk assessment that is based solely upon direct physical consequences might seriously underestimate the full range of consequences of an event. Among the conclusions from this work (Kasperson, Golding, and Tuler 1992; Renn et al. 1992) are the following:

- A high degree of "rationality" is evident in how society responds to hazards (e.g. volume of press coverage is roughly proportional to first-order physical consequences; risk perceptions incorporate aspects of human exposure and management performance);
- Extent of exposure to the direct consequences of a hazard has more effect on risk perceptions and potential social group mobilization than do injuries and fatalities;

- The contention that public perception mirrors media coverage needs further careful empirical study (no perceptual variable – except the ubiquitous dread – correlated with the extent of media coverage once the extent of damage was controlled for);
- The role of risk signals and blame attributable to incompetent risk management seemed particularly important to public concerns (see also Burns et al. 1993). Situations involving blame of corporations or government agencies after the event appear particularly worthy of further study.

Two limitations of this quantitative study bear noting. The outcome variable for the magnitude of secondary consequences was a judgment by experts rather than a direct measure of actual societal impact. Hence, the analysis neither demonstrates, nor concludes, that heightened perceptions as a result of media coverage will *necessarily* lead to secondary impacts and rippling, a point to which we return below. Secondly, the indices of media coverage used were primarily quantitative (volume) rather than qualitative (the content of what is presented in media reports), so did not allow a test of whether the media significantly alter risk representations (a question taken up by Freudenburg et al. 1996).

Qualitative field studies

The qualitative study by Kasperson and colleagues (reported in Kasperson 1992) yielded complementary findings to the quantitative cross-risk work. Six risk events (four in the United States, one in Brazil, and one in Germany) – all but one involving some form of nuclear hazard – were studied in depth. The cases were: a transportation accident involving low-level radioactive material in Queens, New York; a serious 1982 nuclear plant accident in Ginna, New York; a brine seepage controversy at a planned nuclear waste facility in Carlsbad, New Mexico; the closure of a hazardous waste site on Long Island (Glen Cove, New York); a construction accident at a planned nuclear waste disposal facility in Gorleben, Germany; and a radioactive accident in Goiânia, Brazil (Petterson 1988). Components of the amplification framework explored included physical impacts, information flow, social-group mobilization, and rippling effects. Interviews with key participants were conducted in each case. This set of in-depth case studies yielded the following conclusions:

- Even heavy and sustained media coverage does not by itself ensure risk amplification or significant secondary effects. In some cases the secondary effects expected by the researchers failed to materialize. Trust (see also Kasperson, Golding, and Tuler 1992; Slovic 1993) appears to be a relevant critical issue, as are perceptions of the managerial handling of the accident and emergency response;

- The cases pointed to layering of attenuation/intensification effects across different groups and at different scales. Specifically, amplification at the national or regional scale accompanied by attenuation at the local scale may not be uncommon;
- Following on from the first point, it may be that several factors need to be present in combination (e.g. media coverage plus the focused attention of a local interest group, or an accident plus suspicions of incompetence) to generate what Kasperson (1992) terms "take off" (see also Gerlach 1987; Cvetkovich and Earle 1991) of an issue. Other examples of this can be found. Referring to the 1911 Triangle Shirtwaist Company fire in New York, Behrens (1983, p. 373) concluded that "a disaster only prepares the groundwork for change . . . the potential for reform created by a disaster can be fulfilled only if the appropriate interest groups recognize and successfully use the opportunities available to them." With respect to nuclear power, Slovic, Flynn, Mertz et al. (1996) found much higher levels of trust in experts, government, and science to manage the risks in France (where until quite recently this technology has not been a source of significant social conflict) as compared with the United States;
- The economic benefits associated with risks appear to be a significant source of attenuation at the local level (see also Metz 1996).

As a result of both these quantitative and qualitative studies, further research might usefully focus upon the following: case studies giving insight into full social context; cultural studies (particularly those exploring the cultural prototypes drawn upon to interpret risk communications); and investigations of how different communities experience similar risks.

Desired risk

Arguing that studies of hazards and risks have virtually overlooked a range of human activity (e.g. hang-gliding, rock climbing, dirt biking, etc.) involving the *deliberate seeking of risk*, Machlis and Rosa (1990) have explored whether SARF can be extended to this domain of risk (also Rosa 1998b, and this volume chapter 2). Evaluating key propositions and current knowledge about desired risks, the authors reach several conclusions. First, they find the social amplification concept quite suitable for incorporating desired risk, although some terminology (e.g. "victims") may need to be recast. Second, the key variables defined in the framework are appropriate but may need to be broadened to treat such issues as benefits as part of consequences and mass culture (as subsequently incorporated in the framework). Third, individual processing of risk can lead to increased risk-taking, an outcome not addressed in the early conceptual statements or empirical studies. Generally, their application of the social amplification conception led the authors to conclude that "the framework has promise, since it generally performed well against the evidence examined" (Machlis and Rosa 1990, p. 167).

Communications and the mass media

In one of the earliest studies of mass-media coverage of risks and public perceptions, Combs and Slovic (1978) analyzed two United States newspapers for their reporting of various causes of death. They found that homicides, accidents, and some natural disasters systematically received heavy coverage, whereas death from diseases received only light treatment. Whereas the authors noted that these patterns of coverage correlated with lay public judgments of the frequency of these causes of death, they also pointed out that substantial further research would be needed to define the relationships between mass-media coverage and the formation of opinion concerning risk.

Subsequent research suggests how complicated these relations are. Allan Mazur (1984) has examined media coverage of Love Canal and the Three Mile Island accident and argues that the massive quantity of media coverage, independent of the specific content, influenced public perceptions of the seriousness of the events and the political agenda of social groups and institutions. In a subsequent examination of mass media coverage of nuclear power and chemical hazards, Mazur (1990, p. 295) found evidence that "... extensive reporting of a controversial technological or environmental project not only arouses public attention, but also pushes it toward opposition." This may occur, Mazur argues, even when the treatment in the news is balanced. He proposes a theory with four interrelated propositions: (1) a few national news organizations are very influential in selecting which hazards receive most attention each year; (2) public actions to alleviate a hazard or oppose a particular technology rise and fall with the amount of media reporting; (3) public concerns over a risk or technology rise as press and television coverage increases; and (4) it is important to distinguish between the substantive content of a news story about risk and the simple image that the story conveys.

Not all agree. Renn (1991a) argues that the pure volume effect is only one of many influences of the media on public perceptions of risk. Filtering effects, deleting and adding information, mixing effects (changing the order of information in messages), equalizing effects (changing the context), and what he calls "stereo effects" (multi-channel effects) can all be important. Some analyses (e.g. Singer and Endreny 1993, p. 163) argue that the media report on risk events and not risk issues, and on harms rather than risks. Others see the media, whether providing warning or reassuring messages, as extensively framing discourse and perceptions in which the social processing of risk occurs (Wilkins 1987; Wilkins and Patterson 1991; Bohölm 1998). Lichtenberg and MacLean (1991) have pointed out that cross-cultural media research is difficult to conduct because the news media are so diverse and are influenced by the political cultures in which they operate.

Using the 128 hazard events from the Clark University–Decision Research study, Freudenburg et al. (1996) examined the amount of media coverage, public demand for further information, estimates of damage, dread, "outrage" and anger, and recreancy (the misuse of authority or failure to merit public trust; also see this volume chapter 4). As part of their analysis, the researchers read not only the Nexis abstracts but the entire original articles, complete with headlines and accompanying photography and artwork. The authors conclude, despite common beliefs to the contrary, that media coverage overall did not exaggerate risks or display an "anti-technology" bias. Indeed, among the factors examined, only those involving the "objective" severity of the event showed any significant predictive power for the amount of coverage devoted to risk events (Freudenburg et al. 1996, p. 40). Indeed, if anything, the general pattern was for full news articles to de-emphasize the severity of the risks and to provide reassurance. On the other hand, an analysis of television coverage of environmental biotechnology revealed a tendency to focus on extremes, and unknown risks, and to be superficial and incomplete (McCabe and Fitzgerald 1991).

Although the dramatization of risks and risk events in the media has received much attention, the circularity and tight interrelations between the media and other components of social amplification processes (e.g. contextual effects, historical settings, interest-group activity, public beliefs) render it difficult to determine the specific effects of the volume and content of media coverage. There can be no doubt that the mass media are an important element in communication systems, the processing of risk in amplification stations, and, as Vaughan and Seifert (1992) have persuasively argued, how risk problems are framed and socially constructed. And Renn's (1991a) recommended attention to coding, decoding, filtering, and stereo processes remains a highly promising avenue of research. From a social amplification perspective, other interesting questions center upon how the mass media interact with other elements of social amplification processes to construct, intensify, dampen, and modify signals concerning risk and its manageability. In addition to analyses aimed at discerning of media-specific influence components of amplification, the search for patterns, syndromes, or dynamics of interrelationship and the conditions under which they take particular forms is a promising avenue of amplification research.

Hidden hazards

Risk events, when they undergo substantial amplification and result in unexpected public alarms or what some would call "social shocks" (Lawless 1977), often surprise managers and others. No less remarkable is the extreme attenuation of certain risk events so that, despite serious consequences for the risk bearers and society more generally, they pass virtually unnoticed and untended, often continuing to grow in effects until reaching disaster proportions. Kasperson and Kasperson (1991) describe such highly attenuated risks as "hidden hazards" and offer a theoretical explanation for their existence. Hidden hazards, in their view, have to do with both the nature of the hazards themselves and the nature of the societies and cultures in which they occur. The "hiding" of hazards is at once purposeful and unintentional, life threatening and institution sustaining, systematic, and incidental.

The Kaspersons describe five aspects of such hazards that drive attenuation, each associated with differing causal agents and processes. *Global elusive hazards* involve a series of complex problems (regional interactions, slow accumulation, lengthy time lags, diffuse effects). Their incidence in a politically fragmented and unequal world tends to mute their signal power in many societies. *Ideological hazards* remain hidden principally because they lie embedded in a societal web of values and assumptions that attenuates consequences, elevates associated benefits, or idealizes certain beliefs. *Marginal hazards* befall people who occupy the edges of cultures, societies, or economies where they are exposed to hazards that are remote from or concealed by those at the center or in the mainstream. Many in such marginal situations are already weakened or highly vulnerable while they enjoy limited access to entitlements and few alternative means of coping. *Amplification-driven hazards* have effects that elude conventional types of risk assessment and environmental impact analysis and are often, therefore, allowed to grow in their secondary consequences before societal intervention occurs. And, finally, *value-threatening hazards* alter human institutions, lifestyles, and basic values, but because the pace of technological change so outstrips the capacity of social institutions to respond and adapt, disharmony in purpose, political will, and directed effort impede effective responses and the hazards grow. The presence of some of these "hidden hazards" has been documented in subsequent analyses of environmental degradation and delayed societal responses in nine regions around the world (Kasperson, Kasperson, and Turner 1995, 1999).

Organizational amplification and attenuation

As yet, limited attention has addressed the role of organizations and institutions in the social processing of risk. Pidgeon (1997) has suggested that linking risk amplification to the considerable empirical base of knowledge concerning organizational processes intended to prevent large-scale failures and disasters would be an important extension of the framework. Most contemporary risks originate in sociotechnical systems (see Turner 1978; Perrow 1984; Short and Clarke 1992) rather than natural phenomena so that risk management and internal regulatory processes governing the behavior of institutions in identifying, diagnosing, prioritizing, and responding to risks are key parts of the broader amplification process. As Short (1992) points out, large organizations increasingly set the context and terms of debate for society's consideration of risk. Understanding amplification dynamics, then, requires insight into how risk-related decisions relate to organizational self-interest, messy inter- and intra-organizational relationships, economically related rationalizations, and "rule of thumb" considerations that often conflict with the view of risk analysis as a scientific enterprise (Short 1992, p. 8). Since major accidents are often preceded by smaller incidents and risk warnings, how signals of incubating hazards are processed within institutions and communicated to others outside the institution do much to structure society's experience with technological and industrial risks.

Noting the relative void of work on organizational risk processing, Freudenburg (1992) has examined characteristics of organizations that serve to attenuate risk signals and ultimately to increase the risks posed by technological systems. These include such attributes as the lack of organizational commitment to the risk management function, the bureaucratic attenuation of information flow within the organization (and particularly on a "bad news" context), specialized divisions of labor that create "corporate gaps" in responsibility, amplified risk-taking by workers, the atrophy of organizational vigilance to risk as a result of a myriad of factors (e.g. boredom, routinization), and imbalances and mismatches in institutional resources. Freudenburg concludes that these factors often work in concert to lead even well-meaning and honest scientists and managers to underestimate risks. In turn, such organizational attenuation of risk serves systematically and repeatedly to amplify the health and environmental risks that the organization is entrusted to anticipate and to control.

Other studies of organizational handling of risk confirm Freudenburg's analysis and provide further considerations. In an analysis of safety management at Volvo, Svenson (1988a) found that patterns of access to various parties to reliable information about hazards, understanding of the relation between changes in the product and changes in safety levels, attributes of the information network that informs various interested parties about changes in safety (either positive or negative), and the presence of organizational structures for negotiating about risk between the producer and other social institutions were all important. In her analysis of the *Challenger* accident in the United States, Diane Vaughan (1992, 1996) also found communication and information issues to be critical but argued that structural factors, such as pressures from a competitive environment, resource scarcity in the organization, vulnerability of important subunits, and characteristics of the internal safety regulation system were equally important. In counterpoint to these assessments, the well-known DuPont safety culture has sought to identify characteristics that *amplify* even minor risks at the corporation so as to achieve high attentiveness to risk reduction throughout the organization (Kasperson and Kasperson 1993). La Porte and colleagues have examined similar amplification mechanisms in high-reliability organizations that drive performance to error minimization (Weick 1987; Roberts 1989; La Porte 1996), as have Pidgeon and O'Leary (1994, 2000) in their analysis of safety cultures and the use of incident reporting in aviation contexts.

Several theoretical perspectives on organizational processing of risk can be drawn upon within the amplification/attenuation framework. When considering individual responses to hazards within organizations, the idea of psychological denial of threatening information has had a particularly long history (see, for example, Leventhal 1970). Perhaps surprisingly, however, this topic has only rarely been investigated in contemporary psychological risk research, where the current "cold" cognitive paradigm for understanding responses to hazard and environmental threat, based upon the two traditions of cognitive psychology and decision making research, has long undervalued the role of "hot" motivational variables upon behavior and choice. Notable exceptions are the studies by Janis and Mann (1977) on decision making under stress, the related threat-coping model of Stallen and Tomas (1988), and the treatment of worry by MacGregor (1991). More recent work has now begun to explore the relationship between affective variables and risk perceptions (Finucane et al. 2000; Langford 2002; Slovic, Finucane, Peters et al. 2002)

Evidence of a range of broad social and organizational preconditions to large-scale accidents is available in the work of Turner (1978; see also Turner and Pidgeon 1997). As a result of a detailed analysis of 84 major accidents in the United Kingdom, Turner concluded that such events rarely come about for any single reason. Rather, it is typical to find that a number of undesirable events accumulate, unnoticed or not fully understood, often over a considerable number of years, which he defines as the *disaster incubation period*. Preventive action to remove one or more of the dangerous conditions or a *trigger event*, which might be a final critical error or a slightly abnormal operating condition, brings this period to an end. Turner focuses in particular upon the information difficulties, which are typically associated with the attempts of individuals and organizations to deal with uncertain and ill-structured safety problems, during the hazard-incubation period.

Finally, in a series of persuasive case studies of foreign and domestic policy decisions, Janis (1982) describes the small group syndrome of *groupthink*, marked primarily by a strong concurrence seeking tendency in highly cohesive policy making groups. Particular symptoms of groupthink include an over-estimation by members of the group's inherent morality as well as of its power to influence events, a collective closed-mindedness (or mind set) to new information, and pressures within the group towards conformity to the majority view. Janis argues that the groupthink syndrome is responsible for a range of observable decision making defects, including incomplete searches for new information, biased appraisal of available information, and a failure to work out contingency plans to cope with uncertainties.

Despite these valuable explorations, our knowledge of risk amplification and attenuation in different types of institutions remains thin and eclectic. Systematic application of the amplification framework in a comparative study of organizations, issues, and institutions (see e.g. the work comparing regulation of radon, chemicals, and BSE by Rothstein, 2003) might well yield highly useful results, particularly demonstrating how signals are denied, deemphasized, or misinterpreted.

Imagery and stigma

The 1988 article that set forth SARF identified stigmatization as one of four major response mechanisms of amplification processes. Research on risk stigmatization was only beginning at that time, both in the pathbreaking work of Edelstein (1987) and as part of the Decision Research studies on public perceptions of the proposed Yucca Mountain nuclear waste repository (Slovic, Flynn, and Layman 1991; Slovic, Layman,

Kraus et al. 1991; Slovic, Flynn, and Gregory 1994; Flynn, Peters, Mertz et al. 1998). Subsequent work has underscored the importance of stigmatization as a principal route by which risk amplification can generate ripples and secondary consequences (Flynn, Slovic, and Kunreuther 2001).

It is clear from this work that stigma-induced effects associated with risky technologies, products, or places may be substantial. Nuclear energy, for example, once so highly regarded for its promise for cheap, safe power, is today subject to severe stigmatization, reflecting public perceptions of abnormally great risk, distrust of management, and the disappointment of failed promises. Certain products of biotechnology also have been rejected in part because of perceptions of risk. Milk produced with the aid of bovine growth hormone (BGH, or bovine somatotrophin, BST) is one example, with many supermarket chains refusing to buy milk products from BGH-treated cows. Startling evidence of stigmatization of one of the modern world's most important classes of technology comes from studies by Slovic and others. Asking people to indicate what comes to mind when they hear or read the word "chemicals," researchers find that the most frequent response tends to be "dangerous" or some closely related term such as "toxic," "hazardous," "poison," or "deadly." A study of public images of a proposed nuclear waste storage facility provides telling evidence of the potential stigmatization of such a facility (table 1.2).

The ancient Greeks used the word "stigma" to refer to a mark placed on an individual to signify infamy or disgrace. A person thus marked was perceived to pose a risk to society. An extensive literature, much stimulated by the seminal work of Goffman (1963), exists on the topic of stigma as it applies to people. By means of its association with risk, the concept of stigma recently has been generalized to technologies, places, and products that are perceived to be unduly dangerous.

Stigmatized places, products, and technologies tend to share several features (Gregory et al. 1995, p. 221). The source of the stigma is a hazard with characteristics, such as dread consequences and involuntary exposure, that typically contributes to high public perceptions of risk. Its impacts are often perceived to be inequitably distributed across groups (for example, children and pregnant women are affected disproportionately) or geographical areas (one city bears the risks of hazardous waste storage for an entire state). Often the impacts are unbounded, in the sense that their magnitude or persistence over time is not well known. A critical aspect of stigma is that a standard of what is right and natural has been violated or overturned because of the abnormal nature of the precipitating event (crude oil on pristine beaches and the destruction of valued wildlife) or the discrediting nature of the consequences (innocent

Table 1.2 *Images associated with an "underground nuclear waste storage facility"*[a]

Category	Frequency	Images included in category
1. dangerous	179	dangerous, danger, hazardous, toxic, unsafe, harmful, disaster
2. death/sickness	107	death, dying, sickness, cancer
3. negative	99	negative, wrong, bad, unpleasant, terrible, gross, undesirable, awful, dislike, ugly, horrible
4. pollution	97	pollution, contamination, leakage, spills, love canal
5. war	62	war, bombs, nuclear war, holocaust
6. radiation	59	radiation, nuclear, radioactive glowing
7. scary	55	scary, frightening, concern, worried, fear, horror
8. somewhere else	49	wouldn't want to live near one, not where I live, far away as possible
9. unnecessary	44	unnecessary, bad idea, waste of land
10. problems	39	problems, trouble
11. desert	37	desert, barren, desolate
12. non-Nevada locations	35	Utah, Arizona, Denver
13. Nevada / Las Vegas	34	Nevada (25), Las Vegas (9)
14. storage location	32	caverns, underground salt mine
15. government/industry	23	Government, politics, big business

[a] Basis: N = 402 respondents in Phoenix, Arizona
Source: Slovic, Layman, Kraus et al. (1991, p. 693).

people are injured or killed). As a result, management of the hazard is brought into question as concerns surface regarding competence, conflicts of interest, or a failure to apply needed safeguards and controls.

Stigmatization of places has resulted from the extensive media coverage of contamination at sites such as Times Beach, Missouri, and Love Canal, New York. Other well-known examples of environmental stigmatization include Seveso, Italy, where dioxin contamination following an industrial accident at a chemical plant resulted in local economic disruptions estimated to be in excess of $100 million, and portions of the French Riviera and Alaskan coastline in the aftermath of the *Amoco Cadiz* and *Exxon Valdez* oil spills.

Stigmatization of products can also occur and result in severe losses. A dramatic example is that of the pain reliever Tylenol, where, despite quick action on the part of the manufacturer, Johnson and Johnson, seven tampering-induced poisonings that occurred in 1982 cost the company

more than $1.4 billion. Another well-known case of product stigmatiza-
tion occurred in the Spring of 1989, when millions of United States consumers stopped buying apples and apple products because of their fears
that the chemical Alar (used then as a growth regulator by apple growers)
could cause cancer. Apple farmers saw wholesale prices drop by about
one-third and annual revenues decline by more than $100 million. More
recently, the BSE (bovine spongiform encephalopathy) affair stigmatized
the European beef industry resulting in billions of dollars in losses and a
crisis in trust and confidence in risk management in the United Kingdom
(Phillips et al 2000), while the perceptions of the Spring 2001 foot and
mouth epidemic in the United Kingdom (Poortinga et al. 2003) led to
large losses to the rural economy as people cancelled trips to the United
Kingdom countryside and Britain (see Harvey 2001).

Kasperson, Jhaveri, and Kasperson (2001) have extended the social
amplification model, as shown in figure 1.2, to enhance its applicability
to analyzing stigmatization processes. In this adaptation, the early part
of the amplification framework remains the same, with risk events generating information flow and social communication treating the risk. Not
only do public perceptions and imagery emerge or become modified, but
the associated technologies, products, or places become *marked*. Marking involves the selection of a particular attribute of a place or technology
and focuses on some symbol or physical representation of the place. In
Hawthorne's *The Scarlet Letter*, it was the letter A; in Nazi Germany,
it was the yellow star. At Richland, the host community of the
Hanford Reservation in the United States, it is the mushroom cloud in-
signia worn on school sport uniforms. Research by Mitchell, Payne, and
Dunlap (1988) has provided extensive evidence of such marking, imagery, and stigmatization. Labeling, such as the use of the term "dump
site," is an essential part of such marking. Eventually, amplification dynamics and imagery formation can fundamentally alter the *identity* of the
place or technology, so that it is viewed as tainted and discredited by residents of the place, workers in the technology, and by outsiders. And, as a
result, stigma-induced ripple effects and secondary consequences follow.

Extending the current knowledge base of risk-induced stigma and their
effects is, in our opinion, a high-priority area for research on social amplification. Such stigma effects currently raise the specter of gridlock for
important avenues of technology development and for public policy initiatives. Can we anticipate which new technologies may become stigmatized through amplification processes? Can, and should, stigma effects be
counteracted? How can responsible authorities act to ameliorate stigma-
induced gridlock and the associated fallout on trust and confidence? What
are the broad implications for risk management and risk communication?

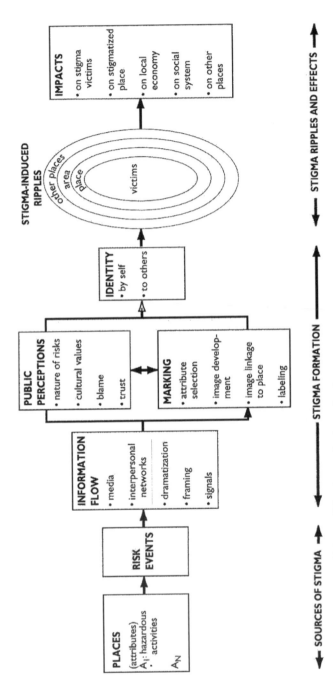

Figure 1.2 Risk amplification and stigmatization.

Trust and confidence

The original framework article (Kasperson et al. 1988) hypothesized four major pathways or mechanisms – heuristics and values, social group relationships, signal value, and stigmatization – in the second stage of amplification. High or growing social distrust of responsible institutions and their managers is certainly a fifth. A broad literature now indicates that recurrent failures in risk management stem in no small part from a failure to recognize the more general requirements of democratic society, and especially the need for *social trust* (see e.g. contributions to Cvetkovich and Löfstedt 1999). Accordingly, risk control efforts have frequently gone awry due to a lack of openness and "transparency," a failure to consult or involve so called "interested" and "affected" persons, a loss of social trust in managers, inadequacies in due process, a lack of responsiveness to public concerns, or an insensitivity to questions of environmental justice. Such interpretations abound across a wide spectrum of environmental and risk debates: global warming, biodiversity, genetic engineering, clean-up of defense and other hazardous wastes, the siting of hazardous waste facilities, and the protection of wetlands. As Ruckelshaus warned:

Mistrust engenders a vicious descending spiral. The more mistrust by the public, the less effective government becomes at delivering what people want and need; the more government bureaucrats in turn respond with enmity towards the citizens they serve, the more ineffective government becomes, the more people mistrust it, and so on, down and down. (Ruckelshaus 1996, p. 2)

Ruckelshaus's dread spiral is reminiscent of United States Supreme Court Justice Stephen Breyer's tripartite "vicious circle – public perception, Congressional reaction, and the uncertainties of the regulatory process" (Breyer 1993, p. 50) – that thwarts effective risk management.

Slovic (1993, 2000) has argued that trust emerges slowly, is fragile, and easily destroyed. And once lost, it may prove to be extremely difficult to recover. He posits an "asymmetry principle" to explain why it is easier to destroy than to create trust: negative (trust-destroying) events are more visible or noticeable than positive (trust-building) events. Negative events often take the form of specific, well-defined incidents such as accidents, lies, discoveries of errors or other mismanagement. Positive events, although sometimes visible, are often fuzzy or indistinct. Events that are invisible or poorly defined carry little weight in shaping our attitudes and opinions. And even when events do come to our attention, negative (trust-destroying) events carry much greater weight than positive events (see Slovic, 1993; also Cvetkovich et al. 2002).

Trust is typically discussed in terms of an implicit relationship between two or more parties. It has long been discussed as a facet of political culture that facilitates the working of the political system (Almond and Verba 1980; Inglehart 1988), and more recently as an important dimension of social capital (Coleman 1990, pp. 300–321; Putnam 1993, 1995). It also functions to reduce complexity in our social environment (Barber 1984), hence making life more predictable. Renn and Levine (1991) list five attributes of trust:

- *competence* (do you have the appropriate technical expertise?)
- *objectivity* (are your messages free from bias?)
- *fairness* (are all points of view acknowledged?)
- *consistency* (of your statements and behavior over time?)
- *faith* (a perception of your good will?)

They argue that trust underlies *confidence*, and where this is shared across a community one has *credibility*. A somewhat different view of social trust is provided by Earle and Cvetkovich (1995; also Siegrist and Cvetkovich 2000; Siegrist, Cvetkovich, and Roth, 2000), who argue that it is similarity in our basic values, rather than attributes of technical competence, that underlies whom we trust or distrust. Hunt et al. (1999) have recently shown that both perceived "truthfulness" and "expertise" are important but perhaps superficial factors as well. One public policy implication of the trust research is that we need to frame the principal goals of risk communication around building trust through participation (Royal Society, 1992; Stern and Fineberg 1996; United Kingdom Interdepartmental Liaison Group on Risk Assessment 1998b). The candid communication by an agency of risk uncertainties to people, however, can signal honesty for some while invoking greater distrust in others. Moreover, given that conflict is endemic to many risk controversies, effective risk communication may follow only if a resolution of conflict is obtained first, perhaps by searching for decision options that address all of the stakeholder's principal values and concerns (Edwards and von Winterfeldt 1987; Renn, Webler, and Wiedemann, 1995; Arvai et al. 2001), or by identifying superordinate goals to which all parties can agree. Despite these difficulties, broad "stakeholder" participation is also increasingly seen, often alas uncritically, as essential to the wider processes of risk assessment and management and a route to success (see, in particular, Stern and Fineberg 1996).

Issues of social trust are clearly important components of the dynamics of social amplification. We know that distrust acts to heighten risk perceptions, to intensify public reactions to risk signals, to contribute to the perceived unacceptability of risk, and to stimulate political activism to reduce risk (Flynn, Slovic, and Mertz 1993a; English 1992; Jenkins-Smith 1991; Kasperson, Golding, and Tuler 1992; Löfstedt and Horlick-Jones 1999). But a host of questions surrounds the interpretation of trust and its effects: there are many types of trust, the processes that create and destroy trust are not well understood, trust (or distrust) exists at multiple levels of the political system, complex attribution issues prevail, and policy responses and their effectiveness are opaque (see Cvetkovich and Löfstedt 1999). From a social amplification perspective, trust is highly interrelated with other components and mechanisms in what we think of as "amplification dynamics." Understanding how trust is shaped, altered, lost, or rebuilt in the processing of risk by social and individual stations of risk is a priority need in social amplification research.

Ripple effects

Since the 1988 framework article, the systematic, cross-hazard study of ripple effects and secondary/tertiary consequences has also been a priority research need. It has yet to occur. The 128-hazard event study did elicit expert estimates, informed by documentary evidence, of event consequences. The results were highly suggestive. The societal processing of risk by media, social groups, institutions, and individuals played a critical role in the overall magnitude and scope of societal impacts. For risk events that were highly amplified, the amplification-driven impacts frequently exceeded the primary (i.e. health, environmental, and direct economic) effects. We also know that ripple effects can be charted and measured along temporal, geographical, and sectoral dimensions. Such a broad-based and systematic empirical study could provide invaluable new information for understanding how social amplification processes affect the rippling of effects, the durability of such effects, possible contagion effects on other risks, and overall impacts of rippling upon social capital, such as trust.

What we now have is some suggestive cases. In Goiânia in Brazil, a strongly amplified radiological accident produced dramatic rippling of secondary risk consequences. As reported elsewhere (Petterson 1988), within the first weeks of the media coverage, more than 100,000 persons, of their own volition, stood in line to be monitored with Geiger counters for indication of external radiation. Within two weeks of the event, the wholesale value of agricultural production within Goiâs, the Brazilian state in which Goiânia is located, had fallen by 50 percent, owing to consumer concerns over possible contamination, even though no contamination was ever found in the products. Even eight months after the event, when prices had rebounded by about 90 percent, a significant adverse impact was still apparent. During the three months following the accident, the number and prices of homes sold or rented within the immediate vicinity of the accident plummeted. Hotel occupancy in Goiânia, normally near capacity at this time of year, had vacancy levels averaging about 40 percent in the six weeks following the São Paulo television broadcast, while the Hotel Castros, one of the largest in Goiânia, lost an estimated 1,000 reservations as a direct consequence of risk perceptions and stigma. Meanwhile, Caldas Novas, a hot-springs tourist attraction located a full one-hour drive from Goiânia, experienced a 30–40 percent drop in occupancy rates immediately following the São Paulo television broadcast. Hotels in other parts of Brazil refused to allow Goiânia residents to register. Some airline pilots refused to fly airplanes that had Goiânia residents aboard. Cars with Goiâs license plates were stoned in other parts of Brazil. Even nuclear energy as a whole in Brazil was affected, as several political parties used the accident to mobilize against "nuclear weapons, power, or waste" and to introduce legislation designed to split the National Nuclear Energy Commission into separate divisions. Increased public opposition to nuclear energy was apparent throughout Brazil. Even international ripples of the accident became apparent as Goiânia became a frequent benchmark and rallying cry in antinuclear publications throughout the world.

Arvind Susarla at Clark University compared two risk events in India, one of which was highly amplified and the other attenuated (see also this volume chapter 8). The amplified event was the discovery of bacterium *Yersinia Pestis* in the city of Surat which led to a plague scare in India. With media reports of increasing evidence of pneumonic plague, rumors about a large number of deaths due to the disease spread in the city. Despite assurances of safety and mitigative measures from local authorities, the rumors triggered widespread public concern and an extreme public response within hours of the initial reports of the plague. At its peak, over 200,000 persons are believed to have deserted the city of Surat, and hundreds of others reported to the public and private hospitals. Authorities in several nearby cities, meanwhile, were alerted to the possible arrivals of plague patients from Surat. Administrative officials responded by ordering a series of precautionary steps, including the medical screening of persons from Surat at the bus and train stations and the closure of schools, colleges, public gatherings and meetings, and theaters. These initiatives amplified concerns and alarm that the disease might spread to other parts of the country. Media coverage of the episode is complex as highly exaggerated death tolls were reported in the English-language dailies whereas Hindi-language newspapers insisted there was no plague and accused neighboring Pakistan of a smear campaign aimed at bringing India's economy to its knees. The combination of public concern, media reporting, and the actions of authorities also resulted in higher-order impacts due to the hazard event. Many countries imposed travel restrictions on people traveling to and from India. Iran's foreign minister postponed his visit to India. Trade embargoes, withdrawal of personnel by multinational firms, and cancellations of many airline international flights reflect the extent of risk ripples produced by the hazard event.

Barnett et al. (1992) report a clear decline (albeit temporary) of one-third, in the use of the DC-10 for domestic United States flights following a serious and heavily publicized crash at Sioux City, Iowa in 1989. Such secondary consequences may emerge only on a case-by-case basis and may require the presence of several factors in order to emerge fully (in this case, the DC-10 had a historically untrustworthy image following a spate of crashes in the 1970s). However, the effects were very temporary (fewer than two months). In a very different social "risk" domain, that of the impacts of media violence, Hill (2001) argues that it is the politics of social group mobilization (around campaigns against particularly violent videos or movies) which is the key driver of secondary amplification effects such as increased censorship and regulation.

Metz (1996) has conducted a historical impact analysis of stigma (stage 2) effects around United States weapons sites. His claim is that, although anticipated stigma or other second-order amplification consequences might be a common response when individuals are asked to *imagine* the future, few of the anticipated negative consequences of siting a hazard in a community (loss of business, decline in land values etc.) were actually manifest in his research *over the longer term*. This is a controversial conclusion, given the central place that stigma and secondary consequences hold in discussions of risk perceptions, and his general argument has drawn vigorous critique (Slovic et al. 1994).

The one theoretical contribution that we know of linking stage 1 processes causally with stage 2 ripple effects is work by Slovic, Layman, Kraus et al. (1991) on stigma effects at the Yucca Mountain nuclear repository site. They designed a series of empirical studies to (1) demonstrate the concept of environmental imagery and show how it can be measured, (2) assess the relationship between imagery and choice behavior, and (3) describe economic impacts that might occur as a result of altered images and choices. The research tested three specific propositions: (1) images associated with environments have diverse positive and negative affective meanings that influence preferences (e.g. preference for sites in which to vacation, retire, find a job, or start a new business); (2) a nuclear-waste repository evokes a wide variety of strongly negative images, consistent with extreme perceptions of risk and stigmatization; and (3) the repository at Yucca Mountain and the negative images it evokes will, over time, become increasingly salient in the images of Nevada and of Las Vegas.

Substantial empirical support was found for these propositions, demonstrating a set of causal mechanisms by which social amplification processes could adversely affect the attractiveness of the area to tourists, job seekers, retirees, convention planners, and business developers and produce adverse social and economic effects.

Despite these cases and the Decision Research theoretical work, it is clear that stage 1 relationships in the SARF have been more studied and are better understood than are those of stage 2. Stage 1 posits that signals from risk events become transformed to influence perceptions of risk and first-order behavioral responses. A relatively extensive set of findings from the risk perceptions literature now exists to suggest this is the case, although much remains to be done to pinpoint the *specific contexts* under which amplification or attenuation occurs. Stage 2 involves a direct link between amplification of risk perceptions and secondary consequences, such as calls for stricter regulation, market impacts, and a generalization of responses to other similar risk events and hazards. In many respects it is stage 2 that is the most important for policy, given the potential here for large economic and social impacts. Despite *prima facie* evidence, stage 2 processes remain rather opaque, based largely upon current case-specific and anecdotal evidence rather than on systematic empirical evidence. It is also less clear what the direct secondary consequences of *attenuation* might be compared to the more visible impacts of amplification. Consequences of attenuation might include, however, the otherwise avoidable direct impacts of the hazard, and the impacts upon trust and credibility if degraded risk management is subsequently revealed in a serious unanticipated accident.

Having surveyed the empirical work that has tested, elaborated, and extended the original conceptual paper, we next turn to a review of critiques and points of debate that have emerged over the past fifteen years.

Critiques and contentions

The framework has prompted general critiques, principally in the set of peer review commentaries that accompanied the original 1988 article in *Risk Analysis*. Although most of these authors welcomed social amplification as a genuine attempt to provide more theoretical coherence to the field, they also highlighted points of issue, as well as avenues for further research. In a subsequent paper Kasperson (1992) sought to respond to many of these critiques. Here we review the various critiques and issues that have been raised, clarifying where we can and identifying unresolved questions where appropriate.

The amplification metaphor

Rayner (1988) has criticized the amplification metaphor itself, concerned that it might be taken to imply that a baseline or "true" risk exists that is readily attached to risk events, which is then "distorted" in some way by the social processes of amplification. He argues that the emphasis on signal and electronic imagery may be too passive to capture the complexity of risk behavior. Rip (1988) worries that the focus of amplification work may be directed to what are regarded as "exaggerated" risks.

It is quite clear, however, that the framework is not intended to imply that any single true baseline always and/or unproblematically exists, particularly in many of the heavily politicized, transcientific settings (Funtowicz and Ravetz 1992) where amplification is most likely to occur. The conceptualization of the amplification process in terms of construction and transformation of signs, symbols, and images by an array of social and individual "stations" and actors is compatible with the view that *all* knowledge about risk entails some elements of judgment and social construction (Johnson and Covello 1987; Holzheu and Wiedemann 1993). The observation that experts and public sometimes disagree about risks is compatible with the claim that different groups may filter and attach salience to different aspects of a risk or a risk event. Amplification and attenuation, then, refer to the processes of signal interpretation, transformation, intensification, and dampening as the dynamics of risk consideration proceed iteratively in society. At the same time, it is clear that risks do have real *consequences* (Rosa 1998a; Renn 1998a), and these may be direct (as are usually treated in technical risk analyses) or indirect results from the social processing of risk (stigmatization, group mobilization, conflict, loss of trust).

The metaphor of amplification does come with some baggage, to be sure. Since the very term amplification, in its more general and common usage, refers to the intensification of signals, the framework nomenclature can be taken to have implicit semantic bias (Rip 1988). The architects of SARF have repeatedly emphasized in their writings that this approach is intended to describe *both* the social processes that attenuate signals about hazards, as well as those involved in intensification. Alleged "overreactions" of people and organizations should receive the same attention as alleged "downplaying" of the risk. In his extensive review of the topic Renn (1991a) discusses the processes and contexts that might be expected to lead to each.

What is amplified or attenuated are *both* the signals to society about the seriousness and manageability *and*, ultimately, the consequences of the risk through the generation, or constraining, of ripple effects. Indeed, the secondary risk consequences will often be connected causally with the various interactions involved in society's processing of risk signals. It is exactly this potential for signal transformation and amplification-driven social dynamics and consequences that has been so confounding to risk managers in various societies.

Is it a theory?

As emphasized in the 1988 article, SARF is not a theory, properly speaking, but "... a fledgling conceptual framework that may serve to guide ongoing efforts to develop, test, and apply such a theory to a broad array of pressing risk problems" (Kasperson et al. 1988, p. 180). A theory, as Machlis and Rosa (1990, p. 164) have emphasized, would require specification and explication of linked concepts, including the application of correspondence rules for converting abstract or inexact concepts into exact, testable ones. We are now beginning to see the first forays into such theorizing, as in the stigma work of Slovic and colleagues referred to above. Progress is also apparent in the empirical work linking events, trust, perceptions, and imagery, also discussed above. Meanwhile, a continuing principal contribution of the framework is its "net" function for catching a broad range of accumulated empirical research, for organizing and bringing into direct analytic interaction relevant phenomena, for theories concerning risk perception and its communication, and for deriving new hypotheses about the societal processing of risk signals (the latter could then, in principle at least, be tested directly).

One limitation of the risk amplification framework, despite its apparent face validity, is that it may be too general (rather as subjective expected-utility theory is) to test empirically and particularly to seek outright falsification. This has led some observers (e.g. Rayner 1988; Wåhlberg 2001) to doubt whether any genuinely new insights can be achieved beyond those already offered by existing approaches. Clearly, the usefulness of this social amplification approach will ultimately stand or fall upon its ability to achieve insights which can be subject to empirical test. Certainly the framework does, at minimum, help to clarify phenomena, such as the key role of the mass media in risk communication and the influence of culture on risk processing, providing a template for integrating partial theories and research, and to encourage more interactive and holistic interpretations. Kasperson (1992) has previously cited three potential contributions of such an integrative framework: to bring competing theories and hypotheses out of their "terrain" and into direct conjunction (or confrontation) with each other; to provide an overall framework in which to locate a large array of fragmented empirical findings; and to generate new hypotheses, particularly hypotheses geared to the interconnections and interdependencies among particular concepts or components. These still seem highly relevant.

Communications and the mass media

The concern has been raised (Handmer and Penning-Rowsell 1990) that the communications model on which the social amplification approach is founded unduly emphasizes too simple a conceptualization of risk communication, as a *one-way* transfer of information (i.e. from risk events and sources, through transmitters, and then onto receivers). So let us remove any existing doubt that this framework, as we conceive it, recognizes that the development of social risk perceptions is always likely to be the product of diverse interactive processes among the parties to any risk communication. Various reviews (National Research Council 1989; Pidgeon, Hood, Jones et al. 1992; Stern and Fineberg 1996) discuss the importance of viewing risk communication as a *two-way process* of dialogue. We would take this even further to note that any risk event generates coverage and signals that proceed through a broad array or fabric of ongoing communication networks. Purposeful risk communication programs nearly always enter a terrain extensively occupied by existing communication systems. Thus, with the United States National Research Council (National Research Council 1989, p. 21), we see risk communication as "an interactive process of exchange of information and opinion among individuals, groups and institutions. It involves multiple messages about the nature of risk and other messages, not strictly about risk, that express concerns, opinions, or reactions to risk messages or to legal and institutional arrangements for risk management." Certainly, applications of the framework should not lose sight of this important qualification, and although it is relatively easy to finger the public and media as the originators of risk communication problems, the communicators are also key parts of the process (Kasperson and Stallen 1991).

In this context, a comment on the role of the mass media is also in order. Some have interpreted the framework to assume that we see high mass media coverage as the principal driver of risk amplification. For example Sjöberg (1999) concludes that the framework predicts that enhanced media coverage should increase perceived risk. This is not the case. Although we find incidents where this has occurred, and some (e.g. Mazur 1990) have advanced this argument, the conceptual work of Renn (1991a) and Pidgeon, Henwood, and Maguire (1999) and our empirical research as well reveal that the relationships among media coverage, public perceptions, and stage 2 amplification processes are complex and highly interactive with other components of the amplification process. Indeed, we have speculated that no single amplification component may be sufficient to ensure "take-off" of the amplification process. We also believe that layering of amplification and attenuation around scale-specific patterns of media coverage may not be uncommon (also Breakwell and Barnett, this volume chapter 3). Indeed, we see the strength of amplification research as oriented to patterns of interacting amplification mechanisms, the nature of the risks and risk events, and social contextual effects. We have also concluded, surveying empirical work over the past fifteen years, that the nature of discourse about risk that characterizes the social processing of the risk is important, including the political competition that occurs to control language, symbols, imagery, and definition or framing of the risk problem.

Individual versus social processes

Two commentaries on the 1988 article expressed the concern that too much attention was given to the individual level of amplification and too little to social alignments, the mass media, and social networks (Rip 1988, p. 195). Svenson (1988b, p. 200) noted that future development of the framework might well benefit from a more articulated system and a broader social psychological approach that would put amplification processes "even more firmly in the societal context." As the foregoing discussion of organizational amplification and attenuation illustrates, the empirical work over the past fifteen years has accorded the social "stations" and processes of amplification as much, and perhaps even more, attention as individual processes have received. Indeed, even the extensions of the psychometric model to notions such as stigma, blame, and social trust have emphasized heavily the interactions between social context and individual perceptions and behavior. And, of course, it is precisely these interactions that are highlighted in the amplification framework.

   With this review of empirical studies and extensions of the social amplification framework, as well as areas of critique and debate, in hand, we next turn to consider implications for public policy and future research directions.

Policy and research priorities

As yet, there has been no systematic exploration of how SARF and the empirical results of the past fifteen years can be applied to various public policy matters. Yet there is an urgent need for social analysts of risk to suggest approaches and processes that have the potential to improve society's ability to anticipate, diagnose, prioritize, and respond to the continuing flow of risk issues that confront, and often confound, society's risk processing and management functions. The recommendations calling for substantial overhauls in existing risk assessment and decision making, whether for an "enlarged concept of risk" and trust-building (United Kingdom Interdepartmental Liaison Group on Risk Assessment 1998a) or "analytic and deliberative process" (Stern and Fineberg 1996), potentially open the door for more socially informed approaches to risk decision making (e.g. see some of the contributions to Okrent and Pidgeon 1998). The scope and structuring of the social amplification framework allows it to generate policy suggestions (with the usual caveats as to what is possible). And from the last fifteen years of work, we do have several examples of substantial policy analysis that draw upon the amplification framework as well as a considerable body of empirical work to inform risk policy questions and ideas for further departures that may enhance management initiatives.

At the outset, it is important to recognize that any policy suggestions proceed from an underlying normative question: is it possible to develop normative criteria for judging the outcomes of social risk amplification as "good" or "bad," rather than merely addressing the pathologies of the most visible manifestations of "over" and "under" reaction? There is no research to date, as far as we are aware, on this critical issue. The question of when social amplification or attenuation becomes sufficiently pronounced, or more destructive than positive to the social construction and handling of the risk, is a complex one. Consider, for example, the case of social controversy over the siting of waste disposal facilities in the United States, an issue that generated widespread disapproval in the form of such acronyms as NIMBY, LULU, NIMTOF, and others, and has often been cited as a classic example of public overreaction. In fact, the resistance to land disposal of wastes has driven extensive waste reduction and recycling at source and, arguably, improved overall waste management.

In practical terms, agencies will still attempt to use the best available scientific knowledge and risk assessments in an attempt to produce estimates of "risk," although as Rappaport (1988) points out whereas scientific risk assessment is evaluated by its *accuracy*, one criterion for evaluating people's attention to risk signals is the *adaptiveness* of the information gained, and the two may not always correspond. Also, as Svenson (1988b) notes, we do not know when risk amplification has involved changes to people's basic mental models of a hazard (which may then, in principle, be judged as correct or incorrect with respect to some standard; see Morgan et al. 2001), or whether the modification of relevant values or thresholds of tolerability to the risk has occurred. Clearly a complete set of judgments oriented to the amplification process will likely be involved in any such evaluation process. And we should not lose sight of the desire of many responsible authorities to *suppress* the flow of signals in society so that control over the risk consideration process can be kept in the domain of the managers.

As noted earlier, two areas of policy analysis have drawn extensively on SARF. The first involves the future of radioactive waste management in the United States. The social amplification concept had its genesis in an ambitious program of social and economic research funded by the state of Nevada and conducted between 1985 and 1995. Included was a broad array of research aimed at assessing the future potential impacts of the proposed nuclear waste repository at Yucca Mountain, including studies on perceptions and imagery, risk signals, patterns of media coverage, possible stigma-related and other ripple effects, and social distrust. Drawing upon this extensive body of empirical work, which covered much of the scope of SARF, a team of researchers, assisted by a well-known science writer, set forth a broad policy analysis entitled *One Hundred Centuries of Solitude: Redirecting America's High-Level Nuclear Waste Policy* (Flynn, Chalmers, Easterling et al. 1995). The analysis argued that given the dismal failure of existing policy, a new approach was sorely needed, one that would be based on such elements as acceptance of the legitimacy of public concerns, an enhanced role for interim storage, a voluntary site selection process, negotiation with risk bearers, and actions aimed at restoring credibility (Flynn, Chalmers, Easterling et al. 1995, pp. 16–18).

A second policy area, one related to the Yucca Mountain case, is the impasse or gridlock over the siting of hazardous facilities more generically in a number of countries. Here the numerous empirical studies conducted as part of the social amplification approach have been an important part of the foundation for several policy prescriptions. Kunreuther and colleagues wedded the amplification concepts to the prescription and compensation research at the University of Pennsylvania's Wharton School and Lawrence Susskind's extensive experience with conflict resolution to develop a new Facility Siting Credo (table 1.3), subsequently tested for its prescriptive power (Kunreuther et al. 1993). Similarly, Kasperson and colleagues have drawn heavily upon social amplification research in arguing for new approaches and procedures in facility siting, including such policy elements as clear demonstration of societal need, steps to narrow the risk debate, approaches that would remain resilient under

Table 1.3 *The facility siting credo*

When planning and building locally unwanted land uses (LULUs), every effort ought to be made to meet the following objectives
Institute a broad-based participatory process
Seek consensus
Work to develop trust
Seek acceptable sites through a volunteer process
Consider a competitive siting process
Set realistic timetables
Keep multiple options open at all times
Achieve agreement that the status quo is unacceptable
Choose the solution that best addresses the problem
Guarantee that stringent safety standards will be met
Fully address (compensate) all negative impacts of a facility
Make the host community better off
Use contingent agreements
Work for geographic fairness

Source: Kunreuther, Fitzgerald, and Aarts (1993).

conditions of high social distrust, building constituencies of support, and use of adaptive institutional processes (Kasperson, Golding, and Tuler 1992; Kasperson forthcoming). The scope of issues covered in these policy prescriptions, the attention to interactive effects, and their links to rippling effects are suggestive of the types of policy analyses that might flow from amplification-based research.

One clear policy contribution could be to draw upon social amplification to improve society's capability to anticipate which new or emerging risks are likely to be highly amplified or attenuated. Given the inherent complexity of risk communication and social processes, it is clear that the framework cannot be expected to yield simple or direct predictions regarding which issues are likely to experience amplification/attenuation effects in advance. A parallel problem – which has in part epistemological and in part practical roots – occurs when researchers attempt to use knowledge of the human and organizational causes of past technological accidents and disasters to predict the likelihood of future failures (see Pidgeon 1988; Turner and Pidgeon 1997 esp. chapter 11). Here some practitioners have adopted more holistic methods, seeking to diagnose vulnerability in large organizational systems through screening against broad classes of risk management factors (see e.g. Groeneweg et al. 1994). In a similar way, knowledge of the factors likely to lead to amplification effects, and the sociopolitical contexts in which they might operate, could conceivably serve as a *screening device* for evaluating the potential for such consequences, particularly with respect to synergistic effects found among factors. Developing such a screening procedure and testing it retrospectively to explain past experience or against samples of new risks could be a particularly useful line of investigation.

Turning to the empirical foundations of social science research on risk, the extent to which existing empirical work reflects North American experience is striking. Clearly, we urgently need to conduct basic investigations on the transferability of the existing findings (for example, whether trust, blame, and responsibility for risk management play as strong a role in Europe or Asia as is reported in the United States), as well as the ways in which different cultural contexts uniquely shape risk communication and risk amplification effects. However, as Renn and Rohrmann (2000) make clear, conducting well-founded cross-cultural risk perceptions research is a formidable task, particularly if we consider the multiple parties present in the amplification/attenuation construct. However, if we start from the standpoint of the key mediators of much risk communication – the mass media – then the framework should be capable of describing and organizing the amplification rules used by media institutions in their role between government and sections of society. How the media interface with the other different institutional players in what Slovic (1998) terms the "risk game" is a key issue ripe for investigation. There is also the question of whether different institutional arrangements can be characterized as operating with predictable sets of amplification or attenuation rules (see Renn 1991a, p. 300), and whether evidence exists of causal links between such institutional behavior and subsequent societal impacts. The influence of regional (e.g. EC) and national legal and cultural frameworks in setting overarching contexts for amplification processes should be part of this research direction.

Social amplification has provided a useful analytic structure for studying stigma-related policy questions (Flynn, Slovic, and Kunreuther 2001), although the existing policy *options* for addressing such amplification-driven processes appear quite limited, as Gregory et al. (1995) have demonstrated. Litigating stigma claims under the aegis of tort law in the United States does not seem to offer an efficient or satisfactory solution. Project developers can, of course, simply pay whatever is asked for as compensation, but such a pay-and-move-on option fails to distinguish between valid claims for compensation and strategic demands based on greed or politically motivated attempts to oppose a policy or program. In addition, claims are often made for economic losses predicted to take place years or even decades into the future, despite the many difficulties inherent in forecasting future economic activities or social responses. Stigma effects might be ameliorated if public fears could be addressed effectively through risk communication efforts, but such a simple solution also seems unlikely. All too often, risk communication efforts have been unsuccessful because they failed to address the complex interplay of psychological, social, and political factors that is at the heart of social amplification and that drives profound mistrust of government and industry and results in high levels of perceived risk and thus opposition. Accordingly, policy responses geared to the interacting factors contributing to stigma at multiple stages of amplification processes are also required.

More open and participatory decision processes could provide valuable early information about potential sources of stigmatization and amplification drivers (see Renn, this volume chapter 16) and invest the larger community in understanding and managing technological hazards. This approach might even help to remove the basis for the blame and distrust that often occurs in the event of an accident or major risk policy failure, and improvements over time in our ability to identify and access the factors contributing to stigmatization may make it possible to predict the magnitude or timing of expected economic losses. This, in turn, could open the door to the creation of new insurance markets and to efforts for mitigating potentially harmful stigma effects. Finally, the societal institutions responsible for risk management must meet public concerns and conflicts with new norms and methods for addressing stigma issues, and improved arenas for resolving conflicts based on values of equity and fairness.

As a concluding comment, we reiterate that a particular policy strength of the framework is its capacity to mesh emerging findings from different avenues of risk research, to bring various insights and analytic leverage into conjunction, and (particularly) to analyze connections, interrelations, and interactions within particular social and cultural contexts. Such strengths suggest that the search for patterns and broader-based interpretations may yield new insights and hypotheses, as research on stigma, social trust, and "take-off" of the amplification process suggests. Elsewhere, assessing risk amplification and attenuation in the particular context of transboundary risks, Kasperson and Kasperson (2001) have pointed to potential "mirror" structures in the social processing of such risks, with social attenuation in the risk-source region and linked social amplification in the risk-consequence area. In global change research, German social scientists have provided new insights into vulnerability to environmental degradation by analyzing "syndromes" of change (Schnellnhuber et al. 1997). Throughout this chapter, and also in our more theoretical writings on social amplification, we have emphasized the potential research and policy value that a broadly based and integrative framework of risk affords. Such meso-level of theoretical analyses within the amplification framework could potentially open up new research questions and potential policy initiatives.

2 The logical structure of the social amplification of risk framework (SARF): *Meta*theoretical foundations and policy implications

Eugene A. Rosa

The social amplification of risk framework (SARF) is the most comprehensive tool available for the study of risk. Theories and frameworks are useful and effective only insofar as they conform to certain fundamental features of logic: clearly defined terms, coherence, internal consistency, sound organization explicated with parsimony, accompanied by a specification of scope conditions, and the generation of testable hypotheses. The first goal of this chapter is to evaluate critically key foundational concepts of the SARF and to strengthen its foundation with a set of metatheoretical principles that have been coherently structured. The second goal is to use these same metatheoretical principles to establish symmetry between SARF and risk policy. Such symmetry should enhance communication between experts and laypersons in the development of risk policy and, therefore, remove some of the obstacles to effective, democratic risk policy.

Genesis of the social amplification of risk framework

The SARF developed in the late 1980s in response to the emergence of multiple perspectives in the rapidly growing risk literature. The multiple perspectives that emerged led, according to Kasperson (1992) one of the leading architects of the SARF, to key disjunctures which came to dominate the field: disjunctures between technical and social analyses of risk; disjunctures within the social sciences themselves (e.g. between

The preparation of this chapter was, in part, supported by the Edward R. Meyer Professorship in the Thomas F. Foley Institute for Public Policy and Public Service at Washington State University. Various versions of this chapter have profited from the critical comments of Thomas Dietz, Riley Dunlap, William R. Freudenburg, M. V. Rajeev Gowda, Jill Griffin, Roger Kasperson, Aaron McCright, Ortwin Renn, James F. Short, Jr., Paul Slovic, and Brian Wynne. The supporting comments of John Searle on my critical, neo-realist approach to risk are also appreciated.

the rational actor perspective (RAP) of economics and engineering and the psychometric paradigm; see also Jaeger et al. 2001); disjunctures between the older natural hazards social science and the newer technological hazard social sciences; and disjunctures over scientific and other claims to knowledge. The literature begged for an integrative framework, such as the SARF.

Assessment and development

Having been subjected to both considerable scrutiny and to a growing number of applications for well over a decade, the time seems propitious for, firstly, assessing the strengths and weaknesses of the SARF. And, secondly, it may be just as timely to suggest directions for the further development of the framework. To date the SARF framework has attracted two separate, but complementary activities: (1) metatheoretical challenges, and (2) a growing breadth in the variety of applications. An example of the first activity is the challenge to the integrative utility of the SARF by cultural theory, the principal, competing integrative framework (see, for example, Rayner 1992, 1988). The second, far more voluminous activity, has comprised empirical work seeking to understand how risk interacts with, among other factors, social, institutional, and cultural processes and how key social variables, such as gender, occupation, ethnic status, and social status shape evaluations of risk (see Pidgeon 1999 for a more detailed summary).

Doubtless we can expect continued growth in the second type of activity and an increase in the cumulative understanding of the empirical status of the SARF. Hopefully, that future body of work will address some of the more neglected areas of past research, including the secondary effects of amplification, such as regulatory changes and economic impacts. In view of this likely direction in the literature another useful effort to further develop the framework would be to proceed in the exact opposite direction; to the very foundation of the framework. Indeed, that is where the argument of this chapter is grounded, not to further empirical considerations, but to fundamental logical ones.

Examining the roots

My overall assessment of the SARF can best be summed up by repeating my conclusion in an article published with Gary Machlis on "desirable risk." Noted there was the soundness and theoretical utility of the SARF, and that the framework "like a net... is useful for catching the accumulated empirical findings and like a beacon, it can point the way to disciplined inquiry" (Machlis and Rosa 1990, p. 164). That assessment serves as the beginning and as the anchor point for the argument of this chapter. The SARF is the most comprehensive overarching framework (net) in the field, and has been an effective orientation (beacon) lighting the way to disciplined inquiry. This conclusion embeds several of the desirable properties of theories and frameworks specified above: coherence, internal consistency, and sound organization explicated with parsimony. That the SARF has stimulated a variety of empirical studies is clear evidence of its capacity for generating testable hypotheses. The metatheoretical foundations of the SARF have yet to be fully evaluated, especially on the criteria of conceptual precision (clearly defined terms) and its specification of scope conditions. The task here, then, is to undertake this evaluation.

The specific aims of this chapter are to evaluate critically the basic logic of the framework and to deepen its philosophical underpinnings so that it can stand up to critical epistemological scrutiny. Just as risk underlies human action whether recognized or not, so do metatheoretical assumptions underlay frameworks, models, and theories whether these assumptions are recognized or not. Metatheoretical assumptions lay the foundation for theoretical frames and should, therefore, be brought to the surface and held up to logical scrutiny. We begin our evaluation with an assessment of the framework's conceptual precision.

The logical status of risk in the social amplification framework

What is the logical status of risk in the SARF? Reflecting on the development of the SARF Kasperson (1992) unpacks the key elements of the framework. As for "risk," SARF's root element, he writes:

Risk, in our view, is in part an *objective threat of harm* to people and in part *a product of culture and social experience*. Hence, hazardous events are "real": they involve transformations of the physical environment or human health as a result of continuous or sudden (accidental) releases of energy, matter, or information or involve perturbations in social and value structures. (Kasperson 1992, p. 154)[1]

This view of risk is a synthetic one. It quite clearly expresses the idea that risk comprises both an ontological and an epistemological domain.

---

[1] In response to some misreading of this conceptualization of risk, Kasperson seeks to clarify by reiterating that: "... risk, as treated in the social amplification framework, is in part the threat of direct harm that happens to people and their environments regardless of their social constructs, and in part the threat associated with the social conceptions and structures that shape the nature of other harms (to people, corporations, social institutions, communities, and values)" (Kasperson 1992, p. 161).

As an objective threat or harm to people, risk enjoys an ontological realism. As an element of the world subject to interpretation, filtered by social and cultural factors, risk enjoys an epistemological lability.

Despite the explication and reiteration of its meaning, the conceptualization of risk used in the original presentation of the SARF (Kasperson, Renn, Slovic et al. 1988) attracted criticisms of the following type: the SARF distinguishes, on the one hand, between "true" or "objective" risk and, on the other hand, subjective risk; and that the latter, due to amplification distortion, virtually always deviates from the true risk. Proponents of the framework have continued to re-affirm a meaning of risk that comprises two complementary domains, the ontological and the epistemological. It is misleading to view risk through the lens of either domain separately. But these efforts have apparently met with only partial success, for they have not quieted such criticisms entirely.

Thus, we find there is a need to address similar criticisms in the most recent work on the SARF. For example, Pidgeon writes:

A number of criticisms have been raised of the amplification metaphor itself. First, that it might be taken to imply that there exists a baseline or "true" risk readily attached to risk events, which is then distorted in some way by the social processes of amplification. (Pidgeon 1999, p. 149)

But, as has been the consistent practice in the past:

It is quite clear that the proponents of the framework do not wish to imply that such a single true baseline always and unproblematically exists, particularly in many of the heavily politicized transcientific settings... where amplification is most likely to occur. (Pidgeon 1999, p. 149)

One difficulty here is a failure to unpack thoroughly the logical (and philosophical) status of the meaning of risk. This may account for the recurring confusion over this key element in the SARF. It also opens the framework to the following challenging question: what, in fact, is being amplified: something real, or only claims about something real? The difficulty may also account for the recent practice of shifting the focus of the meaning of risk from an a priori specification to a consequentialist explanation. So, for example, Pidgeon writes: "Nevertheless, risk perceptions do have real *consequences*..." (Pidgeon 1999, p. 149).

Finessing the logical status of risk is one approach to the issue. However, it circumvents these fundamental questions: what, in fact, is the object of amplification? and, where, in fact, does that object come from? As a consequence, finessing the question leaves the SARF open to the recurrence of these questions. An alternative approach, the one developed here, is to develop the concept of risk in two steps. The first step is to explicate the separate ontological and epistemological statuses of risk, rather than define risk as simultaneously both. The second step is to combine the two domains into an internally consistent metatheoretical framework. This meta-framework's articulated principles are grounded in realism combined with an interpretive epistemology. The adoption of the framework will not likely settle the tension over the logical status of risk once and for all, but it will fortify the foundations of the SARF, making it more resistant to the metatheoretical criticisms of the past.

Meta*theoretical framework*

Our first task is to develop the case that risk is a real phenomenon. Risk as reality, then, becomes the foundation of our metatheoretical framework. Both the development of a "realist" meaning of risk and the building of a framework over that foundation presuppose a world of ontological realism. We refer to the overall metatheoretical framework of reconstructed realism as *Meta*, after the article "Metatheoretical foundations for post-normal risk" (Rosa 1998a) first laying it out. We begin with an argument for the reasonableness of ontological realism.

Ontological realism is the presupposition that a world exists independent of percipient actors. The case for ontological realism was thoroughly addressed in Rosa (1998a). Here is a summation of the *Meta* argument. It begins by posing these pivotal questions. On what foundation can we establish a basis for ontological realism? What class of signals from the world, whether conceived as independent or dependent on our constructs, can we use to illustrate a case for realism? Which of these signals gives us the strongest evidence for this illustration? Do the signals cohere around discernible underlying principles? We address the middle two of these questions first.

Real world constraints The class of signals that seems most compelling in the case for realism, is the one that, after Hayles (1995), represents "constraints." Here constraint is meant to convey the notion of limitation imposed by a world beyond us. Many "physical" constraints may, in fact, be unalterable limitations. If so, they are then beyond human agency. The issue of whether constraints should be viewed as a disembodied interpretation of conditions in the world, versus conditions resting in an embodied construction of the world, need not be resolved in order to take advantage of the power of constraint to reveal knowledge. Constraints, like gravity[2] and the second law of thermodynamics rule

---

[2] There is virtually no cultural knowledge system that claims that someone can step off a cliff on earth and remain suspended in mid air.

out some possibilities and, therefore, provide a more focused way of apprehending reality.

If we ferret out the continuity in the representations of ostensible constraints, rather than the alternative context bound accounts, we can discern a principle for addressing the first question above, namely the question of the foundational basis for realism. The principle to be discerned is contained in the context invariability (over historical time in Western science, and between Western and native representations) in the shared recognition of key constraints, such as gravity. In essence, we have pan-cultural recognition (meaning similar perception and interpretation across gulfs in time and culture) of certain constraints. Such intersubjective agreement, widely dispersed in history and collective experience, suggests that this physical feature of the world is sending compellingly similar signals to us, the percipient observers, wherever or whenever we are. Moreover, it implies that the source of these signals is from somewhere outside our own phenomenological context of interpretation. So, while this is not proof of an external, real world, it does give a compelling coherence to that presupposition.

Chasing the sun   Other pan-cultural knowledges further supports the notion that certain features of the world transcend cultural and phenomenological contexts.[3] Perhaps the most compelling example of such knowledges (owing to its recognition as a physical phenomenon) comes from astronomical observation. In particular, it is human experience with one of the most salient objects in the physical environment – the sun.

The tracing of seasons, one result of the sun's movement across the sky, can be found on the remaining ribs of Ice Age Mammoths at least 37,000 years ago, the work of Acheulean hunters (Hall 1984). And written calendars can be traced back to the last ice age, 20,000 years ago (Aveni 1989). But more remarkable is the fact that virtually every society reaching the

---

[3] The understanding of cultural practices, historically the province of anthropology, has long been prefigured by a deep commitment to cultural relativism, the belief in the unrestricted variability of culture to shape human behaviors. Accompanying that belief in human malleability was a deep skepticism of human universals. In recent years, theoretical opinion has shifted to the position that while culture remains a powerful shaping force, certain universals may lie beneath its force (Brown 1991). As a consequence, a growing variety of universalisms have been identified. Among the universalisms (or pan-culturalisms) of note are the similarity of perception across highly diverse cultures of core facial expressions of emotion (Ekman et al. 1972), the recognition by literally all people "that men and women are different, that babies come from women only, that women have a special role in nurturing infants" (Mazur 1991, pp. 28–29), the universal practice of reciprocity (Gouldner 1960), the universal use of fire (Goudsblom 1992) common color classification schemes (Berlin and Kay 1969), and common approaches to the reckoning of time (Malotki 1983).

stage of development that we call "civilization" knows that the passage of seasons reflects a solar year of 365 days. Such bureaucratically organized societies, typically designated as states, were far-flung in both time and geography. Extensive, highly organized economic systems, rigid patterns of social stratification, and the emergence of classes of specialists, often including astronomical specialists, commonly characterize them.

That annual time is dominated by 365 days in the Occidental world is well known and seldom questioned. It has been this way since before Christ in Roman times; the Julian calendar, a product of the period, sufficed for sixteen hundred years until tweaked by Pope Gregory. Easily overlooked is the fact that ancient Egyptian, Chinese, Javanese, Aztec, Mayan, and Inca civilizations adopted a 365-day calendar, too. Whether for the Asian and African worlds this reflects independent discovery or the diffusion from a common source are subject to ongoing theoretical debate.

Far less problematic is the evidence from the New World. The Mesoamerican states (Aztec, Maya, and Inca), the evidence clearly shows, developed their 365-day reckoning prior to the sudden European incursion in the sixteenth century.[4]

Hermetically sealed by two oceans, whatever ideas they may have developed about time would have taken place in a pristine condition from the start. Hence, when we pry into pre-Columbian systems of thought, unlike Asiatic and African cultures, we can be certain that what we discover about how people make and model their time systems must have been invented and developed independently, devoid of borrowing through social contact, at least from Western civilization. (Aveni 1989, p. 186)

Realism–antirealism consequences The convergence of perceptions and representations across time and cultures is not empirical proof of realism. Adopting a realist–objectivist perspective, instead, reflects the logical choice between two competing presuppositions. On the one hand, if we argue that convergences such as these are evidence of an independently existing reality, we are already presupposing that reality via the reality of the convergences. It, thus, defeats the very point of our attempt to develop a proof of an external reality. Viewing empirical evidence as real embeds the presupposition of ontological realism into the argument at the outset, rather than establishing it on independent grounds. For this

---

[4] A tangible example is at the Mayan ruins of *Chichén-Itzá* where the castle (*el castillo*), the site's largest and most imposing structure contains 365 steps. There are 91 steps on each of its four sides, totaling 364, plus the upper platform (Bloomgarden 1983). Theoretical opinion interprets this as a planned design, reflecting the incorporation of the yearly cycle into sacred architecture.

evidence is only unproblematically real within the presupposition that a world independent of us exists. The argument, thus, begs the question. On the other hand, if we presuppose an entirely constructed, or culturally conditioned reality, we are also presupposing a reality independent of all social constructions that provides the raw material out of which these constructions are formed. For even if our sensations are always unreliable, they are being activated by some external source.

Contemporary realist philosopher John Searle puts the matter this way:

> The ontological subjectivity of the socially constructed reality requires an ontologically objective reality out of which it is constructed . . . a socially constructed reality presupposes a nonsocially constructed reality . . . (Searle 1995, p. 191)

Tying this point back to our astronomical example we can see that pan-cultural and time-distanced convergences occur because however many layers of construction we remove, the signals, wherever they are coming from, must be coming from somewhere independent of the constructions. Furthermore, the signals are received with such similarity that their representations are similar. It makes sense to think of that "wherever" as external reality. In sum, based upon the principle of pan-cultural convergence, and upon the logical choices associated with observed pan-cultural practices, we have sketched a reasonable case for ontological realism. Our task now is to take that case to risk.[5]

Defining risk

Is risk real? We begin with the truism that to abstract is to simplify. Proper metatheoretical frameworks are abstract; they therefore simplify. One tool for accomplishing this simplification is definition. Definitions are useful as tools of abstraction and for bringing intellectual attention to a common focal point so that meanings are clear. Definitions are, therefore, a useful foundation upon which to erect theoretical structure. They are also

---

[5] Searle makes an alternative, but consistent case for realism. He observes that in order to abandon realism we are forced to abandon common sense. From modern computer jargon he borrows the term "default" positions to refer to ". . . views we all hold prereflectively so that any departure from them requires a conscious effort and a convincing argument" (Searle 1998, p. 9). He deepens his point by explicating precisely our key default positions: "There is a real world that exists independently of us, independently of our experiences, our thoughts, our language; We have direct perceptual access to that world through our senses, especially touch and vision; words in our language, words like *rabbit* or tree, typically have reasonably clear meanings. Because of their meanings, they can be used to refer to and talk about real objects in the world; Our statements are typically true or false depending on whether they correspond to how things are, that is, to the facts of the world; and, causation is a real relation among objects and events in the world, a relation whereby one phenomenon, the cause, causes another, the effect" (Searle 1998, p. 10).

useful devices for sorting domains of intellectual agreement from those of contention.

What is risk?

Despite the still rapidly growing literature on the topic of risk (Short 1984; Krimsky and Golding 1992; Beck 1992; Dietz et al. 2002) there is remarkably little consensus over what, in fact, is meant by risk. On the one hand, there has been vigorous debate over the definition of risk (e.g. Fischhoff et al. 1984), while on the other hand, there is an intentional silence about defining risk at all (Douglas and Wildavsky 1982; Giddens 1990) despite book-length treatments of the topic. At one extreme are those who wish to define risk, typically viewing it as an objective property of an event or activity and as measured as the probability of well-defined, adverse events (Kates and Kasperson 1983). The most widely used definition of risk, a convention, is derived from modern positivism; risk is the probability of an adverse event (e.g. injury, disease, death) times the consequences of that event (e.g. number of injuries or deaths, types and severity of diseases) (Wilson and Crouch 1982).

At the other extreme is the constructivist paradigm that at once eschews defining risk while severely criticizing the conventional definition. The harshest criticism has come from a strong form of subjectivism within the constructivist paradigm that is entirely opposed to the notion of objective risk. This strong form, a relativistic view of social constructivism derived from a phenomenological philosophy, views risk as nothing more than subjective perceptions shaped by the filters of culture and social structure (Wynne 1992a). As with most extreme positions, the objectivist and subjectivist views of risk, taken separately, are poor descriptions of reality (Short 1984; Dietz et al. 2002).

Definition

In view of the foregoing considerations a definition of risk is proposed here. This is neither because the definition will necessarily attract universal agreement nor because it will be categorically correct, but because, as noted above, it will be the first brick in the foundation of our metatheoretical framework of realism. The starting-point of our definition is the widely shared presupposition that distinguishes between reality and possibility (Evers and Nowotny 1987). If the future is either predetermined or independent of present human activities, the term "risk" makes no sense whatsoever. Thus, at the foundation of our definition is the notion that certain states of the world which are possible and not predetermined can, objectively, be defined as risk. The fact that these states are not pre-determined means they are probabilistic and, therefore, embedded with some degree of uncertainty.

Despite this "realist" foundation, our ability to identify, measure, and understand risks ranges from the putatively certain to the totally uncertain. To the extent that we are limited in these abilities, risk will appear less and less like an objective state of the world, and more and more like a social construction; a crucial point to be developed later. Furthermore, what individuals or societies perceive as risk and decide to choose to concern themselves as risk are not shaped only by the objective state of risk, but are also shaped by social, cultural, and political factors – as well as the precision of our analytic tools for identifying risk in the first place.[6]

To the idea of possibility, and concomitantly, uncertainty, we add a second presupposition: risk exists only when the uncertainty involves some feature of the world, whether in natural events or in human activities, that impacts human reality in some way. Combining these two dimensions, we propose the following definition:

Definition: Risk is a situation or an event where something of human value (including humans themselves) is at stake and where the outcome is uncertain.

This definition[7] fulfills our present task. It expresses an ontology (a theory of being) of risk, an ontological realism that specifies which states of the world are to be conceptualized as risk. Whether it attracts widespread agreement or not, our definition captures three elements found in nearly all conceptions of risk, even when the term is left undefined and must be inferred from discourse about risk. The first element is the notion that risk expresses some state of reality of human concern or interest. At stake is something of value to humans. The second element is that some outcome is possible; an outcome can occur. The third, implied in the second element but in need of its own specification, is the fact that it seems impossible to talk about risk in the absence of the notion of uncertainty. Environmental and health risks both have as defining features, uncertainty and human stakes. We worry that there is some likelihood, never absolute certainty, that certain human activities, such as types of fuels we consume, will impact the environment in untoward ways. We also worry, for example, that exposure to certain chemicals has some likelihood of causing sickness or death.

---

[6] One of the key strengths of the SARF is the incorporating of these social verities.

[7] This is a slightly modified, improved version of the definition adopted in Rosa (1998a) and Jaeger et al. (2001). The improvement is due to the thoughtful comments of Roger Kasperson and M. V. Rajeev Gowda.

The scoping of theory

No theory or framework can explain all things. This limitation, long recognized for scientific theories (Toulmin 1953), is equally applicable to social scientific theories. The two-part problem is this. First, it follows from the proposition opening this paragraph that predictions are impossible about things not covered by the theory. So, the theory is ineluctably silent in its conjectures about some features of the world. Second, for those predictions that can be derived from the theory there will doubtless be some volume of empirical evidence that fails to confirm its predictions. As a result, "Every general social scientific proposition is both true and false" (Walker and Cohen 1985) because supporting examples and embarrassing counter-examples can always be found for each of them. How does one interpret the contrary evidence? Is the contrary evidence merely a vexing anomaly? Or, does the disconfirming evidence signal a fatal flaw in the theory?

The route out of this dilemma is to delineate the theory or framework's scope. Scope conditions consist of a specification of both the conditions of the world to which the theory applies and the range of its applicability within those conditions. These specifications "conditionalize" theory, thereby delineating the conditions under which propositions and predictions are presumed to hold. Scope conditions, therefore, specify the domain and range of theoretical applicability. This practice is consistent with the structure of theories in the traditional sciences (Hempel and Oppenheim 1948).

Scope domain   The proposed definition not only locates risk in the real world, but also addresses the issue of theoretical scope. The definition embeds a scoping of the domain of risk directly, and a scoping of applicability indirectly. It specifies the necessary and sufficient conditions of risk and, therefore, demarcates risk from other situations or events where human stakes, uncertainty, or both are absent. Thus, risk excludes the following situations or events: those that are "certain," but where human stakes are not involved, such as planetary systems; those that are "uncertain," but where human stakes, at least proximately, are not involved, such as the behavior of sub-atomic particles; and those that are certain and where human stakes are involved, such as fate. These considerations lead to the 2 × 2 table of figure 2.1.

The pattern of the four cells of figure 2.1, derived from our risk definition, provides demarcations between not only states of the world, but also between domains of inquiry and the knowledge systems making claims within those domains. Thus, for deterministic states we find celestial

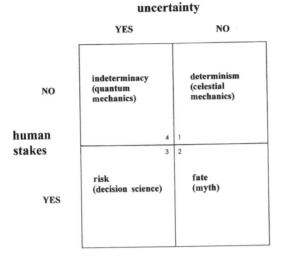

Figure 2.1 Risk: defining dimensions.

mechanics, for indeterministic states we find quantum mechanics, for fate we find myth, and for risk we find decision science. The key derivation of this demarcation is the placement of risk. It occupies a single cell, cell 3, the one in the lower left corner of the figure with the conjunction of uncertainty and human stakes. This, then, it follows, is the proper scope of risk investigation.

Figure 2.2 is a blowup of cell 3, risk, with the two defining features of risk represented by the two axes.

Defining risk in this way uncovers several important features of the concept. First, the definition is consistent with the etymology of the word, which is described in a later section. Second, this representation of risk is consistent with the standard definition of risk in the technical literature as probability times consequences (or outcomes).

Our representation of risk not only subsumes the standard, technical definition but is also more robust. It, for example, easily accommodates debates among experts, among laypersons, and between experts and laypersons (one of several persistent problems produced by insisting on the probability times consequence definition of risk). This is because it points to the challenge of establishing a precise measure of uncertainty as well as a precise measure of stakes involved: these are key points of debate between such groups.

Figure 2.2 is a mapping of the definition into probability space. The horizontal dimension of figure 2.2, uncertainty, is consistent with the

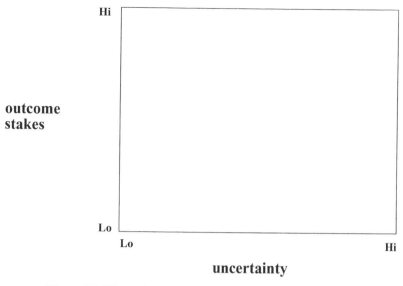

Figure 2.2 Dimensions of risk.

representation of risk in terms of probabilities or odds, as in formal analyses. By definition uncertainty excludes impossible outcomes, on the one hand, and fated outcomes on the other. Similarly, to say that a necessary element of risk is "possibility" means that probabilities of zero or one are removed from consideration. The vertical dimension, human stakes, is consistent with outcomes and consequences; another consistency with conventional and formal analyses.

Our mapping of risk into probabilities, in the range $0 < p < 1$, eliminates by definition the probabilities zero and one. A world where all probabilities about events are zero (the event cannot happen) or one (the event is destined to happen), that is $p = 0$ or 1, is a world of non-risk: a world of fate. This is the world of quadrant no. 2 in figure 2.1. Given the risk and fate states (quadrants 2 and 3) of the world, how does a culture choose one over the other? They choose it through their epistemology: here an epistemological choice based upon their presuppositions about the ontological state of the world.

In which quadrant a culture finds itself is a function of its epistemology and the ontology generated by that epistemology. There is a consequential symmetry between a culture's ontology and epistemology. This means that cultures occupying quadrant 2, let us call them culture type X, will live in a world of shared belief about risk that is incompatible with cultures occupying quadrant 3, type Y. In other words, if the question we wish to direct to these different cultures is: what is the nature of danger in your world?, the answers from the two culture types, X and Y, are fully antithetical. The answers will reflect entirely different presuppositions about the ontological states of the world. Culture X will answer: it is filled with predetermined, certain outcomes. Culture Y will answer: the world is filled with possible but uncertain outcomes. This observation preserves the dignity of prescientific cultures, such as those occupying quadrant 2 who do not normally think of the world in probabilistic terms, because their epistemology is perfectly fitted to their ontology. If the argument is plausible thus far, it then raises the question of whether on this count – a scoping of the conditions of risk in the world – comparison between cultures in the separate quadrants is meaningful.

Scope range   The definition also points to a broadening of the range of applicability of the concept risk. This is so because the definition comprises not only undesirable, but also desirable outcomes. In doing so it expands the range and robustness of risk, a feature virtually absent from any other definition of risk. It also allows us to capture at least two important domains of human risk action: investment risk and thrill risk. In portfolio theory risk is understood to apply to desirable and undesirable outcomes on an equal footing. Investors do not think in terms of a single stock but in terms of a portfolio of stocks where the risk of losing money on one share is balanced against the probability of gaining from another share. Thus, risk's scope includes both losses and gains.

Another domain of social life where gains play a central role is adventure and thrill risk. Despite being generally overlooked in the risk literature, "desirable risk" (risk that is sought, not avoided, because of the thrill and intrinsic enjoyment it brings) is a pervasive feature of social life. The focus of the risk literature has been almost exclusively on dangerous and other untoward risks resulting in definitions, stated or implied, that comprise only undesirable outcomes. The proposed definition can accommodate both danger and adventure within its scope and therefore address a fuller range of human activities. And the applicability of the SARF to such risks has already been demonstrated (Machlis and Rosa 1990), thereby providing an operational delineation of its scope range.

Risk as ontological realism

A logical consequence of defining risk as an objective state of the world is that risk exists independent of our perceptions and of our knowledge claims, subjective judgments, about what is at risk and how likely a risk will be realized. Furthermore, placing risk into an ontological category leaves open the question of our knowability of given risks: the question of the epistemology of risk. It makes no claim that we know, or indeed can ever know, all conditions of the world that are a convergence of uncertainty and of human concern, that is, of risk. Some of our claims to knowledge about risk will be well founded, while others will be beyond our grasp.

One appealing consequence of this feature is that it neither inherently defines away, nor contradicts, the variety of paradigms in the risk field; not the positivistic (technical) paradigm, not cultural theory, not the constructivist paradigm. Indeed, it places debates between paradigms into an arena of disagreement over questions of knowledge: about our perceptions and understandings of risk, and about our understanding of how groups or societies choose to be concerned with some risks while ignoring others. In effect, it defines paradigmatic debates over risk as an issue in epistemology. Operationally, these debates are often over the evidence available from which to infer the probability that a risk will be realized.

Ontological realism and the SARF

Having developed a metatheoretical grounding for the meaning of risk we can now address the question of how that grounding integrates into the SARF. A convenient way for addressing this issue is to compare the meaning of risk in the SARF with the meaning contained in the definition developed above. Here is the previously stated meaning of risk in the SARF: "Risk, in our view, is in part an objective threat of harm to people and in part a product of culture and social experience. Hence, hazardous events are 'real'"... Now here is the definition we just developed above: "Risk is a situation or an event where something of human value (including humans themselves) is at stake and where the outcome is uncertain."

The definitions are similar and compatible in their ontology: both assert that risk is something real. And both incorporate human stakes, implicitly or explicitly. The significant difference is that the first definition "assumes" a position of realism, while the second does not just assume realism, but instead develops an independent argument for realism. Another, less significant difference, is that the first definition focuses exclusively on negative risks (as do virtually all other definitions of risk), while the second definition accommodates both undesirable and desirable risks. Juxtaposing the two definitions leads to two key points. First, the two definitions are similarly grounded philosophically in ontological realism. Accordingly, they are logically consistent. Therefore the incorporation of the second definition into the SARF does not reconceptualize, or otherwise disturb, its basic logic. Second, there are sound reasons to argue for replacing the first definition with the second. The second definition deepens the foundation of the SARF considerably. On the one hand, it does not presuppose the realism that lies at the core of the SARF foundation, thereby exposing it to the vulnerability of an embedded realism bias. On the other hand, the second definition, independent of context, provides a defensible rationale for adopting a position of realism as the core.

The epistemology of risk – *HERO*

Having made the case for ontological realism, what might loosely be called the objective side of risk, we must now address the issue of epistemology, the subjective side. Insofar as our argument for a realist–objectivist ontology of risk is sound, it immediately raises the crucial question: does it ineluctably follow that, on the logic of symmetry, the epistemology of risk is also realist–objectivist? In other words, if the world is ontologically real is our understanding of it too? The extreme positivist position inherent in technical risk analysis answers this question with a resounding "yes." In contrast, it will be argued below that the proper answer to this question is a categorical "no." Knowledge claims about risk may be realist based or constructivist based depending upon the evidentiary basis of our claims to knowledge. That there is no necessary one-to-one correspondence between the ontology and epistemology of risk is due, fundamentally, to the intervening role of human activities: culture, values, institutions, perceptions, and interpretations of our realist world of risk. In short, an amplification process, effectively captured in the SARF, intervenes between risk and our knowledge of risk. As a consequence, the epistemology of risk comprises a continuum ranging from realism/objectivism to relativism/subjectivism.

Limitations to human knowledge

Human perceptual and cognitive capabilities are inherently limited. As a consequence, we can neither generate perfect knowledge about the world, nor can we create a "true" understanding of our physical and social environments; risky ones or otherwise. Facts seldom speak for themselves and considerable ambiguity surrounds even the most basic facts. The world "out there" and our understanding of it can never be isomorphic: human understanding can only approximate the world we seek to explain. Thus, our claims to knowledge about our worlds are always subjective, and always fallible. Many phenomenological thinkers and strong constructivists take this fact as a basis for claiming that all claims to knowledge about our worlds are, therefore, relative; one claim is generally as good as any other.

The position taken here is *hierarchical epistemology*. Connecting it to the ontological realism of our framework, we can refer to their combination as *hierarchical epistemology and realist ontology*, or by the acronym *HERO*.[8] Epistemological hierarchicalism does not deny the fallibility of all knowledge claims. What it denies is that all knowledge claims are equally fallible. Indeed, if all knowledge claims were equally fallible (or equally valid), we all would be living behind a veil of ignorance where there would be no knowledge at all. Instead, hierarchicalism comprises variations in the quality of knowledge claims along a continuum ranging from those of considerable agreement to those of great disagreement. Knowledge claims, while always short of absolute truth, admit to degrees of approximation to what is true.

A very important result of this logic is to make the ontology and epistemology of risk logically independent, but complements of one another. *HERO* is, at once, consistent with epistemological relativism but goes beyond those versions that equalize all knowledge claims or deny the privileging of particular claims. *HERO* admits to differences in the types, the quality, and the aptness of our knowledge.

HERO and the SARF

The SARF delineates the variety of forces and institutions that can intensify or attenuate signals emanating from a risk event. The unstated logic here is fully consistent with the epistemological position developed above. In particular, just because a risk is presumed to be an ontological reality in the world (the SARF's definition, "an objective threat of harm"), it does not necessarily follow that we can come to have objective knowledge of that reality. That goal is generally unreachable because of the inherent limitations in our capacity for understanding and because of the huge volume of "noise" from the social world. A key strength of the SARF is the recognition of this limitation, on the one hand, and the capture of its epistemological process within a coherent conceptualization.

While the basic epistemology of the SARF is logically consistent with the framework developed in *Meta* (Rosa 1998a), and transported to the SARF, there is one key difference worthy of consideration. *Meta*

---

[8] In the original formulation in *Meta* (Rosa 1998a), the ontological and epistemological states of the metaframework were defined as ontological realism with epistemological hierarchicalism, or with the acronym OREH, for short. Many commentators found the idea useful but this terminology cumbersome and difficult to retain when thinking through the entire argument. Hence, we have reordered the terms to produce the more "user friendly" acronym: *HERO*.

developed the idea of *HERO*, that not all knowledge claims about risk are equally valid, or equally fallible, but occupy a broad continuum of acceptability; a hierarchy of credibility. The SARF is silent on this pivotal issue. It does not address the issue of the credibility of knowledge claims. This might be an interesting challenge for future work. For the present, at least, *HERO* can fill that gap.

What might be some key limitations to the argument for realist ontology and a labile epistemology presented thus far? A good share of the argument rests upon the soundness of a definition of risk that is based upon realist–objectivist ontology. Hence, we might point to definitional issues as the Achilles' heel of the argument. Here is one critical line of reasoning along those lines.

Risk and danger: semantics or substance?

Several scholars (e.g. Luhmann 1993) have distinguished between un-recognized risk, on the one hand, and perceived risk, on the other, with the terms "danger" and "risk" respectively. Danger comprises elements of the world that threaten humans in some way. Risk is recognition of danger. The intent here is to demarcate between features of the world that threaten humans but go unrecognized, from those where there is conscious recognition of the threat and, presumably, equally conscious strategies for responding to the threat. Pragmatically, this appears to be an accessible and useful way for distinguishing two key features of the general notion of risk.

Unfortunately, this seemingly straightforward demarcation stemming from its innocent conceptualization poses several challenging conceptual, logical, and epistemological difficulties. Some of these are only vexing in the details, but others raise deep and significant tensions over how we theorize about risk and how we use our theoretical framings to inform public policy. It will be useful to delineate key features of these difficulties.

Etymology

Word origins and connotations of meaning are one issue. As pointed out elsewhere (Rosa 1998a), the word risk according to humanist Peter Timmerman (1986) came to the English language from French in the 1660s, which had been adopted (though its exact origins remain obscure) from the Italian word "riscare"[9] meaning to navigate among dangerous

---

[9] This is the spelling in old Italian, the modern spelling being "rischiare" with the noun form of the word being "rischio."

rocks. The *Oxford English Dictionary* (*OED*) (1982) defines risk as: "hazard, *danger*; exposure to mischance or peril."

The *OED* gives the following as the modern definition of danger, dating from the fifteenth century: "Liability or exposure to harm or injury; the condition of being exposed, the chance of evil; *risk*, peril." The unabridged second edition of the *Random House Dictionary of the English Language* (Random House 1987) provides a nearly identical definition: "1. Liability or exposure to harm or injury; *risk*; peril. 2. An instance or cause of peril; menace."

Noteworthy in the comparison between the dictionary definitions of risk and danger is their remarkable similarity. Both refer to the liability or exposure to harm, injury, peril or, alternately, to risk or danger. Thus, common usages, from which formal definitions historically emerge, converge around common elements. More importantly here, however, is the fact that both definitions imply an *ontological state* of the world: that there is a liability of exposure to some untoward things out there: harm, injury, peril. There is literally no distinction between the "out there" things and our perceptions of them. In these senses the definitions are consistent with the definition we developed above that defines risk as an ontological state of the world, that risk is real.

Definitions are never entirely true nor entirely false. In a theoretical context there is considerable flexibility over the definition of terms. One is generally free to define theoretical concepts in esoteric terms, in formal language, in symbolic terms, in natural language, or whatever pragmatically suits the needs of theory. The usefulness of a given definition lies, not in its truth claim nor in its semantic form, but in its capacity for focusing our perceptions and understanding within a common frame of reference. Defining risk and danger as ontological entities is consistent with common usage of these terms. This means that a theoretically driven definition argued for here, and common usage share the same frame of reference. This is a first-order consistency. But, perhaps the more desirable consequence of this consistency is a pragmatic one; namely, a second order consistency for informing and implementing risk policy. This second consistency is elaborated below.

Policy

The SARF is not only intended to be a theoretical orientation, but also a policy tool for improving risk assessment and management. Policy can be conceived as a bridge over the gap between *what is* and *what ought* to be. Theory is preoccupied with the "what is" side of the bridge. It is the foundation for the bridge. The strength of the bridge (policy) is a function of the strength of its foundation (theory). The more theoretically grounded a given policy, the more defensible is its underlying logic. Policy is also a bridge between expert conceptualizations (theory) and regulatory actions, actions often involving multiple organizations or a wide variety of citizens. To no small degree the successful implementation of policy will depend upon the translation of expert conceptualizations (theory) into operational conceptualizations accessible to policy makers, regulatory professionals, and citizens. It should be evident that this translation will be eased to the extent that all sets of actors have a common frame of reference. Because definitions provide frames of reference, the translation will be eased to the extent that the actors share key definitions. Definitions that are both theoretically rich, yet consistent with common usage (as codified in dictionaries) are in a position to meet this condition.

What is danger?

A second issue is the meaning of danger. Danger, according, to those wishing to demarcate it from risk, comprises unrecognized threats, perils, or hazards. But, this definition fails to settle the matter. Indeed, it opens up a number of challenging questions. If danger is treated as an undefined concept, the residual category from the definition of risk as a perceptual phenomenon exclusively, this raises several disquieting logical problems, perhaps dead-ends. The most elementary issue stems from the natural question: what, then, is danger? Is danger an epistemological convention? Is it all the threatening stuff out there in the world we cannot perceive? If so, danger is an ontological state of the world? If, instead, danger is only a convention for describing the absence of its own recognition by us, then how do we know when danger is, in fact, present? By the parallel definition that risk is only a phenomenon which is perceived, then, by definition, danger cannot be perceived. That being so, how do we know if it is present? Indeed, how can we know if it is ever present? In short, what are the conditions under which we can judge danger? Without a specification of these conditions, doesn't the term danger become nothing more than an undefined semantic residual or a conceptual chimera?

Another interpretation would have it that once risk is defined as a perceptual phenomenon, we can assume that everyone knows what its complement (danger) is. It is sufficient to say that danger is all the unperceived "bad stuff" that everyone knows is out there in the world. It is, therefore, unnecessary to explicate a definition of danger other than to say it consists of threats to humans or what they value that is beyond our percipient recognition? By presupposing a common understanding of the term danger, this commits the well-known fallacy of "begging the question." In particular, it assumes away the very point at issue; namely, when, in fact, is danger present and what, in fact, are the epistemological and ontological states of the terms risk and danger? For example, do the terms imply ontological states at all? Is one real (say, danger) and the other constructed (say, risk), for example? Or, are ontological states merely specifications of epistemological conventions; neither is real nor constructed, but convenient terms for delineating substantive risk topics. Furthermore, begging the question obviates the important, derivative question: how are the ontological and epistemological states, if different, logically connected? In other words, if two states are underpinned by contrary presuppositions (realist ontology and a constructivist epistemology, for example) how is coherence maintained in their parallel use?

What is risk?

Even if we relax our concerns over the question-begging fallacy other logical fallacies await. The first of these are the problems of tautology and the vicious cycle of circularity. We can illustrate the problem by beginning with a definition of risk that implicitly argues that risk does not exist as an ontological entity, but only as an epistemological entity. In this view risk only exists when we recognize it. Risk, therefore, cannot be distinguished from risk perception. One of the most explicit statements of this position comes from Shrader-Frechette who argues: "In sum, there is no distinction between perceived and actual risks because there are no risks except perceived risks. If there were hazards that were not perceived, then we would not know them" (Shrader-Frechette 1991, p. 84).[10]

Thus, in this formulation, risk is entirely a subjective phenomenon. There are no objective conditions in the world where the word risk applies. It is only when conditions in the world are dangerous and are perceived to be so that risk has meaning. Does it follow, then, that there are as many (or

---

[10] Slovic appears to be in complete accord when he writes: "One of the most important assumptions in our approach is that risk is inherently subjective. Risk does not exist 'out there,' independent of our minds and culture, waiting to be measured. Human beings invented the concept 'risk' to help them understand and cope with the dangers and uncertainties of life. There is no such thing as 'real risk' or 'objective risk' " (Slovic 1992, p. 119). However, the apparent accord is virtual, not literal, since Slovic wishes to emphasize the fact that risk strategies and actions presuppose a recognition of risks in the first place; risks must first be perceived. Risks that are out of mind are out of the bounds of strategic choice. Similarly, Fischhoff writes: "Although there are actual risks, nobody knows what they are. All that anyone does know about risks can be classified as perceptions . . . In this light, what is commonly called a conflict between actual and perceived risk is better thought of as the conflict between two sets of risk perceptions: those of ranking scientists within their field of expertise and those of anybody else" (Fischhoff 1989, p. 270).

as few) risks as there are perceptions of what is risky? Or instead, we might ask, what about unrecognized real threats to humans (say, for example, subtle environmental threats to health that are currently undetectable with today's means, or the tens of thousands of untested chemicals in public use)? One answer to this question, a very weak one in my view, is that such threats are merely chimera, absurd creations of our minds. This position leads to the tautological and circular outcome that all threats to humans are perceptual threats, either perceived, reasonable threats or imagined, fantasy threats. Unless we recognize such threats, they do not exist at all.

Another, more reasonable answer to the question would argue, as do Slovic and Flynn,[11] that indeed, unperceived threats to humans (such as the example above) actually do exist in the world. But these threats are not risks; they are "dangers." After all, they are unperceived and, therefore, outside subjective experience. Dangers are "out there" all right; but we cannot perceive them. The possibility that this answer suffers from the question-begging fallacy aside, it may lead us to yet other logical problems. In particular, it can lead us back to the types of circularity outlined above such as defining risk in terms of danger and danger in terms of risk.

Or, it can lead to a parallel problem in logic: the infinite regress. The questioning sequence of an infinite regress might go something like this. Q: What is risk? A: It is threats to humans and what they value that are perceived. Q: What do we call threats to humans and what they value that are not perceived? A: Danger. Q: What is danger? A: It is threats to humans. Q: What is it that threatens humans? A: Unperceived uncertainties in the human condition. Q: What are these uncertainties? A: They are inestimable probabilities. Q: If they are inestimable, do they exist? A: Yes, as dangers, but not as risks. Q: If dangers cannot be perceived, how do we know they exist? A: Because everyone knows there are perils in the world, those that are perceived are risks, so the rest must be dangers. The only sure way of bringing this infinite regress to an end is to define risk or danger, and their relation to one another, with criteria independent of their own semantic complementarity. This is one of the features of the risk definition developed above, and another strength of *HERO*.

Epistemological considerations

One important, final issue here is an epistemological one. Essentially the issue is over the appropriate epistemology for understanding ontological

---

[11] Paul Slovic and James Flynn 1999, personal communication.

states of the world. How do we come to know what's "out there?" How do we come to know when risks exist? One could argue, as do hermeneuticists and other phenomenologists, that the world "out there" and our understanding of it are one. Analytic philosophy, they would argue, has created a false dichotomy between ontology, a world independent of perception and thought, and epistemology, our thinking and claims to understanding of that world. Ontology and epistemology are not distinct phenomena, but exist as a single entity. The world, therefore, is the functional equivalent of our understanding of it. Without mind there would be no world. Remove mind and we remove the world. The logical implication of this is that any phenomenon, such as risk, is the functional equivalent of our understanding of it. For example, we understand the consequences of jumping off a cliff, so this is a risk. We do not, however, know with any certainty whether there are extraterrestrial beings intending to harm us, so this is not a risk.

The phenomenological answer to our epistemological question has several troubling features. It denies a world independent of human capacity. This presupposition (anthropocentric in effect, we may note) is literally impossible to verify or refute unequivocally. One simply accepts it or not. If accepted, it raises questions similar to those examined above: namely, how do we know when risk exists? What evidence can we bring to bear on that knowledge? What do we call threats to humans that are yet undetected? How can we avoid the same circularity or infinite regress observed above in our argument?

Returning to the perspective claiming that risk is exclusively a perceptual phenomenon, that there is no such thing as "real risk," raises several other challenging epistemological issues. First, this conceptualization of risk reduces risk to a perceptual phenomenon. It, in effect, is psychological reductionism. This raises the immediate question: can all risks be reduced to psychological categories? Are there no real risks outside those we find entering the mind? Even if we accept the psychological as a valid perspective, we can ask why, on the one hand, there is often considerable agreement over some risks (such as smoking), or, on the other hand, considerable disagreement about other risks (global warming)? Are these judgments, sometimes concurring, sometimes disagreeing, made solely on the basis of perceptions independent of evidence from the world? Unlikely.

The psychological perspective locates and circumscribes risk in the epistemological domain. So defined, this domain is independent of the world "out there"; it exists independent of ontology. This raises the same key question that troubled us above; namely: how do we account for threats in the world that are unperceived? And, if risk is perception, of what is it a perception? In addition, if risk is a circumscribed perceptual phenomenon, existing only in the realm of epistemology, how does evidence from the world break through to that realm? Certainly it must, or we are left with an understanding of risk that exists independently of the world. If that were so, how can we ascertain whether risk, as perceptions, are real or merely chimera?

Slovic and Flynn provide one proposed solution to the foregoing problem.[11] While risk is coterminous with a perceptual domain (also an epistemological domain), real threats do exist in the world: they are "dangers." Danger, in effect, becomes the ontological complement to risk as epistemology. Unfortunately, this does not settle the matter. For it first raises the serious question examined above; namely: what, in fact, is danger? To say simply that it is threats, or perils, or hazards in the world subjects it to a question begging fallacy. The fundamental problem here is there is no explication of the conditions of the world that define danger. Hence, to say that threats, perils, or hazards are the conditions of danger is not a definition, but a substitution of semantic alternatives. This is so because, in turn, it raises the questions that naturally follow: What are threats? What are perils? What are hazards? Absent a specification of the independent conditions that define these terms opens the obvious possibility of falling into an infinite regress.

These problems might be surmounted if danger were first to be defined independently of risk. Also, since by clear implication danger refers to the ontological state of the world, it should be defined in ontological terms; namely, in terms of conditions existing in the world independent of human understanding. Risk, could then be defined with an independent epistemological criterion, such as the practice of defining risk as perceptual phenomena, a cognitive recognition of danger. Since these procedures produce two independent domains, danger and risk are no longer semantic complements. Rather, they are metatheoretical complements, as they logically should be. But, even if this demarcation were accomplished it would lead to a final requirement: the need to provide a logical link between the ontological world of danger and the epistemological world of risk. Again, *HERO* attempts to accomplish that with a grounded definition of risk.

Systems theory

As noted above, to avoid the logical pitfalls of tautology and circularity, or the abyss of infinite regress, risk and danger must be defined with criteria independent of their own semantic complementarity. One prominent effort to define risk and danger in this way is the work of systems sociologist

Niklas Luhmann (1993). Luhmann's definitions are explicit in their demarcation between risk and danger

In the case of *risk*, losses that may occur in the future are *attributed to decisions made*...The concept risk is, however, *clearly distinguished from the concept of danger*, that is to say, from the case where future losses are seen not at all as the consequences of a decision that has been made, but attributed to an external factor. With respect to *dangers*, however, society faces a problem that *the injured party has not himself caused*. (Luhmann 1993, p. 102, emphases added)

Luhmann's definitions of risk and danger are sociological. The two terms are used to distinguish between risk as agency, and danger as a condition external to decision making. Luhmann provides specific examples:

A first hypothesis is that distinct forms of social solidarity develop differently depending on whether the future is seen from the angle of risk or from the angle of danger. For this reason we judge self-injury by smoking otherwise than we do damage to our health caused by asbestos contamination. In the first case social regulation collides with notions of liberty, and the notion of passive smoking is unnecessary to justify regulation. (Luhmann 1993, p. 102)

Luhmann's examples are revealing, for they raise these two pivotal questions: does claiming that smoking is a risk while asbestos is a danger reflect widespread understanding (including scientific, regulatory, and conventional understanding) of these two threats? Not likely. Nearly everyone would describe both as health risks. Second, and similarly, what is the status of the health effects of passive smoking? In Luhmann's definitional scheme (it is "a problem that the injured party has not himself caused") the answer should be clear: it is a danger. Yet, again, this is at odds with widely accepted usage: passive smoke, to the extent it is a threat to health, is described as a risk. Thus, it is reasonable to conclude that Luhmann's distinction fails the test of ordinary language usage and the collective understanding of the word risk. His is a semantic distinction, not a denotative, nor substantive, nor analytic, nor theoretical one.

The foregoing criticism is not necessarily fatal. Theory building affords the opportunity for considerable definitional flexibility, as already noted above. Theorists are free to define terms instrumentally: that is, instrumental to the logic and structure of the theory, with or without consideration of ordinary language usage. It is possible to view Luhmann's distinction between risk and danger from such a perspective. Luhmann defines the two terms as instruments for leading us to focus attention on a fundamental, ubiquitous social phenomenon: social inequalities. All societies consist of positions or groupings with differential access to resources, prestige, and power. A basic purpose of Luhmann's distinction between risk and danger, perhaps the fundamental purpose, is to lay bare these inequalities. The first inequality stems from distinguishing between those who impose risks, via decision making, from those exposed to the consequences of those decisions in the form of dangers.

In brief, risks are attributed to decisions made, whereas dangers are attributed externally... It shows that the *risks the decision maker takes and has to take become danger for those affected*... The affected party finds himself in a quite different situation. He sees himself as endangered by decisions that he neither makes himself or controls... *He is dealing with danger* – even when he sees and reflects that *from the point of view of the decision maker (perhaps himself!), it is a matter of risk*. (Luhmann 1993, p. 107, emphases added)

The second inequality focuses on consequences. Here the focus shifts from a distinction between decision maker and those affected, to anyone affected by the realization of threats: loss.

Loss itself strikes with unequal force. The wealthy have more to lose, the poor starve more rapidly. (Luhmann 1993, p. 102)

Risks are choices of decision makers; smoking is a risk for those choosing to engage in this activity. Danger, on the other hand, is a threat that the injured party has not caused; it is attributable to the decisions (risks) of others. So, second-hand smoke is a danger. The logic underlying this first inequality precludes the possibility that one can have risks imposed upon oneself by natural hazards, other individuals, or organizational actors. All such impositions, in Luhmann's terminology, are "dangers." While incongruent with ordinary language usage, this definition can be theoretically justified. More troubling is an apparent contradiction where, on the one hand, "dangers are attributed *externally*" while risk is the result of decision making. Yet, when an individual makes a decision that affects the self (such as smoking) as well as others (second-hand smoke), it is a danger, in Luhmann's terminology, for all involved. It is a challenge to ordinary logic to say that a decision by a given individual is a risk but the consequences of that individual's decisions are a danger to all involved and is, therefore, external to that individual.

The more troubling feature of this formulation is the semantic fusion into one meaning that the separate definitions ineluctably lead. The act of decision making by an individual, according to Luhmann, is risk, but the untoward conditions produced by that decision are a danger to that individual. If an individual, as a consequence of a self-decision, imposes danger upon oneself, one is, according to Luhmann, simultaneously in a context of risk and danger. Luhmann himself recognizes the logical consequence of this when he writes: "We are confronted by a classical social paradox: risks are dangers, dangers are risks; because it is a matter of one and the same content observed in the medium of distinction requiring two different sides. The same is different" (Luhmann 1993, p. 107). For Luhmann, the paradox resulting from his logic is a key theoretical strength, for it points to an important dualism, an essential tension, in social reality.

But, there is good reason to question the analytic and logical utility of this interpretation. Risks for Luhmann can only exist as attributions of decisions made. Dangers are then, the semantic complement of risk, attributions of non-decisions. These complementary definitions are empty of a substantive basis for knowing if and when risk does exist. Certainly, no one would claim that all human decision making is an attribution of risk. Humans make countless decisions putatively devoid of risk. And similarly, to complete the complementarity, no one would claim that all non-decision contingencies of human experience are dangers. Yet, a strict reading of the definition would imply just that.

Furthermore, the conceptual space mapped out by risk and danger leaves a large empty section. A very common human decision about risk, recently highlighted in a popular book (Ross 1999), is to know that one is faced with threats (risks or dangers, whatever one prefers to name them), but to do nothing at all. Is a non-decision here a decision? Or is it a non-decision? Whether to apply the term risk or the term danger to this instance very much depends upon an answer to these questions. But, within Luhmann's perspective one would be hard pressed to answer them unequivocally.

Perhaps the most troubling feature of the argument is that the semantic space is self-contained. The semantic space is filled with a set of sociological categories. That Luhmann's theoretical frame defines its foundational concepts, risk and danger, as sociological categories means the frame is sociologically reductionistic. As with psychological reductionism, sociological reductionism raises a number of serious questions: can all risks, or all dangers, for that matter, be reduced to social categories or other features of social systems? If so, does that mean if there were no social categories there would be no risk? This would be a difficult position to sustain. If risk is reduced to sociology does that mean there are no risks independent of social systems? A negative answer here forces us to discredit all specialized knowledge, such as science, that makes strong knowledge claims about risk independent of sociological content. An affirmative answer suggests that risk is an ontological feature of the lifeworld, not a sociological category. If that is so, then this reality should be incorporated in the explication of the meaning of risk, not papered over with sociological conceptualization.

Realism and the SARF

Definition again plays a crucial role in dealing with the logical difficulties raised above. One option is to unpack and elaborate the meaning of risk as stated by proponents of the SARF and to ground that definition in realist ontology. This is certainly a viable option, but one with nontrivial intellectual demands. Another option, to recur to the key point made earlier, would be to incorporate the ontologically realist definition of risk and its associated *HERO* orientation argued for in *Meta* (Rosa 1998a) and above into the SARF. The theoretical advantage from exercising this option rests with the fact that underlying the definition is an already developed foundation: a foundation of metatheoretical logic. Exercising this option also has the advantage of convenience, the convenience of adopting an "off the shelf" tool to fix a theoretical leak.

Metatheory and policy

If *HERO* were to be incorporated into the SARF, as argued above, how can this contribute to policy? The risk field has been punctuated for the past three decades with considerable theoretical and methodological conflict. Yet, amidst this ongoing conflict at least one clear consensus has emerged. There is widespread agreement of the need to devise better procedures for the democratic management of risks in society (Rosa and Clark 1999; Renn, Webler, and Wiedemann, 1995; Beck 1995a; Stern and Fineberg 1996; Rosa et al.1993; Funtowicz and Ravetz 1991; Shrader-Frechette 1991; National Research Council 1989; Wynne 1987; Kunreuther and Linnerooth 1982). One straightforward corollary of this observation is a growing demand for greater grassroots, or layperson involvement in these activities. Indeed, I have recently argued, on pragmatic grounds, for such an extension of "peer communities" to issues of risk and public policy (Rosa and Clark 1999).

Realism and policy

Elsewhere (Rosa 1998b) I developed the rationale for maintaining a position of ontological realism in the development of risk policy. I can do no better than to repeat that rationale in slightly modified form.

In developing my metathoretical structure, in "Metatheoretical Foundations for Post-Normal Risk" (again, *Meta* for short) I had wished, as I do here, to stimulate the risk community to examine the logical structure of its arguments, to develop a framework that coherently preserved the principal modes of intellectual orientation without inherent contradiction, that provided a philosophical foundation for policy bridges and to be attentive and respectful of lay knowledge. Indeed, the latter consideration was a chief reason for adopting an "ontological realist" foundation for the *Meta* framework. As stated in *Meta* it is my contention that "realism – the idea that a world exists independent of percipient human observers . . . is the bedrock of our commonsense ideas of the world around us" (Rosa 1998a, p. 18) And I would also contend that it is the bedrock of how ordinary folks think and act. Laypersons see face validity in a world that is conceived to be real; they are, in short, ontological realists.

This realist assumption has instrumental importance. It is instrumental to the central policy goal stated above, namely the need to do a much better job of democratizing the process for assessing and managing risks. There are sound reasons, such as the principle of symmetry, for coordinating the activities of experts and laypersons with a stipulated ontology[12] and with an ontology that is most consistent with and comes most "naturally" to laypersons. Pragmatically, this approach obviates a difficult challenge of matching expert and lay ontologies. Different ontologies either require, on the one hand, the refashioning of lay presuppositions about the world or, on the other hand, the translation of a foreign, sometimes esoteric, ontology of experts into terms understandable by citizens. The adoption of lay ontology into the philosophical foundation has, instead, the side benefit of preserving the basis and dignity of layperson thought and action, for it neither privileges the ontological presupposition of the expert nor the layperson. It assumes both are on equal footing.

A key element in *Meta* was the idea of "hierarchical epistemology." The basic idea is fairly straightforward. All knowledge claims are fallible. We can never know any feature of the world perfectly. Our knowledge is never entirely isomorphic with the world we seek to understand. Any knowledge claim can, therefore, be problematicized. On this point just about everyone agrees. The more contentious point is that while all knowledge claims are fallible some claims appear more fallible than others: that is, knowledge claims can be hierarchically ordered. This assumption is widely accepted for scientific knowledge (the second law of thermodynamics enjoys far greater certitude than claims of climate change). But, I would argue, it is widely accepted, intuitively in this case, by ordinary folks, too. We can conduct a simple thought experiment consisting of a fieldwork test of this assumption. Imagine an afternoon in a working class saloon in

---

[12] The other logical options, all of which I find untenable, are: to assume that no ontology underlies the presuppositions of either group of actors, or that one does but can be safely ignored, or that an ontology can be recognized but left implicit without mortal damage to knowledge arguments.

North America or a pub in the United Kingdom. My hypothesis is that in the former setting there is a good chance we will hear "bullshit" invoked about lesser knowledge claims whose status is in question, and in the latter setting we would hear something like "humbug," for the same purpose.

It does not necessarily follow that scientists, laypersons, or any other group has a special purchase over where in the hierarchy of credibility to place competing knowledge claims. Indeed, disagreements between such stakeholders often rest upon which version of realism is viewed as most correct. A highly celebrated case of this is, of course, the work of Brian Wynne on the Cumbrian sheep farmers (Wynne 1996). The dispute between the farmers and scientists was not over whether radioactive fallout from Chernobyl was a social construction, nor whether radioactivity truly exists and is dangerous at some level of exposure, nor whether sheep had been contaminated, but instead the disagreement was over the true source of radioactive exposure of the sheep. Whereas scientists argued that Chernobyl was the true and only source, local farmers implicated the nearby Sellafield nuclear plant. Thus, ". . . the two knowledge-cultures expressed different assumptions about agency and control, and there were both *empirical* and normative dimensions to this" (Wynne 1996, p. 67, emphasis added).

Layperson ontology

Couch and Kroll-Smith (1998) have identified a revealing pattern common to the group of environmental movement organizations they studied. These groups did not eschew scientific knowledge (and the ontological realism upon which it is founded). Nor did they choose alternative ontologies. Instead, some group members typically became lay "scientists," in the sense that they familiarized themselves with the scientific and medical knowledge ("appropriating science," in the words of Couch and Kroll-Smith) relevant to their local or individual concerns. Here is the authors' vivid description of this practice:

It is one thing for a young woman cradling an infant to appeal to a government hearing board in the language of home, hearth, and children; it is quite another when this woman clutches her child to her breast and talks in the complicated language of toxicology, discussing the neurotoxic effects of boron or dichlorotetrafluoroethane on her child's cognitive development. (Couch and Kroll-Smith 1998, p. 2)

The typical objections of laypersons, then, is not to science *per se*, nor with the ontological assumption of realism upon which it builds, but to institutions, including science, that attempt to maintain a monopoly on knowledge claims and which sometimes misapply abstract science to the peculiarities of local settings. The core of layperson objections is to challenge presented knowledge that insists that it is the only true reflection of the ontological world.

> While a crisis of trust threatens the institution of science, however, it does not threaten the development or continued utility of scientific knowledge. . . . Indeed, often, they [citizens] become experts themselves. (Couch and Kroll-Smith 1998, pp. 5–6)

Similarly, in his work attempting to apply Habermas' idea of "cooperative discourse" to local settings, Renn (1998b) has found that engaged laypersons do not eschew scientific and technical knowledge. Indeed, they seek the best science and technical knowledge available while also seeking to concretize those abstract knowledges to local settings. Renn describes the general pattern:

> My own experience in organizing and moderating risk discourses in the United States, Switzerland, and Germany has taught me that most participants were not only willing to accept but even demanded the best technical estimate of the respective risks. They often insisted that we conduct expert workshops to collect and organize existing knowledge and separate firm knowledge from educated guesses. (Renn 1998b, p. 58)

Taken together, what do these examples have in common? In my judgment they are all manifest examples of latent, lay ontology. In particular, the examples are a posteriori instantiations of a lay ontology with a preference for realism. Laypersons look to science to expand their knowledge of technical issues and for guidance with difficult choices. Underlying this practice of looking to science for guidance may be the recognition that the realism of science is compatible with lay presuppositions about the world. They also look to science because it is there where they expect to find necessary, but not necessarily sufficient knowledge for decision making.

Policy realism and the SARF

We earlier developed a case for incorporating *Meta* with its realist ontology into the foundation of the SARF. Here we extended the argument to policy; the bridge between theory and application, between "what is" and "what ought to be." Our extension is the result of two separate, but complementary tacks. The first tack emphasizes the fact that laypersons, who it is expected will play an ever-increasing role in risk policy, presuppose a realist ontology in assessing risks of their concern. Thus, it is pragmatically sensible to develop analytic approaches and policy frames built on the same presupposition. Doing so obviates the difficult tasks of the reframing of layperson ontology and translating theoretical and policy ontology into lay terms. The second tack emphasizes metatheoretical symmetry between the SARF as a theoretical and analytical framework and SARF as a policy tool. Such symmetry ensures, among other things, a logical parallel and coherence between the foundations of the framework and of policy. It also expands the intellectual depth of the SARF.

Conclusion

The social amplification of risk framework (SARF) enjoys a status as the most comprehensive overall framework extant for the study of risk. It ostensibly meets certain fundamental criteria expected of fruitful conceptualizations: coherence, internal consistency, sound organization, and parsimony. Disciplined inquiry into the many facets of risk has been systematically and fruitfully guided by the SARF. That the SARF is capable of generating testable hypotheses has been amply demonstrated with a range of empirical studies that either elaborate the scope of the framework's applicability or seek to test its congruence with propositions explicated or implied in the framework. Thus, the principal means for affirming the theoretical usefulness of the SARF has been based upon empirical matters.

The argument presented here proceeded from the other end of the research spectrum. Its goal was to fortify the logical status of the SARF by incorporating an explicit and articulated metatheoretical framework grounded in realism into its core. It attempted to meet this goal by more clearly defining risk (as ontological realism) within the framework and by specifying its scope conditions. The fusing of a realism-based definition into the SARF and the scoping of the framework were drawn from the metatheoretical framework of Rosa, *Meta* (Rosa 1998a). Replacing the original definition of risk within the SARF with the realist-based one proposed here achieved two important objectives: first, the merely implied realism of the original definition is now an explicit, delineated feature of its core; and, second, the burden of performing the difficult balancing act (risk is partly objective harm but partly a product of social and cultural processes) is demarcated and systematized. It was argued that the contents of our metatheoretical framework of reconstructed realism, consisting of hierarchical epistemology combined with realist ontology, or *HERO*, was a more disciplined and systematic way of addressing that requirement. The net effect of the total effort has been to fortify the core of the SARF with a more precise definition of its key concept, risk, with a delineation of the scope of its domain and range, with a clear explication of its ontological and epistemological statuses, and with an explication of the logical connections between the two domains.

Because the SARF is not only a framework for theoretical elaboration, but also a policy tool, the argument was extended to risk policy. The incorporation of a metatheoretical framework into the core of the SARF also provided a basis for establishing symmetry between the SARF and democratic risk policy. Furthermore, it established this basis on the practical grounds of common framing, demonstrating a shared pre-analytic frame between experts and policy makers, on the one hand, and laypersons on the other. Common framing is one essential element in creating effective democratic procedures for the management of risks. The policy utility resulting from this approach, combined with the theoretical utility above, offers a compelling basis for incorporating the framework of reconstructed realism and its contents, *HERO*, into the Social Amplification of Risk Framework.

3   Social amplification of risk and the layering method

Glynis M. Breakwell and Julie Barnett

Risk management has become a dominant concern of public policy and yet the ability of government to anticipate the strength and focus of public concerns remains weak. This has proven to be costly. Rectifying the misunderstandings and assuaging the deep anxieties that surround "scares" and accidents can, and does, cost governments billions of pounds. It is thus vital to understand the genesis and development of such risk impacts. The social amplification of risk framework (SARF) was designed to assist in this endeavor. It aims to facilitate a greater understanding of the social processes that can mediate between a hazard event and its consequences.

The central contention of the framework is that

... Events pertaining to hazards interact with psychological, social, institutional and cultural processes in ways that can heighten or attenuate public perceptions of risk and shape risk behavior. Behavioral patterns in turn generate secondary social or economic consequences. These consequences extend far beyond direct harms to human health or the environment to include significant indirect impacts. (Renn, Burns, Kasperson et al. 1992, p. 139–140)

SARF identifies categories of mediator/moderator that intervene between the risk event and its consequences and suggests a causal and temporal sequence in which they act. Information flows first through various sources and then channels, triggering social stations of amplification, initiating individual stations of amplification, and precipitating behavioral reactions. These also engender ripple effects, resulting in secondary impacts. Within this, the framework identifies two stages. Within stage I the focus is upon the hazard event, the various stations of amplification and their relationships with public perceptions and first order behavioral responses. Stage II of the framework is concerned with secondary impacts. Here there is a direct link between the amplification of risk perceptions

The authors wish to acknowledge the Health and Safety Executive for grant number 3862/R62.080 which supported some of the research reported in this chapter.

and behaviors and secondary consequences. Secondary consequences consist of socio-economic and political impacts.

The purpose of this chapter is to introduce "the layering method." This is designed to describe the nature of the empirical relationships between the variables that SARF suggests are important in driving risk amplification processes. It is argued that such a method is necessary if SARF is to achieve any predictive power. Such a method is also necessary in order to evaluate more fully the propositions within SARF and to assess how useful it is. Before explaining how the layering method works, it is first necessary to situate current empirical work that evaluates SARF in relation to the notion of predictive power.

How useful is SARF?

If the framework is to be useful in informing risk communication initiatives and for understanding when and why particular amplification processes occur, it must acquire greater predictive power. Arguably, it currently has some degree of predictive power at a general level and particularly so within stage I of the framework. However, there is little empirical evidence for the way in which this leads to secondary impacts. Pidgeon (1999) notes that:

despite its prima facie plausibility, Stage II remains very much a hypothesis based upon primarily anecdotal evidence rather than being supported, at the current moment in time, by any systematic empirical evidence. (p. 149)

It has latterly been noted by the proponents of SARF that it does not constitute a theory (Kasperson 1992; Kasperson and Kasperson 1996) and that it should not therefore be expected to yield clear predictions as to which issues are likely to exemplify particular amplification processes (Pidgeon 1999). On the other hand, it is considered that such an analytic framework should be capable of deriving new hypotheses about the societal processing of risk signals (Pidgeon 1999).

The major quantitative study that explores SARF (Renn et al. 1992), set out to try to explore the size and direction of the causal influences between the variables that comprise the framework. Clearly then, prediction *is* a goal of SARF.

Obtaining predictive power

Lack of predictive power in a model is often related to not specifying the right variables, specifying too few of the right variables or not measuring the variables well enough (Breakwell 1994). In the empirical work exploring SARF noted above, by the authors' own admission, the question of how well the various constructs of the framework were operationalized is an issue of concern (Renn et al. 1992; Kasperson 1992). Measuring the variables relating to the physical consequences of the events themselves and to their socio-economic and political impacts was particularly problematic not least because both variables are a product of expert ratings. Ratings of the magnitude of impacts are based upon media reporting. This would also seem to undermine subsequent statements about the strength of the relationship between media coverage and political and socio-economic impacts. Using data about behavioral intentions rather than actual behavior is similarly problematic and may lead to an over-estimation of the strength of the relationships between particular variables.

As far as the inclusion of the appropriate variables is concerned, SARF notes the importance of a number of issues (e.g. amount and content of media coverage, public perceptions, group mobilization, numbers exposed to the hazard etc.). There is now considerable evidence within the risk literature for the importance of these (Pidgeon 1999). However, Breakwell (1994) suggests that the crucial challenge, having listed the factors that are important in determining (for example) risk amplification, is to specify how they interact. That is, in order to be predictive, a model must contain "relational rules" (Breakwell 1994, p. 65). In order to predict aspects of risk amplification these relational rules are likely to be complex, calling upon variables that are hierarchically structured.

Arguably, SARF was born of the recognition that the variables directing risk amplification lie at a variety of levels. Certainly, it was the disjunctures between the many and various strands of risk research that resulted in an appreciation of the value and indeed the necessity of developing a framework that was capable of subsuming a variety of variables that were situated at different levels of analysis. Such disjunctures were seen to limit understandings of the meaning and social causes of risks (Renn et al. 1992, p. 157). Thus the resulting framework is consistent with considering the effects of a range of constructs; from socio-historical context to individual differences.

The way in which these factors interact with each other is clearly vital in effecting particular patterns of risk amplification. This is certainly so when considering stage II of SARF but it is also necessary within stage I. Pidgeon (1999) notes that much remains to be done to investigate variations in the patterns of amplification associated with perceptions of risk and consequent changes in first-order behavioral responses. Noting the specific contexts in which intensification or attenuation occur is unlikely to be a simple matter of the presence or absence of particular variables but is rather likely to involve a consideration of the way in which these factors interact.

A further way in which predictive power can be enhanced is specifically to incorporate a consideration of the time dimension. Change, or the lack of it, as hazard events undergo a variety of amplification processes is crucial within the framework. This cannot be clearly seen with a snapshot simply portraying the configuration of factors evident at any one moment.

It is the contention of this chapter that in order for SARF to be capable of generating models that have predictive strength it is necessary to develop a method that allows exploration of interactions between levels of variables and that ideally this should be done over time. Such an extension would be concordant with, and be a development of previous empirical work by the authors of the framework.

The layering method

The layering method was developed in a project where the aim was to assess the applicability of SARF to informing risk communication in the United Kingdom. We proceeded from the premise that any substantial evaluation of the tenets of SARF should involve a consideration of the way in which the variables interact. A subsidiary aim of the research was to assess the utility and potential of the method for understanding risk events and their impacts.

The key components of the layering method, together with practical implications for collecting and analyzing data are outlined as follows:

- Firstly, the layering method requires data that are situated at various levels of analysis. Data may focus on individual actions, attitudes, or emotions. Information can also be gathered about shared understandings. The unit of analysis here may involve taking account of the effects of group and category memberships. SARF gives primacy to a further level of analysis: the activities of the various "stations of amplification." Finally, data should also access the socio-economic impacts of the risk event. Data are thus collected that act as metrics for a broad range of constructs in SARF. As a minimum, to use the layering method there should be two layers of data.
- Secondly, the layering method includes the time dimension as a systematic focus of the analysis. Thus, whenever possible data should be available over a period of time, and different levels of data should pertain to the same time period. In theory it is possible to use the layering method over the course of a day, a decade, or longer. An important precursor to collecting the layered data is to decide upon the time slice of the hazard that is to form the focus and to be clear as to the rationale for doing

this. The period being studied may of course subsequently expand as an understanding of the relevant amplification processes grows. The ideal of course is that these data should be collected over the life cycle of a hazard. The lifecycle of a hazard is taken here to include all phases in the existence of the hazard. This would include pre-notification, recognition, action to control or remove the hazard and its ultimate endpoint. Obviously for some hazards it is difficult to collect data for each of these phases; indeed it may be difficult to define the start and endpoints of its lifecycle.

- Finally, the layering method uses forms of analysis that examine the relationships of constructs at one time and over time. That is, the method is designed to permit the examination of coterminous change (this refers to the profile of the layers against each other at a single point in time) but more importantly, of sequential change. Here it is the juxtaposition of changes in the layers of data across time that becomes the focus of the analysis.

The layering method is an integrative, multidimensional technique for capturing data and identifying relationships. We are proposing that the layering method can assist with evaluating the usefulness of SARF as it has the capacity to identify relationships between the various components of SARF. As a consequence of this it facilitates the development and the subsequent testing of predictive models.

Using the layering method

Having outlined the conceptual background to the development of the layering method and the requirements of the method itself, this section looks at specific examples of the way that the layering method has been used, and notes some of the insights it has brought.

When using the layering method in the context of SARF to analyze a particular risk issue, ideally data should be collected over a period of time to index chosen variables within the framework. In such a situation thought can be given to the nature of the variables, the best way of operationalizing them and the frequency of time points at which data should be collected. For a variety of reasons, not least the availability of funding for such a task, this may often not be possible. In the research on which this chapter is based, the layering method was applied using secondary data. The examples given will reflect this. Some of the insights gained from the layering method will be given in relation to the BSE crisis in the United Kingdom. A further look at the potential benefits and difficulties of using the layering method will be situated in relation to a consideration of the AIDS/HIV issue in the United Kingdom.

Initially, we aimed to assemble data required by the layering method in relation to both BSE and AIDS/HIV. That is, data that are situated at different levels of analysis and that represent different constructs within SARF over the same time period. This was done with varying degrees of success.

Bovine Spongiform Encephalopathy (BSE)

BSE is one of a class of diseases called Transmissible Spongiform Encephalopathies (TSEs), and is a disease of cattle first identified in November 1986 by the United Kingdom Ministry of Agriculture, Fisheries and Food (MAFF) at its Central Veterinary Laboratory, Weybridge. It was designated as a notifiable disease in June 1988. The events subsequent to this make it the most significant and high-profile risk issue in the United Kingdom of the last fifteen years and arguably one of the most dramatic risk crises of the twentieth century. The nature of the disease itself as well as the risk communications that it has engendered have been extensively discussed, not least within the confines of a major United Kingdom public inquiry (Phillips et al. 2000, volume 1). To date the "BSE crisis," as it is often referred to in the United Kingdom, has not been the subject of a formal analysis from the perspective of SARF although different aspects such as the media coverage (Eldridge and Reilly, this volume chapter 6), the relationship between media coverage and public perceptions (Frewer, Rowe, and Sjöberg 1999) and the way in which products such as beef can become stigmatized (see Flynn, Slovic, and Kunreuther 2001) have been a focus. Having said that, it might be considered an archetypal example of risk intensification with an avalanche of press coverage and a collapse in public confidence in those who manage the safety of British beef. This followed the government's announcement in March 1996 of its concern about the possible link between BSE and the rare human neurodegenerative disease, Creutzfeldt-Jakob Disease (CJD). Following this announcement, which came in the wake of numerous government communications which had stressed the safety of British beef, the European Union placed an export ban on all British beef and beef products, beef sales in other European countries plummeted, and other industry sectors such as abattoirs and agricultural workers were reportedly affected. It has been suggested that other long-term indirect costs might include changed attitudes to the consumption of processed food (Harris and O'Shaughnessy 1997) and detrimental impacts on the condition of semi-natural and coastal grazing marshes as beef farmers increase their intensity of production (Bennett, Tranter, and Mayfield 1999).

	BSE	CJD	MEDIA			
Events	Confirmed cases of BSE	Nos of nv-CJD cases-Incidence and referrals	No of terms about BSE in The Guardian and The Observer; 6 monthly;	National British Press Coverage of BSE, *Miller and Reily*	No types of BSE in Financial Times Jan-Sept 1996 Dornbusch: *Mad cow crises*	British Press Coverage of Salmonela compared with BSE July 1990 and March 1994- *Miller and Reily*

1985	Sept	First cases of Bso diagnosed.
1986	Nov	Date given by Southwood Report when BSE was first identified as an entity.
1987	June	Ministers informed of first outbreak of BSE
1988	April	Committee (Southwood) set up to assess significance of new disease
	June	BSE made a notifiable disease
	July	Min of Agriculture stopped the feeding offal to cattle and sheep
	Aug	Gov orders the staugher of infected cattle
1989	Feb	Southwood Committee reported back
	March	Min of Agriculture asked to ban human consumption of infectious organs
	Nov	Min of Agriculture banned human consumption of any organs known to contain infectious agents - Spefified Bovine Offals (SBO's0 (had been proposed in June)
1990	Feb	Compensation for farmers announced
	Mar/April	EC restrict cattle/SBO exports
	April	Cat diagnosed with spongiform encephalopathy - announced in May
	May	CJD surveillance unit was set up
	May	Prof Richard Lacey: I see no alternative but to eliminate all infected herds, Beef banned in British schools: guidelines on BSE issued to farmers: CMO assurance that beef is safe to eat
	Sept	ban on using cows brains/spinal cord in feed
1992	Feb	Article in Guardian quoting Lacey saying offal ban hadn't stopped spread of BSE
1993	March	CMO repeats 1990 assurance that beef is safe
	June	
	Aug	CJD annual report expresses concern…
	October	
1994		
1995	May	CJD unit identified first case of nvCJD - 3 die in 95
1996	March	SEAC - BSE was potentially dangerous to humans. Press conference held after Mirror leak. Agriculture and health minister statements
		Macdonaids ban British beef; EC imposes ban on exports of all live cattle
	August	
1997		
1998		
1999		

Figure 3.1 BSE secondary data.

It was against this background that data as required by the layering method were collected. Details of this data and the time period for which they were available are set against various hazard notifications relating to BSE (see figure 3.1).

The layering method and BSE

Use of the layering method uncovered several interesting relationships between different constructs of SARF in relation to BSE. Although the BSE crisis might be considered a prime exemplar of risk intensification processes, there were no simple relationships between the volume of media coverage, levels of public concern, government expenditure, and impacts upon consumption of, and expenditure on, beef.

PUBLIC PERCEPTIONS					IMPACTS								
Survey food Risk Questionnaire	RISKPERCEPT M public perceptions data	Smith et al - Risk Decision and Policy	Healthiness perceptions of lamb, pork beef and bacon: MLC 1999	% quite very concerned about 7 different food issues. MLC 1999	Evolution of meat expenditure shares. 1977-95. *Burton and Young*	Household consumption of beef (various cuts) 1995-1999 MAFF	Comparison of beef expenditure (various cuts) 1995-1999 MAFF	% of GB households purchasing beef - MAFF-Monthly 1995-1999	Household food expen -diture 74-99 Beef, lamb,pork and poultry. MAFF	Household food consu -mption 74-99 Beef, lamb,pork and poultry. MAFF	Maff spending on BSE		Dept of Health spending on Funding the CJDSU and TSE funding outside of the area

| 5 data points | 2 data points | small scale - 2 data points |

Use of the layering method suggested that:

- Between 1989 and 1998 spontaneous mentions of concern about salmonella are considerably higher than those concerning BSE and yet this was over a period of time when media coverage of salmonella was almost non-existent
- The variance between the pattern of spend and the trajectories of BSE and CJD may be explicable in relation to the operation of uncertainty
- Different measures of public perceptions depicted different profiles of amplification.

Firstly, our main source of information relating to media coverage of BSE is the work of the Glasgow Media Group. This maps the coverage in the *Guardian* and the *Observer* from July 1987 to June 1996 (Kitzinger and

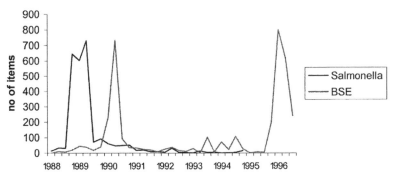

Figure 3.2 British newspaper coverage of salmonella and BSE 1988–96
(Macintyre et al. 1998).

Reilly 1997) and in the British national press from 1988 to 1996 (Miller
1999). The general picture of media coverage of BSE is of two high
peaks of coverage around 1990 and again in 1996 (see figure 3.2). Figure
3.2 also shows the volume of media coverage of BSE between 1988 and
1994 against that covering another food hazard – salmonella (Macintyre
et al. 1998, p. 532). Coverage of salmonella was high in the late 1980s
showing a sharp decline in late 1989 and after that almost tailing off.

This can be set against figure 3.3[1] which relates to some of the public
perceptions data collected. It shows the percentage of women concerned
about a variety of food hazards. These data relate to spontaneous mentions of particular hazards and are presented for the first and third quarters of the year between 1990 and 1998. Two particular points can be
made. Firstly, the graph illustrates the way that the levels of concern vary
to some extent as a function of the way in which the hazard is defined.
The numbers of those expressing concern about "mad cow disease" are
always higher than those expressing concern about BSE, although this
differential is vastly eroded between the first and third quarters of 1996
when the announcement of the possible link with CJD was made. It is
at this point that there are more people expressing concern about BSE.
Indeed, the general trend after the 1996 hazard notification is towards
fewer people expressing concern about "mad cow disease." It can be ten-
tatively suggested that this is indicative of a change in the representation
of the disease: after the hazard notification linking BSE with CJD for the
first time, much greater concern is expressed in relation to the official
scientific name for the disease. The second point is of particular interest

---

[1] Figure 3.3 is from a semi-continuous monitor of women's attitudes to health and diet
(JRA Research 1999). Sample size = 900 per quarter.

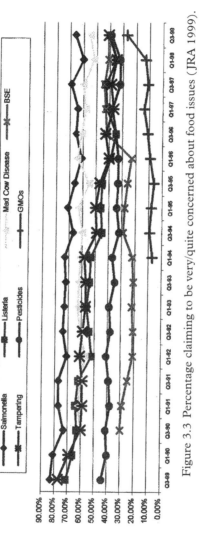

Figure 3.3 Percentage claiming to be very/quite concerned about food issues (JRA 1999).

in relation to figure 3.2 depicting the patterns of media coverage. It is clear that throughout the whole time period there is much more concern about salmonella than there is about BSE. At every data point between 1989 and 1998 spontaneous mentions of concern about salmonella are considerably higher than those concerning BSE. This, with the exception of the first quarter of 1996, is also the case in relation to "mad cow disease."

In contrast to this, after the peak of coverage in 1989, media coverage of salmonella was almost non-existent. It would misrepresent the authors of SARF to say that they suggest a simple relationship between media coverage and measures of public perception and awareness. They do not. They themselves draw attention to the way in which high levels of media coverage are not always related to public concern (Renn et al. 1992; Kasperson 1992; Kasperson et al. this volume chapter 1) However, the apparent lack of a relationship between public concern and the level of media coverage in the group sampled, over a considerable period of time must be considered problematic for SARF. It may be that this is to some extent explicable in relation to the "layering in social amplification of risk processes" (Kasperson 1992, p. 173). This refers to the possibility of amplification being differentially manifest at regional, national, and local levels. However, to be useful the framework should be able to specify the conditions under which particular relationships between media coverage and public concern are likely to exist.

Secondly, the layering method was used to explore the relationship between government expenditure on BSE and CJD and the trajectories of the diseases themselves.

It is commonplace to say that the BSE episode has cost the government millions of pounds. However, the way in which some of these monies were spent in relation to research into BSE and CJD provides an opportunity to consider their relationship with other constructs within the framework.

At the outset it can be noted that it is difficult to know exactly how to situate the variable of government spending within SARF. It is quite feasible that it could be used as a Stage II measure of impact; similarly it could be considered within Stage I of the framework insofar as government departments are social stations of amplification and are creating or responding to the hazard event/notification itself. However this ambiguity is resolved, we would argue that government expenditure inevitably has to be looked at when mapping the social impact of any hazard.

The total spend by the British Government (comprising MAFF; Department of Health; and Research Councils) on research into TSEs to the end of the 1999/2000 financial year has been £140 million.[2] The

---

[2] Personal communication from MAFF.

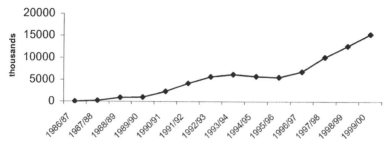

Figure 3.4 MAFF spending on BSE (Breakwell and Barnett 2001).

general picture here is that the amount of spending in this area has been increasing each year and that this was particularly evident after 1996. During this time, £76 million has been spent by MAFF on research into TSEs. Funding by MAFF started in 1987. It initially peaked in 1993/94, declining very slightly in 1994/95 and 1995/96 before increasing sharply every year up to and including 1999/2000 (see figure 3.4).

In 1996, the then Secretary of State for Health, Stephen Dorrell, asked the United Kingdom Department of Health (DH) to provide a programme of Research and Development (R and D) relating to the human health aspects of TSEs. The main research funders were consulted and a research strategy was produced that described the priorities for research and development in the human health aspects of TSE's. The DH Director of R and D had exercised oversight of all research in this area, particularly working through his chairmanship of the funders group which includes funding bodies such as the Biological and Behavioral Sciences Research Council (BBSRC), MAFF, Medical Research Council (MRC) and the Health and Safety Executive (HSE). Each funding body takes forward work most appropriate to its remit as part of a coherent programme.

The DH, and the Scottish Office Department of Health (now the Scottish Executive Health Department) began funding the National CJD Surveillance Unit (CJDSU) in 1990. The CJDSU investigates the incidence and epidemiology of CJD and the Department also funds associated neuropathological work at the CJDSU. Combined funding of the CJCSU is depicted in figure 3.5.[3] Specific research into TSEs was funded primarily by the MRC, BBSRC and MAFF prior to 1993/94 when the Department began to fund research into human aspects of TSEs outside of the CJDSU. Expenditure in this category is also depicted in figure 3.5.

The DH's position at the present time is that since 1996 they have commissioned, or are in the process of commissioning, over fifty research

---

[3] Figures provided by the CJD unit at DH. At the time of writing the figures for 1996/97 and 1997/98 are unavailable.

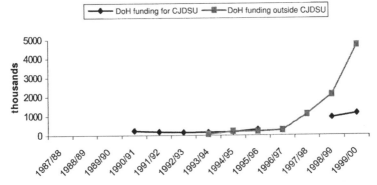

Figure 3.5 Department of Health funding for the CJDSU, and TSE funding outside of the CJDSU (Breakwell and Barnett 2001).

contracts in the fields of epidemiology, strain typing, diagnostics, blood and blood products, and the decontamination of surgical instruments.[4]

It is clear that the timing and levels of spend bear little relationship to the incidence and prevalence of BSE and CJD themselves. Certainly MAFF spending started in 1987, the year that Ministers were first informed of the outbreak of BSE. Department of Health spending in relation to the CJDSU started in 1990 with other funding in 1993. The rise in confirmed cases of CJD is small and there has been a sharp decline in the number of new cases of BSE in cattle; however, expenditure has increased sharply over this time. This may well be attributable to the many uncertainties surrounding CJD: it is unclear how many cases there are likely to be in the future, little is known about the possibility of person-to-person transmission and there is little information about preventative or therapeutic measures.[5] However, there is nothing in SARF that allows specification of the way in which such uncertainty affects risk amplification. SARF does not allow us to distinguish between different types of hazard: that is, it does not build into the framework the notion that hazards with different "personality profiles" may be associated with particular processes of amplification. One implication of this is that SARF cannot facilitate the development of risk communication strategies that take the associated uncertainties into account.

Thirdly, public perceptions data from the Food Risk Questionnaire data set (see Fife-Schaw and Rowe 1996) suggest that different measures within one construct of SARF can depict different profiles of amplification. Food risk perception data were collected both before and after the

---

[4] Personal communication from DH.   [5] Personal communication from DH.

announcement in March 1996. In relation to the question "how worried are you about the potential risks associated with BSE," up until March/April 1996 there is a evidence for a gradual increase in worry about BSE. There is then a sharp decline in ratings of worry after March 1996 to below May 1995 levels. To break this down further, a differentiation in worry levels appeared between people who do and don't have children, with the former becoming progressively more worried. This differentiation again seems to have started before the 1996 hazard notification. However, although the overall level of worry dropped after March 1996, the differentiation between those who did and did not have children was not similarly eroded. Rather it was still evident in June 1996. It is difficult to explain the maintenance of such differentiation without recourse to the way in which processes of self interest can drive patterns of risk amplification.

Overall the public perceptions data are indicative of considerably more complexity than is evident within SARF. Different dimensions of perception changed over the period of the March 1996 hazard notification in different ways. Some changes are gradual, on other parameters there is no change, for others the changes are linked to different life situations (e.g. being a parent). Some changes do seem to be linked to the March 1996 announcement; others, such as the feeling that people can control their exposure to BSE and also the divergence in worry between those who do and do not have children seem to emerge in late 1995.

Having highlighted some of the interactions between different variables relating to BSE, it can be suggested that in order to inform risk management and risk communication initiatives effectively, a focus upon the underlying processes is required to explain the considerable complexity within and between the layers of data. For example, what are the processes that can explain the variety of relationships that can exist between media coverage and public perceptions? Specifically, use of the layering method in this case study highlights what, for SARF, is the more unusual scenario of high public concern running alongside what is effectively the total absence of media coverage. The nature of the relationship between expenditure which continues to rise whilst other indicators are indicative of ostensibly less risk also raises questions about the role of uncertainty in determining the degree and the nature of risk amplification. Finally, the way in which the drop in overall concern masked the maintenance of the differentiation in worry between those that do and do not have children raises questions about the role of self interest mediating amplification processes.

SARF as it stands does not theorize the operation of these processes. These data suggest that if it is to stimulate the development of predictive models, the operation of such processes must be theorized within the framework.

The layering method and AIDS/HIV

To the authors' knowledge, the lifecycle of the AIDS/HIV issue in the United Kingdom, or indeed in the United States, has not been analyzed using SARF. Accordingly the collection of data using the layering method, as well as providing particular insights into some of the relationships within SARF, also has implications for data collection and research practices more generally.

Acquired Immune Deficiency Syndrome (AIDS), the syndrome that damages the body's immune system, was first reported in the United Kingdom in 1981, with the first death from AIDS in the United Kingdom occurring in 1982 (Wellings et al. 1988). The retrovirus which causes AIDS was discovered in 1983 and in 1986 was termed Human Immunodeficiency Virus (HIV) (Berridge 1996). More than 2.6 million people world-wide died from AIDS in 1999, the highest number in any year since the epidemic began (UNAIDS 2000). The steady rise in the incidence of gonorrhoea and other sexually transmitted diseases in the United Kingdom since the mid-1990s has been used by government as an indicator of HIV transmission among heterosexuals, as it appears to be spread within this social group primarily by unprotected sex. It has led to fears that safer sex is being abandoned and speculation that the spread of HIV infection will increase.

A variety of data were collected to act as ciphers for different constructs within SARF. These related to the incidence and prevalence of HIV/AIDS (both in terms of infection and death); modes of transmission; uptake of HIV testing (differentiated by risk status); condom sales; public education campaigns/media events; amount of media coverage; government spending; public perceptions. The complex organizational context within which these constructs operated was also acknowledged.

Use of the layering method reveals that:

- the steady decline in government spending on public education since 1994 largely reflects the declining trend in AIDS diagnoses and AIDS deaths. It bears no relationship to the incidence of HIV in the United Kingdom, which has been steadily rising over the same time period;
- the profile of government spending shows a similar pattern of peaks and troughs to the volume of non-news TV programmes on HIV/AIDS;
- the amount of media coverage of United Kingdom national daily and Sunday press shows a similar profile to the uptake of HIV tests.

Firstly, the relationship between government spending and the spread of HIV and AIDS can be noted. Following the emergence of HIV as

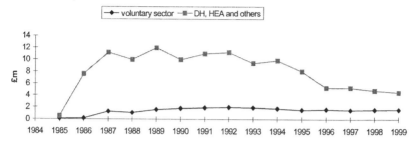

Figure 3.6 Expenditure on HIV/AIDS health education (and National Helpline) and voluntary sector (United Kingdom Department of Health, personal communication).

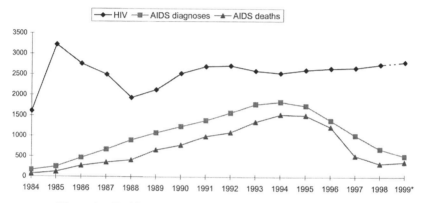

Figure 3.7 Incidence of HIV, AIDS, and number of deaths from AIDS 1984–99 (PHLS 2000).

a public health issue in 1984/85, government spending for HIV/AIDS health education rose dramatically (see figure 3.6).[6]

Since 1994, however, there has been a steady decline of government money made available to the public health sector for health education or promotion. When these trends are considered in relation to the incidence of HIV and AIDS across the same time period (figure 3.7), it becomes apparent that at the beginning of the epidemic government spending closely mirrored the actual occurrence of HIV and AIDS in the United Kingdom.

---

[6] Figures provided are not on a consistent basis. Before 1996/97 figures include HIV/AIDS health education and sexual health plus some contraceptive education and a proportion of Health Education Authority (HEA) overhead costs. From 1995/96 National AIDS Helpline combined with a contract for National Drugs Helpline and from 1999/2000 Drinkline.

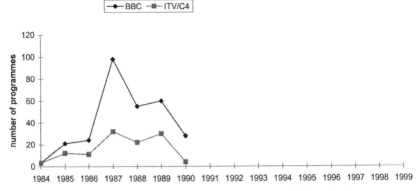

Figure 3.8 Non-news TV programs on HIV/AIDS 1983–90.

However, although the steady decline in government spending since 1994 largely reflects the declining trend in AIDS diagnoses and AIDS deaths, it bears no relationship to the incidence of HIV in the United Kingdom, which has been steadily rising over the same time period.[7]

Secondly, the profile of government spending (figure 3.6) can be set against the number of non-news TV programs on HIV on BBC and ITV/C4. Only two studies relating simply to the United Kingdom systematically explored media representations of HIV/AIDS over a period of time. The data here covered the years 1984–90 and 1988–91 respectively (Beharrell 1998; Miller and Beharrell 1998). Figure 3.8 shows a similar pattern of peaks and troughs between 1985 and 1990; the rise and fall of each mirror one another albeit with the profile of BBC programmes being more extreme. Both indicators show peaks in 1987 when the HEA launched their HIV education campaign.

Whilst these are interesting insights afforded by the layering approach, they immediately beg the question as to why these things are so, what their implications are and where the mechanisms of cause and effect lie. What is the significance of the observed relationship between the trajectories of HIV and AIDS infection and the downturn in government spending since 1994? What are the processes that underlie the similar profiles of government spending and non-news TV programs and what role do these have in the amplification of the HIV/AIDS risk? SARF would seem to be of little help in explaining the way in which these data interact.

Thirdly, looking at the amount of media coverage (figure 3.9) in conjunction with the number of HIV tests (figure 3.10) over the period of 1989/Q2 to 1991/Q3 shows a similar pattern of peaks and troughs. That

---

[7] It is acknowledged that these do not necessarily represent new infections and will also reflect the contribution of imported infections.

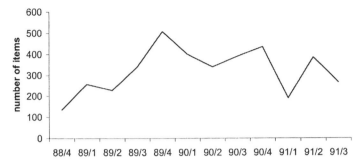

Figure 3.9 Number of AIDS/HIV reports, features, editorials per quarter: UK national, daily, and Sunday press.

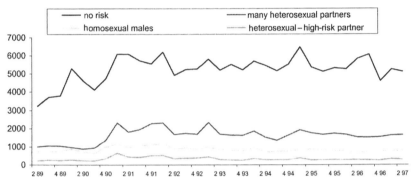

Figure 3.10 HIV tests according to exposure category June 1989–June 1997.

is, for the 3 clear peaks of amount of media coverage (89/Q4, 90/Q4 and 91/Q2) there were subsequent peaks in the numbers of HIV tests (90/Q1, 91/Q1 and 92/Q1).

Layering in this instance is certainly suggestive of a clear relationship between the amount of media coverage and a variable which can be taken as a measure of public awareness. It also raises the importance of understanding the role of time in relation to different amplification processes. However again, from within the framework we are not equipped to specify the *processes* that might be responsible for this correspondence or to hypothesize how this relationship might vary in relation to different risks.

It will be clear to the reader from the graphs that were displayed in relation to AIDS/HIV that even though this is an area where a huge amount of research has been commissioned over the last two decades, it was not always possible easily to align data representing different constructs in the framework over substantial periods of time. This was particularly problematic in relation to public perceptions data. For example, details of 52 surveys of HIV/AIDS from 1981 to 1999 were collected. These studies not only varied in the number of questions they asked and their response options, but also in terms of their sample size, ranging from anywhere below 500 to over 5,000. Similarly, only 13 percent (7) of these studies reported data over two or more data points, albeit not necessarily asking the same questions over time. Comparability across surveys and over time was therefore greatly limited. As noted earlier, information on media responses, newspapers and television, is similarly scanty and hard to obtain.

Even if the information that was collected fulfilled the necessary criteria for truly layered data, it would seem that SARF has little to say about the questions that should be asked of this data. Although the framework itself facilitates and encourages the collection of layered data, SARF itself is not capable of generating specific questions concerning the relationships between different layers of data. Because of this the framework has little of the predictive power necessary to increase our understanding of the dynamics of risk impacts and how these can be affected by risk communications. It is thus presently unable to assist in the asking or answering of questions that will have specific policy implications.

Having said this, the layering approach that is arguably implicit in SARF has produced a number of insights into the relationships between different constructs in the framework. This is indicative of the potential that the method has for developing a much more coherent understanding of amplification processes. The questions raised by the layering method in relation to the interactions between different levels of data raise important questions about the processes that drive risk amplification. SARF is currently not equipped to answer these.

Explanations for all these relationships are likely to involve processes that are situated at different levels of analysis (Breakwell, Millward, and Fife-Schaw 1994). Some explanations are more likely to recourse to intrapsychic and interpersonal dynamics; others to institutional affordances, ideological and social representational structures.

The current analyses also raise the question of how changes in the nature of the hazard itself (for example in relation to medical advances delaying the onset of AIDS) are affected by representations of the disease and relevant health behaviors. SARF does allow in theory for feedback of amplification processes into the hazard event itself so that the objective level of risk that it poses can actually change. However, the way in which this might happen is not theorized, neither is the way in which the new cycle of amplification processes that is then precipitated is similar to the first one. This can be illustrated in relation to HIV/AIDS. It can be suggested that the nature of the hazard itself has to some degree changed as a result of amplification processes. That is, research that has been commissioned has led to medical advances. The application of these has led to the development of new interventions that in turn can affect the nature of the disease in that the prognosis changes and resistances may develop to particular forms of treatment/interventions. Arguably a new cycle of amplification then starts with perceptions and behaviors that, for some groups at least, are constructed in relation to the new hazard status. The introduction of Highly Active Anti-Retroviral Therapy (HAART) has created new challenges (Aggleton 1999), including the extent to which perceptions of the "treatability" of HIV/AIDS impact on the practice of safer sex. In the United States, Australia, and France, there is evidence that this has led to increased optimism about treatment of AIDS. Although no studies have formally assessed this in the United Kingdom anecdotal evidence suggests that there has been a change in the beliefs of homosexual men. Ward (1998), reported the circulation of beliefs that HIV is treatable and therefore there is no need for safer sex; that even if current treatments are not perfect, they soon will be; and that most people with HIV are being treated and so are not infectious.

Conclusions: assessment of the layering method

In conclusion, the layering method has proved to be a valuable tool in extending SARF. In the examples given in relation to BSE and AIDS/HIV it has drawn attention to the way in which an understanding of the processes that link the constructs that SARF identifies and that drive the interactions between them is necessary in order to derive models that have predictive power. It suggests that new analytic concepts are needed if the framework is to have predictive power and to inform specific and effective risk communication initiatives. We would argue that without the adaptation of method that we propose, SARF's predictive and analytic power is limited. Use of the layering method for understanding the social processing of risk facilitates a consideration of the processes that determine the manner in which mediators/moderators operate and the nature of their interactions. It is only when the processes underlying risk amplification are understood that the possibility arises of being able to predict and effect change in the lifecycle of a hazard.

Secondly, there were limitations on the secondary data that were available and this limited the relationships within SARF that could be explored. This has implications for the ways in which research and data collection is commissioned. Data should be systematically collected on a long-term basis. In doing this, particular attention should be paid to identifying key measures that are effective in tracking risk amplification. Having better data structured in a more appropriate fashion would allow more pertinent questions to be asked. An optimal set of core questions should be developed and included in research projects that deal with hazard reactions. This would enable effective monitoring of change over time and the establishment of data sets that permit the layering method to be used to inform policy development.

Thirdly, it can be argued that having situated the data relating to both AIDS and BSE within SARF by using the layering method, the terminology of the framework falls short of being able to capture the complexity of the lifecycles of these hazards. Pursuing an analysis that is focused on the interactions between different constructs of SARF, situated at different levels of analysis, suggests that it is far too simplistic to characterize the lifecycle of a hazard as simply exemplifying intensification or attenuation. Amplification processes change across time, differ across groups and (as Kasperson 1992 points out) there can be evidence of different amplification processes at work at the same point in time depending on the perspective adopted (e.g. local, national) or the particular variables that are the focus of the analysis.

Although not specifically defined within SARF, the notion of amplification clearly refers to the *discrepancy* that might exist between expert and lay points of view, or, where there is amplification of impacts, to the discrepancy between expert assessments of the risk and the magnitude of the impacts that do or do not follow. Where public perceptions are such that the risk is much greater than expert assessments would suggest, we would term this intensification. Conversely, where perceptions/behavior indicate that the risk is much less than expert judgment would suggest, we speak of attenuation. Following on from this we would suggest a third dimension of amplification: that is of *representation*. Bearing in mind the argument about amplification (i.e. intensification and attenuation) indicating a discrepancy between expert and lay perceptions, the notion of representation refers to situations where there is ostensibly no discrepancy. Instead public perceptions and behavior are constructed such that they coincide with expert assessments. Clearly, there is considerable transience in what might be regarded as the representation of the risk as amplification of risk is a dynamic process; new information is constantly being generated and communicated. The transience of clear risk representation is especially evident where there is scientific uncertainty, where expert assessments of the risk are themselves changing, and where there is ongoing conflict. Indeed, such uncertainty and conflict may be instrumental in generating intensification of the risk. However, given these caveats, representation of the risk is generally the position that agencies concerned with regulating risks would like to achieve.

Where the focus of SARF is on informing risk communication strategies, it is also important to facilitate a focus on ways of "undoing" both risk intensification and attenuation processes. De-intensification and de-attenuation can thus be used to refer to the movement towards represen-tation away from the states of intensification and attenuation respectively. When a risk is intensified, it is often the case that the regulators would like to target their risk communications at bringing public perceptions and social impacts into line with expert assessments of risk: that is, they would like to effect de-intensification. Similarly, when risks are attenuated and the public pay little attention to what the regulator might consider to be quite serious hazards, risk communications would then be aimed at de-attenuation. Our work would suggest that these are quite different processes and that this should be recognized in order to communicate risk most effectively.

This level of differentiation is not currently included within SARF, where Kasperson and Kasperson (1996) equate attenuation with the re-straining of amplification. It would not seem in any way incompatible with it. Indeed a similar notion was referred to by Leiss (this volume, chapter 15) who suggested that there was a "holding category" of risks that were neither associated with intensification nor attenuation and that were characterised by the expert and public risk construction being roughly in agreement. This characterization should not, of course, be taken to imply that the public have an image of every risk.

Clearly, there are some domains where it is inappropriate to think in terms of "undoing" amplification processes; for example when risk issues are raised in the context of deliberative processes (see Renn, this volume chapter 16). In such situations the nature of risk amplification is affected by the ways in which regulatory agencies respond to the concerns of inter-ested publics and stakeholders. In fact, unnecessary intensification may be averted by timely action by appropriate agencies. Determining what constitutes unnecessary intensification is, of course, a political process as well as a technical one.

In conclusion, it has been shown that the structure of SARF motivates the collection of data in a way that is quite consistent with the layering method. It has been suggested that the validity of this approach is implicit in the conceptual underpinnings of SARF, and the necessity of such an approach has also been indicated in the empirical work assessing SARF. Use of the layering method in relation to case study material was indica-tive of a level of complexity of amplification processes that cannot be easily subsumed within the current framework as it stands. It has been argued that a consideration of the processes that operate within and between the layers of data will facilitate the development and testing of mod-els that have the potential to identify, explore, and predict amplification processes.

4 Institutional failure and the organizational amplification of risks: the need for a closer look

William R. Freudenburg

Mad cows and oil spills

Had Dickens been alive today, he might still have had reason to write that we live in the best of times, the worst of times. To technological optimists, on the one hand, these are indeed the best of times, and statistical proof is available in the form of life expectancy figures. On the other hand, to many of the other residents of industrialized societies, including such important European theorists as Beck (1992, 1995a) and Giddens (1990), we live in a "risk society."

When Kasperson and his colleagues first spelled out the notion of "the social amplification of risk," they took an important step toward helping us understand this difference in viewpoints. To date, however, much of the empirical attention has been focused on the views of individuals, particularly in the United States. This paper will argue that the work to date needs to be complemented by work that focuses on the organizations that are responsible for managing risks, and on the larger societal context in which we all live. Unlike Giddens and Beck, however, I will be focusing on the risks that are not "truly formidable." If we truly wish to understand technological risks, and how to respond to them, I believe we will learn more by focusing not on the dramatic visions of a nuclear Armageddon, but on more mundane types of risks that have been seen both in Europe and in the United States in recent years – risks such as mad cows and oil spills, which seem highly unlikely to endanger all life on earth, but which nevertheless created significant concern among even the more highly educated members of the general public.

My main points will be two in number. First, if we are to understand public responses to "technological risks" that involve very low likelihood of at least human deaths, we need to correct a fundamental misunderstanding of what it means to say that we live in an "advanced, technological" society. Second, if we are to do a more rational job of managing the risks that science and technology have now brought to us, we also need to focus more attention on what will be needed to get "responsible" organizations to behave "responsibly."

The societal context of technological risks

Part of what puzzles so many observers about the growing sense of public concern toward risks is the fact that, by most of the straightforward indicators, the twentieth century was indeed a time of unprecedented progress in reducing human health risks. The risks that have been the traditional focus of science and technology – the risks of death, as measured by life-expectancy figures – have in fact gone down quite substantially over the course of the nineteenth and twentieth centuries, declining by roughly 50 percent in the case of the United States (calculated from figures presented in United States Bureau of the Census 1975 by Freudenburg 1993), and showing similar patterns in many other industrialized nations.

Perhaps it is partly in response to this paradox that commentators such as Beck and Giddens have emphasized risks that, in effect, could involve utter catastrophe: the collapse of economic growth mechanisms, for example, or the growth of totalitarian power, nuclear or other large-scale warfare, and outright ecological disaster (see e.g. Giddens 1990, p. 171). As Giddens has argued, the concern over such "high-consequence risks" may well "transcend" all values and all exclusionary divisions of power (Giddens 1990, p.154).

To a certain extent, moreover, such arguments seem plausible enough: all of us who value life on earth have a shared interest, for example, in reducing the risks of nuclear conflagration or ecological catastrophe. When examined more closely, however, the arguments become less plausible. In focusing on the dramatic or even the hyperbolic risks, commentators such as Giddens and Beck are largely overlooking the types of technological and environmental risks that are less spectacular, but that are vastly more common, that in many ways are more insidious, and that may ultimately prove to be more significant for society.

Over half a century has now passed since the last use of nuclear weapons in warfare, after all, and yet that half-century has had hundreds of thousands of examples of innocent civilians who have been harmed by "peaceable" nuclear tests on both sides of the former Iron Curtain. In addition, much as Durkheim (1933) would have argued, the specter of shadowy "enemies" with nuclear weapons actually did a good deal to *increase* social cohesion, at least within national societies, but as Short (1984, 1992) and Erikson (1994), among others, have reminded us, the "peaceable" testing and commercialization of the atom have often done just the opposite, often putting the social fabric itself at risk. The remaining "legacy" of nuclear weapons production and testing, moreover, is one that appears likely to present challenges for centuries to come, but mainly for the specific regions playing key roles in weapons production and/or nuclear waste disposal. The socially significant risks, in other words, may have to do not so much with the statistically small but potentially catastrophic threat of nuclear weapons being used against all of us, by those we see as our enemies, but instead, with the everyday yet far more socially divisive threats that "ordinary" nuclear technology poses for some of us, due in large part to the actions of those who claim to be our friends.

To understand this point more fully, it is helpful to avoid (or to correct) a widespread but fundamental misunderstanding about what it means to say we live in an "advanced, technological" society. The corrective can be found in a point made initially by one of the earliest and most articulate proponents of "intellectualized rationality," Max Weber (1946), roughly three-quarters of a century ago. In his lecture on "Science as a Vocation," Weber discussed a question that was evidently a source of confusion for many of his students, as well as for many who were to follow. What does it mean, Weber had been asked, to say that we live in a world of "intellectualized rationalization"?

Does it mean that we, today...have a greater knowledge of the conditions of life under which we exist than has an American Indian or a Hottentot? Hardly. Unless he is a physicist, one who rides on the streetcar has no idea how the car happened to get into motion. And he does not need to know. He is satisfied that he may "count" on the behavior of the streetcar, and he orients his conducts according to this expectation; but he knows nothing about what it takes to produce such a car so that it can move. The savage knows incomparably more about his tools. (Weber 1946, pp. 138–139)

Instead, Weber continued, intellectualization and rationalization mean "the world is disenchanted. One need no longer have recourse to magical means," because "one can, in principle, master all things by calculation."

Yet the availability of this option "in principle" clearly does not mean that the average individual, or indeed, perhaps *any* individual, will be able to "master all things by calculation." Instead, the expectation is that *someone* will be performing the necessary calculations, and that the relevant person will be doing the counting in a way that can be "counted on." Yet it may be precisely this expectation that becomes increasingly problematic as the societal division of labor grows more complex.

In one sense, of course, we do "know more" today than did our great-great-grandparents, at least collectively. Individually, however, to return again to Weber's point, we actually know far *less* today than did our great-great-grandparents about the tools and technologies on which we depend.

In the early 1800s, the vast majority of the citizens of the world (the figure was over 80 percent in the case of the United States) were engaged in raising their own food (United States Bureau of the Census 1975). The life they lived was often difficult, and few of the more affluent citizens of today would truly want to trade places with them. Still, for the most part, those relatively self-sufficient citizens were capable of repairing, or even of building from scratch, virtually all of the tools and technologies upon which they depended. By contrast, today's world is so specialized that even a Nobel laureate is likely to have little more than a rudimentary understanding of the tools and technologies that surround us all, from airliners to ignition systems, and from computers to corporate structures.

Far more than was the case for our great-great-grandparents, in other words, we tend to be not so much in control of as *dependent upon* our technology. Hence, we are dependent as well on whole armies of specialists, most of whom we will never meet, let alone be able to control. For most of us, most of the time, we do find that we *can* depend on the technologies, and on the people who are responsible for them. Everyone who flies to an international conference, for example, will do so on jet aircraft that, while amazingly complex in organizational as well as technological terms, nevertheless generally manage to cover long distances and land quite safely. Despite our *generally* positive experiences, however, even rare exceptions can be profoundly troubling.

One of the reasons is that our increases in *technical* control have come about, in part, at the cost of decreases in *social* control. In this sense, too, we are very much unlike our great-grandparents. In the relatively few cases where they needed to buy an item of technology from someone else, it was often from a "someone" that they knew quite well, or that they would know how to find if something went wrong. Today, by contrast, not only do we have more interdependence; we also have less ability to monitor or to control the countless specialists upon whom we depend. Today's citizens often discover, in other words, that when something goes wrong, be it a car or a computer or a chemical, the "responsible" person or organization can prove almost impossible to find.

Note that this is not an argument that such failures are truly pervasive; my own belief, to repeat, is that cases of "things going wrong" are still more the exception than the rule, and by a considerable margin. In the relatively small number of cases where such failures do occur, however, they may not be much less troubling simply because they are relatively rare. Instead, as Slovic (1993) reminds us, these few but salient failures help to illustrate what he calls the "asymmetry principle": trust is far easier to destroy than to build. If an accountant steals from you even once, after all, that single trust-destroying event is not likely to be forgotten, even if the same accountant had not stolen from you in the past, nor if she or he chooses not to repeat the theft the next year, or for that matter the next year and the next. Such experiences, even when they are rare, are what Slovic calls "signal" events: they send the signal that the system may not be as trustworthy as we would all want to believe.

The core of this problem involves the potential for what I have elsewhere (Freudenburg 1993) termed *recreancy*; in essence, it involves the failure of experts or specialized organizations to carry out the responsibilities to the broader collectivity with which they have been implicitly or explicitly entrusted. The word comes from the Latin roots *re-* (back) and *credere* (to entrust), and the technical use of the term is analogous to one of its two dictionary meanings, involving a retrogression or failure to follow through on a duty or a trust. The term is unfamiliar to most, but there is a simple reason for its use: we need a specialized word if we intend to refer to behaviors of institutions or organizations, as well as of individuals, and importantly, if the focus is to be on the facts instead of the emotions they inspire. The reasons quickly become clear if we reflect on a fact that may tell us something about the societal importance of trustworthiness: virtually all of the common words having comparable meanings carry an exceptionally negative set of connotations. To say that a technical specialist is responsible, competent, or trustworthy, for example, is to offer at least a mild compliment, but to accuse that same person of being *ir*responsible, *in*competent, or of having shown a "betrayal" of trust, instead, is to make a very serious charge indeed. While "recreancy" may not be an everyday term, the need for such a term grows out of the need to avoid the emotional and/or legal connotations of the available alternatives.

How important is recreancy? In terms of public concerns over risk, at least, recreancy proves to be far more important than most of the factors that have tended to be stressed in the many editorials that have been written, in recent years, about the mass media and the public. One recent review, for example, finds that, of fifteen studies that empirically test the hypothesis that environmental risk concerns will be predicted by a lack of technical information, only four support it, while seven encounter significant findings in the opposite direction (Davidson and Freudenburg 1996). In another recent example, Salamone and Sandman (1991) found similarly little support for the common belief that "exaggerated" media reports can be blamed for increased public concerns about risks: even experienced coders often found that, while they often agreed that media reports were "biased," they had remarkably little agreement on something as basic as the *direction* of the bias (for further studies that provide potential explanations for the underlying reasons, see especially Gunther 1992; and Freudenburg et al. 1996).

By contrast (that is, unlike the case with media coverage and public knowledge levels) recreancy and trustworthiness have been shown by systematic research to be key factors behind the increasingly toxic social chemistry that has been associated with an ever-increasing range of technologies. In my own analysis of attitudes towards a proposed low-level nuclear waste facility, for example, I found that sociodemographic variables were only weak predictors of attitudes, being associated with differences of only 7–15 percent in levels of public support for the proposed facility; even values-based and/or ideological items were associated with differences of only 10–25 percent. Each of three measures of recreancy, by contrast, was associated with a difference of more than 40–60 percent. In regression analyses, the recreancy variables alone more than tripled the amount of variance that could be explained by the sociodemographic and the ideological variables combined. As noted in the article from which these findings are drawn (Freudenburg 1993), the growth in interdependence, and in the risks of recreancy, appear to be among the reasons why trust and trustworthiness have been found to be key variables in a growing range of other studies as well.

The social amplification of "real risks"

My second point is that, so long as we focus merely on the ways in which societal *perceptions* of risks are amplified (e.g. through media coverage patterns or individual predispositions) we are missing a significant fraction of the insight that I know to have been possessed by those who first put forth this framework: There are also important ways in which social processes prove to amplify and/or attenuate *risks themselves*. Particularly important in this regard are the societal institutions that are entrusted with the management of risks, but that often fall prey to problems of recreancy.

In many ways, the relevant theoretical context for interpreting this pattern is the one provided not by Giddens or Beck, but by the earlier European theorist, Barry Turner (1978; for an updated assessment, see Turner and Pidgeon 1997; Pidgeon and O'Leary, 2000). Based on a careful analysis of eighty-four accident and disaster reports published by British government sources over the course of a decade, Turner pointed out that such problematic events were not merely a matter of fate or astrology, as suggested by the fact that the word "disaster" has literally evolved from *dis-* and *astro*, or "bad star." Instead, he noted, it was possible to identify a range of factors that were all too common in the creation of "accidents." The title of a later article (Turner 1994) provided a concise summary – "sloppy management" – but the book-length treatment identified additional, systematic sources of "real risk amplification" that continue to be overlooked too often today. These range from the failure to give more than lip service to stated organizational policies or to the concerns of the "external" public, on the one hand, to cases where the strength of organizational belief systems led to disastrous blind spots or gaps in information flows, on the other.

The lasting legacy of United States nuclear weapons production

Despite its importance, Turner's work long remained relatively unknown, particularly in the United States, despite the growing number of analysts who began to struggle with the important issues he raised and who would have benefited significantly from drawing on his work. Rather than attempting to provide another of the "academic" reviews of this growing body of literature that are available from other sources, however (see for example Clarke 1993, 1999; Freudenburg 1988, 1992; Short 1992; Short and Clarke 1992; see also Otway 1992), I will attempt to discuss the relevance of this literature in the context of a real-world policy challenge, that of dealing with the lasting legacy of contamination from United States nuclear weapons production.

To note the obvious *caveats*, although my examples are drawn from what I have learned while serving on a committee of the United States National Academy of Sciences / National Research Council, the views being expressed here are strictly my own; they do not necessarily represent the views of the National Academy of Sciences nor of the other members of the committees on which I have served. The case, however, is a convenient one for underscoring my points: rather than having led to world-wide nuclear catastrophe, the production of nuclear weapons has led to real-world environmental and health hazards that, at least to date, have had more to do with relatively prosaic and localized problems of sloppy manufacturing practices and industrial contamination. Despite the fact that the contamination resulted from building some of the most dangerous weapons ever produced, much of the contamination exists in the form of non-radioactive industrial solvents, although significant levels of radioactive contamination also remain at numerous sites throughout the United States. In either case, unfortunately, there is no known technology today having a practical capacity to clean up many of the resultant hazards. The key problems, accordingly, have been even more "normal" than the "normal accidents" examined by Perrow (1984), save for the fact that the levels and extent of contamination have been not so much ordinary as extraordinary.

The sites in question were contaminated by and still are managed by an agency that is known, somewhat euphemistically, as the United States Department of *Energy*, or DOE. In fact, most of that agency's activities over the years have had little to do with "energy," as the term is normally understood; instead, according to briefings provided for our National Research Council Committee by Department of Energy officials, more than 80 percent of the agency's budget has involved the production and testing of nuclear weapons. The history of the agency traces back through the "Atomic Energy Commission," which went through a transmutation that led to the emergence of DOE in the 1970s; earlier roots stretch back to the "Manhattan Project," which produced the world's first nuclear weapons during World War II.

Part but by no means all of the reason for having a separate agency for nuclear weapons had to do with the rationale of having such activities in the hands of a (nominally) civilian rather than military agency. Unfortunately, in the process of producing the weapons, DOE and its many contractors and subcontractors also produced a remarkably pervasive pattern of badly contaminated sites – a greater problem of industrial contamination than produced by any industry in the United States, and perhaps a greater problem than produced by all other industrial activities, combined.

Even in the context of an agency that has long enjoyed exceptionally high levels of financial support from the wealthiest nation the world has ever known (an agency where expenditures literally amounting to hundreds of millions of United States dollars can be discussed with little incredulity or chagrin) the contamination problems are so extensive and so intractable, technologically, that there is simply no way to "clean up" the vast majority of the contaminated sites to a level that will permit reasonable levels of public access while assuring reasonable levels of public safety. Instead, the vast majority of the 144 sites currently under DOE control fall into two main categories: first, those that are so contaminated with long-lived, extremely hazardous substances that it is clearly not possible to achieve a level of clean-up that will permit public access; and second, those where it is currently possible to achieve only an intermediate level of clean-up and safety (enough to permit some public access to the sites, but not enough to permit unrestricted use).

Both of these categories of sites will thus require what is sometimes called, somewhat euphemistically, "long-term stewardship," or to use a more neutral term, "institutional management." Unfortunately, not only does it prove to be the case that the existing contamination was caused through a series of "man-made disasters" (both in Turner's sense, and in the otherwise sexist, literal meaning of the term, in that virtually no women played important roles in the DOE weapons complex for most of its history) but there is little evidence that the high potential for future cases of recreancy or institutional failure will receive adequate attention in real-world decision making unless significant changes are made. Instead, even though policy documents often reflect realistic understandings of the limitations of physical technologies, those documents will go on to prescribe vague yet unrealistic "solutions" for these limitations, asserting (often in passive voice) that "stewardship" and "institutional controls" will materialize to manage the residual contamination risks, blissfully free from Turner's problems of man-made disasters, often for thousands of years into the future.

Aside from the fact that the entity known as "the United States" has now existed for less than a quarter of one thousand years, raising potentially troubling questions about whether it is possible to preserve systems of warning for longer than it is possible to preserve a system of government, there is also a need to recognize that, unless the future looks very much unlike the past, there are many reasons for concern that are more prosaic and far more immediate – a matter not of centuries or millennia, but of decades or mere years.

Experiences to date with institutional management have of course been less systematically studied than have "hardware" issues, but the existing body of experience suggests that it may be distinctly unwise to assume that human institutions will be able to provide adequate and relatively unproblematic risk management in cases where the best available technology cannot. For example, some of the most common forms of "institutional controls" in policy discussions to date have involved land-use controls, such as zoning and deed restrictions; unfortunately, actual experience to date with land use controls in the United States is anything but encouraging. To note just several examples:

- Love Canal was transferred in 1953 from Hooker Chemical to the Niagara Falls school board with institutional controls very similar to those used today. The school board gave assurances that no construction would take place in landfilled areas, and a deed notice was placed in the land records. Despite these measures, however, adjacent land was developed for housing almost immediately, with home-buyers later reporting they had never been informed of the hazards or the deed restrictions. Within just two years, an elementary school had been erected and opened, literally on top of the landfill (Gibbs 1982; Hersch et al. 1997; Levine 1982; Mazur 1998).

- In Oregon, houses were built on a closed landfill, even though the state had previously notified the county that no use could be made of the site without state approval. After the problem was discovered by state employees, residents' wells were sampled and found to be contaminated (Pendergrass 1996).
- As the National Academy committee learned during its site visit to the Oak Ridge Reservation in Tennessee, where considerable effort is being made to transfer federal properties into private hands, one of the early experiences came from land that was slated to be turned into a golf course. The deed prohibited use of ground water, which was contaminated with radioactive tritium. Within just a few years, however, a well was already being dug to irrigate the golf course with the radioactive ground water.

Some of the reasons why land use controls cannot be relied upon blindly have been discussed in detail by Hersch et al. (1997) and Pendergrass (1996), and some of the legal problems in establishing binding agreements are discussed in detail in a draft reference manual on institutional controls by the United States Environmental Protection Agency (1998). In brief, however, each type of control has its own weaknesses. For example:

- Covenants and easements are generally enforceable only by the party that "owns" the right to prevent restricted activity. Violations of these restrictions can be difficult to detect. If not enforced in a timely way, the covenants and easements may be extinguished entirely by the courts.
- An agreement by a property owner not to use land in some ways is not binding on future owners unless partial ownership of the land is formally transferred in the form of an easement, covenant, or similar document.
- In cases where a formal deed restriction is put in place, it amounts to an agreement between the original seller and purchaser, which can only be enforced by one of those two parties.
- Even when a proper covenant or easement is put into place, it can still become invalid under certain circumstances, such as foreclosure of a pre-existing mortgage by a bank that did not sign on when the covenant was established.

Even local laws, such as ordinances, land use controls and zoning designations, have serious weaknesses of their own. As examples:

- United States zoning regulations are subject to frequent rezoning and variances. In some localities, landowners' rights can supersede zoning rules. Almost everywhere, zoning decisions are inherently political, tending to reflect changing local economic interests rather than embodying policy directions that are consistent over the long term.

- Local ordinances, such as drilling restrictions, are often not enforced effectively by local government agencies. Many such agencies tend to have competing responsibilities, limited budgets, and limited technical competence.
- Even in cases where local government entities have unusually high levels of technical expertise, budgetary and other resources, and political commitment to the enforcement of zoning or other land-use restrictions, there can be no guarantee that the same favorable conditions will remain in place after the next election. One common comment on the United States political system, in fact, is that it is often characterized by reactions to crises. Vigorous enforcement of zoning laws, for example, can provide encouragement to opposing political parties that espouse more "reasonable" or "less burdensome" policies; if policies become so lax that serious accidents occur, on the other hand, *subsequent* elections may well be characterized by a newfound or intensified commitment to safety and regulatory enforcement.

Overall, in the blunt words of an Energy Department study (DOE 1997), "There is little or no evidence demonstrating the effectiveness of enforcing and maintaining institutional controls." A more recent report from the National Academy of Sciences/National Research Council offered an assessment that was still more concise: "Institutional controls will fail" (National Research Council 2000, p. 97).

Yet the problem could scarcely be said to end there. Instead, as pointed out both by Turner and by a growing number of organizational analysts, there is also a need for much greater attention to the kinds of factors that appear to be associated with systematically higher or lower levels of organizational risk management. The relevant factors appear to be both short term and long term in nature.

Short-term factors   First, just as individuals can differ greatly in terms of personality, competence, motivation, and so forth, so too can organizations. Some organizations manage to operate nuclear power plants efficiently, safely, and with a high level of availability; others have been less successful. Some organizations make a serious commitment to worker safety and environmental protection; others do little more than go through the motions. As noted by researchers, organizations often display consistent tendencies and "organizational cultures," which are not merely a matter of summing up the specific personal characteristics of individuals who work in those organizations. These organizational cultures often reveal themselves to be remarkably resistant to change (see for example Deal and Kennedy 1982; Pasternak 1993; Short and Clarke 1992; Lawless 1991).

Part of the reason may be that, as Turner noted, organizations tend to develop more-or-less distinctive ways of viewing the world. In the words of Morgan (1986), "organization rests in shared systems of meaning." Such "shared systems of meaning" can often be helpful; to note only the most obvious examples, they can simplify internal communication, as well as helping an organization to be more cohesive and to carry out its central tasks in a more coordinated way. At the same time, however, these shared understandings have the potential to become so deeply ingrained within an organization's personnel and procedures, so thoroughly taken for granted and "naturalized," as to become almost impossible to change. The problem becomes particularly severe when this organizational belief system includes what Clarke (1993) first termed "the disqualification heuristic": the belief that "it couldn't happen here," or that potential hazards are "not credible." As pointed out by Jennings and Leschine, for example, the native islanders of Bikini Atoll were allowed to return to their homeland despite residual contamination, based in part on dietary restrictions:

Atomic testing at Bikini continued until 1962. Following debris removal and the replanting of vegetation, Bikini Islanders began to resettle in 1972... Bikinians were instructed to avoid eating locally grown foods and to limit their consumption of coconuts in particular. The importance of coconuts in the traditional Marshallese diet was not fully appreciated, however, and the required medical monitoring that was part of the resettlement agreement soon began to detect increasing body burdens for both strontium-90 and Cesium-137. By 1978 the dose levels observed in many inhabitants far exceeded even the highest pre-settlement estimates (also Robison et al. 1997). Reexamination of the scientific judgments that supported the resettlement revealed that the evidence available at the time of the behavior of radionuclides in soils was derived from continental soils and not the calcium carbonate-rich soils of Pacific islands, where cesium readily substitutes for potassium in plant uptake. Coconut trees proved to take up large quantities of cesium under the conditions that prevailed on Bikini. (Jennings and Leschine 2000, pp. 54–55)

In fact, the importance of coconuts and coconut milk in the islanders' diet proved to be so great (despite the dietary restrictions that were announced) that the Bikinians experienced a ten-fold increase in internal doses of radiation from Cesium-137, eventually forcing officials to reconsider not just the implicit assumption that no one would eat that many coconuts, but also the erroneous assumptions that Cesium would "behave" roughly the same way in atoll soils as in North American soils (see also Robison et al. 1997; Simon and Graham 1997).

Independent analysts, unfortunately, have noted particular reasons for concern over assumptions and predictions for environmental and safety management, not just in the case of the Bikini islanders, but across the sites of the DOE weapons complex more broadly and more recently. In a number of cases, the problems appear to have been due in part to the power of the organization's long-established belief system.

This acknowledgment needs to be kept in context: as the open literature generally notes, the primary mission of the weapons facilities – the production of nuclear weapons – does appear to have been carried forward with a high level of competence. Even the most critical authors, in other words, often will take pains to emphasize that at least some of the inadequacies in protecting human health and the environment may have been due to understandable levels of war-time urgency (in the case of the earliest nuclear weapons production) and of subsequent cold-war concerns (in the decades that followed).

In terms of factors predicting the successful performance of institutional management responsibilities, however, a broad range of independent analysts and scientists have consistently identified past experience at DOE facilities as providing virtual textbook examples of the ways in which "responsible stewardship" could prove to be lacking. Similar verdicts have been offered both at individual sites – for example, at Fernald (Sheak and Cianciolo 1993; Hardert 1993), Hanford (Gerber 1992; Jones 1998; United States General Accounting Office 1993, 1996), Oak Ridge (Cable et al. 1999), Pantex (Gusterson 1992; Mojtabai 1986), Rocky Flats (Jones 1989; Lodwick 1993), and Savannah River (Peach 1988; Shrader-Frechette 1993; United States General Accounting Office 1989) – as well as across the weapons complex as a whole (Dunlap et al. 1993; Herzik and Mushkatel 1993; Jacob 1990; Lawless 1991; Morone and Woodhouse 1989; Shrader-Frechette 1993; Slovic 1993; United States Office of Technology Assessment 1991).

Perhaps the earliest clear statement was made by Zinberg (1984, p. 241): "As more of the history of nuclear waste management has become public knowledge, there has been a growing awareness that bad judgment and incompetence have often been masked by military and industrial secrecy." Subsequent analysts have generally concurred with, and, if anything, reinforced the verdict, generally doing little to provide confidence about the commitment to openness and environmental preservation that long-term institutional management will require. Instead, regrettably, DOE and its contractors have often been criticized for having showed greater concern over the release of potentially harmful *publicity* than of potentially harmful substances.

Still, it also needs to be emphasized that DOE is by no means the only organization in which such failures of institutional management have been identified as leading to substantially increased risks. Other illustrations are provided by many of the best-known technological failures of the latter twentieth century. In the case of Three Mile Island, for example, the President's Commission on the Accident at Three Mile Island (1979) began its investigation looking for problems of hardware, but wound up concluding the overall problem was one of humans – a problem of "shared understandings," or of what the Presidential Commission called instead a pervasive "mind-set," both in the Three Mile Island facility in particular and in the nuclear industry more broadly. According to Reason (1986) similarly, the accident at Chernobyl took place while the plant was operating with important safety systems disabled. The explosion of the space shuttle *Challenger* has been attributed in large part to the "push" at NASA, the space agency, for getting shuttle missions launched on a regular schedule (see e.g. Vaughan 1990, 1996). The *Exxon Valdez* oil spill was described even by the *Wall Street Journal* as reflecting a relatively pervasive lack of concern by both Exxon and Alyeska with the companies' own risk management plans (McCoy 1989; for a more detailed assessment, see Clarke 1993).

Longer-term factors   This list could be expanded, but the purpose here is not to point fingers at specific cases of organizational failure; instead it is to raise the point that, if we wish our risk analyses to be guided by scientifically credible empirical evidence, rather than by assumptions or wishes about the way the world would look, it would be irresponsible to accept any risk analysis that treats such common problems of organizational errors as if they simply did not exist. Yet there is also an additional difficulty. Even in an organization that begins with an above-average commitment to safety, or one where managers seek not to put pressure on workers to cut corners, a number of factors can cause real levels of safety to decline over time. In the technical literature (see e.g. Freudenburg 1992; Clarke 1999, National Research Council 2000), this phenomenon has been called *the atrophy of vigilance.*

This broader tendency can be illustrated by considering two of its components: the predictability of complacency and the reality of cost control concerns. The issue of complacency is perhaps the better known. At least since the time when an iceberg got the best of the "unsinkable" *Titanic,* most ships' crews have presumably been operating at an increased level of caution and alertness for at least their first trips through iceberg-infested waters; adrenaline, however, does not keep on pumping forever. Still, even though the ships coming in and out of the Alyeska pipeline terminal in Valdez had not been totally immune from problems, the *general* pattern of experiences, up through 11:59 pm on 23 March 1989, was at least superficially reassuring. Over 8,000 tankers had gone in and out of the port, over a period of more than a decade, without a single catastrophic failure. Based on the empirical track record up to that point, most observers presumably would have seen little reason to expect reasons for any particular concern at that time.

Neither, unfortunately, did the crew of the *Exxon Valdez*. Five minutes later, however, the sophisticated tanker had a less-than-sophisticated encounter. Despite an array of navigational devices having a level of capabilities that early sailors could scarcely have imagined, the ship managed to hit an obstacle that was literally miles out of its course – one that had been known even by the earliest sailors in the area, who had named it after the same Captain Bligh who would later achieve a different kind of notoriety as the victim of a mutiny on the HMS *Bounty*. The accident, coincidentally, took place not just on a Good Friday that happened to be the twenty-fifth anniversary of the 1964 earthquake that destroyed the former city of Valdez, but also during the 200th anniversary year of the mutiny.

In many ways, the eras before and after the stroke of midnight on Good Friday, 1989 – years of reasonably successful operation followed by the largest oil spill in the history of United States – could scarcely seem more disparate. In another sense, however, perhaps they could not be more closely related. It is entirely possible that the accident of Good Friday, 1989, could not have occurred but for the tragic complacency engendered by the dozen good years that had passed before. More specifically, it may have been the very "success" of earlier trips in and out of Prince William Sound (literally thousands of them) that helped to make possible a situation in which the captain had retired to his quarters, and the ship was under the control of a third mate who was "not supposed to" be at the helm. To compound this, Coast Guard personnel on duty were not bothering to monitor even the lower-power radar screens that remained at their disposal after cost-cutting efforts a few years earlier. In the event, eleven million gallons of crude oil fouled roughly 1,000 miles of once-pristine shoreline.

The example of the radar screens points to the problem of cost control concerns. Not just the present-day DOE, but virtually all institutions, public or private, are likely to face periodic pressures to control costs. The sources of pressure may include deficit reduction, private-sector competition, responses to cost overruns, political or other pressures to "cut down on waste and inefficiency," or simply a desire to do more with less. Whatever the original source of the pressure or the nature of the organization, at least one of the responses is likely to be consistent: organizations will generally seek to protect what they consider to be their core functions and to cut back on those they consider peripheral.

Unfortunately, organizations often view safety measures as peripheral or "non-productive." While there is a tremendous range of variation across organizations in what the "core" functions are considered to be – from building bombs to healing wounds – there is virtually no organization for which increasing the safety of its *own* operations is the primary or central goal. Instead, protection of health, safety, and the environment tend to be secondary or "while" concerns: organizations seek to produce energy (or for that matter nuclear weapons) "while" protecting the environment; operate submarines "while" providing an adequate level of protection for the crew; improve production "while" disposing of wastes "in an environmentally acceptable manner," and so forth. Almost never is risk management included in the first half of the sentence, at least in the description of overall organizational goals, as in "increasing the level of safety for workers and nearby communities 'while' maintaining adequate profit margins", save perhaps in cases where risk management professionals use such terminology to describe their activities to other persons in their organizations.

Broader contextual factors

In addition to the factors that influence performance within an organization, it is also important to consider a number of factors that commonly play important roles in the broader contexts within which risk management activities are carried out. These broader factors include broader patterns of *societal/technological change*, such as the fact that future generations will almost undoubtedly possess options for coming into contact with dangerous materials, as well as for dealing with them, that are beyond our capacity even to imagine at present. They include *legal structures and budgets*, such as the fact that, at least under United States-style constitutional structures, there is no such thing as a "binding" legal commitment. Congress not only "makes" laws, but it can "unmake" them, as well, at any time: a promise for future funding from this year's Congress is credible only if the funding is actually appropriated and transferred to a non-governmental entity that cannot simply be "told" by a future Congress to spend the money on something else. Two of the broadest contextual factors, however, deserve additional discussion here; they involve *development pressures* and issues of *trust and trustworthiness*.

Development pressures   Unfortunately, especially if recent trends toward the expansion of metropolitan areas continue into the future, a number of the contaminated sites are likely to be highly attractive for economic, residential, or recreational development purposes. Although the "beneficial reuse" of federal land is often a desired goal, there are also a number of less-than-desirable implications that arise from the potential for future development on or around the sites. In addition to the many weaknesses of land use controls discussed earlier, it is necessary to recognize that state and local governments in particular will often face pressures to maximize jobs and development. In rural areas, authors such as Krannich and Luloff (1991) have noted that leaders often display "desperation" to encourage development, at virtually any cost (see also Freudenburg 1991). Particularly around the outer fringes of urban areas, meanwhile, the predictable pressures to minimize "needless obstacles" to economic development are so well known that urban scholars often refer to cities as being "growth machines" (see e.g. Molotch 1976).

As most public officials are well aware, the residents of any region are likely to have a range of policy desires, not all of which are compatible with one another. At least in the vast majority of United States communities, however, there will tend to be one issue that will be a matter of consensus – particularly for those actors who are most powerful and most attentive to the specifics of local politics. They will be strongly in favor of economic growth, meaning that they will be strongly motivated to attract new economic activities to their own communities and regions, rather than seeing it go elsewhere (see e.g. Block 1987; Edelman 1964; Logan and Molotch 1987; Stone 1989). As a number of researchers have noted, these powerful actors will not only have an intense or "concentrated" interest in the promotion of growth, but they will be "repeat players," capable of exerting persistent, behind-the-scenes pressures on the relevant units of government, long after most members of the general public have lost sight of the issues and records of residual contamination have become lost or forgotten (see also Galanter 1974; Wilson 1980).

Such predictable pressures, to say the least, can make it difficult for such governments to enforce the kinds of vigorous oversight and/or restraints on development that many present-day discussions of "stewardship" seem to envision. As one local citizen put it in an informal comment, "DOE officials come and go, but the profit motive goes on forever." Based on the accumulated research literature, it needs to be noted that development pressures are not necessarily suspect, but they do need to be recognized as predictable and potentially serious sources of influences that can serve to undercut present-day intentions.

Trust and credibility   As noted by a wide range of analysts (see for example Dunlap et al. 1993; Jacob 1990; Slovic 1991) one of the central challenges that needs to be faced in nuclear waste management involves a deep and at times profound legacy of mistrust. It is by now a virtual cliché to note that governmental organizations have suffered a decline of deference in the past three decades, but the significance of the point is scarcely diminished through repetition.

Unfortunately, as already noted, trust and credibility are subject to what Slovic (1991, 1993) calls "the asymmetry principle," or the fact that trust is hard to gain, but easy to lose. Unfortunately, the legacy of past mistakes has led to so much erosion of credibility that independent analysts such as Rosa and Clark (1999, p. 22) have identified nuclear activities as providing "a paradigmatic example, capturing the essential features of technological gridlock... producing a polarization between citizens, on the one hand, and policy makers, experts, and managers, on the other hand, with the net result being impasse over technological choices."

One of the reasons may well be that, rather than responding to the substance of citizen concerns, policy makers of the past have often employed what Freudenburg et al. (1998) call "diversionary reframing" – that is, attempts to divert attention away from the citizens' real concerns by "reframing" the debate as being "about" something else. A particularly pervasive pattern has involved the argument that the citizens are ignorant, ill-informed, or even "insane" (for a review, see Freudenburg and Pastor 1992). Nuclear proponents have often developed sophisticated, professional and well-funded "risk communication" efforts, but even in cases where those efforts have been carried out by professional public relations firms, those efforts have often failed to counteract credibility problems, often backfiring (see e.g. Mazur 1981; Lodwick 1993), and in one case, leading to a "fiasco" (Flynn, Slovic, and Mertz 1993a).

Concluding comments: a call for further research

For the future, accordingly, there would appear to be significant potential benefit in exploring an entirely different approach: not one of trying to divert policy attention away from citizen concerns, but instead, taking them seriously. Not only have a growing number of analysts come to focus on the problems associated with what Turner (1978) originally called "organizational exclusivity," or the "disregard of non-members," but some have also come to suggest that increased "institutional permeability" may deserve much greater attention as an antidote to the blind spots created or reinforced by such forms of insularity (see e.g. Shrader-Frechette 1993; Clarke 1993; Perrow 1984; Freudenburg and Gramling 1992). In simpler terms, although those who are outside of a given brotherhood may well view the world differently than do those within it, such differences in perspectives may well prove to bring advantages, and not merely disadvantages, particularly when the need is to manage increasingly complex sociotechnical systems in a way that is both socially credible and technically prudent. Indeed, although there is a need to repeat one last time the importance of actually carrying out future research, one of the possibilities that clearly deserves to be addressed in such research is that increased institutional permeability – including significant expansions of genuine public involvement in technological risk decision making – might well be able to help *both* in reducing pressures toward societal distrust of recreant institutions *and* in reducing the organizational amplification of risks that remain real, even if they are "man-made."

Part II

Risk signals and the mass media

5   Trust, transparency, and social context: implications for social amplification of risk

Lynn J. Frewer

One element which is an important part of the social amplification of risk framework, and merits further empirical investigation, is the role of public trust in different institutions (for example, regulatory bodies, industries, or non-governmental organizations) in mediating public responses to potential hazards, and any resulting risk amplification or attenuation effects. Social psychological theory offers various frameworks for assessing empirically the importance of trust, and its constituent components, on attitude change. It is proposed that incorporating insights from these theoretical perspectives into the study of the social amplification of risk may provide the basis for empirical tests of the model in future research.

The social amplification of risk framework was proposed to explain why "risk events with minor physical consequences often elicit strong public concern and produce extraordinarily severe social impacts" (Kasperson, Renn, Slovic et al. 1988). Pidgeon, Henwood, and Maguire (1999, p. 70) have commented that the social amplification of risk model serves as "a useful analytical tool for describing and integrating relationships between rival theories of risk perception and communication, and for deriving new signals about the societal processing of risk signals." However, it is recognized that empirical tests of the model are difficult (Sjöberg 1999), implying that further hypothesis generation might be useful if the model is to be tested and used as a predictive tool in scientific research aimed at understanding public responses to different hazards, and to inform the development of effective risk communication about these hazards.

Public trust in institutions has been recognized as being an important part of the social amplification of risk framework, and merits further empirical investigation. The importance of trust in risk management is discussed in detail elsewhere (Cvetkovich and Lofstedt 1999). In the current context, it may be useful to investigate the role of trust (and distrust) in mediating risk amplification or attenuation. It has long been recognized that risk management is not confined simply to understanding risk perceptions held by individuals, but must also focus on the behaviors and interests of societal institutions entrusted with the management of risks (Freudenburg and Pastor 1992). In particular, there has been much recent concern expressed regarding the ability of organizations to communicate issues of risk, particularly within the public sector. Trust may be particularly important within the public sector. The public sector has been identified by the public as a risk *generator*, as well as a risk *regulator*. It has additional responsibility for communicating about those risks for which it has responsibility to regulate, and, to some extent, maintain (Smith and McCloskey 1998). It is not surprising that the public perceive some degree of vested interest associated with communicators who simultaneously claim to protect the public interest but also assume responsibility regarding risk creation and continuity, as well as public relations regarding the efficacy of regulatory processes in terms of public protection.

Public responses to risks appear to be determined, in part, by perceptions that a particular event was caused by managerial incompetence (see also Freudenburg, this volume chapter 4). This may result in the event itself providing a signal of future risk from the same hazard or similar risk events (Burns et al. 1993). Thus, the extent to which people trust or distrust risk managers may determine how people process risk information. Risk information from a trusted source is internalized by the receiver of the information, and contributes to the way that an individual perceives and responds to a particular risk. Risk information from a distrusted source may be disregarded as unreliable or self-serving, or even result in influencing risk attitudes in an opposite way to that intended by the information content itself. An alternative way of expressing this might be through the social amplification of risk framework. Risk information from a trusted source might result in risk amplification if it contains information regarding, for example, the increased dangers associated with a given hazard, but attenuate risk perceptions if the information contained in the risk communication emphasizes the lack of danger from the same potential hazard. Converse effects may occur if an information source is distrusted. Dynamic shifts in trust in institutions and risk managers may also determine changes in public responses to a particular risk with time, and account for some of the temporal variation associated with the social amplification of risk model.

Evidence which has been put forward as supporting the role of trust as a mediating variable in the social amplification of risk framework has tended to be qualitative, and somewhat atheoretical. None the less, there is evidence that trust is important enough to merit further empirical investigation. For example, Kasperson and Kasperson (1992) reported that heavy media coverage may not, by itself, herald risk amplification or secondary effects – rather, trust may be a critical issue in the mediation of whether amplification occurs, as is public perception of the *effectiveness* of the handling of the hazardous event by the authorities, which will, in turn, impact on the extent to which the authorities themselves are perceived to be trustworthy.

It is useful to examine further advances in understanding the importance of trust in risk communication since the 1988 paper by Kasperson and colleagues was published, and to explore ways in which these more recent findings might be incorporated into the social amplification of risk framework. Other psychological components contributing to trust and distrust in an information source or institution may usefully inform this analysis. For example, the extent to which the public trust information sources might be driven by public perceptions that the source of a risk communication message is acting in the best interests of the public, rather than protecting a vested interest or acting in a self-serving way. Perceptions that an information source is systematically distorting risk information, or selectively reporting the "truth" about different hazards for reasons of self interest, may result in distrust. The manipulation of trust variables may provide the possibility to test empirically the influence of source characteristics on the extent to which changes in risk perceptions occur, which can then be further interpreted within the social amplification of risk framework.

Trust and distrust: psychological determinants and underlying constructs

A useful first stage in understanding the role of trust in the processes embedded in the social amplification of risk is to determine how trust (or perhaps honesty) and credibility (expertise) influence the way in which risk messages impact upon the risk perceptions held by the receivers of these risk messages. Social psychological theory may provide insights into how trust influences communication processes within the social amplification of risk framework.

The importance of source characteristics such as credibility and honesty has long been recognized in social psychological models of communication and attitude change (Petty and Cacioppo 1984). There is evidence that trust is multidimensional, although recent reviews of risk-related research in this area have not been conclusive (Johnson 1999). Two major dimensions have emerged from the social psychological literature as being important in determining trust: that of "competence" (that is, the expertise held by the communicator and the extent to which they are able to pass on information about a particular subject area); and "honesty" (the extent to which a communicator will be truthful in communication of information). Expertise without honesty is unlikely to result in long-term changes in attitude formation (Eagly et al. 1978). Moreover, trust appears to be linked to perceptions of accuracy, knowledge, and concern with public welfare. Distrust is associated with perceptions of deliberate distortion of information, being biased, and having been proven wrong in the past. Sources which are perceived to be over-accountable (responding to the requirements of an external institution), or to be protecting a vested interest, are not trusted to the same extent as sources which are not associated with these attributes. However, public beliefs that a source is not accountable and is likely to sensationalize information may also lead to distrust (Frewer, Howard, Hedderley et al. 1996).

It is reasonable to expect that underlying constructs which determine trust and distrust in information sources will also have some direct impact on amplification and attenuation mechanisms. Specifically, highly trusted sources (particularly those which are perceived to express high levels of concern for public welfare) will increase amplification effects if risk information is attributed to them as a source, but attenuate perceptions of risk if they are perceived to provide reassuring information. The converse will occur if a source is highly distrusted, or is perceived to sensationalize information. Sources perceived to be over-accountable may have less impact on attenuation or amplification, as they will be perceived to be providing only partial information regarding the real issues associated with the risk.

Social psychological theory provides a firm theoretical basis for understanding the potential importance of trust in risk communication, and it is possible to extrapolate experimental findings to make predictions regarding the potential influence of trust upon the processes embedded within social amplification. There is substantial evidence within the literature that processing biases influence the way that people respond to incoming risk information. Freudenburg et al. (1996) have argued that the media may not necessarily "blow risks out of proportion." Instead, the media may attenuate the kind of reporting that is critical of large-scale industries which are primarily profit driven. The authors report that only objective information (such as the amount of damage, or number of casualties resulting from an incident) appears to have a strong impact on risk perceptions. Keynote effects (use of headlines, photographs, and loaded words) actually give the impression that the authorities are acting more responsibly rather than less responsibly, and that social amplification may be due to the selective perceptions and biased information processing of scientists and engineers as much as within the reporting of particular risks.

The elaboration likelihood model (ELM) has been proposed as a model which can predict whether persuasion or attitude change will occur, following a communication about a particular issue (Petty and Cacioppo 1986). The impact of source characteristics on responses to risk messages provides a framework in which such effects might be systematically investigated. The ELM proposes that people may adopt attitudes for reasons other than their understanding and evaluation of persuasive arguments contained in a message. That is, attitude change may occur in the absence of argument scrutiny (for example, because of an individual's beliefs about information source characteristics).

The basic premise of the model is that there are two routes to persuasion, the "central" route and the "peripheral" route. The central route involves in-depth processing of the incoming information, and external cues do not influence whether the information is processed in a thoughtful and complex way. However, if peripheral processing is adopted, external cues associated with the information are utilized to permit simple inferences about the merits of the content of the information to be made without recourse to complex cognitive processing. There is considerable support within the social psychological literature to support the model (Eagly and Chaiken 1993). Perceived information source characteristics (for example, source credibility or honesty) have been shown to be influential determinants of attitude change if peripheral processing is used (Priester and Petty 1995). The model has been applied successfully to the study of the influence of source characteristics in risk communication (Frewer, Howard, Hedderley et al. 1997). However, the influence of source characteristics appears to be dependent on the perceived characteristics of the hazard itself (Frewer, Howard, Campion et al. 1997). Source characteristics appear to be more influential in influencing risk perceptions for hazards where there is reduced optimistic bias (the individual's tendency to rate their own personal risk from a particular hazard as less than that applicable to a comparable person with similar situational and demographic characteristics), or where the hazard itself is perceived to be under societal, rather than individual, control.

In terms of social amplification of risk, it may be useful to attempt to utilize the ELM to test the effects of source credibility on amplification or attenuation of risk perceptions. Even if people get their risk information from the media, this information is often attributed to a particular source, or sources, which may introduce an additional layer of complexity in assessing the importance of trust. The media themselves (and their different manifestations) are also associated with different levels of public trust and distrust, and this might be expected to directly influence public responses in the absence of other source cues. It is possible to liken risk amplification to a widespread and dynamic change in risk attitudes within the population. Such changes in attitude are temporary and short lived by definition, implying that they are more likely to be the result of peripheral processing. This *may* mean that people are making greater use of the contextual information which is associated with the risk messages, than the risk information content of the messages themselves. Presentation is more important than content.

More enduring or long-lasting changes in risk attitudes, on the other hand, may not be described as "amplification" as understood by the social amplification of risk model. Rather, there has to be a major shift in the way in which individuals incorporate new incoming risk information into the way they assess hazards in terms of potential riskiness. Under these circumstances, it is possible to argue that people receiving the risk message are utilizing a central route to process the information resulting in lasting and enduring attitude change. It is also important to remember that measuring responses aggregated across whole populations may obscure individual differences in social amplification processes. It is individual-specific risk perceptions which will mediate risk-related decisions and behaviors, should such a direct link between risk perception and behavior be proven. The importance of individual differences are discussed further in a subsequent section.

Other dual processing models of risk perception have been utilized in the study of risk perception and communication. For example, Epstein (1994) has proposed the existence of two parallel, interacting modes of information processing, the first described as "rational" and the second described as "emotionally driven experiential." Recourse to the latter, "affective" heuristic appears to be made by individuals when attempting to make decisions about risks and benefits associated with different hazards under conditions of time pressure, when more rationalistic approaches to decision making are not possible (Finacune et al. 2000). Whether trust in risk information also activates the affective heuristic may be a worthy topic of future research.

The media debate about risk often focuses on conflict between different actors in the debate about risk, particularly between pressure groups and more establishment national institutions such as governments (Frewer, Raats, and Shepherd 1993/94). Regulators and scientists often express concern about the undue influence that pressure groups appear to have on public opinion about risks, particularly in the processes surrounding amplification. Another element, therefore, that might usefully be considered within the context of trust and the social amplification of risk is that of pressure group influence on the prevalent attitudes held about a particular topic at any given time. Understanding if and how pressure groups attempt to influence prevalent attitudes, and the role that trust has in determining the extent of this influence, may help interpret the roles of different stakeholder groups, non-governmental organizations, and other pressure groups in the media debate about risk, as well as provide the opportunity to understand the potential impact of risk communication emanating from these groups on the risk communication process. Interest and pressure groups have been identified as both information sources and information transmitters within the social amplification of risk model (Renn 1991a), and it is important to understand whether trust is involved in defining the extent to which such groups can influence social amplification or attenuation of risk.

Pressure groups are associated with different social networks and structures, and may have a central role in social amplification processes in that they may take advantage of, or even identify and provoke those initiating risk events which trigger amplification, actively seek media coverage, directly and/or indirectly seek to influence people's perceptions of risk associated with a particular hazard of interest, and act at a social level to influence other groups (Baggot 1995; Rawcliffe 1998). The question arises as to whether trust and distrust in pressure groups is likely to influence the extent to which they influence public opinion via amplification mechanisms.

The way in which these pressure groups are perceived in social terms (particularly in terms of trust-related issues, such as attributed motivation to change social "norms") may determine the extent to which such groups are able to act as agents of social change. Examples from laboratory experimentation cast some insight into how these social processes occur, although clearly it is inappropriate to extrapolate from a tightly controlled experimental situation to the wider social context without further empirical justification. Such experiments have shown, for example, that consistency in message construction is an important element in changing attitudes about a particular topic (Moscovici and Large 1976). However, pressure groups perceived to be protecting a vested interest are unlikely to result in group influence (Maass and Clark 1983). If, however, they are perceived to be acting in order to protect the welfare of the public, as well as being believed to be expert on the subject of the risk under discussion, they will be highly trusted, as well as being more likely to promote amplification or attenuation of the risk through information dissemination via the media and other information channels which is deeper and enduring (Moscovici 1985). Under these circumstances, it has been postulated that "in-depth" processing of the risk information will occur. Such in-depth processing will only occur if the pressure group is highly trusted, and perceived to be dissociated from promotion of a vested interest and concerned with protection of the public. It is postulated that, as the debate between the pressure group and the dominant institution becomes more polarized, public risk perceptions will continue to align with the view promoted by the pressure group because of these trust related factors. Of course, the activities of distrusted pressure groups may also provoke shifts in risk perception which oppose the information content of risk communication messages, which may also impact on amplification or attenuation.

A primary motive of regulatory bodies in conducting public involvement exercises is restoring public confidence in risk regulators and regulatory practice. The question arises as to whether increased public involvement in the formulation of government policy will lead to improved public confidence in regulatory practice, reducing the potential for risk amplification and attenuation via other, less "official" information channels. One school of thought posits that public distrust of science and scientific institutions is by no means a bad thing if it causes people to be more skeptical when evaluating scientific issues such as those associated with different risks. Members of this school of thought would argue that public mistrust is a positive benefit, as skepticism reduces the likelihood of the public being misled by inaccurate or misleading statements (Wynne 1992b).

This has been particularly important as trust in government to provide food risk information remains low, particularly in the United Kingdom (Miles and Frewer 2000). It is assumed that acceptance of new technologies (for example, the use of genetic modification used in food production) is based to a great extent on perceptions of the associated risks (e.g. Flynn, Slovic, and Mertz 1993b), and that perceptions of risk are influenced by trust in the information provided by various sources (McGuire 1985; Worcester 1999). It has also been assumed that individuals who trust an institution or regulatory body perceive the institution or regulatory body to be more credible, and its hazard policies more acceptable (e.g. Sandman 1993; Johnson and Slovic 1995; Johnson 1999).

Assuming that distrust is linked to perceptions that risk information is being hidden from public scrutiny, or systematically distorted to protect a vested interest (Frewer, Howard, Hedderly et al. 1996), by increasing transparency in regulatory practice, and involving the public in the decision making process itself, distrust ought to decrease. Increased trust in regulation *may* mean that people are less amenable to the effects of amplification and attenuation via the media, or other information channels, as their beliefs about the risks associated with a hazard will be more closely aligned to risk communication messages produced by "official" channels. Increased consumer confidence will have a direct impact on consumer responses to information produced by a particular source. Reassuring information from a trusted source about genetically modified foods, for example, may result in reduced risk perceptions associated with genetically modified food products.

An alternative explanation is that, rather than trust influencing risk perceptions held by an individual about a particular hazard, both trust and risk perception are related to *other* attitudes held by an individual about this hazard (Eiser 1994). In other words, those individuals opposed to a potentially risky technology or activity regard it as more dangerous than those individuals who support its development and application. Likewise, those with more favorable attitudes towards a particular technology may be more inclined to trust reassurances about its safety compared to those individuals who hold negative attitudes (Dunlap et al. 1993). If this is the case, then increasing trust is unlikely to make people more accepting of regulatory decisions regarding different hazards. However, it is arguable that increased public involvement in risk management, and democratization of scientific process is a good thing *in itself* (see Pidgeon 1996), independent of impact on acceptance or rejection of potential hazards arising from the development and application of scientific processes. This is probably the most convincing argument for involving the public in risk management decision making, rather than utilizing public involvement and consultation in an attempt to increase public acceptance of potentially hazardous activities or events.

Individual differences and temporal changes in trust

Individual differences in trust and risk perception may be important determinants of whether or not social amplification occurs. Trumbo (1996) has classified individuals as risk amplifiers or risk attenuators, although distinctions of this type are likely to be dependent on individual differences in the perceptions of risk associated with the hazard producing the amplification or attenuation effect, as well as trust and other psychological factors of relevance to risk perceptions. It has been proposed that serious hazards might systematically become hidden if, for example, they disproportionately affect marginal groups (Kasperson and Kasperson 1992). Presumably, if these groups recognize they are more at risk than other members of the population, increases in risk perceptions from the hazard will occur in those groups who are most at risk. This type of response appears quite appropriate: increased risk perceptions are an appropriate response to the recognition of a sudden new threat. A secondary response, however, may be increased distrust in risk regulators, particularly if these regulators are perceived to be inadequately protecting the marginal groups now recognized to be at greater risk. As a consequence, risk perceptions associated with other hazards regulated by the same institutions might be increased differentially for members of the marginalized group.

Research conducted in Arizona has indicated that, following a serious contamination incident, latent feelings of inequality in the community were increased. Whereas the accident amplified perceptions of environmental risk, other aspects of the risk also resulted in secondary effects, such as a decline in housing prices (a risk-induced discount was observed when compared to those in adjacent and similar areas, despite reassurances from government sources that the residual contaminants were within safe limits). One interpretation of this finding was that trust in risk communicators was not high enough to result in risk communication which was believable (Pijawka et al. 1999) and thus offset risk communication efforts (Flynn, Peters, Mertz et al. 1998). A further interpretation was that people felt socially excluded from the risk management process, and so did not respond to reassuring risk messages provided by risk managers.

Research in the United Kingdom has been conducted which has been directed towards understanding demographic differences in risk perception, public priorities for risk mitigation and preferences for public involvement in the risk management processes (Frewer 1999). The results indicate that women, members of certain ethnic minorities, and people in poorer socio-economic groups perceive more risk from different hazards, whilst simultaneously expressing greater preferences for public involvement in risk management processes. This may imply that these individuals perceive that they are excluded from risk management processes. One result of this type of effect is that amplification processes associated with particular risks may vary according to the extent to which individuals perceive that risk management processes are inclusive. Individual perceptions of social exclusion and disenfranchisement may result in increased sensitivity to risk messages transmitted by the media. Individual differences in perceptions of risk associated with particular hazards may explain the "layering of attenuation and intensification effects observed to occur across different groups and in time" (Kasperson 1992). Similarly, individual differences in information sources and institutions may interact with these perceptions to produce quite diverse individual responses to risk amplification.

Increasing public participation in risk management processes (and, by implication, transparency in regulatory systems) may reduce systematic differences in trust which result from perceptions of social exclusion, and thus homogenize some of the differences in amplification attributable to perceptions of social exclusion (Rowe and Frewer 2000). Against this, increasing transparency in the risk analysis process may result in greater unpredictability in risk perceptions and risk related behaviors experienced by individuals as the inherent uncertainties in risk management become a focus of public debate.

BSE and genetically modified foods

There is some evidence that a social amplification of risk perceptions associated with BSE ("mad cow" disease) occurred in the United Kingdom in March 1996 (Reilly 1998), following the announcement by the health minister at the time that there was evidence of a causative link between BSE and new variant CJD (Creutzfeldt-Jakob Disease) in humans. The pattern of media reporting in the United Kingdom maintained a saturation level of reporting for about ten days, then dropped off to a very much lower, but constant, level of reporting, similar to that observed following the Chernobyl disaster ten years earlier (figure 5.1). Impacts on risk perceptions associated with Chernobyl were not very great, and very short lived (Braxton et al. 1997). This reporting appeared to have very little impact on psychological variables associated with risk perception, either in the United Kingdom or in other European countries surveyed – France, Spain, Norway, and Sweden (Sjöberg, Janson, Brenot et al. 1999). However, beef consumption drastically and immediately reduced following the announcement within the United Kingdom, although beef and beef products were still available for sale in the shops. Inspection of meat consumption patterns indicated that the British had, by 1997, returned to consuming beef and beef products at the same level as they would have done had the BSE crisis not occurred (Ministry of Agriculture, Fisheries and Food 1998). Economic, rather than psychological, indicators may have provided the best barometer of amplification processes in the case of BSE. It is suggested that the amplification effect was triggered by lack of trust in those responsible for regulating the risks associated with BSE (the "real risks" being perceived to be hidden to promote vested interests or self-serving biases). Reducing beef consumption was a relatively easy precaution for most of the population to choose to take in this climate of distrust in science and regulators, although increases in risk perception for most members of the public appeared to make a relatively unimportant contribution to food choice behaviors.

It is likely that amplification processes appear to operate differently under circumstances where people perceive that they cannot protect themselves, as in the case of genetically modified foods where poor traceability of ingredients, and disparate labeling practices, means that avoidance

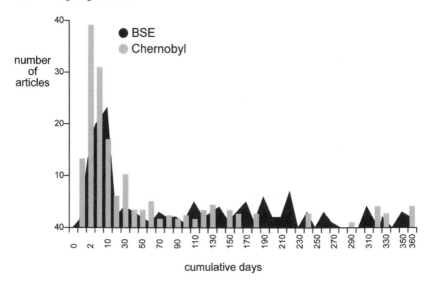

Figure 5.1 Media coverage of Chernobyl and BSE. Comparison of patterns of media coverage about the Chernobyl accident in 1986, and the announcement by the United Kingdom Minister of Agriculture regarding the potential link between BSE and new variant CJD in humans in 1996. Day 0 on the graph is when each event actually occurred. The figures are representative of United Kingdom broadsheet newspapers (*The Times* and *Sunday Times*, the *Guardian* and *Sunday Observer*, and the *Daily* and *Sunday Telegraph*). Although no tabloid newspaper data are available for the Chernobyl accident, a similar pattern of reporting about BSE was observed for tabloid reporting of risk in 1996 (Braxton et al. 1997).

of genetically modified foods may not be possible for most people. In addition, a second type of concern, related to the potential for genetically modified organisms to have negative and unpredictable impacts on the environment and ecosystem, differentiates genetically modified foods from BSE for British consumers (Miles and Frewer 2001).

The high profile media debate about genetically modified foods has resulted in increased risk perceptions associated with genetically modified foods among the United Kingdom public. At least some demographic groups have become more convinced of the negative aspects of genetically modified foods (Frewer, Miles, and Marsh 2002).

Spring of 1999 was associated with heightened media reporting in the United Kingdom about the risks of genetically modified foods. This increase in reporting followed the release of data purporting to demonstrate potential dangers associated with genetically modified potatoes, and the subsequent furore associated with public perceptions that the real scientific "truth" was being hidden to promote the vested interests of the scientific community and the food industry. Such self-protectionism aligns with public distrust in scientific institutions described earlier in this chapter. Examination of attitudes comparing the extent to which people held positive or negative beliefs about genetically modified foods following this increased level of media attention varied according to demographic variables: for example, age. Older people became more convinced of the negative aspects of genetically modified foods relative to younger people, although there was no difference between these two groups prior to the increased levels of media attention. Younger people did not change their views following the increased media attention at all (figure 5.2). This may be because younger respondents were more aware of the issues and had already developed firmly established attitudes, as they had been provided with more information through formal educational processes and so forth. They were therefore more likely to filter incoming information to reinforce attitudes already held, and behaved in an *attitude consistent* way following increased media reporting of the harmful consequences of producing genetically modified foods. In other words, a priming effect was observed: increased exposure to risk information simply primed the recall of already existing attitudes (Fazio 1989). Older respondents, on the other hand, were more likely to attend to the negative information presented in the media, which they then incorporated into the types of beliefs held about genetically modified foods. This might be because older respondents had been less exposed to risk-benefit communications and scientific information about genetically modified foods. As a result, they were more likely to attend to media reports about risks and other negative aspects of genetically modified foods, resulting in more negative attitudes towards their introduction into the marketplace. However, the available data did not substantiate the hypothesis that older people were more likely to *trust* the media reports, resulting in greater internalization of risk messages, as there was no difference between age groups in terms of trust in the information provided in the media. In any case, the media typically present disparate arguments from different actors in the debate about risk, and the media debate about genetically modified foods was no exception. How people attend and process information from different information sources must be assessed, as well as whether or not individuals believe that the media in some way "filter" what information they present from different sources in order to produce a systematic distortion in what is actually reported about a hazard.

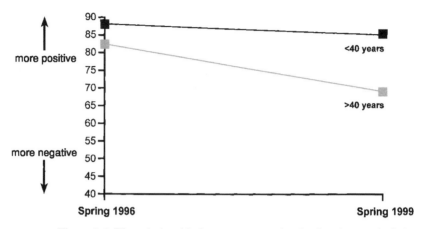

Figure 5.2 The relationship between age and attitudes. Age made little difference to British people's negative attitudes towards genetically modified foods prior to saturation levels of reporting about them. Increased levels of reporting (predominately negative in tone) resulted in older people developing more negative attitudes in Spring 1999 (significant at $p < 0.05$ level) although this effect was not observed for younger respondents. Whether older people will retain this increased negativity towards genetically modified foods in the long term will be assessed in the future.

Conclusions

Trust (in information sources and risk managers) is potentially an important element in the social amplification of risk framework, and one that deserves further empirical attention. It is, however, a mistake to use trust as an explanatory variable which can ultimately explain all facets of the risk communication process, as the way in which people process incoming information is dependent on many different social, cultural, and cognitive factors. The assumption made by some risk managers, that if only the public trusted regulatory processes then risk communication practice (and unwelcome amplification or attenuation effects) would be unproblematic, is unlikely to be true. None the less, it may be possible to model some of the types of amplification and attenuation processes through controlled empirical investigation *via* the mediating effects of trust and distrust. For example, the extent to which an individual trusts a particular pressure group may mediate responses to risk information emanating from that pressure group. The extent to which an individual trusts or distrusts risk regulators *may* determine whether risk perceptions increase or decrease following the announcement of the occurrence of a hazardous event, or activity. In any case, individual, demographic, and social group differences must be taken into account when attempting to relate trust to risk amplification and attenuation processes – taking the aggregated responses of the population overall as an indicator of the influence of trust on social amplification or attenuation of risk is unlikely to be insightful or meaningful.

It may be useful to apply theories developed in social psychological theory to generate hypotheses regarding predicted patterns of amplification and attenuation of risk. Initially, this research might be better conducted in a controlled environment in order to test the strength of effects, although the results should then be extrapolated to real world situations where models can be tested in ecologically valid situations. It is important to develop new methodologies with which to test the social amplification of risk framework, if the model is to have predictive rather than explanatory value, and it is also probable that understanding the importance of trust and distrust in science, scientific institutions, and risk regulators may contribute to the development of such methodologies in a potentially significant way.

6   Risk and relativity: BSE and the British media

John Eldridge and Jacquie Reilly

If we follow Popper's metaphors of the searchlight or the net, we recognize that there is always an element of selectivity about what we study linked to various purposes and interests. The question he always asked was "what is the problem?" This is why different disciplinary and interdisciplinary approaches can be found in the study of risk. Different problems are posed – though they may at some point be linked with other problems which others are trying to solve.

According to the German sociologist, Ulrich Beck, we now live in a "risk society": obsessed with the risk of accidents, technological errors, ecological disaster, professional miscalculations, and scientific discoveries hurtling out of control (Beck 1995b). Risk has become a defining concept in public and political debate and the mass media are seen to play a key role in this social transformation. Pressure groups seek to attract media attention in their campaigns for safety measures, experts complain of media "scare-mongering," industries and government bodies employ special "risk communicators" in an attempt to maintain (or woo) public confidence, and journalists themselves describe the attractions of scientific controversy and risk disputes (Adams 1992; Friedman et al. 1986; Hansen 1994; Sandman 1988).

Risk and the media

Several studies suggest that the media are paying increasing attention to scientific uncertainty and have been instrumental in generating public concern about particular threats (Cole cited in Goodell 1987; Goodell 1987; Peters 1995). However, media reporting has also been shown, at times, to eschew emphasizing risk in favor of offering reassurance (Schanne and Meier 1992). Furthermore, some researchers argue that the media have failed to address fundamental dangers integral to corporate practice, uncritically presented technological developments as "progress," overlooked severe threats to public health and only belatedly attended to crucial social problems brought into the public domain via other avenues (Banks and Tankel 1990; Medsger cited in Goodell 1987; Schoenfeld et al. 1990).

At the very least it is obvious that media coverage of risk is selective. Even if risk is inherently newsworthy, not all risks can be in the news all of the time. Research also consistently demonstrates that the media do not simply reflect experts' assessments of the most "serious" risks and reporting does not parallel incidence figures. For example, coverage of river pollution may bear an almost inverse relationship to the level of that pollution (Kepplinger and Mathes 1987 cited in Lichtenberg and Maclean 1991) while incidents of salmonella poisoning diverge completely from the amount of media attention this form of food poisoning attracts (Miller and Reilly 1995).

We would argue that theoretical accounts of "risk society" often oversimplify the media's role. Far from being eager reporters of risk, the press and television news are ill-adapted for sustaining high-level coverage of long-term threats. Media interest is rarely maintained in the face of ongoing scientific uncertainty and official silence or inaction. In spite of this, pressure groups can use the media to force an issue onto the public agenda in the face of official denials; and the media can serve as one avenue for public information and political/policy leverage for those who believe that risk assessment is "too important to leave to the experts." However, the media cannot be assumed to be automatic allies in the "democratization of risk."

Although the media are identified as important in the growing field of "risk theory" there has been a lack of detailed analysis of their role. A focus on "cultural consciousness," the fragmentation of authority and the spiraling of real risk, fails to explore how the battle for the definition and validity of different risks is fought out.

The mass media are not indiscriminately attracted to risk. In fact, the mainstream news media are ill designed to maintain attention to any particular future threat (however "real" or "imaginary"). Individual stories will attract attention when there are decisive scientific statements, major disasters, fresh human interest stories, official reactions, and/or when major organizations or governments come into conflict over the extent of the danger. However, many risk debates, much of the time, do not fall into these categories and, regardless of the concern of certain journalists, news structures do not encourage sustained risk coverage. There are three main reasons for this.

Firstly, risk is often characterized by uncertainty and the absence of conclusive scientific evidence ("virtual risk," Adams 1995). This leads to "going round in circles" and the "we need more research" approach which is so frustrating for journalists. Scientific uncertainty per se, is *not* attractive to journalists – it is new and apparently definitive findings and *controversy* that draws media attention.

Secondly, unless governments (or other official bodies) adopt the precautionary principle, risks may be ignored or appear to be resolved at the official level which, in turn, dampens the story's news value. The irony here is that it is precisely this failure to adopt precautions which may increase risk.

Thirdly, and perhaps most important of all, risk, by definition, concerns *projected* assessments. Risk is a concept based on predicting the future. This is in conflict with the basic news principle that emphasizes the events of the day. Press and television news, far from focusing on risk, may actually tend to ignore very distant and hypothetical threats. Many potential risks will not be reported as risk stories unless or until the dangers are manifest in some way; hence the journalist's comment that the risks around human genetic research were "speculation, not really news" and the remark that BSE could not re-emerge as a major story in the early 1990s because: "we needed dead people." The news media are better at retrospective than prospective reporting of risk, and retrospective risk reporting is inherently limited.

The literature on policy processes tends to focus on interactions between government and interest groups, neglecting the media's role. Similarly, sociological theories about risk have given only cursory attention to relationships between experts, policy makers, and the media. Indeed some grand theory about, for example, a "generalized climate of risk" (Giddens 1991), obscures discussion of why some risks appear more significant than others as well as why risks emerge, and fade away, when they do. Drawing attention to the complexity of these situations challenges naive but common assumptions about how the mass media work.

BSE and the British media

The BSE story has been one of the most dramatic "risk crises" in Britain in the last twenty years. It has been an extremely long running and complex saga with a definite risk narrative. The existence of this new disease, Bovine Spongiform Encephalopathy (BSE) was first announced by the Ministry of Agriculture, Fisheries, and Food (MAFF) in 1987. In April 1988 the British government set up a committee (Southwood) to assess its significance. Southwood reported back in February 1989. On the potential danger of BSE to humans, the report concluded that it was:

Most unlikely that BSE will have any implications for human health. Neverthe-less, if our assessments of these likelihood's are incorrect, the implications would be extremely serious." It also stated that: "With the long incubation period of Spongiform Encephalopathies in humans, it may be a decade or more before complete reassurances can be given. (Southwood 1989 paragraph 9.2, p. 12)

So, while scientific knowledge had not ruled out the possibility that BSE could be transmitted to humans, the Ministry of Agriculture, Fisheries, and Food (MAFF) stated that the report's findings meant that there was no risk to humans and beef was safe. This position did not change until March 1996.

The handling of the BSE issue and its implications for human health has been subject to controversy throughout its history. This issue involves "risks" associated with modern agricultural policy, the effects of intensive farming, the threat of zoonoses, and the role of government in ensuring the safety of animal and human health. BSE raises questions about how scientific uncertainty was translated into risk judgments, and policy deci-sions, who influences those decisions and how (see Phillips et al. 2000). What we want to look at here, from a sociological point of view, is the role of the mass media in the communication process.

BSE involved a dramatic risk crisis with coverage across every media outlet and format. Its profile was distinguished by a peak of mass media concern in 1990, followed by a relative lull until 1996 when it became a major risk story again. As with other issues it is clear that the level of media coverage given to any given issue does not necessarily mirror the incidence of the disease/problem in reality (see figure 6.1). This does raise questions about criticisms constantly levelled at the mass media concern-ing "scaremongering," "sensationalism," or actually creating "scares" or "panics" (Miller and Reilly 1994, 1995; Kitzinger and Reilly 1997) and demands that we look more closely at how the mass media actually work.

What we observed were a number of key elements within the mass media which helped to frame media attention and influence the profile given to BSE.[1]

Journalists' training

Journalists' willingness to explore a specific risk is influenced by their con-fidence in that area. This is partly a question of training, but also of their *perceptions* of their knowledge. Some clearly took on a campaigning role.

[1] The research cited arises from a project entitled "Media and Expert Constructions of Risk" (ESRC: L211252010, 1994–96) which looked at the rise and fall of different risk crises (including BSE) within the public arena. The focus of the study was that in order to understand "risk reporting" we need to examine the processes by which certain risks emerge (or not) in the mass media. For further details please contact the authors.

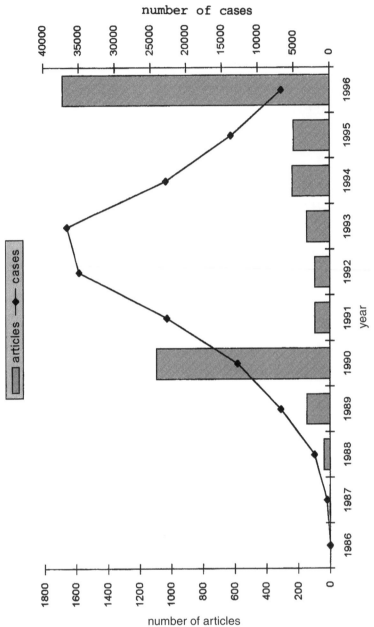

Figure 6.1 BSE: number of cases of infection in the United Kingdom against the number of articles in United Kingdom national newspapers (1986–96).

It was David Brown of the *Daily Telegraph* who is credited with coining the phrase "mad cow disease." While the name, unsurprisingly, "wasn't the favourite of the agricultural industry" he claims that giving it such a catchy title was, in his words, a "public service": He said that at the time:

> The National Farmers Union didn't think that it was a particularly good thing to do but at the same time they couldn't get anyone interested in how the farming industry was going to fight the disease. They knew it had to be stopped, they knew it was serious and where was the money? The treasury is only going to produce 50% of the money needed, how do you persuade the treasury that you get the other 50%? There is only one way and that's through public pressure, through MP's . . . there is no public perception of urgency . . . the title of the disease summed it up. It actually did a service. I have no conscience about calling it mad cow disease . . .

At another level some journalists felt that once the political aspects of the issue were perceived to have been cleared up (lifting of European bans in 1990) the uncertainty surrounding and complexity of the science could did not make "good copy."

News values, "fresh news," and policy announcements

The lack of coverage of BSE following 1990 was partly explained by the fact that certain risks were seen as very distant, they were, one journalist commented: "*speculation not news.*" The seeming lack of policy activity also undermined media interest. The media profile of BSE was also directly influenced by political events. BSE had a great deal of news momentum during 1990 because of the level of policy/official activity, but this attention declined when there appeared to be a political resolution to the problem. Thus there were 1,092 newspaper items about BSE in 1990, but only ninety-three in the following year. Journalists who maintained a personal interest during this time were thwarted by editorial decision making:

> They [the editors] lost interest in the subject because nothing was happening. Of course that was the whole point, nothing was happening to destroy this thing, but in newspaper terms I wouldn't be given the space to say that every day or every week . . . what had to happen for the full scale go ahead of a major story was dead people . . . (Broadsheet journalist)

"Human interest"

BSE was identified by journalists as directly relevant both to themselves and to their readers. The view was that any of us could be infected by eating beef. At times, the topic provided human interest stories in the form of individuals who appeared as "living proof" of the dangers (e.g. film footage of people apparently dying of CJD helped to maintain the momentum of media coverage in 1996).

Media templates

The media attention given to BSE, in part, built on a history of concern about food management. For example, there was already a well-developed interest in the United Kingdom in food safety because of salmonella and listeria which were high profile public issues throughout 1988–89. Secondly, by 1989, other countries began to be interested in the disease (Australia had already banned British beef cattle exports in July 1988). Germany, Italy, and France banned British beef imports. The issue, in British terms, became political and economic. European countries claimed they were protecting the public health. John Gummer treated this as powerful vested interests playing at protectionism. Thirdly, in Britain, local councils began banning British beef from the menus of 2,000 schools. The death of a domestic cat from a spongiform encephalopathy caused alarm, opening the debate on transmission and bringing the potential threat to humans a little closer to home. As one food industry representative put it: "Everything would have died down had it not been for that bloody siamese cat."

The media's initial attraction to BSE is easy to explain in the light of the factors already identified. The potential implications for human health were obviously relevant to the general public. Secondly, media interest was already primed to food crises stories, so it could be reported as further evidence of a crisis in the management of food risks and another reason to distrust government policy. Thirdly, 1990 saw a rapid build up of both self-referential and interactive news momentum; and finally, although BSE could not, at first, offer stories around human transmission, it could introduce individual case studies such as "the ruined farmer." It also had the added appeal of "good pictures": Daisy the staggering mad cow, the Minister for Agriculture feeding his daughter a beef-burger and the dramatic image of burning cattle carcasses (TV news reporters, in particular, stress the importance of good film footage to ensure coverage, see also Jacobs 1996).

Crucially, the spread of a new, mysterious, and rapidly increasing cattle disease had huge political/economic as well as potential health implications. It also involved clear government responsibilities and responses. Journalistic interest in the story was increased by the behavior of the main government department involved in the crisis: the Ministry of Agriculture, Fisheries, and Food (MAFF).

At the center of this whole issue is the role of science. Had more been known about the BSE agent, clearer statements about diagnosis and treatment could have been made. But, what became clear quickly was that until *scientific* uncertainties about mad cow disease were cleared up, reassurances about the safety of British beef were not entirely convincing, and no firm resolution to the problem could be reached.

While no one believed that the government wanted to infect the population with a potentially fatal disease, decisions on BSE could not have been made based on pure science alone. Because of the lack of science what should have been a scientific debate opened up into an economic and political one within MAFF. BSE remained in the public sphere because controversy surrounded the subject.

Ultimately, although all the above factors contributed to media attention it was sociopolitical events which led to the original rise of the BSE story. These are traditionally events with high news values, especially the European dimension. In addition, this range of circumstances mobilized science, education, farming, food, political and economic correspondents, rapidly increasing the space into which BSE news could be inserted.

The importance of such events becomes even clearer when tracing the *decline* in media interest in BSE. While the first peak of *media* interest appeared in 1990, interest rapidly declined toward the end of that year and the next major peak did not occur until 1996. Given recent events, one of the most fascinating questions is: why did media attention lapse between 1990 and 1996 (when very clearly the disease itself was not in decline)?

The fading interest had nothing to do with a change in MAFF's activity, nor any kind of scientific resolution, nor a decline in the spread of BSE. Rather, coverage reduced because there was a resolution of sorts on a political level. A compromise solution was instituted that reinstated beef imports to Europe so long as they were certified to come from BSE-free herds. However, as we argued in 1995:

The central issue of human transmission was not resolved by the European community decision. Indeed, it can be argued that the certification of British beef exports to Europe made the official position less credible. (Miller and Reilly 1995, p. 322)

In spite, or perhaps because, of the outstanding scientific uncertainty, the decline in coverage toward the end of 1990 was sustained for the next five years, with only the occasional minor peak. BSE retained the potential to re-emerge but required further scientific evidence or renewed official action. At this stage, MAFF's efforts to control the story were actually quite effective.

The general low level of media interest in Britain during 1991–95 was due, in part to the feeling that BSE had exhausted its news value. There were also very few new events to maintain a momentum of media concern. While a number of journalists remained intensely interested in BSE, they fell foul of editorial decision making and the demands of hard news. One specialist correspondent commented:

Scientists continually said "we don't have the data, we need further research" . . . so we tended not to write about it . . . It just doesn't make very good copy, to simply say "we don't know, we need further research," "we can't answer that." However honest that is, it doesn't play very well in terms of headlines. (broadsheet specialist)

At the same time the lack of policy activity meant that editors lost interest in the subject because "nothing was happening." This reaction frustrated some journalists, because, as one broadsheet specialist pointed out:

Of course that was the whole point, *nothing was happening* to destroy this thing; but in newspaper terms I wouldn't be given the space to say that every day or every week.

The period 1991–95 thus saw a relative lull in coverage. The "information vacuum" created by MAFF still allowed for some dissenting voices to be heard occasionally, and much lobbying still focused on the media in an attempt to bring about changes in practice (e.g. in relation to abattoirs). However, blips which did occur, in the main, were linked to high news-value events rather than the successful strategies of dissenting sources (for example, during 1992 further action from Europe again caused a brief flurry of reports and, in 1993 there were some suspected new cases of CJD). BSE did not capture the headlines again until March 1996 and then the change was very dramatic indeed.

By the end of 1995 there were ten new cases of CJD which had appeared in younger people. These cases were similar to each other both in clinical symptoms and in the pathological damage that appeared in the brain (in similar areas to those found in cows with BSE). John Pattison, chair of the Spongiform Encephalopathy Advisory Committee (SEAC) suggested that projected cases of BSE in humans, calculated on current information, could represent a major public health problem. Under Pattison's headship SEAC decided that the news had to be made public and this led to an explosion of media coverage, even exceeding the previous peak of interest in 1990. Not only did BSE have all the high news values it had in 1990 but this time health interests were finally brought into play. In addition, the government cover-up/failure angle was all the stronger and European interventions were dramatically strengthened in 1996 with demands for a major culling policy. This time around too, the risk was less hypothetical and the case studies of individuals apparently dying of CJD were there for the cameras. As one journalist said, before his news desk would countenance giving a lot of attention to BSE: "We needed dead people, well, we've got them now" (broadsheet specialist).

"Public opinion"

The media respond to the assumed opinions of their target audience, depending on factors such as those outlined above and on specific page or newspaper identity. The desire to be seen to mobilize public opinion or prompt investigations and policy responses can also influence coverage, especially in some formats such as television documentaries, encouraging strong single messages highlighting risk. Journalists also respond to "public opinion" as represented by other media output or by colleagues. This creates a self-referential media momentum, whereby media coverage generates further attention in an upward spiral, eventually leading to "news fatigue."

Within the above context, a number of additional factors can be seen to influence who is heard, which views are reported, how and when:

The nature of the assessments

On the one hand journalists work with notions of balance along a continuum of "reasonable" opinion. On the other hand uncertainty is less newsworthy than certainty and "moderate" opinions less attractive than "extreme" points of view. Experts also reported straightforward misrepresentation of their findings in order to support a particular storyline and some, very experienced, public commentators remarked that they had never had such problematic contact with the media before. It seems that when journalists cover risk stories they are more likely to challenge (or distort) experts' views, not least because the definition of "expertise" itself comes into question.

Story initiation, timing, and source resources

Official experts have the status to initiate newsworthy events, in particular, press conferences. This allows for a high degree of news control. Careful briefing, pressure of deadlines and official status can be used to maximize the chance that official assessments will be transmitted uncontested. However, in some cases, lay assessments of risk may enter the media far in advance of organized professional response. Although lay pressure groups may lack authority and material assets, they may be able to respond quickly and use other resources (including their human interest value) to mobilize publicity.

Pressures not to talk to the media

Some experts withheld their opinions from the media, because they themselves resisted exposure or, in some cases, they felt pressurized or were directly prohibited from expressing them. One BSE expert commented:

> I've had criticism from my own health authority about getting involved in political aspects . . . it wasn't for me as what was described as a "back-room researcher" to be commenting on these things of national importance.

Source credibility

In addition to the power of official bodies to set up "news events" and influence what was said in public, journalists are predisposed to accord official sources (e.g. those on government committees) greater credibility than unofficial or lay sources. Journalists are also more likely to rely on "*mainstream*" professionals than "*lone voices*" and are influenced by the generic status of particular professions (e.g. the relatively high status of doctors and scientists versus the dubious status of therapists and psychologists). However, this intersects with the perceived independence of the experts and their personal credibility. Crucially, once a story is defined by journalists as a "risk story," or an official cover-up is suspected, then the authority of official sources may be undermined.

The above factors interact so that voices which gain access to the media at one point in time, may later be muted. For example, in 1990 the media were receptive to Professor Richard Lacey who appeared on television news and was widely quoted in the press arguing that BSE was dangerous to humans. Although failing to conform to some journalists' standard definitions of credibility, Lacey gained attention partly because of an official information vacuum. Journalists viewed MAFF as uncooperative and exercising unacceptable levels of control over the news agenda. After 1990, however, a political resolution with Europe and the absence of fresh scientific evidence, combined with consistent government reassurances, to mute coverage. Alternative voices were increasingly isolated and became "old news." As one broadsheet specialist commented:

> It wouldn't have done me any good to wander up and say "Professor Lacey is still very worried that we might all get some weird brain disease from moo cows." The news desk would say: "Sod off, we know that, he's said it before."

As such, the relationship between expert/policy assessments and the media can be two-way; the media do not simply represent such assessments, they actually feed into assessment processes. Finally, other elements can play a part in the process which impacts on how mass media coverage of an issue develops.

Lobbying

Lobbying has forced certain risks onto the political agenda. It was not until June 1986, seven months after the first diagnosis, that MAFF informed ministers of the new outbreak and a further ten months elapsed before the government moved to have the threat assessed. MAFF also attempted to keep the nature of the disease to itself for as long as possible. When MAFF announced the existence of the new disease in October 1987 it did so in the Short Communications section of the Veterinary Record (journal of the BVA). The government also kept tight control of information on BSE and journalists were given very little information. The effects of this policy were two-fold:
• Secrecy and conspiracy became the key major news themes. Lack of information from official sources has made it easier for journalists to write about cover-ups and government inaction.
• It created a news vacuum which could be filled up by other sources, opening the way for different players to engage actively with the media to establish positions of credibility, to debate and ask questions.

Government action had the effect of mobilizing people into action. So, for example, according to the BVA:

There was pressure from everybody, there were pressures from veterinary surgeons, pressures from public health, pressure indeed from farmers in the South who were having multiple cases on farms, and I'm sure that there was almost panic within the department, what do we do now with this new disease?

The very strictness of the official government line meant that those who "disagreed" with it had to find ways of communicating their ideas. One scientist working on encephalopathies at the time said that:

What came from all this was that the media were the most efficient and effective way of getting anything done about a serious and dangerous disease. Mr. Waldegrave did not reply to letters, other MPs could not understand, government organisations (PHLS) had been told to do nothing...there was a consensus of ignorance among the medical profession and large numbers of experts who deliberately did not say anything, even though they knew the risk was bad...So, the media were the only route by which information could reach the population.

So, willing alternative experts could easily be found and used as a balance to what little official information was being offered. This allowed the debate to widen and introduced a conflict at the level of science over the behavior of the BSE agent and its potential consequences for animal and human life.

The public as voters/consumers

Politicians may be most likely to become actively involved in promoting policy when the issue is seen as of widespread public concern. They are also increasingly seen as both an audience and a problem for expert and policy makers. A Health and Safety Executive report, "Use of Risk Assessments Within Government Departments," describes how communicating to the public is viewed:

> pressure groups and the media have tended to exaggerate insignificant risks, often at the expense of ignoring larger more common-place ones. Departments agree that, as a result, the public is confused and treats government assurances of the safety . . . with considerable scepticism and agree that a government-wide strategy on risk communication would be beneficial. (Health and Safety Executive 1996, p. 37)

Crucially, "the public" are brought into risk assessment and policy making as consumers of goods and services. Such manifestations of "public opinion" are combined with particular images of lay people and models about their relationship with experts/policy makers. One dominant model presents lay people as irrational and ignorant, another views them as consumers of scientific information, a third emphasizes the citizen's "right to know."

The perception of lay people as consumers of science, to some extent, as having "rights" to information, is now influencing some policy. This is clearly seen to be of legitimate "public interest" in a way that animal feeding practices were not. By contrast, perceptions of the public as irrational but powerful consumers have heavily influenced government responses to BSE. "Public opinion," then, is rarely directly canvassed, but is the specter at the table of many decision making, implementation and publicity processes. How these processes operate depends on the model of public rights / expert duties adopted, the public opinion being assumed, the "fit" between the risk-source and the specific individuals "at risk," who is assigned responsibility, the resources and strategies of pressure groups and the potential effect of public reactions.

Conclusions: reflections on the media and the social amplification of risk

So, how does this approach to risk and the media relate to the social amplification of risk framework (SARF)? The work which we undertook was never intended to "test" the adequacy of the SARF theoretical position. It began with a different problematic, namely to consider the social processes that took place in and through the media relating to the risk discourses about food. The most immediate theoretical point of contact related to the work of Beck (1995b) and, to a lesser extent, Giddens (1991). But it was concerned with the process of social amplification, notably with the work of Cohen (1972) on moral panics. This has led us into a critical conversation with their work, whereby we have tried to show the ways in which empirical media research might modify or contest their general positions. However, given that the SARF model deals crucially with the issue of amplification it is reasonable to suppose that there might be some affinity. If it is so then it would be a pleasing example of serendipity rather than of an intended research strategy. We will take up some specific points from the original SARF paper (Kasperson et al. 1988, reprinted in Slovic 2000) as regards our own work.

There is a general point about the status of the model. The title refers to "a conceptual framework." Within the text the call is made for a comprehensive theory "capable of integrating the technical analysis of risk and the cultural, social and individual response structures that shape the public experience of risk" (Slovic 2000, p. 234). Later in the paper it is made clear that what is on offer is "not a fully developed theory of social amplification of risk" but "a fledgling conceptual framework that may serve to guide ongoing efforts to develop, test and apply such a theory to a broad array of risk problems" (Slovic 2000, p. 236). In the concluding paragraph the rationale for setting up this conceptual framework is described as being to build: "a comprehensive theory that explains why seemingly minor risks or risk events often produce extraordinary public concern and social and economic impacts with rippling effects across time, space and social institutions" (Slovic 2000, p. 245).

This leads to an invitation to scrutinize, elaborate, and even offer competing views along with empirical work that will provide tests and insights for the next stage of theory elaboration. Within this general orientation there is, then, room to breathe, especially since, if need be, it offers the opportunity for expressing dissent and offering an alternative perspective. At the most general level the treatment of the social amplification of risk is a dynamic one, as it is in our work. Its strategic choice of a processual analysis rather than a static cross-sectional approach is one that we share. The authors of the SARF paper confront a paradox. Why is it that:

apparently minor risk or risk events as assessed by technical experts, sometimes produce massive public reactions, accompanied by substantial social and economic impacts and sometimes even by subsequently increased physical risks? (Slovic 2000, p. 233)

One way to pursue this – and we think an important one – is to undertake case studies.

In the BSE case the role of technical experts was in part visible through the mass media. But it was clear that the experts were not all in agreement. On the one hand the Chief Vet, a leading figure in the government's advisory group of experts, was for the most part reassuring the public that beef was safe to eat, whilst expert scientists who were working on the topic were not prepared to do that. Their responses varied from caution based on the fact that the relevant experimental data needed time to deliver results to warnings that not only was there a risk to cattle beyond the government's projected estimates but also of a cross-species development of the infection, including humans. The nature of what was "at risk" changed in emphasis: the cows themselves, the beef industry in Britain, agricultural arrangements in Europe, other species, human beings. It was not therefore simply a matter of "technical experts" as a category but different bodies of expertise relating to a set of issues that became highly politicized. Moreover, what began as something defined by the government and their "official" experts as a minor risk, came to be experienced as a major risk with extensive ripple effects. The case which we have here described has a slow burn character to it. It was not in the first instance defined in panic terms either by the popular or broadsheet press or television news. But once the growing gap between reported rates of BSE and the official estimates was evident this became more difficult for the government to contain public concern. And, of course, crucially, when the official announcement was made concerning the link between BSE and one variant of CJD the slow burn was ignited into an explosion with huge consequences for government credibility among the public at large. This particular case stands not so much as one of general distrust of technical experts in the first instance or of lay people thinking all along that they knew better than the experts, but rather one of the loss of credibility of both experts and politicians as the significance of this new knowledge broke through and was assimilated. The fact that we were able to track this in a very detailed way both in terms of the encoding and decoding of the media messages is what gives this case its value.

As time passed, the BSE experience, because it had led to a break down in trust between politicians and the public, with the credibility of some experts damaged in the process, did have ripple effects of the kind suggested in the SARF model. Just as the nuclear accident at Three Mile Island may have led to increased public concerns about other complex technologies, such as chemical manufacturing and genetic engineering in the opinion of the SARF authors, in the BSE example there were consequential effects on public views concerning the "new genetics" and the development of GMO crops. This, as it were, became embedded in cultural terms in British society. Even though the scientific issues were entirely different it was the credibility of scientists and politicians as social groups that had been undermined. This is why the image of the then Minister of Agriculture, John Gummer, feeding his daughter with a hamburger, whilst telling the public through this manufactured media event that it was absolutely safe, remains in the public consciousness as an iconic representation of why politicians cannot be trusted. The fact that it is now also treated as a joke – the ex-minister became a figure of fun – is an indication of how deeply embedded into our culture doubt and skepticism now are. But it should be noted that this amplification of risk perception is connected with the loss of trust in significant authority figures. From a policy point of view there is obviously an interest in how this process can be attenuated. Essentially this points to the need for active and authentic work to be done on trust-building exercises. This is not the place to pursue the matter but it is clear that such action will have to go far beyond public relations exercises, which were part of the problem in the first place.

What this case study does illustrate in detail is the contention in the SARF paper that "the news media tend to become battlegrounds where various participants vie for advantage" (Slovic 2000, p. 241). What we have been able to show is who these participants are and the context in which they operate but also in part seek to shape. The social construction of reality in and through the media is an on-going and contested matter. The SARF model does draw our attention to elements in the media process which can contribute to the amplification process: the volume of information, the degree to which it is disputed, the extent to which it is dramatized and the symbolic connotations of the information. In our view it is not the volume of information per se that matters. In this respect, as in so many other kinds of news stories, it is at least possible to have information without understanding, or at least very little understanding. But BSE did emerge over an extended period as a drama in which the actors themselves disagreed as to its meaning and significance and as to when the curtain would fall on it (which it still has not). And the symbolic connotations of the information varied in the encoding and the decoding process. As we showed, and as Barbara Adam (2000) has also subsequently pointed out, a story which began in the media as a science and veterinary matter, turned into a health hazard issue, then a matter of European politics and into a beef crisis. She comments:

> Within that media career of BSE, stories abound about scientific discovery, competition and protectionism, government incompetence and cover-ups, competing approaches to health regulation in continental Europe and the United Kingdom, beef wars and bankruptcies, innocent victims and human suffering. (Adam 2000, p. 127)

Although the authors of the SARF model are aware of the many complexities they cautiously express the hope that some prediction of the processes may be possible. Obviously this would be useful for policy purposes. For our part, we are not sanguine about this. Not only are we dealing with complex patterns of interaction, but also with reflexive agents variously located in the action, together with the unintended consequences of purposeful action.

Social amplification, as conceptualized in the SARF model is a metaphor drawn from a form of communications theory which "denotes the process of intensifying or attenuating signals during the transmission of information from an information source to intermediate transmitters, and finally to a receiver" (Slovic 2000, p. 236). Metaphors can be fruitful and indeed they have a valuable function to play in social theory. But in applying the metaphor here care needs to be taken. In the communications theory context we might suppose there is a real empirical base against which to measure amplification and attenuation. This carries with it the idea that corrections could be made to prevent "distortion" caused by either of these processes. But if we try to do that in risk analysis we encounter problems. This is because there is no unambiguous or one-dimensional benchmark against which "distortion" can be measured. In the BSE case, for example, the question of what is at risk and who is at risk are the subject of competing, sometimes conflicting, definitions and answers, as we have already shown.

Does this leave us adrift in a sea of multiple subjectivities and interpretations? To begin with we need to recall that at the center of the SARF model is a preoccupation with perceptions of risk and risk events. These, of course are the subjective ways in which people see the world, which in some respects they may come to share with others, hence the interest in public perceptions. Indeed, the SARF model represents a version of how social scientists perceive perceptions! Interwoven with the more mechanistic amplification metaphor is an approach derived from symbolic interaction, as the reference to the work of Blumer (1969) makes clear. This is an approach which certainly emphasizes social process and works out the implications of the ways in which people come to define situations as real in the course of their social interactions.

It has become something of a social science truism that if people define situations as real they are real in their consequences. But that is not the only reality, so to speak. There can be situations that people do not define as real but nevertheless are real in their consequences. This point was elegantly made by Robert Merton:

Total subjectivism leads us astray by failing to provide a theoretical place for systematic concern with objective constraints upon human action. These social, demographic, economic, technological, ecological and other constraints are not always caught up in social definitions. To ignore these constraints is mistakenly to imply that they do not significantly affect both the choices people make and the personal and social consequences of those choices. (Merton 1976, p. 176)

As one of us has argued elsewhere (Eldridge 1993) there is an interplay between the "subjective" and "objective" aspects of social reality and the task of social science is to offer explanations that go beyond perceived experience or common sense. This means that we have to allow not only for the situations that people define as real but ask under what conditions those definitions come to be present. We also have to allow for the possibility that some socially induced situations are not generally defined as real and to understand the circumstances in which that does come to be the case. Admittedly working through this can be difficult and demanding but it does imply that not all interpretations are as good (or as bad) as each other. For this reason pluralist definitions of reality do not entail relativist explanations. Indeed, this allows us to consider that some (subjective) constructions of reality, which may be real in their consequences and can even result in socially produced ignorance can be misconstructions in the light of what Merton termed the objective constraints on human action. This enables us to look critically at the issue of propaganda and the role of rhetoric as they are mediated in and through the media. After all, we do not have to buy in to conspiracy theories on the grand scale to recognize that sometimes we have to contend with propaganda and the suppression of information on the part of the powerful. Whatever the rhetoric of risk that may be deployed by various interests for diverse purposes with BSE we are dealing with a disease that kills cattle and crosses species, including the human species. That is the underlying brute reality. There are interpretations that are consistent with this reality. Others may be offered but they are expressions of false consciousness. So we conclude that relativism, like patriotism, is not enough.

7   After amplification: rethinking the role of the media in risk communication

Graham Murdock, Judith Petts, and Tom Horlick-Jones

This chapter responds to the challenge from the proponents of the social amplification of risk framework (SARF) a decade ago, that future research should focus on the *interaction* between risks (as conventionally calibrated) and "the psychological, social, institutional, and cultural processes" which generate interpretations that may "heighten or attenuate public perceptions of risk and shape risk behavior" (Kasperson 1992, pp.157–158). In particular the discussion tackles a core, unresolved question at the heart of SARF relating to the mass media's pivotal role as a "station" for relaying "signals" and constructing public representations of risk (Kasperson and Kasperson 1996, p. 97).

SARF was presented as a "fledgling conceptual framework" rather than "a fully developed theory" (Kasperson, Renn, Slovic et al. 1988, p. 180), and its proponents expressly invited "scrutiny, elaboration, and competing views" (p. 187). However, while primarily intended as a stimulus to debate within the professional risk research and policy making communities, there were suggestions that SARF could also provide a productive departure point for broader assessments of the state of democratic life. The dispute over the nuclear waste facility at Yucca Mountain Nevada, that had served to prompt questions about risk amplification mechanisms, confirmed an apparent increasing breakdown of trust between citizens and governments. In common with many political scientists and commentators Kasperson and his co-workers saw this evaporation of trust affecting "all social institutions and public orientations towards particular policies or decision areas" (Kasperson, Golding, and Tuler 1992, pp.176–177) although it appeared particularly marked in relation to risk issues.

This work was funded (1997–99) by the United Kingdom Health and Safety Executive on behalf of the Interdepartmental Liaison Group on Risk Assessment as one of three research projects on the social amplification of risk. The opinions and conclusions expressed are those of the authors alone and do not necessarily reflect the policies or views of the sponsoring departments. The authors also gratefully acknowledge the data collection and analysis undertaken by two research staff, Shelley McLachlan and Diana Hargreaves.

The centrality of debates around risk in modern democracies had been persuasively argued by the German social theorist, Ulrick Beck, in his book *Risk Society*. He suggested that whereas governments in the past had been judged primarily on their ability to deliver "goods" (higher incomes, better working and living conditions, greater consumer choice), they were now increasingly expected to protect citizens (and their descendants) from the "bads" presented by environmental, technological, and other risks. For Beck, notions of progress were giving way to fears for safety and security and belief in science as the midwife of social improvement was being edged out by the insecurities created by the advent of the nuclear age and advances in biotechnology. As a result, the "conflicts of a 'wealth-distributing' society begin to be joined by those of a 'risk-reducing' society" (Beck 1992, p. 20). It is against the backdrop of this general shift that Kasperson and his colleagues saw risk research providing "a risk beacon" shining a strong light onto "deeper questions of social organisation and processes and into the nature of democracy . . . and social justice" (Kasperson 1992, pp. 177–178).

We shall argue that while SARF has helped to initiate research activity, the framework itself cannot offer a satisfactory account of risk communication and responses in contemporary democracies. Our argument is developed in the context of developments in social and political theory and a long history of mass communications research that point strongly to alternative frameworks than those presented by SARF. We draw for empirical evidence on our recent research into media representations and public understanding of risk in Britain (see Petts, Horlick-Jones, and Murdock 2001). The media analysis entailed an extensive quantitative content analysis of risk reporting in the major daily newspapers and terrestrial television channels in the first half of 1999 together with detailed qualitative studies of the coverage of selected risk areas, including GM foods, a major rail crash, and the "Y2K" ("Millennium") computer "bug." Audience responses and understandings of both general risk concerns and experiences and the case study topics, were explored through group discussions. Small groups viewed selected television coverage taken from the main content analysis sample, and in addition individual "accompanied reading" interviews were held in which a cross-section of focus group members were asked to read and talk about their responses to copies of their normal daily newspaper containing risk items selected by the research team. Like all case studies, Britain and its media are "peculiar" in many ways. However, we would argue that the general approach outlined here can be applied to a wide range of national conditions.[1]

---

[1] Our research also included an analysis of how lay publics make sense of risk issues, although it is not discussed in detail here. The role of such interpretative practices in risk perception is discussed in the chapter by Horlick-Jones et al. this volume, chapter 11.

Modeling communications: highways and arenas

The first major problem with SARF's central metaphor of amplification, and the sender–message–receiver model of communication on which it rests, is that it cannot deal adequately with the complex social organization of risk communication. Faced with such criticisms, Kasperson and his colleagues have responded by trying to accommodate them within their framework: stressing its flexibility, and the complex social interactions that it acknowledges (even if it is difficult to present these diagrammatically). However, this explanation still underplays over three decades of research and theorizing in media and communications studies that points insistently toward alternative approaches. SARF is isolated from key developments in social and political theory and, inevitably given its date, from more recent debates about the constitution and mechanisms of citizenship in complex democracies. As a result there is an unresolved tension at the heart of the SARF project, between the logic of the amplification metaphor on the one hand and the wider ambition to illuminate the operations of democracy on the other. The first is rooted in a transmission or transportation model of communication in which authoritative "messages" travel from centers of expertise and legitimated power to lay publics. The second presupposes a dialogic model in which the claims of the powerful are continually tested in open debate.

As Mary Douglas has argued, SARF's central metaphor carries an implicit political bias (Douglas 1997, p. 126). Although its proponents are at pains to point out that in the language of electronic engineering, from which they borrow the term, "amplification" refers to the attenuation of "signals" during the process of transmission from senders to receivers as well as to their intensification (see Kasperson et al. 1988, p. 180), the thrust of their research defines the central "problem" as removing unnecessary "noise" in the major channels of communication so that authoritative information can travel undistorted.

This focus on how the public acquires a false or exaggerated view of hazards and is prompted to respond in inappropriate or disproportionate ways is also central to the extensive literature on the amplification of deviance and the construction of moral panics. Following Stanley Cohen's seminal research on the panic about disruptive youth, sparked off by media coverage of the clashes between rival teenage gangs of Mods and Rockers in England in the mid 1960s (Cohen 1972), the study of moral panics has become a well-established sub-field within both criminology and media studies (see Thompson 1998). The SARF discussion does not appear to have recognized this earlier work on amplification although it does address many of the same communicative processes. However, there is one important difference between the two research traditions. SARF tends to focus on centers of cultural and economic power, arguing that amplification processes too often devalue their expertise and stigmatize their operations. In contrast, deviancy amplification research tends to focus on the powerless, arguing that media labeling and subsequent official and public over-reaction reinforces their marginality and confirms their subordination. For proponents of SARF the central problem is "information transfer." For deviancy theorists it is securing the conditions for a democratic debate to which all parties contribute and through which dominant labels and understandings are subjected to close interrogation.

The ideal of open rational debate as the touchstone of the democratic process has been most forcefully advanced by Jürgen Habermas in his immensely influential model of the political public sphere as a communicative bridge between the concerns of civil society and the operations of state and government (Habermas 1989). However, as Habermas readily acknowledges, this ideal has been thoroughly compromised in practice by the progressive capture by major centers of corporate and governmental power of opportunities to speak in public, particularly in the major public media, and the consequent relegation of citizens to the role of spectators. Investigating the resulting power struggles over command of the agenda of public debate has been a major focus of research in political science and political sociology. One important strand in this work presents the public sphere as a gladiatorial or sporting arena in which competing power-holders battle for advantage and public support.

Ortwin Renn (1992a) for example, has applied the arena model developed within policy analysis to political conflicts over risk but has pointed to its limitations, arguing that it cannot account for the perceptions or motivations of individuals. He is correct, but his discussion deals with only one, relatively limited variant of the model. The perspective sketched here draws on general attempts within recent social theory to overcome the structure/agency dichotomy.

This metaphor of the arena forms the basis of a number of conceptual models, the most notable of these is Pierre Bourdieu's work on "fields of action." Bourdieu's model of fields is part of a cluster of concepts that form the basis of a comprehensive theory of the dynamic relations between situated action and structural formations. In common with Anthony Giddens (1984), whose theory of "structuration" has the same basic objective, Bourdieu aims to explain how "structures are constituted through action, and reciprocally how action is constituted structurally" (Giddens 1976, p. 161). The model which we outline here draws heavily on Bourdieu's ideas but adapts his notion of fields rather than applying it strictly. In the spirit of the metaphor's emphasis on fields of play, we can usefully outline its basic features with the example of the field of professional football.

This is made up of the various football clubs together with the game's organizing bodies. As with all fields, it is a "structured social space, a field of forces" (Bourdieu 1998, p. 40) within which the various clubs struggle not only to win particular games and trophies, but also to alter the field's overall organization and governing rules so as to consolidate their longer term position and expand their effective scope for action. The top clubs may form an elite league for example and negotiate lucrative but exclusive television rights to their games. A club's capacity to secure a "win" in these various contests depends on the stock of resources or "capitals" they command. Bourdieu distinguishes four main forms of capital: economic, social, informational, and symbolic (Bourdieu 1987, pp. 3–4). Economic capital consists of assets and cash that can be used to secure key operating resources and fund lobbying, advertising, and public relations activities. Social capital consists of resources based on connections with influential figures and membership of key trade and advisory groups. Informational capital derives from command over data with strategic value within the field. In the case of companies this would include patent rights and intelligence on consumers and competitors. Symbolic capital is generated by a player's accumulated reputation and status within the field. For our present purposes we also need to add a fifth form of capital, communicative capital, consisting of competence in the arena of public communication.

The size and composition of an agent's overall stock of capital will determine both their relative position within the field of play and the array of choices open to them, but it will not determine their strategy in any particular instance. This will be as much a matter of improvisation as of calculation. Key games can be won by creative responses to the run of play or lost through failure to anticipate and prepare for competitors' interventions. It is this indeterminancy that ensures the field's continual dynamism.

Not all change is generated by action within the field however. Players also have to respond to changes in their surrounding environment. Bourdieu sees society as being made up of an array of specific sub-fields embedded, like Chinese boxes (or perhaps, Russian dolls), within the overarching spaces staked out by the economic and political fields. Changes in the organization of these master fields impact on the operations of specific fields by creating new opportunities and presenting new problems. As well as responding to the actions of other players within their immediate field of operations for example, major corporations operating

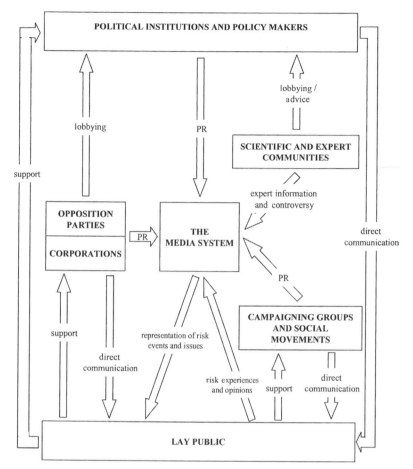

Figure 7.1 The field of mediated risk communication: earlier versions of this model can be found in Renn (1992a, p. 183) and in Durant and Lindsey (1999, p. 5).

in risk sensitive areas such as nuclear power and biotechnology have to negotiate general shifts in regulatory climates, labor markets, and international trade.

Our general model of the field of mediated risk communication is shown in its basic form in figure 7.1.

This shows six major sets of players – government and state agencies, opposition parties, campaigning groups, corporations, scientific and expert communities and the media – engaged in a continual contest for position and advantage in which the struggle for command of public communications and attention plays a central role. This competition revolves around four main stakes:

(1) *Visibility.* The ability to control when and how news about strategic information and action will enter the public domain together with the ability to conceal or suppress potentially damaging publicity.
(2) *Legitimacy.* Having one's arguments treated as credible and authoritative.
(3) *Precedence.* Establishing the dominant definition of the situation and commanding the agenda and terms of debate.
(4) *Trust.* Maintaining and if possible enhancing public trust and support.

Work conducted within the SARF framework tends to concentrate on the amounts of coverage given to different issues and actors rather than the terms on which this publicity is secured. Separating these different dimensions of communicative activity allows us to construct more fine-grained accounts of the ebb and flow of advantage within the risk communications field. As many actors have discovered, attracting news attention may initiate a new run of play, but "the real battle is over whose interpretation, whose framing of reality" commands the debate (Ryan 1991, p. 53). During the dispute over the disposal of the Brent Spar oil platform in the North Sea for example, Greenpeace activists secured substantial publicity for their views by occupying the platform and releasing photographs of the subsequent "battle" in the sea around it. However, their efforts to convert this visibility into legitimacy were only partly successful with several major British daily newspapers expressing strong antagonism to their position (Hansen 2000). The theoretical position we adopt here also insists that control over communications is about secrecy as well as publicity.

SARF's conception of power is derived from Max Weber's classic definition of it as the ability to compel compliance with "rules and commands independent of the subjugated group's convictions" (see Renn 1992a, p. 185). However, as Steven Lukes (1974) has forcefully pointed out, this is a one-dimensional model which ignores power's other two faces: the ability to prevent the public airing of issues, and the structural power accruing to an actor's dominant position in the field of contest. In their discussion of "hidden hazards," Roger and Jeanne Kasperson point to significant continuing risks that have been "attenuated" (receiving less coverage than they argue they merit) because "they lie entangled in society's web of values and assumptions which either denigrates the importance of the consequences or deems them acceptable [and] elevates the associated benefits" (Kasperson and Kasperson 1996, p. 103). This functionalist emphasis on prevailing values avoids the thorny question of how particular assumptions and frames of meaning rather than others achieve centrality. They cite smoking as an instance of a "hidden hazard."

However, this example requires some attention also to concerns that the major tobacco companies have suppressed evidence on the causal connection between smoking and cancer.

Lukes' insistence on the importance of structural power is also difficult to accommodate within SARF since the framework presents the various actors in the area of risk communication in classically pluralist terms, as competing and interacting more or less on a level playing-field. In contrast our model's emphasis on the differential stocks of capital that actors possess follows Bourdieu in presenting fields as invariably structured around relations of dominance and subordination. Major corporations, for example, enjoy special advantages since they can convert their stocks of economic capital into other forms of capital. They can augment their social capital by inviting prominent politicians to serve on directorial or advisory boards. They can increase their informational capital by funding key research and intelligence gathering activities. They can bolster their communicative capital by employing professional lobbyists, public relations firms, and advertising agencies to manage their public communication operations. As Powers and Andsager's (1999) study of the career of American debates around breast implants shows very clearly, effective corporate public relations can shift the framing of issues, in this case moving it from a concern with health risks to a focus on the problems facing implant manufacturers.

In contrast to classical structuralist arguments, however, our model does not assume that the privileged positions these resources deliver are fixed. On the contrary, actors' continual efforts to maintain or improve their relative positions are the central dynamic within the field. As the recent debates over genetically modified (GM) foods in Britain show, economic capital cannot always be converted unproblematically into symbolic capital because public trust in large corporations is continually contested by definitions of the situation that draw on deep-seated reservoirs of populist distrust of "big business." To understand this we need to investigate the interplay between public representations and audience interpretations and responses in their full complexity.

The field model sees audiences as *active participants*[2] in the contest of positions rather than as simply "receivers" or spectators. In his account of the arena model and its limitations, Ortwin Renn argues that its central metaphor "leaves the impression of politics as a game" in which citizens participate purely as spectators (Renn 1992a, p. 195). In the field model they play a double role. Firstly, they are a key stake in the struggle. In the marketplaces for commodities, votes, and ideas their continued support

---

[2] The role of agency is emphasized in "interpretive" studies of risk perception (see Zonabeud 1993; Walker et al. 1998; Horlick-Jones et al. this volume, chapter 11).

cannot be taken for granted. It has to be repeatedly won and retained and its withdrawal can have real material consequences. As the British debate over GM foods clearly demonstrates, consumption is now a political as well as an economic activity. Consumer campaigns are designed not only to maximize choices within the marketplace (by clearly labeling foods containing GM ingredients for example) but increasingly to challenge the general organization of food production by initiating boycotts of products manufactured under conditions that activists find ethically or environmentally unacceptable. Secondly, members of the public are often the principal actors in the dramas and debates played out in public representations of risks. As we will see this is particularly true of the tabloid media. Furthermore, lay publics are not merely passive spectators of the game on the field and absorbers of information and messages. They are considerably more active than this bringing their own "capitals" to bear on their responses to what they are seeing and hearing.

In their analysis of disputes over the siting of nuclear facilities, Kasperson and his colleagues argue that developers need to step back from the immediate ebb and flow of action and see the situation in *"systems and historical perspective"* (Kasperson et al. 1992, p. 182). The diagrammatic representation of SARF does not provide for this insight, particularly its suggestion of amplification as a chain of consequences emanating from an originating event. In contrast, the field model makes clear that players' responses to particular events are fundamentally shaped by continuing patterns of interaction within a relatively durable system of relations. Moving from a focus on specific events to a consideration of these systematic determinants of action is particularly important to a proper understanding of the role of the mass media in the field of risk communication

Although the mass media are shown as a single box in figure 7.1 (similar to SARF's representation of them), we do not present them as a more or less undifferentiated relay mechanism. On the contrary, we see them as a series of sub-fields of action, each with its own distinctive history and rules of engagement, in which practices are shaped by continuing competition between and within media organizations. As Bourdieu notes:

To try to understand what journalists are able to do, you have to keep in mind a series of parameters: first, the relative position of the particular news medium [within the general field of news production]; and second, the positions occupied by journalists themselves within the space occupied by their respective newspapers or networks. (Bourdieu 1998, p. 40)

These positions, taken together, structure what particular journalists are required to deliver and their relations to potential sources of information.

To understand how these general conceptions shape the field of risk reporting in Britain it is necessary to grasp the importance of the division between tabloid and broadsheet news.

Organizing accounts: tabloids and broadsheets

In his analysis of the relations between the growth of communications and the development of modern democracy in early nineteenth-century England, Habermas (1989) distinguishes two major spaces for debate and representation. The first of these, the political public sphere, he sees as centered around the coffee houses, clubs, and other meeting places of the new commercial, political, and professional elites, with the newspapers of record, like the London *Times*, the *Manchester Guardian*, and *The Daily Telegraph*, all founded between the French Revolution and the accession of Queen Victoria, playing a crucial mediating role between private conversations and public pronouncements. In this conception, the "serious" press act as a trading floor on which strategic information is exchanged, the credentials of speakers scrutinized, and the implications for action debated. As Habermas notes, however, access to this new communicative space was restricted to the bourgeoisie. The populus gravitated towards the alternative public sphere centered around popular literature and the new entertainment-oriented popular press led by the *News of the World* (est. 1843).

These cultural forms focused on "the chronic and persistent problems of life – love, trust, betrayal, responsibility, death" rather than the immediate political issues of the day and the relative merits of competing courses of action which were the stuff of the political public sphere (see McGuigan 2000, p. 5). Their producers operated more as celebrants at a ritual than transportation agents (Carey 1989, p. 8). They were less interested in imparting information than in representing shared beliefs, exploiting the ancient identity between "communication" and "community." To cement these ties they set out to foster relationships in which authors and audiences "talked heart to heart," united by a shared fascination with "what was 'human,' " as defined by heroism and suffering on the one hand and exploitation and criminality on the other (Habermas 1989, p. 50).

There was also a third communicative space, which Habermas does not mention, but which is central to our argument here. It consisted of the various public shows and spectacles that proliferated in the nineteenth-century city from funfairs and circuses, to exhibitions of human oddities and the popular melodramas played in the penny theatres. A large part of their attraction lay in their visuality and their ability to surprise and shock.

Many observers saw this emphasis on sensation as posing a significant danger to democracy.

The "ideal" democratic citizen was a sober individual, diligently searching out relevant information, carefully evaluating its validity, engaging in rational debate on its implications, and registering eventual choices in the calm and seclusion of the ballot box. For many commentators the logical sequences of written language and agreed rules of turn-taking in debate were essential guarantors of the rationality of this process. Because images work associatively rather than sequentially they saw them slipping beneath the perimeter fences of rationality and encouraging emotive reactions. In the process the citizen moved from sovereign individual to member of a psychological crowd. As the influential French writer, Gustav Le Bon, argued in his book, *The Crowd*:

The simplest event that comes under the observation of a crowd is soon totally transformed. A crowd thinks in images, and the image itself immediately calls up a series of other images, having no logical connection with the first. (Le Bon 1969, pp. 35–36)

It is no accident that Le Bon should have made this observation in 1895, the year of the first commercial cinema showing in Paris. By then popular culture was already highly image intensive following the innovations in lithography and ink technology that had produced much more vivid advertising posters and the introduction of the half tone process which allowed photographs to be printed in newspapers for the first time. It was against this background that a new cheap popular daily press was launched either side of the century's turn, led in Britain by the *Daily Mail*, the *Daily Express*, and the *Daily Mirror* (est. 1904), all titles that are still very much in business.

From the outset these papers were aimed squarely at a mass market and drew on styles of writing and presentation that combined information, debate, storytelling, and attractions. Readers were invited not simply to keep themselves informed, but to enjoy a well-told story featuring "ordinary" people and the chance to see something out of the ordinary, something spectacular and visually arresting (Ekstrom 2000, p. 468). Contemporary observers recognized immediately that they were now looking at two distinct newspaper systems (see for example Wilcox 1900). On the one side stood the "serious" titles concentrating on political and business news and offering extensive space for commentary and analysis and on the other stood the "sensationalist" press built around visual images and human interest stories. This division between broadsheet and tabloid titles (as they came to be called) remains a fundamental feature of the British national newspaper market. This is in marked contrast to the United States where the daily press is built primarily around regional and city markets and where best-selling tabloids like the *National Inquirer*, appear weekly rather than daily. These national characteristics might explain SARF's presentation of the press as though it were a more or less unitary system, although we readily recognize that it is easy to fall into the language of singularity just as it is in talking about "the public."

Many commentators regard tabloid journalism as a debased form of "serious" reporting. However, we would argue that it is more useful to see it as a parallel news system "with its own internal coherence and rules of engagement." Whereas "broadsheet" risk coverage trades in the activities and pronouncements of the powerful, tabloid stories tend to show individuals as victims of "untoward and often uncontrollable circumstances" or present the "achievements of ordinary people" and communities in the face of adversity (Langer 1998, p. 35). They are "not translating the opinions of the powerful 'down,' but depicting the world of 'everyday' people with all their trials, tribulations and triumphs" (p. 30).

By illustrating the concrete consequences of catastrophic events, "such as images of...people crying over destroyed homes, a grief-stricken mother and her suffering child, a forlorn domestic pet, or an emaciated wild animal, the uncertainty of future risks is given concrete form and content" (Bohölm 1998, pp. 126–127). By personalizing the impact of remote forces and providing potent points of identification, human interest stories invite readers to see themselves as members of an extended community of "ordinary" people that transcends geography, class, and party. This certainly helps to maximize market share but it also has social implications. As Helen Hughes pointed out in her pioneering essay on the human interest story, "moral speculations are not evoked by news of court procedure; they take form on the reading of an intimate story that shows what the impact of law and convention means as a private experience" (Hughes 1937, p. 81). By trading in identification and empathy she argues, tabloid news, at its best, can cement the habits of the heart and sense of shared conditions on which democracy depends.

Constructing imagined communities nevertheless also involves the erection of boundary fences to keep "outsiders" out. For every "us" there is a "them." In tabloid reporting the "world of 'Them' is the world of the bosses... 'the people at the top,' 'the higher-ups'... [who] 'aren't really to be trusted,' 'are all twisters really...are all in a click [clique] together'" (Hoggart 1966, p. 72–73) This is a classically populist world view. It pitches a romanticized ordinariness against an exaggerated arrogance, "Middle England" against the metropolitan elite, common sense against accredited expertise, practical experience against bookish learning (Taggart 2000).

This populist structure of feeling emerged repeatedly in the interviews and focus groups we conducted; reference to "the suits" being common

Table 7.1 *Principal prompts for risk items (United Kingdom stories only)*

actions /experiences by	The Sun	Daily Mail	Daily Telegraph
lay actors	38%	14%	4%
government/politicians	14%	14%	26%
scientists/experts	6%	24%	28%
pressure groups	3%	10%	4%
corporations	3%	6%	2%

Source: Petts et al. (2001).

(Petts et al. 2001). However, it fits uneasily with conventional party allegiances, being altogether more pervasive. In the 1997 British General Election for example, the country's best-selling tabloid daily newspaper, *The Sun*, urged its readers to cast their vote for New Labour. Just over a third (38 percent) did. The remainder was split more or less equally between those who voted for one of the other main parties and those who did not vote at all. Interestingly, amongst readers of the "establishment" broadsheet, *The Financial Times*, 39 percent did not vote at all.

Our research results underlined the importance of the broadsheet/tabloid division in organizing styles of reporting and presentation in the British press. Table 7.1 shows the principal prompts for risk stories in the leading titles in each of the three main segments of the national daily newspaper market; the broadsheet *Daily Telegraph*, the mid-market *Daily Mail*, and the tabloid *Sun*.

These results demonstrate the different structures of news attention in the tabloid and broadsheet press very clearly. Whereas over a third (38 percent) of all risk items in *The Sun* are human interest stories prompted by the experiences or actions of "ordinary" people, the corresponding figure for the *Daily Telegraph* is only 4 percent, with the mid-market *Daily Mail*, which straddles the two styles, falling in-between. Conversely, the *Telegraph* is over four times more likely than *The Sun* to base items on the activities or pronouncements of certified experts and almost twice as likely to base them on governmental or party political initiatives.

These differences were further underlined by the pattern of quotation. 80 percent of all the risk items coded in *The Sun* quoted a member of the public as either the primary or secondary speaker compared to only 23 percent of items in the *Daily Telegraph*. Conversely, whilst almost half (46 percent) the *Telegraph* items quoted a scientist or accredited expert, they spoke in only 6 percent of *Sun* stories.

These differences confirm that in the British case at least, we are dealing with two parallel systems of press reporting, one working from the top-down, the other operating from the bottom-up. But does this distinction also hold in the other major popular news medium of television?

Televizing issues: public service and market competition

Despite its centrality to popular mediated experience, television has received little systematic attention in risk communication research. The reasons are mainly practical. Press stories can be coded on any desk-top and their main features taken in with a single sustained glance. Television news items can only be viewed on videotape and their sequential nature and their complex combinations of oral, written, and visual materials requires researchers to play them back a number of times to record and check their observations. The personnel and time needed to undertake comprehensive, large scale, studies of televised news are therefore beyond the means of most university-based research projects (Hargreaves and Ferguson 2000, ch. 4, p. 9), obliging them to either ignore television altogether, to work with much smaller samples, or to code only basic or selected aspects of the presentation (e.g. Cottle 2000).

Historically, television in Britain has been governed by a public service ethos which saw its central role as providing the information and access to rational debate that citizens required to act as competent members of a democratic polity (see Murdock 1992). It emphasized "objective" reporting, untainted by sensation, the relay of expert evidence and opinion and the impartial chairing of legitimate debate. As its first Organizer of Programmes explained in 1924, the BBC's "unique position gives the public an opportunity they have never had before of hearing both sides of a question expounded by experts," allowing "the 'man in the street' to take an active interest in his country's affairs" (quoted in Smith 1974, p. 43). This paternalistic solution to the management of a mass democracy was consistently challenged however by those inside the organization who championed "ordinary" people's right to speak for themselves. As a consequence there was always an underlying tension in the BBC's practice between deliberative and delegative models of democratic representation.

With the launch of the commercial ITV (Independent Television) system in the mid 1950s a third mode of address was introduced into this uneasy relation between paternalism and participation: commercial populism. This beckoned viewers to join an imagined community of "ordinary" people for whom consuming the products and lifestyles shown in the advertising breaks was assuming a more and more central role in everyday life and political judgment. Its styles borrowed heavily from tabloid traditions of storytelling, display, and attraction.

With the rapid rise of cable and satellite channels over the last decade terrestrial broadcasters (who had previously enjoyed monopoly access to television homes) have faced intensifying competition for audiences. Between 1991 and 2000 the average audience share commanded by the BBC's main channel, BBC1, fell from 38 percent to 28 percent, and the share of its main terrestrial rival, ITV, dropped from 43 percent to 30 percent. Both channels have responded by assigning a greater share of transmission time to programs featuring ordinary people and everyday lives: talk shows, game shows, "docusoaps," soap opera, and lifestyle programmes (Arlidge 2000). News too has become more populist with the major bulletins giving more space to human interest stories. Between 1993 and 1996 for example, the percentage of running time devoted to human interest stories on the ITV early evening bulletin increased from 8.9 percent to 15.6 percent and from 1.7 percent to 8.9 percent on the competing BBC bulletin (Harrison 2000, pp. 182–183). Despite this shift towards tabloidization, our content analysis results confirm that overall the BBC continues to be more strongly oriented to political and expert sources than ITV. Of the United Kingdom risk items carried on the Corporation's early evening bulletin, 88 percent featured elected politicians or members of the government as primary or secondary speakers compared to 17 percent of the stories in the competing ITV bulletin. Conversely, ITV news was more likely to feature the testimony and opinions of members of the public. These differences help to explain why many of our respondents continued to see the BBC as a more authoritative news source:

I don't know why, but you take it more seriously. You know if it's BBC1 News, it's going to be accurate. (Thirty-four-year-old special needs assistant in a primary school)

Yeah, the BBC seems more professional. It just seems straight down the line . . . sort of the facts. (Nineteen-year-old, male video-store clerk)

This evidence underlines once again the importance of seeing the news system not as an array of relay posts or "issue multipliers" (Renn 1992b, p. 501) but as a set of institutional actors responding to the changing terms of play in different ways. Although the BBC's stocks of economic capital have been depleted by falls in the real value of the license fee which funds its operations, it can still draw on the reserves of symbolic capital it has accumulated in its historical role as "the voice of the nation" in times of trouble and crisis.

The personas and reputations of news outlets play an important role in framing audience responses to particular stories. To some extent they take them from whence they come. At the same time, their interpretations remain heavily dependent on the ways in which they negotiate the various layers of meaning mobilized within the text itself.

Making sense: messages and meanings

As Kasperson points out in relation to nuclear waste debates, "publics typically have long memories and employ broader contexts" when assessing the arguments advanced in relation to recent events (Kasperson et al. 1992, p. 182). It is impossible, for example, to explain the intensity of public reaction to plans to introduce genetically modified crops in Britain and the skepticism which greeted government assurances of safety, without placing the "event" squarely in the context of popular memories of the mismanagement of the BSE crisis, including the official evidence that:

The Government was preoccupied with preventing an alarmist over-reaction to BSE because it believed that the risk was remote. It is now clear that this campaign of reassurance "was a mistake" resulting in "confidence in government pronouncements about risk being a casualty." (Phillips et al. 2000, volume 1, p. xviii)

This example strongly suggests that the media coverage of risk is more usefully approached not as a series of discrete responses to bounded events, but as the latest episodes in an intersecting series of continuing narratives about chance, choice, science, power, and accountability.

In *Mythologies*, his celebrated dissection of French popular media in the 1950s, Roland Barthes (1973) argues that mediated communications always operate at three levels: denotation, connotation, and myth. The first corresponds to the manifest content, the second consists of the associations sparked-off by key phrases or images, and the third connects the item to deep-seated values and world views that confirm or challenge prevailing relations of power.

The importance of connotation and myth is recognized in SARF arguments. Kasperson and his colleagues see "specific terms used in risk information are seen as potential triggers of associations independent of those intended" (Kasperson et al. 1988, p. 185) and concede that "the symbols present in messages are key factors in shaping decoding processes" (Kasperson et al. 1988, p. 180). However, taking these arguments to their conclusion indicates the need for a more interactionist framework than the source-receiver model where risk stories offer a more complex array of possible meanings which audiences actively interpret in different ways depending on their prior experience and stocks of cultural knowledge. As recent work in media and cultural studies has repeatedly demonstrated, mediated communication is as much about symbolic exchange as it is about information transfer.

In our own recent work we have drawn on insights from linguistics and visual analysis to explore two key aspects of the way news constructs the meanings it offers to audiences: framing and anchorage.

Representing risk: frames, anchors, and images

Framing has been defined in several different ways in media analysis, but we are using it here to refer to the ways that news coverage draws boundaries around an event or issue, classifying it as an instance of "X" rather than "Y." Confronted with any happening, journalists need to answer the question "What have we here?", firstly for themselves and secondly for the audience. In doing this they draw on past incidents that appear to be similar and which audiences are likely to remember. In this sense all "news" is in fact "old." Indeed, as we argued earlier, rather than thinking of news stories as reports about distinct and separate events we need to approach them as episodes in continuing narratives built around particular master themes and central motifs. At the same time, frames are not fixed. Like paintings, accounts can be re-hung and placed in different positions in the gallery of popular representations, suggesting new contexts of interpretation and connections to other events and issues. This gives struggles over the initial framing of events a central role in the organization of public understandings and responses.

Framing always works through connotation and myth as well as denotation. Its success depends firstly on activating chains of association that reinforce a particular construction of events and connect it to basic beliefs and values, and secondly on finding resonant linguistic tags and images that, like a weight thrown over the side of a boat, anchor these meanings and prevent them from drifting. The extensive use of the phrases "Frankenstein" and "mutant" and the popular play on words around the idea of vegetation during the debate on GM foods in Britain, provide particularly clear illustrations of these processes in practice.

Mary Shelley's cautionary tale of Frankenstein, a scientist who sets out to create a perfect being and ends up making a monster who destroys him is "one of the most important myths of modernity" (Turney 1998, p. 3). It provides us with our most enduring images of the unintended consequences of technological intervention in general and biological experimentation in particular. The fact that the creature is assembled from elements taken from a variety of different sources also resonates strongly with fascinations and fears around ideas of artificial mutation and alteration. Familiar from countless comic books, pulp fictions, and popular films, the story's ubiquity forcefully underscores the need to approach popular texts not as isolated artefacts but as nodes in a dense network of intertextual connections marked by multiple borrowings, adaptations, and parodies.

The newspaper language deployed in the British GM foods debate, particularly in the tabloid and mid-market papers, drew extensively on both the Frankenstein myth and the idea of mutation. The tabloid *Daily Mirror* for example, chose to launch its campaign for more information to be printed on food packaging under the slogan "Label Frankenstein Foods," whilst headlines such as the *Daily Express*'s "Blair Battles to Calm Public Fears Over Mutant Foods" (19 February 1999) evoked deep-seated fears about the long-term effects of eating GM foods.

Western cultures draw a sharp division between the human and vegetable domains. Humans possess consciousness, animation, and free will, vegetables do not, which is why people who lose these faculties (such as patients with severe brain damage) are often dubbed "vegetables" in common speech. Play on the idea that genetically modified crops might make people more vegetable-like in this sense was a consistent theme in press representations. Examples include portraits borrowing the technique developed by the Milanese painter, Arcimboldo, depicting faces composed entirely of vegetables, and the *Guardian* cartoon of 16 February 1999. This showed Tony Blair standing in front of a mass of back-bench Labour MPs depicted as carrots wearing rosettes with the slogan "Modified Labour." The only exception is Ken Livingstone, who at the time was lobbying to be adopted as the Labour candidate in the forthcoming elections for Mayor of London in the teeth of concerted opposition from the Prime Minister. An adviser is whispering in Blair's ear, "Don't look now Boss, but we seem to have neglected to modify one of the vegetables." This image deftly linked the mounting media commentary on Tony Blair's centralized style of leadership and intolerance of within-party dissent with the widespread publicity given to his strongly voiced support for GM foods and his seeming lack of responsiveness to public concerns. This connection was also suggested by a *Daily Mirror* front page depicting the Prime Minister with the familiar facial features of Frankenstein's monster. This digital merging of identities was a playful but powerful anchor to the paper's questioning of the close relations between some of the leading agribusiness and biotechnology companies involved in developing GM crops and senior members of the New Labour Government.

The anchors provided by resonant phrases and images also help to establish links to more general belief systems, including religious systems. Despite the widespread belief that we live in a predominantly secular age, religious iconography remains a rich source of popular representations, particularly in matters of life and death (see also MacGregor's account of Y2K in the United States, this volume, chapter 10). As Asa Bohölm has argued, after analyzing the press photographs accompanying stories marking the tenth anniversary of the accident at the Chernobyl nuclear reactor, written accounts of the event in terms of science were consistently "challenged by the visual material presented in the media [which] portrayed an event preordained by divine forces striking at a sinful humanity" (Bohölm 1998, p. 139).

Religious symbolism was also widely deployed in the GM foods debate, sometimes appearing in unexpected contexts. On 5 March 1999 for example, the satirical magazine, *Private Eye*, carried a cartoon showing two elderly men walking past a trial field planted with GM crops with a line of men with scythes working in the background. They were dressed in the black hoods and cloaks of the Grim Reaper, the traditional harbinger of death in Christian iconography. The caption read: "Harvesting already, I see."

Our research confirmed the general importance of imagery in risk communication. Over half of all the newspaper items we sampled in our cross-sectional content analysis contained at least one image, usually a news photograph, and very few of the television news items analyzed were confined solely to shots of the presenter in the studio, reading direct to camera. The great majority contained some additional visual material. There is no reason to believe that these results are in any way exceptional, and yet most work on the media coverage of risk has focused on the written copy in press stories and ignored the visual content, and, as noted earlier, has paid surprisingly little attention to television.

"Messages hidden in fiction writing or entertaining movies... may be powerful agents in creating images of objects" (Renn 1991a, p. 298). However, the issues of connotation, myth, and intertextuality that this observation opens up fit uncomfortably with the metaphor of signaling, which is too one-dimensional to capture the layered nature of mediated communications and its complex links to wider formations of discourse and representation. When audience members read a newspaper story or look at a television news bulletin they encounter relatively enduring frames and anchors that presuppose certain generalized cultural knowledge. Two decades of research in media and cultural studies have explored the social dynamics of audience activity in some detail (e.g. Murdock 1989; Morley 1992; Moores 1993). This work has advanced three arguments that are central to the case being made here.

Firstly, it sees people's media activity as an integral part of their continuing attempts to make sense of the world and their situation by drawing on the interpretive resources provided by personal experience, local knowledge, and mediated communication. Consequently, every encounter with media materials involves a complex chain of assessments, comparisons, and judgments, based on negotiations between "situated" and "mediated" knowledge.

Secondly, patterns of response and judgment are grounded in the enduring templates of classification and judgment inscribed through socialization, within the family, the neighborhood, and the education system. These habituses, as Bourdieu calls them, provide the generalized schemes of thought, perception, and appreciation through which people order and evaluate their social and symbolic experiences (Bourdieu 1984). Bourdieu locates these schemas in particular class locations, though other commentators have drawn attention to the importance of other dimensions of stratification, particularly gender, ethnicity, and age, in regulating access to underlying meaning and value systems and the vocabularies through which they are expressed. In our research we made some attempt to respond to these stratifications, with initial analysis particularly confirming the need for greater attention to ethnicity. Although Bordieu views habituses as relatively durable he accepts that they are subject to modification and change as actors move from one location to another or are persuaded to alter their position.

Thirdly, following on from that last point, people's understandings of, and responses to, media are seen as being continually refined and modified through everyday conversation and argument.

These starting-points have far-reaching consequences for the way we approach audience activity. Methodologically they suggest that in-depth interviews, biographical narratives, and modes such as focus groups which approximate as closely as possible to the conditions of everyday conversation, are likely to produce richer insights into the negotiation of media meanings than standard questionnaires or self-completion tests. Theoretically, they help to explain not only the consistent social patterning of media preferences and in-group communalities in interpretations and judgments (as products of a shared habitus), but also individual variations in response (as the outcome of particular biographical careers).

Communication and democracy revisited

Running through the interviews and focus group discussions we conducted was a consistent demand, particularly from working-class respondents, for ordinary people to have more opportunities to contribute to public debates on risk issues. One young woman, who had left school at sixteen without any qualifications, put the case particularly forcefully:

I'm just a little person [...] But you want to put your hand up, don't you and say "I've got an opinion. It might not count for very much, but I've got an opinion"... I want to sit [...] and say, "Look I'm sorry but I don't particularly understand about GM foods or whatever" I want to talk the way I want to talk.

This position was rooted in the classical opposition between "them" and "us" at the heart of populism. Interestingly though, while politicians were invariably seen as belonging to "them" independent scientists were classified as honorary members of "us":

> When you ask politicians you know ... it's beside the point. Just getting a polit-ical slant on it rather than an objective scientific basis of it all. Because we all want to be informed [...] and we need people to explain it to us in layman's terms. (Local government officer)
> I'd have liked to have heard from a geneticist, is that the right word, someone who knows about genes and stuff, who will explain what they are doing. But not some politicians. (Unemployed furniture restorer)

This division has also emerged strongly in recent national surveys. When asked in a recent opinion poll who they would trust to advise them on the risks posed by pollution, only 4 percent nominated politi-cians and 6 percent government ministers. In contrast, 60 percent said they would trust an independent university based scientist, though sig-nificantly, less than a quarter (23 percent) claimed they would trust a government scientist (MORI 1999).

These trends underlie contemporary debates on, and practical re-sponses to, the changing relationship between risk communication and the democratic process. Official encouragement (e.g. Stern and Fineberg 1996; Royal Commission on Environmental Pollution 1998; House of Lords 2000) is being given to the replacement of top-down forms of in-formation transfer with dialogic fora that bring together the values, ques-tions, anxieties, and experiences of ordinary people, the provision of inde-pendent and accessible expositions of the current state of scientific debate and uncertainty, and sustained debate on the social and ethical implica-tions of current initiatives. However, despite the encouragement, clear definition of means to achieve this within existing regulatory and policy making frameworks still requires attention. Philosophical constructs of "discursive" and "deliberative democracy" founded in Habermas' (1984) ideal of "no force but the force of better argument" underpin criteria for, and analysis of, effective communication (Webler 1995; Gutman and Thompson 1996; Barnes 1999; Petts 2001). The aim is to address four basic issues: where are we going? Who gains, and who loses, and by which mechanisms of power? Is it desirable? and what should be done? (see Flyvbjerg 2001, p. 162).

As we have seen, the development of current forms of mass media has produced a broken-backed response to the problem of creating an inclusive public sphere, in which tabloid forms privilege grounded experience and popular voices, and broadsheet and public service forms orientate themselves around expertise and official viewpoints. However, the dramatic expansion of information media combined with the current emphasis on deliberative processes creates an environment in which information and expertise are no longer protected, revered, and unchallenged. The arrival of the Internet, and its growing integration into the flows of press and broadcast journalism, opens up, for the first time, opportunities to go beyond the historic dichotomy. News items and documentary features are no longer self-contained. They are becoming departure points from which readers and viewers can launch further explorations of the issues, exchange information and experience, and talk to journalists, program makers, and other players in the field of risk. Mobilizing the communicative opportunities opened up by digital media to develop more open, inclusive, and interactive dialogues on risk is one of the major challenges facing risk communications in the coming decades.

Conclusions: on communicating with the media

We conclude that SARF at best provides a highly simplistic understanding of the role and influence of the media in the amplification and attenuation of risk. At worst it could serve merely to aggravate tensions between risk experts and managers and lay publics through its failure to provide a coherent and full understanding of the impact and operations of these plural and symbolic information systems and their relationships with their consumers. Of course, it is not helpful merely to say that the argument is more complex than SARF suggests. SARF has been useful in raising important research questions. However, considering the media–lay public relationship we need to move beyond SARF to execute more effective risk communication.

Most importantly we need to move towards a design-based and user-centered approach to communication; that is communication which is based on an understanding of existing lay knowledge and beliefs prompted by asking the question "do we know what lay publics know and want to know rather than what we want to tell them?" This requires detailed analysis of how different lay publics talk about and respond to specific risk issues and their media preferences and how these change with time.

It also requires a clear understanding of the roles and actions of the different parties on the risk "field," in this case particularly the media.

Communication with the media by government and other official bodies requires a more proactive and media-specific communications plan that responds to the divergent styles and badges of the individual media and is responsive to their preferences in terms of narrative forms, visuals, and lay language, etc. It suggests a relationship with the media that is ongoing, diverse, responsive to lay interests and engaging as opposed to reactive and source-focused.

8 Plague and arsenic: assignment of blame in the mass media and the social amplification and attenuation of risk

Arvind Susarla

Societal responses to hazard events are perplexing. In the past, people have equated these societal responses with the potential injuries and deaths resulting from the hazards. More recently, however, hazard researchers have identified additional factors, such as mass media, organizational responses, and nature of the hazard, that shape societal response to hazard events. In other words, there is no linear relationship between societal responses and the injuries and deaths that result from a hazard event.

What factor(s) coalesce with the magnitude of the event to explain societal response to hazard events? This question remains a challenge for hazard researchers. Two hazard events described below demonstrate that societal responses depart from the magnitude of the event. These events characterize human experience of risk and provide an opportunity to explain how interactions with some hazard events produce intense societal reactions, while many others remain unnoticed.

In September 1994, reports on the reappearance of the bacterium *Yersinia pestis* in Surat indicated recurrence of the plague in India. Word of the plague quickly spread through the mass media and social networks. Despite local authorities' assurances of safety, rumors of a large number of deaths because of the plague occurred in the Surat. Public concern about the management of the hazard was widespread.

Within hours of the first appearance of the reports on the plague, an estimated 200,000 people deserted Surat. Hundreds of people arrived at the public and private hospitals of the city seeking assurance that they were

This chapter is derived from my doctoral dissertation research and I am grateful to Roger Kasperson, my dissertation supervisor, for advising through the entire process of shaping this manuscript. Paul Slovic and Nick Pidgeon not only gave helpful suggestions but also invited me to write this chapter after listening to my presentation on this subject at the Society for Risk Analysis Annual meeting. My peers at the Clark University gave valuable feedback on draft versions of this paper. Jeanne X. Kasperson helped me to organize ideas and thoughts expressed in this paper. I am thankful to all for their support and assistance, however I am solely responsible for errors that may have remained in the paper.

not infected. Meanwhile, civic authorities in several cities were alert to the possible arrival of potential plague patients from Surat. Precautionary measures included medical screenings of people from Surat at the bus and the train stations, and the closure of schools, colleges, and theaters. These preventative steps indicated the deep concern of the civic authorities that the disease might spread to other parts of the country.

Media coverage of the episode was dramatic. Local newspapers reported deaths of thousands of people because of the plague. This combination of public concern, media reports, and preventative measures instituted by the authorities sent mixed signals to foreign governments. Several countries imposed restrictions on people traveling to and from India. Dignitaries postponed official visits to India. Trade restriction, withdrawal of personnel by multinational firms, and cancellations of international flights were some of the ripples produced by the plague hazard.

In stark contrast, the social attention accorded to another hazard event – arsenic pollution – at first inspection is inexplicable. In West Bengal, groundwater in six districts[1] of the state were contaminated with arsenic. The total geographic area affected is equivalent to the size of Belgium, and the arsenic pollution several orders of magnitude higher than the recommended standards for drinking water by the World Health Organization (WHO). Water supplies in roughly 7,000 wells in 430 villages contained arsenic levels that were between twenty and seventy times the WHO's maximum permissible limit; in some wells the contamination was 200 times the limit. The arsenic pollution directly harmed over 175,000 people (Chatterjee et al. 1995; Das et al. 1994).

Yet only a modest degree of public attention can be discerned. The initial report of the arsenic contamination appeared in the newspaper in 1979. Although a large number of people was affected, initiatives of the government and the non-governmental organizations were limited. The number of people exposed and the scope of the contaminated area continued to rise over the time; however, there were no political campaigns to spotlight arsenic pollution as a major public issue. The combination of very few state initiatives, limited media coverage, and inattention of political and non-governmental institutions is baffling.

In this chapter I discuss the portrayal of blame in the news items of the two hazard events to interpret its influence on amplifying risk signals and risk consequences in one case and attenuating them in the other. Existing empirical evidence on blame is scant and the concept has proven to be complex. None the less, it is necessary to explore the relationship between

---

[1] This number was reported in December 1996. However, the numbers both of affected districts and of the people harmed continue to rise (Chowdhury et al. 2000).

societal practices of blame and changes in the policy agenda, procedures
for hazard management, and public policies that may correct or prevent
future occurrences of hazard events. As an initial step, I examine the
similarities and differences in the portrayal of blame in the two cases.

Background

Figure 8.1 depicts the locations of the two hazard events. The plague
occurred in Surat, which is located on the banks of the Tapti River in
Gujarat, a western state of India. Most people there speak Gujarati. As
a commercial center, Surat is well connected with other cities and towns
of India through railroads and roads. Over the past two to three decades,
an increase in the trade of diamonds and textiles, manufacturing of industrial goods and services has resulted in rapid population growth for
the city, with many immigrants. Growth of the infrastructure facilities
in the city, however, did not keep pace with the needs of the increasing
population and many illegal settlements developed. The haphazard rapid
urbanization of Surat was also accompanied by a severe deterioration
in environmental conditions. For instance, the discharges of untreated
effluents have polluted the Tapti River.

Several weeks before the plague episode the city experienced unprecedented rains and the water level in the Tapti River rose submerging settlements on the banks and killing livestock. Soon after the floodwater
receded, according to the newspaper reports, there was a shortage of
drinking water in the city and bodies of dead animals littered the streets.
Their removal by the Surat Municipal Corporation (SMC) was slow,
threatening an outbreak of epidemics. The flooding over extended the
infrastructure facilities and resources of the SMC. Just before news reports of the plague appeared, newspapers had been highlighting public
dissatisfaction with the workings of the SMC in addressing problems
arising from the flooding of the city.

The arsenic pollution, on the other hand, occurred mostly in the
rural areas of West Bengal. West Bengal, an eastern state of India,
adjoins its neighboring country of Bangladesh, and shares boundaries
with other Indian states, such as Orissa and Bihar. Most people of the state
speak Bengali. West Bengal has sustained its economic growth through
the modernization of agricultural activities, especially in the rural areas.
In the decades 1970s and 1980s a particular emphasis of agricultural
policies was to increase agricultural yields per hectare. The agricultural
development plan promoted sowing high-yielding variety seeds and using fertilizers and pesticides. A reliable supply of water was crucial to
the success of this plan. Thus the Public Health Engineering Department (PHED) of the state government was entrusted with developing a

Figure 8.1 Map of India.

network of tube wells[2] in the state. These wells were able to provide large quantities of water the farmers needed to grow paddy crops. The farmers reduced their dependence on rains to irrigate their lands. Instead of cropping for one season, which was dependent on rains, many were able to grow crops in two seasons. As a result farmers increased their profits from farming.

In parallel with these changes in agricultural policies, federal and state governments instituted a shift to the public health policy aimed at

[2] Tube wells are tubular contraptions that are dug into the depths of the earth to tap subsurface water. A pump at the ground helps to extract the water.

reducing the number of deaths from malaria. The strategies included spraying of DDT pesticide and eliminating *pukurs* (a Bengali term) as a potential source of malaria.[3] Over time, the state government encouraged people to adopt other sources of water, such as groundwater and drained the pukurs. With reluctance, people switched to tube wells as the alternate source of water. The insert in figure 8.1 highlights the arsenic-affected areas of the state, which strangely coincides with the geographic area that received much attention in implementing agricultural and public health policies described earlier.

The hazard events occurred against these backgrounds and they provide an opportunity to investigate the widely differing societal responses in the social and cultural setting of India. Below I provide an overview of the framework applied to examine the two hazard events.

Theoretical framework

How do we explain social attention and response to the plague in Surat that resulted in ripple effects? How can we explain social attenuation of the arsenic hazard despite its significant health threat?

In 1988, researchers at Clark University in Worcester, Massachusetts and Paul Slovic at Decision Research in Eugene, Oregon collaborated in an effort to understand societal processing of risk. They proposed a conceptual framework called the social amplification of risk. The premise of the framework is that events pertaining to hazards interact with psychological, social, institutional, and cultural processes in ways that can heighten or attenuate perceptions of risk and shape risk behavior (Kasperson, Renn, Slovic et al. 1988; Renn, Burns, Kasperson et al. 1992).

In the original version of the framework a risk event E is initiated, which can be characterized by certain attributes such as numbers exposed, location, and voluntariness. Information flows via the mass media, social networks, and other mechanisms that portray the event using various "signals" or interpretative messages. Individual and institutional responses, such as acceptance or defiance, produce ripple effects that begin with the immediately affected parties and spread outward along spatial and organizational lines to, for instance, local government and states-wide environmental and public interest organizations. Beyond these ripple effects, the authors of the framework envision a set of third-order impacts in

---

[3] A pukur is a small pond of water usually located in the yard of every house. Larger ponds also exist in the village for communal uses. The pukur is the source of water for daily household activities, such as bathing and washing clothes and dishes. Rainwater replenishes pukurs.

which regulatory changes, litigation, and loss of confidence in governing institutions ensue.

The authors acknowledge that several variants of amplification and attenuation can be anticipated. The crucial point, however, stands: the framework addresses the social context to explain why certain events produce social and economic consequences that are seemingly incommensurate with their direct health and environmental harms (see Kasperson et al. 1988; Kasperson 1992; and Renn et al. 1992). In other words, the framework allows us to account for information processes, institutional structures, social-group behavior, and individual reactions that affect people's responses to various events and risk experiences.

Jeanne Kasperson and her colleagues analyzed signals, or interpretative messages, to show how they direct the processes of social amplification and attenuation of risk (Kasperson, Kasperson, Perkins et al. 1992), establishing a foundation for in-depth investigation into the notion of "risk signals." The robustness of the framework has also been demonstrated by applying it to several hazard events. However, thus far the framework has been applied predominantly in the context of the United States and Europe, while the present investigation extends application of the framework to the context of India.

Blame and risk consequences

Mary Douglas (1992) and Paul Farmer (1992) have documented blaming as an important societal practice. Douglas contends that danger and blame have been present in societies for a long period of time, mainly to control and differentiate one social group or individual from another. The same idea is prevalent in the practices of contemporary organizations. Michael Baram (1997) theorizes that companies that employ incident analysis as a means to improve safety performance may find that, among other factors, the potential for employee blaming may impede organizational learning. He notes that management has incentive to blame employees who report an incident, thus shifting the responsibility and possible liability onto the employees and preserving the existing safety procedures. Blame rituals commonly address organizational risks, in both technological and non-technological events. Das (1995) and Countinho and Banerjea (2000) report practices of blame in Indian settings that were intended to reduce organizational risks. For instance, documents from the court proceedings of the technological accident in Bhopal show that the forms of blame include hiring, firing, transferring, prosecuting, and punishing (Das 1995). Research studies have also revealed motivations that underlie practices of blaming and praising in organizations.

Most researchers have found blaming victims is dominant and widespread (for example, see Singer and Endreny 1993).

Little is known, however, about the social, political, and policy consequences of blame conventions. Interaction of numerous factors in a supportive social and political environment may govern the societal impacts of attributing blame. The mass media are one of the factors that may be crucial in shaping the ultimate consequences of blame because of its agenda setting function, which has already been theorized in the literature (McCombs 1981). Hazard researchers have examined the media's agenda setting role because they believe media attention to hazard events and public concern about those events may be connected. The reason for this belief among researchers is rooted in their understanding that peoples rely principally on mass media as a channel of information. Researchers have also shown that the mass media report on only a small number of hazard events because of their constraints of time, space, money, and the perceptions by editors of readers' interests. In other words, only a select number of hazard events are highlighted in the mass media. People, on the other hand, do not have direct experience with most hazard events. For example, not many people have experienced a volcano at first hand, but many experience it indirectly by receiving information through the media. While several channels of information may shape risk perception of a volcano, the mass media play a significant role through their accessibility, immediacy, and penetration at various scales of geography in people's experiences to hazard events. In other words, the mass media are performing an agenda-setting function by reporting on certain hazard events. Several clarifications on agenda-setting function have also been reported in the literature over the past two decades.

In the following sections, I report on the nature of blame signals in the editorials, news items, headlines, and photographs that pertain to the hazard events. In the plague example I hypothesize that an interaction with the event caused heightened public concern and resulted in the amplification of economic, political, and social consequences. By contrast, public concern and response were attenuated in the arsenic hazard, despite its effects on a large number of people due to arsenic toxicity and widespread contamination and while the risk consequences continued to mount, the management response remains weak and ineffective.

Methodology

I chose local language newspapers to identify media reports on the two hazard events. *Gujarat Mitra*, a Gujarati language newspaper, was used for news items on the plague hazard and *Anandabazar Patrika*, a

Bengali language newspaper, for news items on the arsenic hazard (the full set of sources used for illustrative quotations throughout this chapter are referenced in the Addendum). Two separate investigators familiar with the local languages identified all news items on the hazard events, using a format and procedures produced by the author. The items included news reports, editorials, authored articles, news agency reports, and letters to the editor. Since the plague event was episodic, we scanned the newspaper for a total of six months, from July to December 1994. The time frame included the months of July and August, prior to the episode, to ensure that no relevant news items were missed and December, despite negligible reporting in November, to assure complete coverage of the hazard. Adopting a similar strategy, we scanned the newspaper for news items on the arsenic hazard for a period of eighteen years, starting in January 1979 through December 1996. The first news item, however, was identified in 1983. Arsenic pollution coverage continues to the present. I chose the cut-off date of December 1996 to coincide with my field visits to the study area. The newspaper searches yielded a similar number of news items for the two events – 119 items for the plague and 113 items for the arsenic pollution. The news items were translated into English, forming the raw data for further investigations.

I then read the articles to identify the signals of blame. In their simplest form, risk signals are messages about hazard events that affect people's perception of the seriousness and/or manageability of the risk. Risk signals, or simply signals, convey messages that are inferred, interpreted, and generalized and that, more importantly, go beyond the concrete and factual information to display a certain degree of abstraction. In the taxonomy of signals developed by Kasperson, Kasperson, Perkins et al. (1992) blame was identified to be a significant class and included both villains and victims of blame. They also report that it is important to identify not only whether a victim and villain is present but also who or what that villain and/or victim is *or* is claimed, purported, or perceived to be by the mass media. In the present study, signals of blame were discerned in a similar number of news items for each hazard: forty such news items for the plague hazard and thirty-six news items for the arsenic hazard (see table 8.1). This finding is striking because of the similarity in not only the total numbers of news items with blame signals, but also in the total number of news items about the hazard events.

Interpreting blame signals

To interpret signals of blame four broad categories are developed. These categories are: *number of signals*; *flow of signals*; *blaming the victim*; and *multiple dimensions of blame*. After analyzing the number and flow of

Table 8.1 *Similarities and differences in the identified signals*

source of signals	number of signals in the hazard event	
	plague	*arsenic*
editorials	5	
letters to the editor	2	
special or authored articles	6	12
news items with no author	23	24
news agencies	4	
total number of news items in which blame signals were identified	40	36

signals, I discuss the nature of victim blaming in the two cases. The signals are then organized along multiple dimensions of blame, namely: *foci in signals*; *familiarity with the blamed*; *spatial proximity of the blamed to people*; and *comprehensiveness in assigning blame*. Each of the dimensions is discussed below in detail, and is followed by conclusions on how blaming in the two cases might have contributed to the social amplification and attenuation of risk.

Number of signals

First, I counted the signals in the two events. A variance in the number of signals could provide some gross indication of the prominence accorded to the two hazards. There were 123 signals in the plague hazard as compared with 56 in the arsenic hazard.

Besides the number of signals, the origins of the signals in the newspapers also provide clues to the likelihood of reaching the readers. Wide ranges of types of news items form the sources of signals; risk signals were sprinkled throughout the newspaper in the plague hazard. However, in the arsenic hazard case all the signals were restricted to either the authored articles or news items. Table 8.1 shows the type of news items from which the signals were identified in the two cases. The larger number of signals, and their location in more varied types of news items, may well have enhanced the likelihood that signals in the plague hazard would reach readers as opposed to the case of arsenic hazard.

Flow of signals

Continuous or intermittent flow of signals can facilitate or hamper the public scrutiny of risk. Figures 8.2 and 8.3 depict the life cycle of blame signals in the two hazard events. Two points are apparent. First, blame

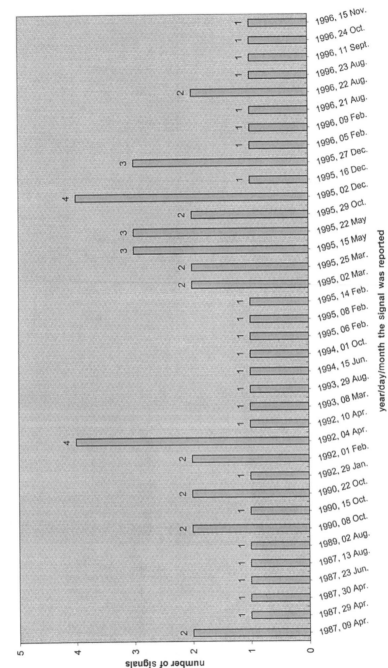

Figure 8.2 Flow of blame signals in arsenic hazard.

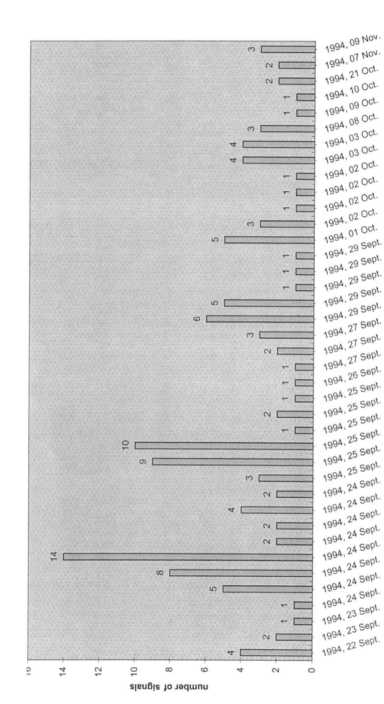

Figure 8.3 Flow of blame signals in plague hazard.

signals occur unevenly in the arsenic hazard case, but they are found continuously throughout the reporting of the plague hazard. In the arsenic hazard there were no signals until 1987, four years after the initial reporting on the event. Furthermore, over the entire period of the media coverage there were a few years in which there were no risk signals, for instance, in 1988 and 1991. On the other hand, signals were present for the entire reporting period of the plague hazard. Second, the maximum number of blame signals identified on any particular day of reporting is four in the arsenic hazard case, which is far less than the fourteen signals identified in the plague case.

Risk signals ebb and flow with both hazard events. With the plague, signals accelerate in a short time, soon after the initial reporting, but they also disappear rapidly. The episodic nature of the plague hazard may have generated this pattern in the flow of signals. However, signals flow in a similar pattern in the arsenic hazard, which is a chronic event. Thus, the nature of the hazard (acute or chronic) does not explain the flow of signals observed in the two cases. There is a remarkable coincidence between the spikes in the flow of the signals and timing of the major events associated with the arsenic hazard. A major contextual event (say, announcement of a commission of inquiry) associated with the arsenic hazard coincided with a spike in the flow of signals. However, a distinct and close link between critical decisions associated with the plague hazard and the flow of blame signals is not apparent because numerous decisions were undertaken in a short time period and the signals were present densely throughout the reporting. Thus, the readers of the plague hazard encounter the signals often in a short span of time. This pattern of reporting carries the potential for strong signaling for the readers of the plague. However, in the arsenic hazard there was a similar pattern in the flow of signals, although with a much lower intensity and hence suggests a weak signal for the readers.

This similar pattern in the flow of signals in the two events suggests the need for a close examination of the link among the nature of the hazard, the number of news items, and the signals. Further, the links between risk perception and the duration for which the readers encounter the risk signals also require further investigation.

Blaming the victim

In the plague reports, very few signals blamed the victims. No statements blamed the victims in the news items on the arsenic hazard, despite scanning the media coverage for eighteen years. This finding is intriguing because numerous studies report evidence of victim blaming.[4] Three interlinked reasons – namely, scientific uncertainty, complexity in the management structure of the hazard, and ambiguity in the identification of vested interests – may explain why minimal victim blaming occurred in the media reports of the two cases.

In both hazard events one or more hazard management organizations addressed the risks associated with the hazard. The structure of these organizations suggests that the hazard management organizations are geographically widespread, with hierarchically layered responsibilities. In the plague hazard, public health personnel in the health ministry of the state government and at the SMC were responsible for addressing adverse consequences of the hazard. A close scrutiny of the organizational behavior in the arsenic hazard reveals that none of the organizations explicitly addressed the presence of the arsenic in the groundwater as a risk event. In other words, the hazard management structure is dispersed in both cases and ambiguous in the arsenic case.

In general, the state government is responsible for initiating measures to mitigate the consequences of the hazards. The state government has a constitutional mandate to provide safe water and to protect public health. In other words, both health and water issues belong to the state government, as opposed to foreign policy, which is under the jurisdiction of the federal government. Given this context, state government has the primary responsibility of initiating steps to mitigate the potentially harmful consequences of the hazard events.

It is difficult to identify organizations that exclusively addressed the arsenic hazard because a controversy surrounds the characterizing of the risk. The community of medical doctors and health professionals perceived the risk to be a health problem, and, accordingly, the health ministry and an array of organizations that provide health services – from the state level to local villages – can be viewed as the appropriate hazard management organizations. On the other hand, arsenic-contaminated water pumped from the ground was the source of the risk. Hence, many decision makers perceived the water problem to be a risk so that PHED was the appropriate hazard management organization. The services provided by PHED are not under the purview of the health ministry. Is it a water problem or a health problem? This issue remains unresolved to date. Thus, it is difficult to identify clear management responsibility in the arsenic hazard.

---

[4] Some hazard researchers hypothesize that the mass media will blame victims of the hazard and not the sources of the risk. This is because newspapers in India depend on corporations and governments as a major source of revenue (Jeffrey 1997).

A review of public documents and newspaper reports reveals that the cause of the arsenic hazard is unknown, both to the scientific community and the public. Over the years (1979–96), there have been numerous explanations as to the source of arsenic in the water; however, the evidence has been poorly substantiated and the problem remains unresolved. Furthermore, due to technical, commercial, environmental, and financial reasons, attempts to remove the arsenic from the water have failed. Consequently, an answer to the arsenic problem continues to be elusive. Again, this is in sharp contrast to the plague hazard where the cause is well documented. There was a widespread public perception that the doctors and the medical professionals could cure the plague. In other words, there was significant perceived scientific uncertainty about the arsenic hazard, but minimal such uncertainty about the plague hazard.

In sum, the state government had a pivotal role in managing the arsenic hazard. But the state government had no knowledge of the cause(s) or solution(s) to the hazard. Under these circumstances if the state government had shifted the blame onto the victims, then public debates may eventually have unmasked the complicity of the hazard managers. For these reasons there may have been no victim-blaming statements in the entire media coverage of the arsenic hazard.

In the plague hazard, the locus of victim blaming was on plague patients and migrants to Surat who were portrayed as potential carriers of plague bacilli. For example:

The city is in the grip of plague. The patients are under treatment at the New Civil hospital and a considerable number of patients have fled at their own risk, neglecting medical advice. (*Gujarat Mitra* 29 September 1994a)

The plague epidemic is felt after heavy rains, floods, and/or earthquake. Maharashtra, a neighboring state, is under the plague impact. The city of Surat has just come out of the floods. Moreover, migrants of affected Maharashtra have come here in large number and in the prevailing circumstances nine persons succumbed to fever and bloody cough in a single day. The municipal authorities, including the commissioner and the health officer, suspect plague epidemic. (*Gujarat Mitra* 22 September 1994)

Patients who fled from Surat have created an atmosphere of horror in the entire Gujarat. (*Gujarat Mitra* News Service 2 October 1994)

Unlike previous studies, victim blame statements were minimal in the news items of the plague hazard and were non-existent in the news items of the arsenic hazard. Thus, a question arises: who was blamed in the news items?

Multiple dimensions of blame

Taking a small sample of the signals, I developed four dimensions of blame, each of which captures a distinguishing feature of blame. These dimensions are: *foci in blame* statements; *spatial proximity* of the blamed to the public; *familiarity* with the blamed; and *comprehensiveness* in the assignment of blame. Table 8.2 briefly describes each of these blame dimensions. These four dimensions help to assess the role of the signals. Table 8.3 summarizes an initial assessment of the signals.

Foci in signals   I proceeded to decipher the foci of assignment of blame by examining every signal. Who was assigned blame in the risk signals? Was there a pattern to the assignment of blame? The inquiry led to the development of two broad categories. In the first category I gathered signals with a very broad locus of blame. In the second category I placed signals with explicit locus of blame on individuals and organizations. This categorization reveals an absence of specific blame on individuals and organizations in the news items on the arsenic hazard. Hence, rudiments of a pattern in the assignment of blame emerged. A further examination led to distinct patterns in assignment of blame and the message conveyed.

Collective blaming in the news items   In both events several signals assigned blame to the "authorities" and the "state government." The risk signals illustrated collective blaming. In the news items, hazard managers were characterized as the authorities. However, many different individuals and agencies were engaged in the direct management of the events, for example, employees of the local, state, or federal government. Blaming "authorities" thus indicated a collective blame, and not a specific blame on particular managers.[5] Similarly, placing blame on the state government assigned blame collectively to many public sector employees and organizations. Below are examples of blaming authorities and the state government.

Authorities ignore the diagnosis of expert doctors, hide information from the Chief Minister, and justify their decision of not disclosing the facts to the public because they do not want unwarranted danger, excitement, or concern to spread among the people. (*Gujarat Mitra* 24 September 1994a)

Authorities are criminally negligent. (Editor *Gujarat Mitra* 24 September 1994b)

People are horrified by the plague that hit Surat and have lost faith, despite government announcements. (*Gujarat Mitra* 25 September 1994a)

---

[5] Senior doctors serving as medical professionals as well as administrators are excluded from the category of authorities.

Table 8.2 *Multiple dimensions of blame*

S. no.	*dimensions of blame*	*explanation of meaning in the dimension*
1	Foci in signal statements	In this dimension, locus of the blame is examined. The foci of blame are placed explicitly or specifically in some signals, while in others blame is diffuse. A closer exploration of signals when blame is placed ambiguously may reveal a richer interpretation. A direct assignment of blame, on the other hand, may sharply derive an association and meaning in the statement to enhance the strength of the signal for the readers.
2	Familiarity with whomever is blamed	Among the individuals and organizations assigned blame, the signal potential enhances for the public if the blamed is familiar. For the readers, familiarity with the blamed comes about by way of frequent interactions, which may enhance signal strength. On the other hand, if the blamed individuals and organizations interact infrequently with the readers and do not form part of their daily lives, then, signal strength is weakened for the readers. For example, people are familiar with the workings of the Surat Municipal Corporation as part of their daily lives, hence a blame signal is hypothesized to be significantly enhanced for the readers. If, on the other hand, the foci of the blamed are sharp but remote from public daily lives, as in the example of the World Health Organization, then the signal potential may be considered weak. Familiarity with the blamed allows for bringing in past experiences and assists the readers to interpret the signals in a broader social context.
3	Spatial proximity of the blamed to the public	Proximity to the organizations and individuals that are assigned blame shapes signal strength for the citizenry. For example, a local organization by way of its closer spatial proximity may invite greater public attention. On the contrary, distant organizations, for instance, rarely invite public consideration and scrutiny, thereby diminishing the strength of the blame-signal.
4	Comprehensiveness in assigning blame	A comprehensive assignment of blame includes an array of hazard management activities, starting from hazard identification to post-hazard management. When a wide range of decisions and decision making processes of managing the hazard are blamed, then the assigned blame is comprehensive and the signal potential can be judged to enhance for the readers.

Table 8.3 *Qualitative assessment of the hazard events*

		hazard event	
S. no.		*plague*	*arsenic*
1	number of signals	high	low
2	flow of signals	continuous	intermittent
3	blaming the victim	very few signals	none
4	foci in signals	individals by name and by designation; local hazard management organizations, and several signals with ambiguously identified locus	no individuals are blamed, only one organization is blamed, and several signals with ambiguously identified locus
5	familiarity with the blamed	high	low
6	spatial proximity of the blamed to the public	close and high	distant and poor
7	comprehensiveness in assigning the blame	high with an array of decisions and decision-making processes highlighted	low with very few decisions and decision-making processes discussed

Both the federal and the state governments spread propaganda that the plague epidemic is now coming under control. (*Gujarat Mitra* 29 September 1994a)

There is hardly any need to say that the plague epidemic of Surat is not a heavenly but a stately calamity. (S. Joshi *Gujarat Mitra* 3 October 1994)

A similar blame was assigned in the arsenic news items:

Despite recommendations from arsenic specialists to prevent people from drinking contaminated water, the recommendations are still on paper. (S. Basu *Anandabazar Patrika* 15 May 1995)

Authorities neither seal the contaminated tube-wells nor provide safe water. (*Anandabazar Patrika* 8 October 1990)

The news reports of the arsenic hazard consistently assigned most blame to the state government. The mass media first directly blamed the state government in 1987, noting, "due to negligence on the part of the state government and lack of required medicines, people are staring at an uncertain future" (D. G. Thakur *Anandabazar Patrika* 9 April 1987). News reports of the 1980s contained very few blame statements; a few risk signals in the early 1990s blamed the state government. The signals implicated the state government for being negligent in addressing concerns of the citizenry. By 1995, the emphasis in blame shifted to high-light the fact that governmental statistics misinformed the public and to indicate that there was an apathetic response in addressing public concerns about the arsenic hazard:

Seven districts of the state are already affected by the fear of arsenic pollution. Except at Kaliachak in Maldah district, the government has not taken any initiative to change the source of water at any other places. (*Anandabazar Patrika* 6 February 1995)

The number of arsenic deaths and persons affected increases as we go down from district to block to village-panchayat to the village level itself, according to government accounts. Clearly, this fact shows the extent of negligence and wrong statistics. (*Anandabazar Patrika* 22 May 1995)

Pradip Basu Dhar, Executive Engineer of Public Health Engineering Department of the North 24-Parganas district, has noted that government has declared these areas as arsenic-sensitive in the year 1984. He also agreed to the fact that people of these areas are drinking polluted water due to lack of publicity about the issue by the government. (S. Basu *Anandabazar Patrika* 22 August 1996)

Thus, although the blame was placed on the state government in both cases, the reasons varied. In the plague case, news items blamed the state government for making unrealistic claims, spreading propaganda, and acting as a source of the calamity. In contrast, in the arsenic case blame was placed on the state government because it was viewed as negligent in upgrading water and health infrastructures and failed to inform people about the causes and remedies of the problem. The state government, in turn, blamed inadequate finances for any shortcomings in the management of the arsenic hazard. The government's role as a guardian of public interest was thereby undermined. Similarly, news items of both hazard events blamed the authorities for neglecting hazard prevention measures.

Blaming the state government and authorities illustrates collective blaming. Such signals do not, pointedly, reflect the *specific* locus of blame but do help us to portray the *reasons* for blame.

"Sharp" blaming in the news items   Nine individuals or hazard managers were assigned blame for their role in the management of the plague hazard, but no individuals were assigned blame in the reports of the arsenic hazard.

Of the nine individuals that were assigned blame in the plague case, three were employed at the SMC, two officers were in charge of the city administration, and the rest were political ministers. These individuals held leadership positions and had the power to mobilize resources that could have reduced the potential consequences of the hazard. There was extensive reporting of the decisions made by the government officers and the political ministers. This finding suggests that individuals within an institution can be held accountable.

News items also sharply placed blame on local hazard management organizations. Plague news items most frequently blamed the SMC, particularly the health and filarial departments.

Despite warnings from the city doctors, the Municipal Corporation handed over the city to the epidemic. (*Gujarat Mitra* 25 September 1994b)

The central and state governments, along with the Municipal Corporation administration, are spreading a propaganda that the plague epidemic is now coming under control. (Editor *Gujarat Mitra* 29 September 1994b)

The mass media also came under scrutiny for their reporting of the plague hazard. Initially, the government-owned mass media were blamed because "in broadcasting details of the plague epidemic, blunders had been committed" (*Gujarat Mitra* 24 September 1994c). One week after initial reports of the plague, an editorial claimed that All India Radio (AIR) and Doordarshan (the government-owned television network) had broadcast fabrications, and that newspapers had similarly exaggerated the event.

They published inflammatory reports, pictures, and death photos. (Editor *Gujarat Mitra* 29 September 1994b)

Government mass media failed to provide adequate and credible information. (V. S. Patel *Gujarat Mitra* 3 October 1994)

Most newspapers have forgotten the ethics of sticking to the truth. (*Gujarat Mitra* 21 October 1994)

A small percentage of the signals assigned blame to private medical dispensaries, medical laboratories, Ashakta Ashram hospital, and the local district collectorate. In comparison, throughout the media coverage of the arsenic hazard, there were no statements blaming individuals, which is surprising because we scanned eighteen years of reports on the arsenic hazard. In those news items, PHED was the only organization explicitly assigned blame. This agency uses geological and engineering science to develop the tube wells. Before commissioning the tube wells, PHED conducts chemical testing of the water; after installation, PHED provides regular maintenance. A news item in 1987 noted that PHED did nothing to mitigate the harmful consequences of the hazard, despite public complaints. No blame appeared for five years thereafter. Blaming of PHED occurred occasionally and at intervals of several years. The signals indicate that blame was directly placed on the PHED.

There is a tussle between the Health Department and the Public Health and Engineering Department. A responsible officer of the Public Health and Engineering Department noted that high levels of arsenic would be found if the investigation is conducted. (D. G. Thakur and A. P. Chakraborty *Anandabazar Patrika* 4 April 1992)

In sum, the focus of blame in the plague hazard was placed sharply on individuals within the hazard management organizations that were identified by their name or title. In comparison, no individuals were assigned blame either by name or designation in the news items of the arsenic hazard. Likewise, three differences were observed in assigning blame to hazard management organizations. First, in the plague case, blame was on familiar and local hazard management organizations, such as the SMC. In the arsenic case PHED was blamed and, unlike the SMC, it was an unfamiliar organization to people. Second, throughout the reporting of the plague case, blame was assigned to the hazard management organizations. In contrast, in the arsenic case the blame on PHED was intermittent. Lastly, numerous hazard management organizations were blamed in the plague case, however, only PHED was blamed in the news items on the arsenic hazard.

Discussion: the signal potential of collective versus focused blaming
In the plague case, sharp placement of blame on *local* hazard managers and organizations enhanced the likelihood of alerting the readers to the foci of blame. Such signals may be strong for the readers. In addition, people in Surat had had frequent direct and indirect interactions with local hazard managers and management organizations. Hence, in the plague case, sharply focused blame strengthened the signal for people who had prior experiences with the hazard managers and hazard management organizations.

By contrast, the strength of the signals blaming the PHED in the arsenic case may not be as strong because people do not routinely interact with the PHED and, unlike SMC, PHED is not a local organization. Also because most people have minimal or negligible interactions with the PHED, prior experiences are not numerous enough to influence people's perception of the workings of the PHED.

The institutional context for managing the hazards was also different, and may therefore have also strengthened the signals for readers of the plague hazard. Decision makers all along perceived the plague as a health hazard and thus the onus of mitigating the risks was with distinct departments, offices, and ministries of the state government. However, when the plague hazard occurred, an administrator who was an officer appointed by the state government headed the SMC. This had occurred because the

term of the members elected to the SMC had expired and new elections
of representatives had not yet been held. Soon after the first reports of the
plague appeared, the state government appointed a senior bureaucrat as
officer in-charge to direct and coordinate the plague hazard management
operations. The powers of all the hazard management organizations were
either suspended or consolidated, as this officer directly supervised all of
their operations. In fact, the management structure for the plague hazard was far simpler than the initial review of the organizational structure
suggested.

Only a few officers appointed by the state government directed the
daily handling of the plague case. The newspaper extensively reported
on the organizational change invoked to manage the plague hazard. *Collective* blame (on "authorities" or "state government") may have been
relatively salient for the readers of the plague hazard precisely because
specific blame was also present in the news items, directed at people at
the helm of organizations in the revised hazard management structure.
In brief, the institutional context to manage the plague hazard, that is
the perception of plague as being a health hazard and the relatively less
complex management structure to manage the hazard helped to convey
a stronger signal to the readers and the public.

Unlike in the plague case, the arsenic hazard was contentious among
the decision makers of the state government. Since the arsenic hazard
was not explicitly categorized by decision makers in terms of the kind of
problem it was, there were potentially many hazard management organizations, at various geographic scales, that could address the issue. Hence,
the organizations that would address arsenic as a "health hazard" were
different from those that would do so if the issue were to be characterized
as a "water problem." Ultimately, there was confusion amongst decision
makers in characterizing the arsenic hazard, and numerous organizations
involved in managing aspects of the arsenic hazard. The fact that decisions in the hazard management organizations were spatially widespread
and layered as a hierarchy compounded the difficulty in identifying the
focus of signals with collective blame. And, even with a complete reading of a news article the institutional context for managing the hazard
remained unclear for many readers. Hence, collective blaming conveyed
a weakly focused signal to the media readers in the arsenic case.

In sum, the analysis shows that both collective and focused blame
signals are employed in newspaper reports of a hazard.

Familiarity with the blamed   This second dimension (see table
8.2), familiarity with the blamed, signifies the strength of the risk signal.
One can argue that if an individual, for example, is blamed sharply but is

unfamiliar to the readers, then the signal is weak. Blame laid on doctors, officials, and experts illustrates the potential significance of this dimension. Hence, in the plague case, medical doctors, practitioners at the private medical laboratories, and the paramedical staff at the city hospitals were all blamed. Senior medical doctors at the public hospitals played dual roles; they performed the duties of both a medical professional and an administrative decision maker.

"Compel the fleeing doctors to return" (*Gujarat Mitra* 24 September 1994d) stated one headline, "Ved-Katargam Empty: What will people do living here when the doctors have fled?" (Editor *Gujarat Mitra* 24 September 1994e) declared another. The initial news items blamed the doctors, and the readers encountered dramatic news reports:

General practitioners, MD physicians, surgeons, all have closed their clinics, locked their houses, and left Surat. (Editor *Gujarat Mitra* 24 September 1994e)

People ridicule the fugitive doctors whom they considered as the lamps of faith and respect. They have fled when they were required most. (*Gujarat Mitra* 24 September 1994f)

The diseases flee at the sight of doctors; here the doctors have fled at the sight of diseases. (*Gujarat Mitra* 24 September 1994f)

The phrase immediately above was highlighted as a bullet within the text of the news item, enhancing the possibility of public attention. Soon after, blame shifted onto the Indian Medical Association (IMA) for its weak initiatives to ensure the return of doctors.

The medical association must summon the deserting and cowardly doctors. The association must blacklist the doctors, like the soldiers who defy the order to return. The people will surely blacklist and boycott such doctors. (*Gujarat Mitra* 25 September 1994c)

In contrast, in the arsenic hazard the entire community of doctors was assigned blame.

In a letter, the president of the Indian Medical Association (IMA), Ashoknagar branch wrote that doctors at the School of Tropical Medicine were investigating arsenic pollution in this area. Unfortunately, they left the place without completing the work. (*Anandabazar Patrika* 1 February 1992)

Most people are unfamiliar with the doctors at the School of Tropical Medicine, a specialized hospital with an emphasis on research and teaching. Daily interactions with the doctors at this hospital are minimal for the people of the state because the school is located in Calcutta and it is expensive to consult them often. Accordingly, the doctors blamed in the news items on the arsenic hazard did not form part of people's daily lives, unlike the doctors who were assigned blame in the plague hazard. In the plague hazard, it is apparent from the signals and a complete reading of the news items that the Surat doctors and medical personnel were assigned blame. Most doctors not only pursued their medical practice there but also lived within the city. The people knew the doctors and strong ties existed between the doctors and the local community. In the plague case the newspaper portrayed the blame on doctors in a dramatic headline and highlighted the blame within the text of the news item, which surely would have grabbed the attention of newspaper readers.

Thus, it can be argued that while blame was placed on doctors in both of the events, blame in the plague hazard may have had much more effect than in the arsenic case.

Spatial proximity of the blamed to the public   Table 8.2 briefly describes the dimension of spatial proximity of the blamed with the public. To illustrate this dimension of blame, I analyzed statements that assigned blame to politicians and political parties. They all, either directly or indirectly, supervised workings of the hazard management organizations and many had resources that could shape the outcome of events.

The politicians blamed in the plague hazard included elected representatives to the Gujarat State legislature, ministers in the state government, health ministers of the state government, and politicians in general. Below I list several signals from the plague hazard that assigned blame to the politicians.

Ministers in the state government are the real culprits who thrust appointment of part time administrators to the city administration. (Editor *Gujarat Mitra* 24 September 1994b)

In general, ministers just watch the situation and, instead of accepting the reality, they seek technical escape. (Editor *Gujarat Mitra* 24 September 1994b)

The public life of Surat has been damaged within the past five to seven years and some representatives have contributed the most. Every political party seems to be in a race to damage the public life of Surat. (*Gujarat Mitra* 24 September 1994c)

Surat has two publicly elected representatives in the Gujarat State legislature. One is the health minister and the other is a minister in the state government. The blame on the elected representatives and ministers of the state government was strong in the newspaper. People's representatives were assigned blame because they "shirked their responsibilities to remove public fears" (*Gujarat Mitra* 25 September 1994c). Other commentators suggested:

Plague is a gift from politicians. (J. B. Lekhadia *Gujarat Mitra* 1 October 1994)

Talks and visits by politicians are hypocritical because the bulk of the anti-plague medicines were procured only after the plague had spread its empire in all respects. (J. B. Lekhadia *Gujarat Mitra* 1 October 1994)

Local politicians are aptly thought of as plague mice. (S. Joshi *Gujarat Mitra* 3 October 1994)

In contrast, in the arsenic case only the Chief Minister and the Governor of West Bengal were blamed. A letter written to the editor of the newspaper alleged that they both failed to respond to requests from an individual seeking financial assistance.

In both hazard events, politicians were viewed skeptically. The premise in this dimension of blame is that, as the spatial proximity of the blamed to the location of the hazard increases, the strength of the signal diminishes for the readers. Three reasons help me to hypothesize this outcome. First, there is a widespread and popular belief among the people that distant decision makers are far removed from the local realities and hence they inadequately address public concerns in their decisions. Second, the number of layers or filters of decisions increases as the spatial distance increases, which results in many tradeoffs, compromises, and complexity in arriving at decisions. Lastly, direct accountability to the people affected by these decisions declines as the spatial distance increases.

Surprisingly, in both hazard events the blamed were located in the capital city of the state but with some distinctions that shaped the stronger signal strength in the plague hazard than in the arsenic hazard. In the plague hazard although the newspaper assigned blame to individuals in the capital city, the interpretation was that many local risk managers were blamed. This is because readers closely associated the blame with the health minister or cooperative minister in the state government, who were Surat representatives and were therefore accountable to them in the next cycle of elections. In contrast, in the arsenic hazard blame was placed on only two politicians and only one of them was an elected representative. The offices for both the Chief Minister and the Governor were located in Calcutta, which limited direct contacts with the people of the state. The Chief Minister was also not a direct, elected representative of people in the arsenic-contaminated area. Hence, it may be concluded that the signal strength was stronger in the plague hazard because local politicians were blamed, as opposed to distant ones in the arsenic hazard.

Comprehensiveness in assigning blame   I chose blame assigned to the "administration" in the news items to investigate how comprehensiveness in the assignment of blame contributes to the strengthening of signals. Table 8.2 provides a brief description of this dimension. In the news items on the plague hazard signals of blaming the administration included:

People of the Ved-Katargam areas are entrusted into the hands of God and have no faith in any government administration. (*Gujarat Mitra* 24 September 1994f)

People have lost all faith in the administration and they are verbally attacking representatives of the administration, whether he may be an ordinary employee of the collector's office, or that of the municipal corporation, or the administrator himself. (*Gujarat Mitra* 24 September 1994f)

Unpardonable negligence and passiveness of the administration summoned the plague. (P. G Mavlankar *Gujarat Mitra* 29 September 1994)

The administration is often caught unawares and successive administrations thrust upon Surti people are mostly responsible for this blot. (Editor *Gujarat Mitra* 29 September 1994b)

In contrast, in the arsenic hazard only a couple of risk signals assigned blame to the administration.

The district secretary of the Congress party, Sabitri Mitra has blamed the district administration for being reluctant and negligent. (*Anandabazar Patrika* 16 October 1990)

The people of Har ka tola are financially stable and they only want the administration to give attention to their village. At least once, the administrative team should come and visit. (D. G. Thakur and S. Chakraborty *Anandabazar Patrika* 4 April 1992)

The administration was blamed both for the process by which decisions were made and for the decisions themselves. In news items on the plague hazard, there was a wider ranging discussion of bureaucracy in local management organizations. Administration was portrayed as indifferent and negligent. Further, official responses were presented as delayed, with no coordination among government officials, suggesting that they had a passive attitude to managing the hazard. In the arsenic news items, however, the district and the state government administration were blamed for not providing sustained commitment to reduce the impacts of the hazard.

The decisions were expansively discussed in the news items on the plague hazard and hence provided the readers with an in-depth understanding of issues in risk management. Besides a comprehensive discussion on risk management decisions, the emphasis of the signals was on decisions taken in the local hazard management organizations. In addition, a complete reading of the article and the presence of statements with sharp blame strengthened the signals for the readers of the plague hazard.

In contrast, in the arsenic hazard, there was blaming of the decisions of the district and state administrations. Accordingly, one can argue both that the strength of risk signals was relatively stronger in the plague hazard than in the arsenic hazard, and that public perception of the manageability of the risk was higher in the former case.

Conclusions

Mass media reports on hazard events can be conceptualized as early signals to draw attention to issues of governance surrounding a hazard. Applying a risk signals approach and extending the social amplification and attenuation of risk framework has allowed the advance of a number of propositions on the nature of blame that merit further investigation.

There was no victim blaming in the arsenic case, and the amount of victim blaming in the plague case was negligible. This finding is intriguing because the media literature often suggests victim blaming will characterize newspaper reporting. I identified three linked reasons that may have contributed to a lack of blaming of the victims of the arsenic hazard. They are scientific uncertainty, complexity of the hazard management structure, and ambiguity in identifying explicit vested interests. But negligible victim blaming in the reporting of the plague case continues to be baffling. In other words, the evidence from the two hazard events suggests the need for an in-depth examination of the relationship between mass media reporting and victim blaming.

Risk signals have multiple dimensions that help to organize different forms of blame and to influence signal strength. The strength of signals in both the cases was assessed along four dimensions and yielded interesting hypotheses. The two cases suggest that signal strength is enhanced when there is *focused* blame and diminishes with *collective* blaming. Collective blaming diffuses the locus of blame and thereby reduces its influence on the strength of the risk signal. The second dimension identified suggests that strength of risk signal increases when the blamed are familiar to the people. Thirdly, signal strength may decline with increase in spatial proximity of the blamed to people. In other words, local politicians and decision makers draw considerable attention when blamed, as opposed to those located far away from the epicenter of the hazard event. Lastly, the fourth dimension suggests that when blame is laid comprehensively on local bureaucratic decisions then the signal strength is enhanced. The robustness of these results, however, needs to be tested further, because only indirect evidence of public reactions to the hazard events was gathered in this study. Other cases will have to be investigated in order to delve into the notion of "multi-dimensionality of blame."

More broadly, the methodology of risk signals allows enriching of the current focus on two primary factors – media coverage and content analyses. Conventionally, in the hazard literature either *amount* of media coverage or the *content* of news items is examined. In the "signals" approach, media coverage is also in itself a risk signal. The current methodology shows how analyses of media reporting can include both quantity of coverage as well as the content of news items.

NEWSPAPER SOURCES REFERENCED

Anonymous. 8 October 1990. "Arsenic in wells: severe scarcity of water in the villages of Maldah" *Anandabazar Patrika.*

Anonymous. 16 October 1990. "Death toll in Maldah rises to 25" *Anandabazar Patrika.*

Anonymous. 1 February 1992. "When water is the cause of death – Part I" *Anandabazar Patrika.*

Anonymous. 22 September 1994. "Surat in the grip of deadly epidemic: 35 dead" *Gujarat Mitra.*

Anonymous. 24 September 1994a. "Unfortunates succumb to death in absence of exact diagnosis of the plague in this complicated epidemic" *Gujarat Mitra.*

Anonymous. 24 September 1994c. Tetracycline arrives in the city but chaos in distribution" *Gujarat Mitra.*

Anonymous. 24 September 1994d. "Compel the fleeing doctors to return" *Gujarat Mitra.*

Anonymous. 24 September 1994f. "Rander-Adjan road haunted: more police reinforcement sought" *Gujarat Mitra.*

Anonymous. 25 September 1994a. "The first camp of the exodees on one hand and the hell of dirt on the other hand" *Gujarat Mitra.*

Anonymous. 25 September 1994b. "At last, Surat declared plague hit" *Gujarat Mitra.*

Anonymous. 25 September 1994c. "The plague crisis: the final and the biggest warning to Surat" *Gujarat Mitra.*

Anonymous. 29 September 1994a. "The fugitive plague patients can be imprisoned and fined Rs.1000" *Gujarat Mitra.*

Anonymous. 21 October 1994. "The newspaper that made no exaggeration in the critical situation of exactly one-month old plague affected Surat" *Gujarat Mitra.*

Anonymous. 6 February 1995. "Arsenic: the commission appeals to the centre to arrange finance" *Anandabazar Patrika.*

Anonymous. 22 May 1995. "All the water is poison water" *Anandabazar Patrika.*

Basu, S. 15 May 1995. "Municipal elections 1995: arsenic in water is the main problem" *Anandabazar Patrika.*

Basu, S. 22 August 1996. "To explain the danger of arsenic seven affected youth on the road" *Anandabazar Patrika.*

Editor. 24 September 1994b. "Few words of advice to the authorities and officials" *Gujarat Mitra.*

Editor. 24 September 1994e. "Ved-Katargam empty: what will people do living here when doctors have fled?" *Gujarat Mitra.*

Editor. 29 September 1994b. "Surat cannot afford to remain unaware about the plague" *Gujarat Mitra.*

Gujarat Mitra News Service. 2 October 1994. "Dismiss Kundanlal: demand by Ashok Bhatt-BJP" *Gujarat Mitra.*

Joshi, S. 3 October 1994. "Who is responsible for the plague of Surat?" *Gujarat Mitra.*

Lekhadia, J. B. 1 October 1994. "Plague and Surat: the industrial city" *Gujarat Mitra.*

Mavlankar, P. G. 29 September 1994. "Unpardonable negligence and passiveness of the administration summoned the plague" *Gujarat Mitra.*

Patel, V. B. 3 October 1994. "Wrath of the plague, people, and social responsibility" *Gujarat Mitra.*

Thakur, D. G. 9 April 1987. "Cancer affects 200, even then they drink arsenic contaminated water" *Anandabazar Patrika.*

Thakur, D. G., and Chakraborty, S. 4 April 1992. "Diseases are spreading in the villages of Kaliachak due to arsenic pollution in water" *Anandabazar Patrika.*

Part III

Public perceptions and social controversy

9 The dynamics of risk amplification and attenuation in context: a French case study

Marc Poumadère and Claire Mays

The social amplification of risk framework (Kasperson, Renn, Slovic et al. 1988) seeks to forge links between the technical assessment of risk and psychological, sociological, and cultural perspectives on risk perception and risk related behavior. We present a case study illustrating and elaborating the central hypothesis of the social amplification of risk framework (SARF), in which hazards interact with psychological, social, institutional, and cultural processes in ways that may amplify or attenuate public responses to the risk or risk event.

While an important body of research drawing on SARF has been published in the years since the seminal paper by Kasperson et al., attempts to connect the framework to risk issues in their local context are few. With the case of the "spontaneous fires" observed in the French village of Moirans-en-Montagne in 1995–96, we examine the process of both amplification and attenuation in a community context.

Furthermore, most of the existing body of research rests upon situations where the risk issues and conflicts around them are already exacerbated, and the positions of the actors involved are already polarized. In most reports, risk objects or situations are often already well defined and summarized by catchwords (such as BSE, AIDS, radwaste, tobacco, and so on) that can give the impression that the risk object pre-exists both the conditions that bring it into being, and the analysis. In this study, we demonstrate that *responses* to the risk event actually *define* the risk itself: the construction of the event, psychologically and socially shared in interaction and in collective sense making, itself shapes the danger.

The framework was originally developed around a typical sequence in which experts (scientists, technologists...) define risk through their assessments, a definition which then becomes attached, challenged or unchallenged, to a given risk event. This definition flows with the signals amplified or attenuated through relay stations, moving out from the expert circle across, for example, the media, and arriving finally at a non-specialist level before "rippling" out again across economic institutions and arenas. The Moirans case, however, is characterized by a different flow. Local actors seize upon a series of mysterious risk events, identifying, interpreting, and dramatizing them. Only in a second phase do technologists and other experts join this public forum and adopt, with interest, the definition "in-the-making." These latter players will actively develop and refine scientific and technological hypotheses on the hazard and the possible causal mechanism lying behind the risk events. The media join the process at a third stage to take up the risk definition under construction, bringing it to the attention of a larger public and a new range of specialists who add their own contributions. Finally the entire edifice collapses when a radically different hazard is acknowledged to be indubitably the mundane source of the risk events!

In the first part of this chapter we document the case through press reports, moving from a description of the fires to the search for explanations and the application of expertise, at the same time illustrating the reactions of the local community. We subsequently review the features of the case illustrating tenets of SARF. After examining the unusual flow of risk communication in this context, we analyze the peaceful co-existence of the different players who construct risk around the "technologically marvelous." Policy implications for future cooperative risk management are then considered.

The case: mysterious fires in Moirans-en-Montagne

From November 1995 to February 1996, Moirans-en-Montagne, a small town of 2,200 inhabitants in the French Jura, an eastern mountainous region, was the seat of an unexplained phenomenon. More than a dozen apparently spontaneous house fires occurred during that period. One fire had tragic consequences: a firefighter and a resident lost their lives on 20 January 1996. Other fires caused varied material damage.

In this section, we present the case in a literal manner, using vocabulary[1] and information as reported by the regional[2] and national[3] press, and by a specialized press agency.[4] These sources will allow us to convey the point of view of players involved in situ: victims of house fires, members of the local population, firefighters, city officials, and a large

---

[1] The case phraseology is almost entirely obtained from press reports; we have reconstructed the case chronologically. Occasionally we place quotes around a phrase to emphasize and recall that the specific choice of words is not our own, but belongs to the journalists who reported the events. Italicized quotes are verbatim interview statements by involved actors, as reported in the media. In all cases we have translated literally and idiomatically from the French.

[2] *Est Républicain, Le Progrès, Indépendant du Jura, Liberté de l'Est.*

[3] *Le Journal du Dimanche, Le Monde.*   [4] Enerpresse.

array of professionals and experts (physicists and electricians, police, justice, and specialists of paranormal phenomena).

Description of the fires

Starting in November 1995, a series of house fires plagues Moirans. Many fires occur in the same street, *rue des Cares*, near the gendarmerie, and are without serious consequences. While little damage is suffered, the trained volunteer firemen are puzzled and worried by the apparently spontaneous character of the fires: there are none of the usual signs to explain how or why flames break out in one location or another.

On Sunday 7 January, observers of one fire will see thick, gray, acrid smoke, coming from the garage of *rue des Cares* resident Charles Raffin, but no flames.

On Saturday 20 January 1996, at 1.30 in the afternoon, firemen intervene at the home of Charles's brother, pensioner Jean-Pierre Raffin. A fire of little gravity has taken hold in the ground level workshop. As the firemen pack up their equipment after successfully extinguishing the fire, a second blaze takes hold in an unexplained manner on the second floor, in the wardrobe of a bedroom. This time the damage will be considerable. The house is given a maximum alert status and regular rounds are made. At 8.16 that evening, just after a watch has come by to verify that the Raffins are doing well, a third fire ignites (the fourteenth in the entire series). Flames devastate the upper story of the house. Firemen arrive on the scene within two minutes. Jean-Pierre Raffin escapes, but his wife Annie Raffin, fifty-four, is caught upstairs. Experienced volunteer fireman Gérard David, forty-seven, father of two, enters by an upper window in an attempt to save Mrs. Raffin, but both perish in the flames.

A judiciary inquest is opened for "involuntary destruction and fire," and for manslaughter. It is revealed that the clothes of the victims do not appear to have been consumed by flames, while the bodies, however, are covered with burns as if they have been in an oven. These paradoxical observations remain unexplained.

The fireman appears to have died neither from electric shock, nor from asphyxia or smoke inhalation (his face does not show burns, an indication that he was wearing his mask throughout). The very high temperature reported by all witnesses is thought to be the cause of the victims' deaths. Whereas firemen's leather jackets are designed to withstand temperatures of up to 800°C, the garments of the several firefighters involved all appeared to have suffered serious damage (a photograph shows one jacket inexplicably retracted across the back and shoulders). Helmets too were damaged although made of Kevlar, a synthetic material suitable for intervention in extremely hot zones.

Firemen report that the flames they have seen are atypical: small and undulating, of a strange orange color, advancing by waves against the draft, jumping from walls to ceiling, burning more fiercely in the upper part of the room as if they were consuming gas vapors. The flames are reported to attack unusual targets, such as a sack of cement. Brass door-knobs and faucets in the Raffin house are found to have been altered by the heat, indicating that temperatures approached the metal's melting point of 1350°C. Furthermore, in one room, the plaster on the walls is found to be completely disintegrated by the heat.

Following the fatal fire, *rue des Cares* is closed. As water is observed to be inefficient against the odd flames, a special extinguishing powder is kept on hand. A 24-hour watch is also observed, allowing firemen to reach any new site within three minutes of receiving the alarm.

To minimize stress to the population, the firefighters cease to activate their sirens when they are called into action: sometimes several times a day, at short intervals.

The search for explanations

Early January 1996   While the fires had been breaking out ever since the preceding November, in January 1996 they begin to occur at an alarming rate, concentrated over periods from Friday noon to Sunday evening.

"People think" there is an electrical phenomenon involved in the fires. Indeed, a high voltage underground cable was laid by Electricity of France (EdF) in the summer of 1995. This 20,000 volt line lies twenty meters from *rue des Cares.*

The Town Hall goes on official alert. The Mayor requests that Electricity of France "take the problem in hand." The local EdF unit manager is present to observe the acrid smoke and absence of flame at the 7 January fire. He then orders captors to be placed on the underground network of lines providing electricity to the *rue des Cares* quarter of Moirans.

On Saturday 20 January the fatal fire takes place in *rue des Cares.*

Sunday 21 January   The day after the tragic fire a crisis cell is formed by the Mayor, grouping Town Hall officials, gendarmes, firemen, and EdF. The assistant regional director of EdF has made the trip to Moirans, and makes a statement to the local press:

As of today, our measurements show no fault on the network. At this time we have no scientific explanation for the phenomenon. Once the EdF network is out of the game, we have to look at other possibilities: magnetic fields or high frequencies. Along with the Town Hall, we are trying to get in contact with all the neighboring industries to learn if they have high frequency machinery.

Such machinery is used to join plywood, and is frequent in the toy industry, of which Moirans is one of the French capitals.

High frequency emissions from a source in or near Moirans, it is hypothesized, could cause an electric arc involving the metallic structures of victims' houses (in reinforced concrete, for instance). A phenomenon of induction could result. High frequency currents are those found in microwave ovens, and the arc phenomenon would be similar to what happens when a metallic object is placed in such an oven.

The assistant regional director continues:

High frequency currents are outside EdF's domain, but if we have to bring experts all the way from the other side of France, we'll do it. For the moment, we're asking Télédiffusion de France[5] to perform the measures. Whatever the cause, this series of fires is not to be related to the EdF works carried out in the neighborhood last year – as public rumor would have it. We put the overhead wires underground, on the contrary, to improve safety and to preserve the environment.

However, in order to redouble security and reassure residents, EdF cuts off the neighborhood from the grid and provides electricity from a mobile generator.

Monday 22 January   The Mayor consents to requests for telephone interviews by television stations. A formal press conference, too, is held at the Town Hall, grouping the members of the crisis cell now enlarged to the public prosecutor and her staff. The Mayor states:

In Moirans, we believe in Santa Claus, because we're the toy capital. But we don't believe in the supernatural. Some media have already started reporting that certain residents are ready to entertain supernatural explanations . . . It's understandable in such a situation that people should have such thoughts.

The Town Hall has received phone calls from diviners and sorcerers, exorcists and adepts of vibration ever since the fatal fire. Denying that an exorcist has been summoned, the local priest declares himself to take the side of profane modern science over supernatural hypotheses; for their part, the gendarmes entirely reject paranormal explanations. The local EdF unit manager reports that captors in service during the fires have revealed no fault on the lines.

---

[5] TdF: a public company charged with matters of television frequencies and transmitters.

By this time the public prosecutor has obtained the help of two independent experts, specialists in electricity and in fires. On site since Sunday, they have twenty-four hours to report to the inquest. The latter expert is seeking traces of magnesium or other incriminating starter materials. However, no traces of any accelerator have been found, and the criminal thesis is called one of the least likely at this point in the investigation. How could human intervention be seen in the fire that started inside a non-electric cabinet, in the presence of the owners who had been victims a few hours earlier of another fire? And how could human intervention be responsible for the simultaneous flare-up of an unplugged television and a sack holding cement in a closed cellar?

With the "total exclusion of the criminal cause," the fires are "generally attributed by public opinion to an electric phenomenon," sums up one regional paper.

In line with the hypotheses developed in Moirans before the fatal fire of 20 January, the prosecutor has also summoned research units from four public service industries: Télédiffusion de France, France Télécom, the National Radiocommunication Center, and the Atomic Energy Commissariat (CEA). The latter are called in to check for the presence of radioactive materials (and will eliminate that hypothesis in the next days).

A self-styled "heretic" (unorthodox) researcher, employed by the National Center for Scientific Research (CNRS), has announced he will visit Moirans on his own time and perform measures in line with his own theories. The Town Hall is checking his credentials.

Tuesday 23 January   Most experts arrive on Tuesday and meet with the crisis cell. More than ten experts are ready to get to work. EdF has called on the neighboring Lyons Region Engineering Center experts. The regional Science and Industry Inspectorate (DRIRE) joins the inquest to verify the high frequency machinery in the toy factories.

At a new press conference, the high frequency hypothesis still has the place of honor. The electric hypothesis (short circuit or fault on the lines) has been excluded, and the criminal thesis is not retained: the fires have started in conditions that appear to exclude, for the time being, any human intervention. "It must be said that the fires of Moirans have very definite particularities," explains one regional paper.

Each fire has started in metal, in the form of induction. The metal itself is actually the source of the fires! A closet clothes rod is at the origin of one fire: intense heat made white smoke escape from the metal. The phenomenon of induction by microwave (the atoms in the metal vibrate and provoke very intense heat) may be caused by high frequency emissions.

Such graphic explanations are offered by regional papers through Saturday 27 January, as for instance:

The hypothesis of high frequency currents could explain a set of the facts observed at last Saturday's fire [when the bodies, but not the clothes, of the two dead were found to be burned]; these currents may have acted like a gigantic microwave oven, literally "cooking" the victims. A hypothesis far from confirmed . . .

The experts detect a fault in a transformer near the house in which the two people met their death. According to quotes this transformer was observed to make an abnormal rumbling noise and to provoke surges. However no causal link is established between these faults and the fires.

At this time several additional hypotheses are also circulating. Swamp gas, or a field mouse that might have gnawed through cable insulation, are invoked. The fires may be the revenge of World War II victims of the firing squad, or are related to the death of a local healer. The Mayor receives dozens of letters from occult specialists. Parapsychologists from various regions of France and even Switzerland come to visit and study the phenomenon. One of them suggests that local victims of the Thirty Years' War (in the seventeenth century) are responsible for the "scratches" he believes were to be found on the bodies of the two dead. The media have also come to town. According to a later account in a national paper:

Marvel: the halogen lamps have hiccups, pipes go *"crr, crr"*. Special envoys from television news peer suspiciously at the high voltage line that supposedly produces a microwave effect (*sic*), and lean over the trench in which it was recently buried. They open their microphones to weirdoes, telepaths and diviners who wander through the main street. They follow EdF experts, looking over their shoulder at the lines presumed guilty.

The Mayor states, "*We need a scientific and reasonable approach. We are open to all hypotheses, all competences.*" Permission has also been granted to the controversial researcher to install his devices within the security zone. Jean-Martin Meunier, a physicist near retirement, wants to evaluate the idea he has been researching for decades. A geological fault, he says, when in movement could liberate ionized hydrogen. This hydrogen gas when in the presence of oxygen might produce a high-temperature incandescent flame. The hypothesis of hydrogen transport has the advantage of explaining the orange color of the flames as well as the exceptionally high heat; the presence of metal near each seat of fire would serve to ignite the flames. Meunier is happy to explain his theories, with detailed charts, to any listener.

As it is the Alsatian physicist's theory is perhaps the least fantastic of all. But he cannot prove his statements. Last year, a house near the eastern city of Nancy whose concrete foundations heated up to 800°C, and a worker who received an electric shock from an iron bar while working underground, lent support to his theory; however, he has never been on the spot to record the release of hydrogen.

Friday 26 January   The gendarmes ask the "crazy professor" to pack up his equipment, sodden under the rain, and to go home. In the evening, a barn burns three kilometers north of Moirans. Investigators see no relation between this fire and the series in town. It is the third time in two years that this barn has burned, probably lit by a pyromaniac, whereas in Moirans, the criminal track is all but abandoned. Still, a fireman is troubled by two white marks on the metal door of the barn, resembling traces of a blowtorch; these remind him of the odd flames he witnessed in Moirans.

Saturday 27 January   At 4 am on the Saturday morning, the Mayor, experts, and firemen are called to a house in south Moirans. An elderly resident has been awakened by a sound like gunfire, and the floor tiles in her second floor kitchen have suddenly heaved up to a height of five centimeters over a surface of four square meters. This is a phenomenon familiar to seismologists, who describe it thus: the foundations of houses resist, and repercussions of telluric movements are then seen on the more vulnerable upper floors. This event convinces more than one resident that something is happening underground in Moirans. Even though no cracks are to be seen in walls, the Mayor would like the scientific experts crowding his town to measure any quake activity. (Eventually the Institute of Global Physics in Strasbourg will come, but record no results.)

Over the course of the week, engineers have placed sensors that should have detected any high frequency transmission. Thomson, a private electronics multinational, has carried out measures as well. But no emitter has been found to support the microwave theory. The sensors placed in early January by EdF (in places where electric meters click forward speedily or where gutters are heard to vibrate for hours) have still produced no data that can explain the fires (nor the odd noises). In private, the experts admit they are perplexed.

Saturday 3 and Sunday 4 February   Two more fires break out: one in the cellar of Charles Raffin, *rue des Cares*, the next in a perambulator parked in the entry hall of a building in which three other fires have previously taken place.

Monday 6 February   In an exchange of communiqués, the Paris headquarters of EdF states that the absence of any defect in network insulation demonstrates that the electrical hypothesis was *"completely exaggerated and premature"*; the Mayor of Moirans recalls that he *"never pointed a finger at EdF"* and hopes Saturday's fire will *"provide some clues to the experts. I have confidence in the investigators."* He states that his townspeople are becoming exasperated by the fires and by the fact that these may encourage petty arson.

Late in the afternoon, the public prosecutor finally announces the arrest the day before of an arsonist, related to the Raffin family, one hour after he lit Sunday's perambulator fire with a simple cigarette lighter. He admits to responsibility in seven fires, but denies causing the fire in which two people died.

And so, where there's smoke, there's fire; where there are spontaneous fires, there's someone to light them. The experts may have played the role of . . . smoke screen; while the media were focused on the results of Saturday and Sunday's electrical readings, the gendarmes were following persons they had suspected from the time of the fatal fire. The investigators are keeping quiet, though, about the methods used by the pyromaniac to set off his fires, probably by delay.

The Mayor is relieved, if pained to learn of the "human dimension" of the story; residents show their satisfaction that the spectacle has come to an end, and that Moirans will no longer be seen as the cursed village.

Epilogue   At the suspect's trial in November 1996, the captain of the gendarmes reports that twenty gendarmes and judiciary police investigated the criminal hypothesis throughout, keeping an eye on three persons. The difficulty was that no trace of accelerator was ever found at the site of a fire.

The fire expert admits that *"a mountain was made of this affair"* and accuses EdF of having *"misled everyone."* *"Certain fires had no scientific explanation, and so we thought of a voluntary gesture."* Taken to task by the judge for thinking of anything *but* arson at the time of the inquest, the expert affirms: *"You really have to work at it to ignite a fire with a cigarette lighter. We said to ourselves: there has to be an accelerator."*

Reactions of the population

The media document the reactions of the Moirans population. We translate from a number of press reports published shortly after the fatal January fire.

The Lançon couple, who own a house at the entry of *rue des Cares*, have been the victims of three nascent fires. "*The first time was about ten days ago; I was coming in from a drive when I noticed smoke coming out of the ground floor. I immediately took the car out of the garage, thinking it was the cause. That's when I realized that I was wrong: the fire had started simultaneously in two bedrooms side by side, on a little corner table and on a bed.*" That was not the end of Mr. Lançon's troubles. "*When I went upstairs, [another] bed was just beginning to take fire.*" The owner manages to put out the fires before the arrival of the firemen. He will not be so successful the following Saturday: "*A big cupboard in the garage took fire. I couldn't do anything, the heat was so intense.*" Fortunately, the firemen quickly manage to put out the fire. The damage still is great. Since that day, although Mr. Lançon claims he's not afraid, he does feel some worry. "*I don't dare put my car in the garage anymore.*" Still and all, he does not want to leave his house. (*Regional press*)

The residents of Moirans are not at all panicked. Everyone knows there must be a scientific, concrete explanation to the fires and that they must just wait a little longer to have it. "*We are afraid, still, given that we know a fire can start anywhere, anytime,*" says one lady who however does not live near the Cares quarter. Strangely, the calmest are those who do live in that neighborhood. Too calm, perhaps, to the mind of the authorities. Yet another safety measure has been taken: residents of fire-damaged houses have been relocated to friends' homes or to the hotel at the town's expense. Local elected officials and firemen have requested that all neighborhood residents leave their residence. Few have accepted. "*If I'm home when a fire breaks out in my house, I might be able to stop it*" says one man. But it's that "*might be*" that bothers the authorities. When you know the power and rapidity of the fires, you are right to be worried. (*Regional press*)

All possible safety measures have been taken to reassure the Moirantans, sirens are silenced, but their anxiety is growing. The inability of the experts to determine the cause of the fires brings them little by little to doubt. Strangely, the Moirans residents most concerned are the most unruffled: Mr. Raymond Lançon, victim of several fires, stays on in his house during the day. "*Calm, yes, I'm calm.*" However he prefers to sleep at his sister's place every night "*as long as the cause has not been found. For the fire to follow the electric lines, it must be electric*" he says, sure of his reasoning. All the victims who were lodged in the hotel at the town's expense are now staying with family or friends. The curious who stroll along the safety perimeter are paradoxically more worried: "*If I lived here, I'd already be out,*" says one lady walking with friends, her face grave. "*We're afraid, we don't know where the fires come from,*" she says, worried although she lives in a distant quarter. The "esoteric" rumors are racing through the village, but reason still resists. The priest has even tried to dissipate all doubts by taking the side of the scientific explanation. Throughout the day, numerous residents follow the experts in their ballet, on foot, or in their truck bristling with antennae, across the forbidden zone. Empty, the house in which the drama took place is protected from the threatening rain by canvas, and continues to pose a somber riddle. (*Regional press*)

In the absence of tangible elements, people cling to the wisdom of elders. Bernard Grossiord, head of the local EdF unit, who has been criticized for not knowing how to measure subterranean electricity, recalls the experience of ancestors who always sent a horse into a field to test the current with its iron shoes. The farmers talk about the haystacks that, at summer's end, take fire spontaneously because of fermentation. In the case of the barn burned last Friday, this explanation is unacceptable. The hay, two years old, was dry. People talk, talk, to combat their nervousness. A speed race is being run against the inexplicable. Wednesday, Judge Berthet should receive the autopsy reports for the two victims, and in a week or two, lab results for the blood and lung samples taken. Awaiting these concrete elements, the Mayor of Moirans, himself a medical doctor, is impatient. Jean Burdeyon would like to know, to be able to reassure the population, and mourn in peace his friend, fireman Gérard David, whom all Moirans called "the tough guy." (*National press*)

Analyzing the case through the social amplification of risk framework

The social amplification of risk framework (Kasperson et al. 1988; Renn 1991a; Kasperson 1992; Pidgeon 1999) will be utilized in this section to examine how our case illustrates shared construction of risk. The model serves to analyze social relationships with risk as they are expressed around given risk objects or situations. Changes in collective behavior can be explained as resulting from the amplification or attenuation any particular risk may have received. The notion of "particular risk" is important; indeed the risk event must be considered to pre-exist the process of amplification or attenuation, giving a baseline against which the dynamic may then be evaluated.

In the case that we have just presented, the risk is tightly tied to its social context: to the extent that one may even ask the question (as we do in the next section), just what is the risk at hand in this situation? By which processes does the risk become an object of collective concern? We will suggest, in the analysis of the Moirans case, that those processes point to other, perhaps less evident, objects of collective concern.

Much has been written and debated about the idea that different actors (for example, experts and members of publics) hold different definitions of technological risk. We subscribe to this view, which SARF itself helps to elucidate. The Moirans case invites us to look beyond even the transversal definition of risk as a threat to health and safety, to another even closer to the heart of humanity: in which risk may be experienced as a threat to persons, objects, and relationships of importance. In general, as in Moirans, the aspects of the situation that mobilize risk perception behavior and adaptation, may not be limited to those which have direct implications for health and safety, but rather, may be those aspects which threaten more covert features of social organization and relations. In the

Moirans case, those aspects are repressed fears associated with the buried cable, otherwise accepted for economic and social reasons.

In this section, we review the Moirans case on three major dimensions examined by Kasperson et al. in their original formulation of the framework: signal amplification in communications theory; structural aspects of social amplification; and informational mechanisms of social amplification. We will examine whether a process of amplification or attenuation has taken place, which transmitters are involved, and whether "ripples" or secondary effects occur. Throughout, we formulate hypotheses that would call for detailed qualitative field research; accordingly our account may be regarded as the first phase of a larger study.

Throughout, as well, we will be drawn to the view that while the Moirans case not only provides excellent illustration for many tenets of the social amplification framework, it provides at the same time some provocative counter-examples. Rather than diminishing the value of the framework, this analysis suggests that the framework is supple and robust enough to represent the contradictions inherent in the human experience of risk. While based upon signal theory, a model criticized for its flattening of social communication, SARF appears, through the Moirans case, on the contrary to render the Escher-like dimensionality of social risk perception.

Signal amplification

Knowing as we do the end of the story – that is, that the Moirans fires were lit by a pyromaniac – we can say that risk amplification did indeed occur. After all, there was no underlying technological hazard that, if left unidentified, would inexorably continue to produce spontaneous fires. The arsonist's actions were explicable and followed a pattern he had established for himself. The risk events, as the gendarmes eventually proved, needed no elaborate electrophysical explanation.[6] The consequences, even if tragic, were limited to temporary community disruption and two deaths. The happenings in Moirans, in and of themselves, *should have* attracted the attention only of the victims, their loved ones, and the institutional representatives (firemen, the Mayor, local police, the court, fire investigator...) charged with managing and mitigating such situations. As it is, many more players were mobilized: local residents, regional and national media, and various scientific experts in electricity,

---

[6] We use the term "electrophysical" to designate the ensemble of dominant technological hypotheses: that an electric fault was to be found on the underground grid, producing surges or propagating electromagnetic fields, or that high frequency emissions from some other source were responsible for a microwave effect or arc phenomenon.

microwaves, seismology, radioactivity, and so forth, on through to specialists in the paranormal. The scope of activity of the institutional representatives was also enlarged beyond their usual mission. Amplification has thus occurred, but perhaps not according to the expected pattern; we note the *absence* of visible opposition between proponents and opponents of some risk-producing activity, which typically fuels the social amplification process. In such a situation, opposition could have built against the buried cable and the health risks attributed to this technology.

Shared construction of the risk event   A strong amplification dynamic finds its origin in *the shared construction of the risk event* in Moirans. This risk event is limited, at the start, to the mystery of the spontaneous fires and to the menace that weighs upon the residents of being themselves victims of the next fire. The risk event then takes on another contour with the shared construction it undergoes. "People think" there is an electrical phenomenon involved. Interpreted as the manifestation of something electric, and furthermore of "something going on underground," the fires become something needing the attention of Electricity of France; EdF in turn will think the fires call for the attention of microwave specialists. The involvement of more than just those actors who *should have* participated signifies that the fires are of special interest, bringing publicity and finally input from specialists offering a range of alternative constructions. The luxuriant development of risk information transmitters, to cite the communications theory upon which SARF reposes in part, is itself an outstanding feature of the amplification seen in Moirans.

The role of symbolic factors   The Moirans dynamic also illustrates the role of *symbolic factors* in signal amplification, held by Kasperson et al. as perhaps the most potent elements in social amplification. Symbols include such things as the prestige, or other features, of an information source. Electricity of France, a large public service institution, mobilizes to attend to fires in Moirans, and successfully solicits other, well-known, respected national institutions to mobilize as well. The public prosecutor further lends the prestige of Justice when she officially mandates these experts. At one point a dozen individuals branded with the greatest technological acronyms of France are at work investigating the Moirans mystery.[7] One newspaper among the seven that we consulted reports,

---

[7] Note that the French public may accord a relatively high degree of trust towards engineers of such institutions; in a comparative survey study, the French public differed from United States residents in avowing trust towards "experts and engineers who build, operate, and regulate nuclear power plants" (Poumadère et al. 1996; Slovic, Flynn, Mertz et al. 2000, p. 89).

apparently in error, that Telecom was present as well (Telecom is the second utility familiar, along with EdF, to every household in France). This outstanding presence lends symbolic importance to the set of electrophysical hypotheses, and to the process itself of risk definition.

Repetition of factual statements   Kasperson et al. point out that a

factual statement repeated several times, especially if by different sources, tends to elicit greater belief in the accuracy of the information . . . An elaborate description of the inference process may distract attention from the accuracy of the underlying assumptions. (Kasperson et al. 1988, p. 180)

In Moirans, a heterogeneous set of actors takes up the chorus of electrophysical causes, and moreover, devotes visible efforts to studying those causes. The fascinating technical discourse interpreting the unusual ignitions and attributing them to a microwave effect may have distracted from the banal but likely criminal thesis.

Note, however, that it is possible to over-amplify the description of the inference process and thereby destroy the credibility of the underlying assumptions: the independent researcher obtained entry to the restricted zone in Moirans to measure hydrogen transmission, but as newspapers recount, his eager display of "sketches and diagrams" and his claim to "challenge Newton's universal theory of gravitation" finally wore on the patience of gendarmes, and "the inhabitants of Moirans had a great deal of difficulty believing this crazy professor."

Institutional and role constraints   "Signals passing through a transmitter may be amplified or attenuated according to institutional rules, role requirements, and anticipated receiver interests" (Kasperson et al. 1988, p. 181). One may guess that the gendarmes attenuated any signals they had of the criminal nature of the fires; being good police practice, this facilitated their shadowing of suspects.

The Mayor stands out as an amplifying transmitter, taking up the early public rumor that an electric phenomenon was at stake and requesting that the local unit of the national utility "take the problem in hand." Two aspects of his role may have influenced this behavior. Any mayor is by definition the representative of his townspeople, bound to represent their concerns to outside parties. He is charged with both the administration of town affairs and the protection of his citizens and their interests, including the management of all safety issues affecting the village. Finally, the "premier magistrate" as a mayor is known in France,[8] quite normally is led to weigh, judge, and decide the community matters that are brought before him, as well as indicate a course of action. The Mayor of Moirans had more than just this role, however. It is stated once, in all the newspaper clippings consulted, that this Mayor is by training and profession a medical doctor. We can see in his actions the additional reflection of the ethic of care to which a physician subscribes, reinforcing perhaps the administrator's duty to protect his townspeople. Also, a physician is more likely to have faith in science, and to appeal to science to furnish explanation: "*We need a scientific and reasonable approach.*" This aspect of his role may have directed the Mayor's attention to a technological cause, to an explanation in which science was intrinsically present, and which scientists could naturally come forward to elucidate.

The village priest "takes the trouble to distance himself" from supernatural explanations, denying that a diviner is in fact an exorcist called to town, and to state that he sides with secular modern science. This gesture is interesting in that it takes its force from the *overturning* of expected institutional role requirements: the caricatured expectation being that a priest might favor a traditional theory of malign intervention, and call upon the tools of the Church. Here, thus, is an example of the equal value of SARF elements when taken in the positive or the negative: alignment or non-alignment with role demands each contributes to the amplification of one risk interpretation.

What of anticipated receiver interests? As discussed above, the focus on an "electric phenomenon" reflects the measure of respect accorded to public opinion. However, the case again shows a subtle variation on the social amplification framework: in Moirans, one is tempted to speak not just of receiver interest, but also of the flourishing interest of transmitters themselves. Witness the eagerness with which the entire range of experts, from respectable institutional engineers to paranormal illuminati, rush to Moirans to investigate and elaborate their own pet theories.

Structural aspects of the social amplification of risk

"The information system," suggest Kasperson et al., "may amplify risk events in two ways: intensifying or weakening signals that are part of the risk message; [or] by filtering the multitude of signals with respect to the

---

[8] Mayors are pre-eminent figures on the French sociopolitical scene: there are some 36,000 of them administrating sometimes tiny collectivities, for some sixty million inhabitants. This high ratio is unusual in Europe and in the world.

attributes of the risk and their importance" (Kasperson 1988, p. 181). Among the key amplification steps identified, a number appear to apply to the case of the spontaneous fires.

- *Filtering signals.* In Moirans, any signals that suggest the fires are due to arson are apparently left aside, or coupled with doubt and thereby diminished in news conferences, or actively crushed in the Press: numerous are the media reports that the criminal thesis is the least likely, that human intervention is "totally excluded."
- *Processing of risk information (use of cognitive heuristics to draw inferences).* The frequency of outbreak in *rue des Cares*, for instance, led to inferences that the fires were due to some feature of the street itself: the buried high voltage cable.
- *Attaching social values to the information.* Attitudes in Moirans appear to reflect both values of faith in science and technology (*when something strange and bad happens, we can call on science*), and in a more covert way, values of rejection of technology (*when something strange and bad happens, technology must be responsible*). Again, the Moirans dynamic is composed of a tension between contradictory attitudes about science and technology.
- *Interacting with one's cultural and peer groups to interpret and validate signals.* In Moirans there are many such groups (professional corps of firemen or gendarmes; the heterogeneous crisis cell; neighbors and residents...) Actors seem indeed to interact strongly within and across groups; see our discussion below of the Moirans risk experience.
- *Engaging in group or individual actions to accept, ignore, tolerate, or change the risk.* In Moirans we are struck by actions to *investigate* the risk. In parallel with the investigations launched by the Mayor and Edf, reinforced by the crisis cell and public prosecutor, note that residents come to stroll and look around *rue des Cares*, in the same way as technologists visit the area. The news media suggest that these inhabitants come to get a thrill of fear; perhaps they are also actively participating in this way in an important village research event.

Informational mechanisms of social amplification

Attributes of information about a risk that may influence the social amplification include *volume*, degree to which information is *disputed*, and *symbolic connotations* of information (Kasperson et al. 1988, p. 184). Clearly risk information abounds in Moirans for several days or weeks, and symbolism touches on a range of connotation from scientific sophistication to esoteric enlightenment to the pathos of untimely and violent death. The very mystery of the fires' origin, and the clash of theories, signify uncertainty. Kasperson et al. also point to *cultural bias in interpretation*; it is present in Moirans when EdF, responding to the Mayor's call, orient subsequent development of hypotheses into electrophysical channels (or *"mislead everyone,"* as the fire expert will bitterly state in court).

Dramatization and labile fantasy Another key informational attribute is extent of dramatization. "Experience with dramatic accidents or risk events increases the memorability and imaginability of the hazard, thereby heightening the perception of risk" (Kasperson et al. 1988, p. 184). Dramatization is found in the eye-witness accounts of the volunteer firemen, and relayed by the press: the death of an esteemed and skilled colleague, the jacket abnormally burned, the inexplicable ignitions, the unheard of high temperatures, the unusual appearance and behavior of the flames, and so forth. The firemen enjoy a definite degree of credibility inasmuch as they are professional experts and habitués of fire; the fact that they can be puzzled and shocked by their experience deepens the drama.

The Moirans case suggests that an aspect of dramatization may be the recourse to *fantasy images and labile associations*. We take note of the vague borders here between science and the imaginary. The scientific scenario of a microwave effect shows as much labile creativity, in context, as do the hypotheses of radioactive phenomena, seismic eruptions or paranormal occurrences. All of these generous visions of causality are pursued and elaborated with equal enthusiasm and seriousness by their various advocates, who receive support and encouragement from players ranging from the courts to local residents to the town priest.

The Mayor acted here as a relay station, declaring that the situation must be addressed in a scientific spirit, while at the same time welcoming *"all competencies,"* thereby signifying that the range of explanations worth considering might be very great – as great as the mystery itself.

Mobilization of latent fears: hypothesis of strong attenuation at the base of strong amplification "High volumes of information mobilize latent fears and enhance the recollection of previous accidents or management failures" (Kasperson et al. 1988, p. 184). In Moirans, an important recollection of a past event *precedes* the strong amplification and attendant volumes of information: that past event is the emplacement underground of the high voltage line just six months before the first mysterious fires. From early January (when, we may expect, the frequency and regularity of the fires produced some volume of exchange among concerned players), this cable becomes the object of causal attributions. We may put forward the hypothesis that this cable was also the object of latent fears, and that the population's fears at the time of the cable's installation were repressed. That is, the fears were not given full expression and consideration, and thereby integrated into overt representations or translated into active opposition or rejection of the cable. Instead they remained covert, in the form of a lingering, perhaps unspoken suspicion of the danger posed by the presence of the line. The fires then provide a triggering event permitting these fears to emerge.

The hypothesized repression of these risk concerns might be an example of a very thorough process of *attenuation*,[9] whose relays and mechanisms may be more difficult to identify and capture than are those of amplification. In any event, they appear to have been relatively less described in the social amplification literature. Note that in our hypothesis, the wide amplification of the risk event represented by the fires is in fact *dependent upon* the deep attenuation of the prior, repressed risk event (burial of the cable). Moirans in this perspective introduces another level of dynamic into SARF: *the degree of amplification may sometimes be a function of the degree of prior attenuation in the given social context.*

Information flow   Information about risk and risk events flows through two major communication networks: the news media and more informal personal networks. [. . . These latter] include the linkages that exist among friends, neighbors, and co-workers, and within social groups more generally. Although relatively little is known about such networks, it is undoubtedly the case that people do not consider risk issues in isolation from other social issues or from the views of their peers. (Kasperson et al. 1988, p. 185)

We shall not attempt, in this paper, to portray the flow of information through the media, although that flow is clearly of central importance. We will indicate in this section, however, some socioeconomic issues at play in Moirans. In a later section we give extensive consideration to social psychological dynamics underlying the flow of information among groups, thereby providing a theoretical basis for future explorations of social networks.

In Moirans itself, residents may have a special relationship with electricity, for it is used extensively in the regional toy and plastics industry (numerous generators and transformers are to be found in the area), and

---

[9] Attenuation, in the Moirans case at least, transposes to the collective level in terms of the concept of *denial* put forward by Freudian psychodynamic theory. Denial is a mechanism of defense, allowing individuals to form a compromise between the psychological necessity to repress certain threatening representations or thoughts, and the constant environmental reminder of the basis of those thoughts. Denial allows persons to embrace a sort of intellectual acceptance of the threatening situation, while the underlying affective reaction of fear and rejection is withheld from consciousness.

Table 9.1 *Contextual factors and social amplification of risk in the Moirans case*

levels	contextual factors	social amplification/ attenuation of risk	timescale
level 1	*historical and structural conditions*: key elements of the local culture mountain/wooded area ⇓ toy industry ⇓ industrial use of electricity provision of jobs (1 per family in Moirans)	familiarity with, dependency upon industrial use of electricity ⇒ *risk attenuation*	≥1 generation
level 2	*introduction of a new technology*: the buried cable • technological change • socio-economic continuity with level 1	perception of change downplayed; ⇒ denial; *risk attenuation*	<1 year
level 3	*triggering event* unexplainable fires • active search for continuity with levels 1 & 2	release or recovery of suppressed representations; ⇒ *risk amplification*	a few weeks

each Moirans family counts at least one member employed in that industry. Table 9.1 portrays in summary fashion the linkages between local geography, socioeconomic development, and hypothesized risk perception behavior. It draws attention to different levels of involvement with the Moirans "risk event," and treats attenuation or amplification as dynamic manifestations within a continuity of representations and relationships.

The portrayal of extensive, dynamic linkages underlying amplification and attenuation in Moirans will not be further developed in these pages. Field research might elucidate the way in which electricity, as a vital feature of family and social benefit, takes on the aspect of an outstanding source of risk, in an imagination-charged and mysterious context. It might also indicate whether an attenuation process at the time of cable installation, and again after the resolution of the fire mystery, corresponds in Moirans to a defensive mechanism of denial, or perhaps of reduction of cognitive dissonance (Cramer 2000).

Ripple effects Kasperson et al. (1988, p. 182) suggest that risk amplification will spawn behavioral responses which in turn will result in secondary impacts: among these are enduring perceptions and attitudes, stigma effects, social disorder, changes in risk regulation, monitoring and management, and increased economic liability, and repercussions on other technologies.

Are there technological ripple effects in the Moirans case? The secondary consequences of the amplification of risk could have taken the form of a demand that the underground high voltage cable be displaced away from the residential area. This demand, easy enough to formulate on the local level should the experts have come to agreement on an electric causality to the fires, could then have served as a precedent and a stimulus for other demands on the national level. Indeed a national campaign in France to bury electric lines throughout the 1990s had elicited isolated and tenuous expressions of concern for the potential health and safety effects of underground electromagnetic fields. Moirans might have catalyzed the re-emergence and amplification of those concerns and resulted in a massive demand to reconsider the burial policy, and to take action in residential areas, especially, one may anticipate, in any place where an underground line was found to co-exist with, for example, a recent case of childhood leukemia.

As it happened, however, the amplification process came to an abrupt halt with the identification of the arsonist, and to our knowledge Moirans did not feed the potential or ongoing debates over EMF in other localities.

The risk-shaping effect of the local context

The role of the social context in risk communication has been analyzed by Slovic and MacGregor (1994). However, the communication processes described rest upon identified risk events, in the same way as a tire fire in a rural Ontario community produced responses in local residents that could be carefully documented by Eyles et al. (1993). In the Moirans case, the risk communication process bears on both local contextual social factors, and an unidentified hazard. This leads us to examine the systemic structure of risk communication where the risk at hand is itself in the process of definition. It appears that, in such a situation, several levels of risks must be considered.

Defining the risk: the systemic structure of risk communication

Just what is the risk event in Moirans? A first answer lies in the fundamental, and operational, definition of risk as a threat to something – persons, objects, relationships – held to be important. In Moirans, the notion of threat certainly existed in the local population: although the spontaneous

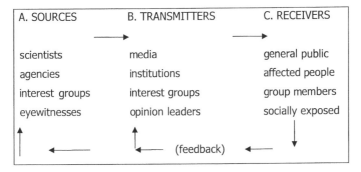

Figure 9.1 Organizational structure of risk communication (Renn 1991a).

fires were concentrated in one street, their cause being unknown, no resident could be certain that he or she would not become a victim. Even without going so far as to entertain the idea of a fire breaking out in one's own house, the sense of community order and safety was certainly threatened; awareness of this is reflected in the decision to silence firemen's sirens to minimize population stress. This stress, along with the two deaths and material damage, are among the direct consequences of the Moirans risk.

As for the general population in France, the news was brought by the media, and not by local witnesses or affected people as in Moirans. Before commenting on what kind of risk can have been perceived by the general population, let us look at one aspect of SARF: the systemic structure of risk communication (labeled organizational structure by Renn 1991a). Portrayed in figure 9.1, Renn's model presents a flow from the risk events and their characteristics toward sources, transmitters, and receivers, with a feedback loop back across those three levels.

In the Moirans case, it appears that Renn's contentions are supported: science, as carried by experts in high frequencies or radiation, plays an important role as a source of risk communication, and the media have effectively played the transmitter role.

In addition to scientists, firemen are a major source of risk vision in Moirans; their credibility is linked to their direct expertise in the matter.

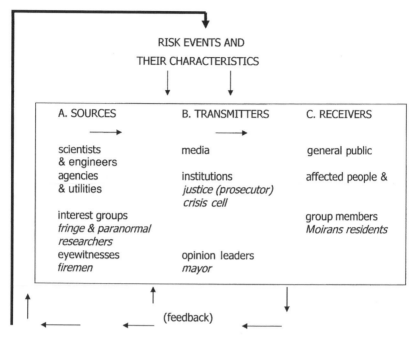

Figure 9.2 Double loop of risk communication in Moirans.

In Renn's source categories, they are an intermediate group, with characteristics of both eyewitnesses and scientists.

The local population, too, is active. The mysterious nature of the fires is more readily invested with credibility than the solid common sense of provincial French people would have suggested. Clearly, the local public and affected persons are not passive receivers. Such a receiver role can be more readily attributed to the general French public, whose knowledge in the case is constructed not in social interaction but in taking cognizance of the information provided by the media.

Looking again at figure 9.1, we see that the Moirans case suggests a need to add a second loop, showing feedback upon the risk events from the social interactions among the various Moirans players (figure 9.2). It is their discourse that lends risky dimensions to events which in themselves could appear banal and circumscribed. The specific social context provides the specific risk characteristics. Indeed the characteristics of the risk event in Moirans did not pre-exist its construction by sources: eyewitnesses, firemen, administrators, technical experts, and the local population at large. These characteristics are amplified by the media and by the influx of new experts. The whole soufflé collapses when the pyromaniac is eventually caught, and a much-attenuated interpretation must be given to the source of risk. At that point the model reverts to the single-loop version of figure 9.1, with arson representing a relatively weak risk signal.

Levels of risk

It is worth looking further at the different levels of risk experienced and communicated in an idiosyncratic way by the different players involved.

For firemen, their work itself is often associated with risk. They are ready to fight fires at any time and in any circumstances, and yet there seem to exist implicit boundaries to their activity. Within these boundaries, they perform their work and, even though exposed, probably consider it to be an acceptable or "normal" risk. In Moirans, however, firefighters felt they were outside the ordinary boundaries: they faced fires surprising by their physical form and their unaccustomed dangerousness (one of their number died). Despite the extraordinary nature of the fires, the men did not shirk from their duty, but developed new responses they believed to be more adapted, such as stocking powder (to replace water) for extinguishing a future fire. These "soldiers of fire" communicated their perception of the flames as both strange and exceptionally dangerous, and contributed in that way to constructing the risk event.

The local public, including the victims and eyewitnesses, also seemingly preferred the vision of mystery attached to the fires, rather than the banal supposition that a pyromaniac was at work.

The Mayor held an open attitude in order to examine all "scientific and reasonable" hypotheses, which included, as we have seen, the consideration of causes quite removed from those commonly, or indeed ever, seen in the case of house fires. "Reasonable" here may be understood in two ways: first, in the sense that the Mayor was excluding the paranormal or mystic explanations offered; second, in the sense that he invited reliance upon rational scientific method. An outside or ex post observer might object that rationality is not really present here, if one takes as a criterion that the scientific model chosen be adequate to the physical nature of the situation. On the other hand, it may be said that the decisions taken proved to be socially adequate.[10]

In fact, the risk event in question in Moirans, as it became constructed, never existed before the interaction and communication of these players.

---

[10] This could open discussion of social rationality, that is a rationality based upon the acceptance of social representations and dynamics, even when these contrast sharply with the dominant cognitions in society (e.g. Jaeger et al. 2001).

The constructed risk event never took place, and perhaps never could, on the physical plane.

A risk event, still, may exist here in the manner suggested by Renn's schema (figure 9.1), in the underground emplacement of the cable. The installation of the 20KV line a few months before the fires apparently took place in a calm atmosphere. It seems possible, however, that this installation inspired some worry. When something later goes wrong near the site, the collective imagination designates the cable as a likely culprit for the fires. Why should fear of the possible consequences of this underground cable and current have been repressed? Was the fearful position associated with rejected images of backwardness or anti-technologism? Were the concerns in conflict with the dominant risk-benefit analysis, electric energy being tightly linked to local jobs? Or were images of potential effects upon the body and health from this unfamiliar installation so horrible that they were buried like the cable itself?

Several levels, thus, of risk are present in the social context of Moirans-en-Montagne. The mystery is first suggested by firefighters, then taken up willingly by the eyewitnesses and local public, relayed by the Mayor, and just as willingly adopted by the scientific experts, who contribute thus to the amplification of the risk event. For these experts give a rational consistency to the unleashed imagination of the firemen and public, whose preference goes to what could be labeled the "technologically marvelous" exemplified by the cable, buried in the ground as many, perhaps, preferred it would remain buried beyond consciousness.

Rather than objecting to the population's doubts concerning the underground line, or dismissing it as a causal factor, authoritative players accept and take the doubt seriously, pushing the investigation even farther, on the scientific and technical levels, than demanded.

The social context at large, thus, contributed greatly to shaping the risk event, while players implicated in this context carry and to a certain extent, manage the shaping process. In other words, the social context was not overwhelmed by the events, despite their mysterious and menacing nature.

In the midst of uncertainty and stress caused by the mysterious fires and their mortal and psychological impact, the public authorities (the Mayor, the courts, the police, and even the firemen) and institutions (in the sense of social norms, conventions, and codes) continued to provide direction and structure, whatever the judgment one may make a posteriori of the decisions produced. That the public authorities continued to function without rupture suggests that the risk event should not be described as having evolved into a crisis situation (Lévy 1998).

There was thus no real loss of orientation in the population of Moirans: traditional signposts were replaced by others that appeared to be adapted to the situation, and loaded with meaning. An activity of collective sense making, a shared process of definition, developed and produced a risk event hitherto unseen. The residents of Moirans continued to think and interact, and in this unusual situation, different thought modes and content cohabited without some hierarchy of rationality to impose one mode of thought as superior to another.

The Moirans risk experience

A major hypothesis has been proposed for the analysis of the strange occurrences in Moirans. That is, the buried high voltage line resurfaced in people's minds when unexplained fires appeared, reflecting both repressed concerns about the technological installation and a taste for the technologically marvelous (rather than for the banality of arson). Indeed, we may state with confidence that if reported as just a series of arsons, the Moirans fires would not have burned very long in the regional media, and even less in the national media.

In this section, we consider elements of the community risk experience, in particular the co-existence of plural risk representations. Not only did this co-existence prove important, as discussed above, in shaping the risk: it was also a peaceful co-existence among typically opposed groups of players. This contrasts with most reports of risk communication experiences, which describe *conflicts* between opponents and proponents, blaming of institutions, and stigmatization[11] (Slovic, Layman, Kraus et al. 1991). Loss of trust is also a frequent phenomenon in such situations (Slovic 1993), as are outrage and feeling of betrayal (Horlick-Jones 1995).

This peaceful co-existence does not represent the sole condition for the shaping of risk. Typically, conflict as well contributes to that definition process in society. Some advantages of the peaceful manner are to be found in the definition process itself, and in its consequences. As to process: not all persons enjoy conflict. As to consequences: the technological choice of burying power lines has not been reconsidered on the basis of this experience; that economic ripple has been avoided.

We will thus look more closely at this dynamic of co-existing plural risk representations, and at what made it a "peaceful" one.

---

[11] Whether any form of stigmatization may be observed in Moirans of course is a question not yet closed, as such a phenomenon can develop over a longer period than the critical period discussed here.

The co-existence of plural risk representation

Social representation, as studied by social psychologist Serge Moscovici and colleagues since the 1960s (Moscovici 1976; Moscovici and Hewstone 1983), is the process through which common sense or shared vision is produced. The content of such collective knowledge is also designated by the noun social representation. Potter and Wetherell (1987) point out that social representations provide agreed codes for inter individual communication. To the extent that persons share similar representations, they enjoy mutual understanding. Their exchanges are founded upon assertions that appear to be coherent and clear, that require no further explication. The theory of social representations here does not lay emphasis on the necessary coherence between such assertions and rational, impersonal, and non-context-dependent knowledge. It is indeed simply the shared basis of representations that furnishes their adequacy and their clarity in social interaction.

In contrast, a too heterogeneous set of representations among participants in interaction cannot provide the shared vision of an external, stable reality that is necessary to establish interaction. In such a setting, interpretations of basic facts are divergent, misunderstanding arises, and disputes or conflicts appear.

Risk communication situations most often correspond to this latter process, and thus it may be useful to examine more closely the way in which the heterogeneity of social representations produces such a dynamic.

Human rationality and risk communication

We may use Asch's stimulating work in social psychology (1951, 1955, 1956) to question more closely the topic of rationality and risk communication. Asch considered that research should not be concerned so much with what exists, but rather with what is understood to exist. He gives, on this basis, the following concept of human rationality: people are recognized as rational beings to the extent that others understand their construction of the world around them. And for Asch, social perception, like the perception of ordinary objects, is situated in social relationships.

Asch's best-known studies are those on persuasion and on the effects of social pressure. His most celebrated experiment uses sticks of unequal length. In that study, a small group of subjects are asked to designate which stick is shortest, medium, or longest. All but one subject are confederates of the experimenter, and together come to agreement upon a measurement classification that goes against the obvious right answer, clearly perceived by the sole naive subject. How will this subject respond?

What strategies will be used to try to influence the cohesive group to change their perception? Will the subject buckle under and adopt the manifestly incorrect view? Asch's interpretations and developments on the effects of pressure by a majority (if one considers the number of persons directly involved in the situation) are well known. If one considers the cognitive content of the representation created for Asch's experiments, it is very much a minority view (an unusual interpretation of reality) that is dominant in the situation. This suggests a parallel with Moirans, in which the unusual interpretation of the fires becomes dominant.

Yet another aspect, less often discussed, of Asch's experiments may be of value in understanding what happened in Moirans.

Asch noticed, beyond the fact that the targets of pressure gave up or preserved their independence of thought, that they were profoundly disturbed by the gap between what they saw to be and what they believed to be the vision of the others in the group. It is clear from these observations that the sense of reality is partially social, and that when others do not share this sense of reality, the foundations of our vision of the world, or alternatively our feeling of social cohesion, are shaken.

The point we wish to make is that the interactions implied by the communication of risks generally contain the elements that lead to such profound upset. In many cases, adopting another's risk definition involves such choices, between abandoning one's own vision of things or ceding one's sense of social belongingness and harmony. The conflicts around risk issues are above all, for the players involved, composed of disturbing feelings of gap between their vision and that which they believe to be the vision of others. By insisting upon the social dimension of our sense of reality, Asch allows us to frame risk conflicts, at least in part, in cognitive and existential terms. The consequences for social management of risks are numerous. This framing focuses attention on the fact that multiple forms of knowledge and views exist outside the bounds of a given vision or discipline, and the dominance it exercises by giving an a priori definition of what is the "real" risk at hand, or the priority that should be given to risk reduction. A shared sense of reality is a necessary prerequisite to communication inside or across any of these bounds.

Entente in risk communication

It appears to us that this shared sense may be designated by the term of *entente*. Entente is a social condition for communication in something of the way that oxygen is a necessary constituent of our atmosphere. As with oxygen, entente's existence and role only becomes apparent when it comes to be in short supply (hence the large volume of research on conflictual or failed risk communication). In the domain of risk, any player can deprive another or others of entente by imposing, intentionally or not, a vision of reality that contradicts the others' beliefs and sense of reality.

For an outside observer, the points of disagreement, the divergent visions that form obstacles to successful communication may be easily identifiable. But for those persons who are caught in the impossibility of achieving entente, the first stage is one of shock, of loss of meaning and of radical incomprehension. In dealing with risk, the chances generally are high that one player or another will find himself at some time in this situation. Various fields of knowledge and of understanding are apt to become involved in the construction of the risk situation, each with its own logic. And the knowledge and interpretations of the public are apt not to limit themselves to the concepts and methods of an established risk discipline.

Chateauraynaud and Torny (1999), in their study of three public health risks in France (asbestos, nuclear energy, and BSE), examine the role of the "whistle-blower." Not all risk alerts are well received and adopted by relays; their evaluation involves an assessment of the whistle-blower, who is easily suspected of incompetence, pathological anxiety, or ill intentions. Hautin (1999) analyzes media responses to recent nuclear issues in France and posits a sequence of argument in the development of risk polemics: from technical exchanges, debate moves to the public scene, and is then stemmed (if only temporarily) by political and legal discourse. In the Moirans case, it must be said that while many actors (prosecutor, scientists, Mayor, media, administrators...) were engaged in evaluating the alert, none stopped its evolution but rather, each favored the adoption of a highly unlikely risk hypothesis.

The case of Moirans appears to constitute an exception to the general relay tendency in risk situations. Several aspects of the Moirans shared risk construction appear important here. With regard to the fires, a constant menace for the population, we notice a successful propensity to place the cause or source of these fires outside the scope of what is mundanely human (preferring a marvelous explanation to a human explanation). As it happened, the presence of the high voltage line allowed the risk to be constructed outside the banal (if tragic) criminal realm to attain another dimension. The response to the mystery is sought in science and in technology. Here, the "technologically marvelous" is close to the paranormal, which itself is another explicit part of the risk construction.

The marvels of technology

Another exemplary aspect of this case is the way various *institutional* players take on board the technologically marvelous hypothesis. The prosecutor follows the lead given by the collaborating Mayor and EdF unit head, and calls on experts in electricity, high frequency transmission, radioactivity, etc. These players in turn show themselves willing to test hypotheses on electromagnetic fields, the microwave effect and so forth. The entente among players is not broken. One could in effect imagine one of these experts insisting upon the very low probability of such fires having an electric origin, underlining the usual fact that repeated fires are often arson, and labeling the attention turned on alternate, technological causalities as irrational. Why this was not the case, or why if it was the (unreported) case the technologically marvelous none the less continued to dominate favored explanations, calls for further investigation. The Moirans case could have sparked conflicts among players and provoked rejection of underground cables and loss of confidence in EdF, the managing institution. In other words, the case could have transformed itself into a risk communication crisis. The unusually harmonious entente among players, the tacit agreement to pursue a shared risk construction, prevented this.

Policy implications

The "spontaneous" fires of Moirans did not produce, as might have been expected, a typical crisis of risk communication pitting technological discourse against public understanding. Quite the contrary, science was called upon to provide answers in a wide-open process of questioning. The risk communication process itself seems to have been both spontaneous and successful, in terms of both risk shaping and coping with stress. No player appears to have made explicit reference to risk communication principles, nor called upon experts in that field, in public relations, or otherwise. On the grounds of the Moirans risk experience, what practical or policy implications can be drawn?

Risk, science, and the public: a creative encounter

We observe, with the elements of this case, an absence of rupture between the public (active locally) and the other actors involved (judge, Mayor, technologists and other experts). We see, as a corollary, an absence of polarization and of conflict among the different actors. Since conflict is often found in risk situations characterized by uncertainty, we should ask how this unusual situation has come about.

We notice that the public in Moirans does not reject, a priori, science and technology. The burial of the cable was effected without manifest opposition. We hypothesized above that a collective defense mechanism of denial was in play, allowing the potential risks of this technological arrangement to remain far from consciousness. When the reality of the buried cable resurfaced, the Moirans actors turned principally (but not exclusively) to science to find a satisfactory explanation for the mysterious fires. If we wish, then, to understand the rejection of science and technology that is more typical of risk situations in which the public becomes passionately involved, we must look at the use of science in those contexts, and at the attitudes of those who identify with science. As an example, science may be rejected in contexts where the public observes that it is used rigidly and dogmatically by political or technocratic authority to justify decisions "in everyone's best interest." In such a context, the roles allocated to the public are typically limited to passive acceptance, or to forming an "obstacle" to progress or a "challenge" to policy (Mays et al. 1997, 1999).

In Moirans, the determining factor in the welcoming attitude seen may well be the use made of science: principally, to respond to the open questions posed by residents. Recourse to a sole scientific discipline would have artificially restricted the debate within the narrow boundaries of excessive specialization. Here, the application of several types of scientific (and non-scientific) knowledge allowed the collective frame of reference to remain open.

The Moirans public set the order of the day, laying out the questions to be addressed. Technologists responded to expectations, or even to strong desires, by contributing their knowledge resources. The institutions involved accommodated this process instead of imposing a split between the real world and socially constructed risks (Wynne 1982).

Collective adaptation and coping

Research has shown the health impact of risk situations upon populations. Even in the absence of hazardous substances, stress and traumatic disorders can occur if there is continued exposure to a threat (Baum 1987) or even the bad news announced with a threat (Poumadère 1991). The people of Moirans are subjected to a number of stressors. First of all, fires of unknown origin ignite. The mysterious phenomenon repeats itself and lasts over time, culminating in the death of two residents.

Indicators of adaptation are seen: firemen, for instance, drive to new calls in silence, having observed that their sirens – the prototypical signal of alert – enhance residents' anxiety.

A parallel may be drawn with the psychological defense mechanism we hypothesize was applied to the burial of the cable: the silencing of discourse on the potential risks of this technological installation, evacuated the anxiety that novel event may have caused. Denial is classically an individual response, and some reservations may be expressed about the extension of this notion to describe a collective practice. Still, some elements exist to encourage such an extension.

Baird (1986) showed that smelter workers were not only less likely than non-employees to consider the smelter as a personal health hazard, but also appeared less concerned with environmental pollution in general; such perceptual culture resembles collective denial. Studies of risk perception have highlighted the role of local value placed upon economic and social goods (Fitchen et al. 1987), as well as community capacity to make sense of risk impacts and to cope in a collective manner (Eyles et al. 1993).

In Moirans, risk is not predetermined but is largely mysterious, and thus open to some collective fantasy in the process of risk construction. While the situation of spontaneous fires is certainly stressful, some added stress may be hypothesized in the presence of repressed fears associated with the buried cable. The risk construction process itself, the active search for explanations to a mysterious situation, may be interpreted as a collective process of coping. In this way, the very process of risk amplification and attenuation appears as an implicit strategy of collective adaptation or coping with danger.

Social determinants of risk communication

Moirans highlights the fact that risk construction is deeply embedded in the social context of interaction. The Moirans case also questions the nature of risk when taken outside that context. Risk assessment and comparison do call for the separation of the risk from its setting, but in this case the determining aspects of the risk situation are to be found in large part in that social context.

Policy recommendations, on the strength of the Moirans experience, will thus rely more upon the dynamics of the social context, than upon a hypothetical, a-contextual relationship between the analyst and the risk event per se. The recommendations offered by the Moirans analysis may be most suited to local risk situations, in which individuals from different quarters interact directly and share the work of construction. Guidelines can be drawn from observations of how the Moirans risk communication setting was apparently kept free from polarization. The rationale behind such guidelines is that polarizations are factors that reduce efficiency in risk management, on both the social and the technical levels.

Guidelines for social risk communication

• Each player on the risk scene is attentive to avoid depriving others of their feeling of "entente";

- Science and the irrational are not seen to be mutually exclusive: they can exist side by side in the construction of a risk event;
- Scientists put their skills to the service of community risk construction, rather than opposing that construction; science is "on tap, not on top" (Stirling 1999);
- No player spends time and energy asserting that his worldview is right and that he can prove the others wrong; not even those who will ultimately be proved right by events;
- Pre-existing or emergent concerns, doubts, worries about various objects in the environment are not dismissed, but taken on board as the starting point for expertise and evaluation;
- Such openness may be shared by commissioned experts, who are invited to avoid imposing a priori a conclusion based upon their previous expertise or experience. Rather, they engage with local expertise as if they were researchers embarking upon some new experiment;
- Traditional rationality has its place as well: the gendarmes' investigation follows its own course, although silently and with a hypothesis less spectacular than others;
- Institutions and their representatives (for example, Mayors, the judiciary, firefighters, et al.) can aim at providing the formal framework to ensure that a risk event which mobilizes community members will be addressed in an ongoing manner;
- This framework may have highly formal aspects and yet should be open enough to accommodate the expression of different worldviews;
- Risk amplification and/or attenuation may be recognized in context as an implicit collective strategy of adaptation and coping in the face of overpowering stress or repressed anxiety.

Conclusions

The case of the Moirans fires reminds us that risk is so intricately embedded in its social context that it is difficult, if not impossible, to identify it a priori. Beyond the debate on real vs. perceived risk, it can be said that risk assessment theories and methods in fact provide a means to extract risk, as an object of research and measurement, from its social context.

We have examined, with this case, a situation in which, to the contrary, players from inside and outside the community construct a risk event very much *within* the social context. Once that shared construction has commenced, and the risk event comes into being, SARF can be applied, and various aspects of amplification (for example, ripple effects) can be interpreted or predicted in the light of the particular social dynamic at hand.

Further research could thus bear usefully on what *precedes* the appearance and definition of risk in a given community; that is, on the dynamics that precede and shape the emergence of a designated risk event. This case study brings to attention a potentially important observation: a community may seem quietly to accept a new technological input (in Moirans, the burial of a high voltage line), while in fact repressing fears and anxiety. Only when an opportunity arises (here, mysterious fires) will an outlet for risk expression be found.

It can be objected that the real risk at hand was that of human intervention of a banal, if tragic, sort, and that the other risk interpretations were errors in a social process of causal attribution. This would be missing two important points. First, this position is only possible post hoc, now that the end of the story is known. Second, it would deny the actual Moirans risk experience in all its phases and dimensions, including the entente shared by a heterogeneous group (composed of the public, scientific experts, and decision makers) as to the potential role of the buried high voltage line.

This case shows that scientific or technological risk hypotheses (the electric, microwave, telluric, nuclear, or hydrogen effect) are not systematically rejected by the public. On the contrary, when they appear as part of a desired answer to a mysterious phenomenon, they may be taken up with much attention and seriousness.

On this basis, the place and role of the public in risk analysis may be reconsidered. An international trend is seen toward heightened involvement of the general public in risk issues. In most cases (and contrary to that of Moirans), such public involvement is problematic from the point of view of other actors: public perceptions, attitudes, and demands are commonly thought of as obstacles to projects. Such polarization among actors is reinforced by entrenchment in a purely disciplinary position. A multidisciplinary approach to risk is already one type of response to the difficulties encountered in the past by risk managers. Another step now is taken with the inclusion of local criteria in risk evaluation. Opening the very definition of risk to the ensemble of actors, official and unofficial, and accommodating that opening with novel organization and procedures, are steps apt to encounter resistance from established systems. The Moirans case indicates that mutual acceptance of the roles and visions of the ensemble of partners is possible and may be beneficial: such mutual acceptance is exemplary of a democratic model under which all members of a society are able to exercise their unique capacities. In other words, not only is public involvement in risk issues an empirical fact in democracy, it represents an opportunity for democracy to strengthen itself.

Indeed, the risk amplification and attenuation seen in Moirans constitute a democratic process through which members of the local population investigate and elaborate a past risk event in a way that had been inaccessible to them at the time. Throughout this process, the tools of political and public management are faithfully employed, not to refuse, replace, or render "rational" the collective construction of risk, but to allow it to run perhaps a needed course.

10   Public response to Y2K: social amplification and risk adaptation: or, "how I learned to stop worrying and love Y2K"

Donald G. MacGregor

As the world approached the change of the millennium, intense public interest became focused on the possible consequences of potential failures in computer technologies. These potential failures arose because the mechanism for storing and calculating dates failed to differentiate adequately between the turn of the previous century (1900) and the turn of the millennium (2000 or "Y2K"). In many industrialized nations, much effort was expended by government and industry to insure that critical computer systems, such as Air Traffic Control and financial systems, had been properly "debugged." Though no official tabulation of Y2K costs has yet been done, estimates reported in the media suggest that in the United States approximately $100 billion was expended by government and industry to identify and correct computer problems relating to the Y2K bug, and to prepare for possible disruptions at the turn of the millennium. On the world level, media estimates for Y2K remediation and preparedness are in the $450 billion range. However, despite this high level of effort, press reports left the impression that some systems were inadequately prepared and that regional and local computer systems may have been, in many cases, completely unprepared. Thus, the potential consequences of the "millennium bug" (as some have called it) were not entirely predictable. Indeed, newspaper reports yielded predictions of everything from minor inconveniences (e.g. bank difficulties for a day or two) to major failures of critical infrastructure, including financial markets, electric power control and distribution, telephone service, and food distribution.

Though technical experts generally predicted that problems were likely to be either non-existent or minor, they could not conclude with certainty that no problems would occur. Thus, the broad public, exposed to an

This research was supported in part by the National Science Foundation under Grant no. SBR–9974421 to Decision Science Research Institute, Inc. Special thanks to Joel Blumenthal of the NSF Office of Legislative Affairs for making available the Gallup poll results. Thanks as well to Bruce Tonn, Paul Slovic, James Flynn, Nick Pidgeon, M. V. Rajeev Gowda, and numerous media commentators and writers for delightful conversations about Y2K.

array of press reports concerning Y2K and its possible consequences for their lives, could only conclude that the problem was not completely understood and that certain solutions had not been achieved.

Some anecdotal evidence at the time suggested that, among the general public, concerns about Y2K could translate into behaviors that would not only have a significant impact on society, but could also in and of themselves exacerbate or bring about conditions that were beyond those predictable solely from computer-failure events. For example, many financial planners reported a desire among their clients to move all or part of their portfolios to cash in anticipation of what they perceived as impending failures of the financial markets. Because individuals could exercise control over their liquid assets, they were able effectively to buy insurance against what they perceived as Y2K risks; the price of such insurance to the individual being the loss of opportunity for financial gain in the markets. However, if sufficient numbers of individuals "move to cash," that movement alone could influence markets and (potentially) the perceived need for greater protection. Other examples are available, including potential hoarding of food reserves. Thus, there existed the potential for the behavior of a relatively small number of individuals to "signal" to others the need for them to behave accordingly. Their motivations need not be related to Y2K itself, only to the perceived behavior of those responding to Y2K.

This paper takes a retrospective look at Y2K, and uses concepts from the social amplification of risk framework (Kasperson 1992; Kasperson, Renn, Slovic et al. 1988) to frame the Y2K issue. Y2K is a potentially useful context for applying and extending the social amplification of risk framework because it grew out of a relatively minor technical problem that attained a high level of public attention over a relatively short time frame (approximately two years), and for which a resolution of the risk was at a fixed point in time. Thus, the dynamics of social amplification can potentially be seen more clearly than in contexts where a risk issue is more slow to emerge, or for which the risk issue is a long-standing problem (e.g. radiation risks). Moreover, the social impact of Y2K went well beyond the technical consequences (e.g. computer failures) and in the United States at least, extended into beliefs about major social revolution, including cataclysmic change in society. Thus, these "ripple" effects extended outward from beliefs about the impact of Y2K on our technological environment, to impacts of Y2K on our fundamental ideology about the appropriate role of technology in human societies.

Empirical data for this examination come from two sources. One source is a set of survey studies conducted in 1998 and 1999 by the Gallup polling organization for the National Science Foundation and a United States newspaper *USA Today* (1999). The surveys were conducted by telephone during 9–13 December 1998 and again during 5–7 March 1999.[1] This time span traversed a significant increase in media attention to the Y2K issue occasioned by the change in the new year.

A second data source is a set of survey studies conducted by Decision Research in 1999. The surveys were conducted by telephone during September and again during December, just before the turn of the millennium.[2] Both the Gallup and Decision Research surveys were Random Digit Dial (RDD) household surveys of the adult population of the United States.

Perception of Y2K

It's far too late, and things are far too bad, for pessimism. (*Dee Block, Founder, Visa International*)

Perceived significance of Y2K problem

As might be expected, the three-month interval between the two Gallup survey administrations resulted in a greater awareness of Y2K issues. In the United States, the turn of the new year from 1998 to 1999 was accompanied by a great deal of media coverage of Y2K, much of which included speculations about the potential seriousness of the problem and what individuals might do personally to manage or mitigate Y2K-related hazards. However, the more people became aware of the Y2K issue, the less they appeared to perceive that it would result in significant problems either in general or for them personally (see table 10.1).

As the 1999 calendar year progressed, concerns about Y2K moderated and even attenuated. From October 1999 to December 1999, general concern about Y2K declined (see table 10.2). For most people contacted in the Decision Research Y2K Survey, levels of concern remained the same or decreased over the nine months prior to questioning.

In general, respondents did not see Y2K as a major problem for them personally, though most expected at least minor difficulties. However, the difficulties were anticipated to be of some duration, ranging from a matter of a few days to weeks or months. From December 1998 to March 1999 there was a slight decrease in the proportion of respondents who thought that Y2K problems would last only a few days, as opposed to longer periods (see table 10.3).

It appears from these survey results that media reporting of Y2K tended to lead to a decrease in the perceived severity of Y2K problems, as

---

[1] Gallup survey results are used by permission of the National Science Foundation, Office of Legislative and Public Affairs. Respondents were 1,032 individuals 18+ years of age randomly selected from all United States households.

[2] $N = 406$ and 405 for the September and December surveys, respectively.

Table 10.1 *Perceived seriousness of Y2K-related problems*

	major problems %	minor problems %	no problems %	DKNA %
"Do you think that computer mistakes due to the Year-2000 issue will cause major, minor, or no problems at all?"				
December 1998	34	51	10	5
March 1999	21	65	12	2
"Do you think that (Y2K) will cause major, minor, or no problems at all for you personally?"				
December 1998	14	53	30	3
March 1999	9	56	32	3

	a great deal %	some %	not much %	nothing at all %
"How much have you seen or heard about the (Y2K) problem?"				
December 1998	39	40	13	8
March 1999	56	30	11	3

Source: National Science Foundation/*USA Today* Gallup Poll (1999).

evidenced by both a reduction in the perception of Y2K as problematic for society and for individuals personally, as well as a reduction in the duration of Y2K-related problems should they occur.

Personal Y2K risk management

A distinctive aspect of the Y2K issue is the potential for individuals to undertake self-protective actions that could potentially mitigate or manage the impact of Y2K on their personal lives. For example, individuals concerned about possible power outages caused by Y2K-related computer problems could purchase oil lamps, power generators, or gas-powered heaters. Since the actual Y2K event would occur near midwinter for many people in the United States (and other nations as well), press reports on Y2K frequently mentioned this as a possible inconvenience or difficulty. Likewise, potential problems with the operation of

Table 10.2 *Degree of concern about Y2K*

	not at all %	slightly %	somewhat %	very %
"In general, are you (very, somewhat, slightly, not at all) concerned about the Y2K problem?"				
October 1999	29.9	39.8	22.0	7.7
December 1999	36.2	41.1	15.8	6.7
	increased[a] %	same %	decreased %	
"In the past nine months, would you say that your level of concern about Y2K has decreased (substantially, slightly), stayed the same, increased (slightly, substantially)?				
October 1999	14.1	49.4	35.8	
December 1999	15.8	45.3	37.9	

[a] Response categories "substantially" and "slightly" are collapsed.
Source: Survey of Public Perception of Y2K, Decision Science Research Institute (1999).

Table 10.3 *Perceived duration of Y2K-related problems[a]*

	few days %	several months %	several weeks %	more than a year %
December 1998	23	30	38	11
March 1999	15	30	37	7

[a] Rows may not total to 100% due to DKNA responses.
Source: National Science Foundation/*USA Today* Gallup Y2K Poll (1999).

financial systems were also reported in the press, possibly leading people to anticipate keeping additional sums of cash on hand at the turn of the millennium. However, it appears that people's intentions with regard to Y2K-related perceptions varied widely depending on the specific type of potential disruption. Table 10.4 shows the percentage of individuals expressing intent to take protective actions for a number of possible problems.

The results in table 10.4 are interesting from the perspective of the relative importance that people appear to place on some self-protective

Table 10.4 *Percentage of individuals reporting "probably will"*
undertake specific Y2K-related protections

	December 1998 %	March 1999 %
obtain confirmation of financial records	65	66
avoid air travel around 1/1/2000	47	54
stockpile food and water	26	39
withdraw and set aside cash	31	30
buy a generator or wood stove	17	24
withdraw all money from bank	16	15

Source: National Science Foundation / *USA Today* Gallup Y2K Poll (1999).

behaviors. As early as December 1998, over half of the respondents planned to obtain special documentation or confirmation of key financial records, such as bank accounts, retirement accounts, and credit records. Nearly half (47 percent) also planned to avoid air travel near the turn of the year. At the March 1999 survey administration, almost 40 percent planned to stockpile household supplies and nearly a third planned to set aside cash. Some significant increases in the rate of Y2K self-management also appeared between the two survey administrations, particularly for food/water stockpiling and for air travel avoidance. A more detailed perspective on Y2K self-management of risk can be seen in table 10.5 that shows awareness of potential Y2K disruptions, as well as whether those surveyed had considered a plan for dealing with the disruption.

By October and December of 1999, most people were aware of the potential disruptions to major technological infrastructure such as electrical power, water, food, and finances. Large numbers were also sensitized to the possibility that social disruption and unrest (e.g. crime, vandalism) might occur at the turn of the millennium. In general, about half or more of the respondents in the Decision Research Y2K Survey had considered some type of plan to deal with potential disruption caused by water, food, or cash shortages. Slightly smaller percentages had considered a plan to deal with electrical outages; not a surprising result since this type of disruption is much more challenging to deal with than water, food, and/or cash. Only about a third of respondents had considered a plan to deal with social unrest. Again, few options were typically available, though advertisements and marketing of firearms in the United States increased during this period, suggesting that self-protection through gun ownership may have been viewed by some as a possible risk management measure.

Changes in levels of preparation between October and December 1999 for possible Y2K disruptions are visible on a small scale in the percentages

Table 10.5 *Percentage of individuals reporting awareness of potential disruptions due to Y2K*

disruption	heard of disruption %	considered a plan[a] %
electrical power outage		
October 1999	87.2	46.6
December 1999	90.6	52.0
water shortage		
October 1999	70.9	64.9
December 1999	70.4	68.8
food shortage		
October 1999	71.6	61.9
December 1999	78.8	58.4
cash shortage		
October 1999	83.2	57.7
December 1999	85.5	55.0
social unrest/crime		
October 1999	62.5	30.8
December 1999	66.5	37.2

[a] Only respondents who had heard of disruption were asked if they had considered a plan.
Source: Survey of Public Perception of Y2K, Decision Science Research Institute (1999).

of people who considered some type of plan. Only for two of the five disruptions (i.e. food shortage, cash shortage) did the percentage of respondents considering a plan not increase. The largest change was for social unrest, which was also the potential disruption people least anticipated over the course of the year. Here again, media attention during the last part of 1999 emphasized social risks, such as crime and vandalism. Also, as more people expressed an indication that they might personally hold cash in anticipation of cash shortages, authorities began warning people about the potential for robbery.

An interesting aspect of these results is the contrast they bear to those in tables 10.2, 10.3, and 10.4. Taken together, it appears that as respondents became more aware of the Y2K issue and (potentially) its meaning for their personal lives, they became slightly less concerned (tables 10.2 and 10.3), and tended to see the problems occurring from Y2K as of lesser duration (table 10.4). However, with greater awareness of Y2K issues, they also were more likely to undertake greater self-management to decrease (ostensibly) the potential impact of Y2K on their personal lives. Thus, the more media attention was paid to the Y2K issue, the more their concerns about Y2K were "translated" into personal protective actions.

This may have given them a greater perception of control over an issue so large and (potentially) incomprehensible as their focus of concern was directed to those things that they *could* undertake as part of a personal risk management strategy.

Does this mean that, on balance, the overall effect of Y2K as a media event was an attenuation of risk perception? There is good reason to argue that, on the whole, it does not. Indeed, people likely became more aware of Y2K as an issue that went well beyond a simple matter of problems with dates in computers, and extended into potentially real consequences for their personal lives. Those impacts could include not only inconveniences relating to the availability of money and food, but also potential risks to health and safety.

The apparent attenuation of concern may actually be an amplification of risk through mechanisms of self-protective behavior. Thus, concern is transformed through, for example, the "work of worry" (e.g. Janis 1958; MacGregor 1991) into a productive risk management strategy that is it-self a response to a risk issue. Those strategies can consume significant amounts of not only time and energy, but also of capital resources. Indeed, the more individuals who plan and undertake such strategies, the greater the likelihood that others will as well through processes of social modeling, facilitation, and group-related behavior. Thus, the practical significance of survey results such as those shown in tables 10.4 and 10.5 may be misinterpreted and under-appreciated; for example, it may re-quire far less than 50 percent of the population to initially undertake a self-protective behavior for others to follow suit, even if those others have initially expressed an intention not to undertake that same behavior. We know relatively little about how risk management behaviors undertaken by individuals influence the likelihood that others will undertake those same behaviors. We can only speculate that, since risk perceptions evolve from and are facilitated by social processes, personal behaviors intended to control exposure and/or reduce risk are determined and guided in the same way. Therefore, each individual's "guide to action" is derived in part from their personal perceptions of risk and its need for reduction, as well as by what they experience others around them perceiving, believing, and doing.

Risk–risk trade-offs in self-protective behavior

Prevent what you can, manage what you can't. (*James Lee Witt, Head, US FEMA*)

People face many risks in life. Some of the most studied have been soci-etal in scope; for example, chemicals in the environment, nuclear fuels, automobile hazards, and communicable diseases. For some risks, individual responses in terms of self-protective behavior are difficult or impossible to undertake. Thus, individuals concerned about the effects of industrial chemicals on ozone depletion can do relatively little to protect themselves, except perhaps through the mechanisms of participatory democracy (should it exist in their country) to help bring about change through regulatory or political processes. However, for some types of hazards individuals can take actions that they perceive as risk reducing. For example, people concerned about motor vehicle accidents can reduce their personal risk through more vigilant driving habits, by wearing a seat belt, or simply by driving less to reduce their exposure. In general, these personal risk management strategies work to the net benefit of the individual; by wearing a seat belt drivers reduce their potential injury should they be involved in an accident without exposing themselves to any additional risk from the fact of wearing it.

However, some prescribed self-protective behaviors (e.g. seat belts) are not always (or by everyone) perceived as risk reducing. Recent public concerns in the United States about risks associated with air bag deployment in motor vehicles reflected a perception that (at least some) drivers perceive themselves to be at greater risk from exposure to the risk reduction technology than they are without it. Indeed, early in the United States motor-vehicle seat belt implementation program, a common concern among the public centered around a perception that individuals could be trapped in their cars by a seat belt and, therefore, sustain injuries (or even mortality) that otherwise would not occur were they "thrown clear" of their vehicle. Such views were sometimes advanced as reasons why the inconvenience of wearing a seat belt might not be justified in terms of risk reduction.

But, let's look at the other side of risk reduction. Are there occasions when people may sometimes undertake self-protective measures that could expose them to greater hazard than the hazard that they intend to manage? Can self-protective behaviors based on perceptions of a risk or hazard potentially lead to greater likelihood or severity of harm than if no self-protection was undertaken? Drawing from the Y2K case, there may be reason to suspect that people do not make the same kinds of risk–risk trade-offs that a technical analysis might suggest that they should. As an example, consider the Y2K personal risk management strategy of purchasing an electrical power generator or kerosene lanterns to offset the perceived risk of loss of electrical power. Both devices require the storage and use of volatile fuels, which in themselves constitute a safety hazard due to their flammability. The same fuels also pose environmental hazards if not stored, handled, and disposed of properly. In addition, power

Table 10.6 *Y2K preparedness measures and associated risks*

perceived Y2K hazard	preparedness measure(s)	preparedness risk(s)
loss of electrical power	• power generators • oil lamps • gas heaters	• gasoline storage (fire, fumes) • suffocation (CO, improper placement of generator) • physical injury (e.g. starting generator, unloading from truck) • electrocution • fire hazard
food/water shortage	• stockpile food • stockpile water	• contamination • spoilage • poisoning (self-purification of water) • food shortages
money/cash shortage	• stockpile cash • withdraw funds from banks	• crime • cash shortages
social disruption	• acquire firearm(s)	• accidental discharge of firearm • unintended/unanticipated use of firearm

generators also pose the hazard of electrocution, since their use often involves connections to existing electrical circuitry in the home. Various types of lamps, candles, and stoves (e.g. butane, propane) carry the risks of exposed flame. Table 10.6 presents some commonly proposed Y2K self-protective actions, along with the risk the action is intended to mitigate, as well as risk created by the action itself.

How do people weigh these risks against the risks of, for example, power outages of varying duration? What psychological mechanisms come into play that may mitigate against a full consideration of risk in personal Y2K risk management strategies? Tentative answers to these questions can be gained by examining how people's actions with regard to hazards are guided. One source of potential guidance is "folk wisdom" or homilies that often serve as rules of thumb or epithets. For example, *better safe than sorry, a stitch in time saves nine,* or *look before you leap* all offer precautionary words of advice to the individual that prudence is sometimes appropriate. Indeed, the essence of these relatively simple principles sometimes appears in more formalized risk management strategies such as the "precautionary principle" (e.g. Foster et al. 2000). However, homilies such as these go in one direction only. That is, they fail to caution the individual against actions that might in themselves create the potential for hazard. Thus they don't coax or guide the individual into considering fully the risks of self-protective behavior. For example, oil lamps purchased to offset the risk (or inconvenience) of power failure on the principle *better safe than sorry* may focus "safety" more on being safe from power failure than being safe from fire. Individuals who adhere very strictly to such risk management adages may actually undertake a greater number of self-protective actions, and may expose themselves to greater overall risk than those who are more considerate, choose more deliberatively, and with awareness of offsetting risks.

Self-management of risk is also guided by many of the principles that have come to us through risk perception research. Risks perceived as ones for which individuals have relatively little control over exposure draw significant psychological attention (e.g. Slovic 1987, 1992). Hypothetically, people can be expected to be concerned about a risk issue as large and omnibus in its potential impacts as Y2K and, therefore, seek means to control their exposure. Personal risk management strategies that emphasize compensating for power outages, storing food, and maintaining cash on hand are all mechanisms of personal control and may have decreased the perceived personal impact (and risk) of the Y2K event. Concerns about Y2K itself as an issue may be exacerbated not only by general media coverage, but also by disagreements between technical, scientific, and government experts about the extent and seriousness of the problem, or even disagreements about whether there is a problem and who will be affected. Conflicts between experts can generate within the general public (deep) feelings of concern that arise from a perception that "if the experts don't know then who does?" In these situations, uncertainties are heightened and risk perceptions are elevated.

Other research in risk perception suggests that risks and benefits tend to be perceived in terms of a balancing mechanism; when perceptions of risk are increased, perceptions of benefit decrease, and vice versa (e.g. Alhakami and Slovic 1994). More recent research on the role of affective processes in risk perception suggests that risks and benefits are evaluated in terms of an underlying encoding along a "good–bad" psychological continuum, with the result that things perceived as "more good" are thereby perceived as "less bad" (e.g. Peters and Slovic 1996; Finucane et al. 2000; MacGregor et al. 2000). As a result, the kind of trade-off evaluation of risks and benefits that would be expected from normative theories or models of risk analysis fail to be appreciated or employed psychologically.

In the Y2K case, we might expect similar mechanisms to be at work as a guide to both risk perception as well as self-protective behavior. Indeed, many of the risk management measures that appeared in the media (e.g. storing food, cash, candles, lanterns) are relatively low-cost means of self-insuring against what may be perceived as a quite large and incomprehensible risk. The benefits of computer technologies that brought on the Y2K crisis (if it can be called that) may have paled somewhat in light of the voluminous Y2K risk "discussion." Thus, it is very likely that Y2K was not perceived as a risk offsetting years of benefit from technology. Rather, the benefits of technology are called into question even more as the risk issues are discussed and implications for people's personal lives are drawn more clearly.

From the perspective of self-protective behavior and risk–risk tradeoffs, such behaviors are planned and potentially undertaken with anticipated benefit of risk reduction. Thus, Y2K self-management of risk is hypothetically perceived in terms of the benefits that the behaviors will produce (e.g. light, heat, food, available cash). As a result, the perceptions of risk associated with the behaviors producing these benefits are likely to be attenuated, perhaps more so than they would be under other circumstances. For example, people may have intuitively discounted the risks of, for example, oil lamps in the home more when they were purchased because of Y2K concerns than if purchased at some other time.

Furthermore, the affective processing associated with risk perception may work against people intuitively decomposing a self-protective action to reveal underlying risks that should also be of concern. For example, if the purchase of a power generator is viewed as an aggregate benefit in light of Y2K concerns, then the encoding of the generator as a "good" may at least partially inhibit tendencies to see its other "bad" qualities that can potentially expose its owner (or family) to harm. Thus, fuel may be encoded as a feature of a generator and not as a separate hazard associated with the generator. However, people may see a heightened risk from storing additional gasoline in or around the home if the risk was evaluated outside of the context of owning a generator for Y2K purposes. This general tendency may be particularly exacerbated in the case of firearms purchased with the intention of self-protection against social disruption associated with Y2K. For example, an individual purchases a gun to reduce the perceived risk of crime, and the perception of that hazard focuses attention and thought on scenarios or circumstances in which possible use of the firearm is anticipated. That focusing hypothetically reduces one's ability to conceptualize or recognize other classes of situations in which the firearm might be used in which its owner or others are exposed (e.g. domestic situations, cleaning or handling of a firearm, children tampering with a firearm).

Worldviews and perceptions of Y2K

Y2K provides an opportunity to understand the technological vulnerabilities that can arise from human shortsightedness. (*US Senator Robert F. Bennett, Chair, US Senate Special Committee on the Year 2000 Technology Problem*)

How many have said a prayer to God and asked for things to slow down? We may get that prayer answered. (*Kathy Garcia, Y2K Community Organizer*)

On the surface, Y2K was a technical matter, a "glitch" created by idiosyncrasies in how computers are programmed and dates are stored. However, Y2K also stimulated awareness, interest, and response at another (and much deeper) level that went beyond its technical features. This was, in part, reflected in the content of media coverage of Y2K, as well as anecdotal, public comments about Y2K and its broader meaning.

An interesting feature of the Y2K phenomenon is the degree to which it became a community preparedness issue, and the role that churches and religious organizations played in facilitating and organizing Y2K preparedness. Though Y2K was ostensibly a potential failure of technology, the public response was (at least in part) somewhat like that for a natural hazard, such as a hurricane. In this light, Y2K appeared to carry with it some features of an "Act of God" in that the meaning attributed to Y2K goes beyond its technological features and may extend into deeper worldviews having religious themes.

Worldviews are general attitudes or beliefs that predispose people toward different outlooks and that influence their judgments about complex issues, such as social policy and organization (Buss et al. 1986; Cotgrove 1982; Dake 1991; Jasper 1990). Though research on worldviews has been motivated in part by the desire to identify dimensions along which individuals can be differentiated in terms of their viewpoints regarding technology in society, a single individual can hold multiple worldviews depending on situation and social circumstance.

A good example is the "fatalist" worldview, an outlook which many people hold at least in some situations or in some contexts of their lives. This perspective need not necessarily be interpreted pejoratively to mean personal defeat. Fatalistic thought is a common means of interpreting the world and embodies the sense of inevitability that is present in most of the world's historical religions (e.g. Smith 1986). For example, in a 1984 Yankelovich poll, 39 percent of a public sample agreed that "When the Bible predicts that the earth will be destroyed by fire, it's telling us that a nuclear war is inevitable" (Jones 1985). Modern (and non-religious) fatalism can also reside in secular views about apocalyptic events, such as nuclear war and environmental destruction. Wojcik (1997), in a comprehensive review of apocalyptic theories, notes that in traditional religious apocalypticism "Faith and fatalism are... interwoven into the fabric of apocalyptic thought: a profound fatalism for a world believed to be irredeemably evil is entwined with the faith for a predestined, perfect age of harmony and human fulfillment." However, secular apocalypticism appears devoid of an underlying redemptive meaning and moral order, and thus is "characterized by a sense of hopelessness and despair" (Wojcik 1997, p. 4).

The sense of an approaching apocalypse may be a major attitudinal theme for a significant portion of the American public. Within this theme, catastrophic occurrences bring about devastation on a vast scale, destroying most of humanity and its trappings. Along with this destruction comes a cleansing and a rebirth, and (in many themes) a survival of the righteous or the "true believers." Thus, in the apocalyptic view, the world is not a continuous process of growth and evolution, but a cyclical process of expansion and *de*volution, in which the future is finite and inevitable. As philosopher and theologian Martin Buber notes, in apocalyptic thought "everything is predetermined, all human decisions are only sham struggles" (Buber 1957, p. 201).

Though the public is quite supportive of efforts to restore the environment (as evidenced by their endorsement of attitude statements), their individual propensity to act can be compromised by other attitudes and views that suggest a belief in either a personal incapacity for effecting real change or belief in an inevitable future that is simply a matter of fate. Indeed, many of the images that have been used to identify environmental problems may actually contribute to this sense of fatalism. For example, most images in the media are those of environmental catastrophe. While images of disaster and environmental collapse can serve to draw attention to environmental problems, they do not necessarily suggest or indicate the behaviors needed to produce the opposite state of the image. These images may actually confirm apocalyptic beliefs, at least for some, thereby exacerbating their feelings of the futility of human action in the face of what they see as the ultimate fate of humanity.

The potential role of religiously based worldviews in public reaction to Y2K can be glimpsed in table 10.7. Here we see a moderate relationship between survey respondents' self-expressed importance of religion in their lives and anticipated preparations for Y2K, particularly for actions involving stockpiling of essential goods. These data, of course, do not provide a firm basis for conclusions about religious views and the impacts of technology on society. However, they suggest that religious beliefs are a potential component of worldviews that need to be studied

Table 10.7 *Percentage of individuals reporting "probably will" undertake specific Y2K-related protections according to importance of religion*

	Religion "extremely important"	Religion "less than very important"
obtain confirmation of financial records	65	62
avoid air travel around 1/1/2000	48	46
stockpile food and water	37	17
withdraw and set aside cash	36	27
buy a generator or wood stove	23	11
withdraw all money from bank	22	11

Source: National Science Foundation / *USA Today* Gallup Y2K Poll (1999).

further. We speculate that the Y2K issue was viewed in part as a "signal" that humanity has exceeded its ability to manage technology, and for those with deep religious worldviews and convictions as a sign from God that humanity has in some ways strayed from the appropriate path. In this sense, the Y2K event may have represented as much a spiritual crisis as it did a technological one, the meaning of which could only be fully understood by individual reflection on the (appropriate) relationship between humanity and technology. Such reflection may have led individuals to explore and examine their underlying values, which in turn may have led (at least some) people to consider lifestyle changes which they may have already been predisposed toward. "Ripple effects" may have occurred at a psychological level in which widening and deepening levels of psychological questioning accompany Y2K.

Y2K: environmental options and opportunities

The Y2K bug provides us with an extraordinary opportunity to ask ourselves the profound questions which have been buried by our wealth and our technology. It is a time for us to ask what we really value and how we can preserve the ecological systems on which all life depends. It is a wonderful time to be alive. (*Robert Theobald, Economist and Futurist*)

The Y2K experience may also reveal a special sense in which technological failure and its social impacts are both a source of concern and of satisfaction. Thus, Y2K has both approach and avoidance properties. Sometimes there may be comfort in fears – they are things that people can prepare for, they can draw meaning from them, they are purposeful activities. At the very least, Y2K may have provided many people with the rationale they needed to (at least partially) withdraw from a hectic, over-energized society and lifestyle, or to at least question their role in modern life.

Ripple effects can also occur because Y2K themes interlink with other prevalent attitudinal themes in society and for which individuals may have strong affinity. One such theme is environmental protection and "sustainable development." For example, an announcement for a Y2K preparedness workshop conducted through Portland State University with the cooperation of the City of Portland, announced the following through its Internet site:

In addition to "Y2K 101: an introduction to the Y2K problem," workshop topics will include sustainable approaches to:

- non-hybrid seed cultivation
- food storage
- urban gardening
- energy conservation
- alternative transportation
- water purification and storage

- bartering skills
- community building skills
- fuels and other energy sources
- working with Y2K-triggered emotions
- community and household preparedness

We speculate that perceptions of Y2K activated and signaled other thematic associations relating to environmental protection and restoration that are themselves related to views about the wisdom of minimalism and conservation. These in turn may be predictive of lifestyle attitudes (and possibly future behaviors) in the direction of less reliance on technology and, in some cases, society itself.

Y2K in the year 2000 – the morning after

Frankly, I think we'll be lucky if (on January 1, 2000) the (Global Positioning System) just doesn't come on, because then we'll know we have a problem. Our bigger fear is going to be that the system seems to work fine but the data is unreliable. That's a far worse problem. (*John J. Hamre, US Deputy Defense Secretary*)

Much of the media coverage of Y2K focused on the actual change of date from 31 December 1999, to 1 January 2000, and the possible impacts on computer technologies. However, some technical experts proposed that many of the "real" problems would not actually appear until well into the new year. Some of these problems can occur because computers fail to operate reliably; others because seldom-used computer functions activate only as circumstances require.

However, technology often fails to operate as it is intended. Indeed, accidents, failures, disruptions, and the like are a "normal" part of technological operations (Perrow 1999), even without Y2K. The question is the meaning of such failures, the attributions given to their cause, and the effects of these attributions on perceptions of technology and technological risk management. For example, will power outages that routinely occur during the winter in many parts of the United States be attributed to a normal failure of that technology, or will they be seen as a broader and perhaps more insidious carryover of Y2K? Will some technologies become further stigmatized (should they fail, even "normally") simply because they have failed in the year 2000? Will confidence and trust in technology and, particularly, the institutions and individuals that manage it, erode further because failures are conveniently attributed to a new and more fundamental technological problem in the form of the "Y2K bug"? This can be conceptualized as a special kind of ripple effect in which a strong metaphor for technological failure enters the cultural lexicon and becomes a defining feature for how technology is perceived. Thus, technological failures and crashes may become collectively viewed through a single, over-arching concept that provides a convenient explanatory mechanism for why such failures occur, and provides as well the kind of conceptual simplicity that promotes media reporting. Indeed, the famous "Watergate" incident in United States politics during the Nixon administration has provided a metaphorical base for the many "gates" that have since made news (e.g. Irangate, Monicagate, White Watergate), to the extent that many United States citizens recognize the meaning of the term when it appears in the media (including its negative affective loading and suggestion of political/moral impropriety) without knowing the event from which it arose. Thus, social amplification processes may bring about fundamental change in the cultural references and language people use to think and reason about technology.

International response to Y2K

The globalization of computer technologies has caused problems like Y2K to have both national and international impacts. However, the general tenor of concern and response to Y2K was not everywhere equal around the globe. For emerging nations who lack basic infrastructure, relative inattention to Y2K is understandable in light of their more pressing concerns. None the less, even among industrialized nations, concerns about Y2K varied considerably. Indeed, in Great Britain government officials faced difficulties energizing both public and private organizations to be sufficiently concerned to take steps toward Y2K preparedness. Experiences in other European industrialized nations (e.g. France, Germany) appear to have been similar.

Why, then, did Y2K engender so much concern and response in the United States, while other nations with similarly sophisticated technological infrastructure appeared to have been more cavalier? Answers to this question are only speculative at this point, but perhaps provide a hint of how different nations' experiences with social disruption and upheaval condition them to respond differently to novel situations. For example, most European nations have, within recent history, experienced major disruptions to social and technological infrastructure due to wars. Britain managed to exist as a society during heavy bombing during World War II, once in 1940 and again in 1944 under rocket attack. Likewise, Germany and France have lived through similar devastations. These events are part of the social histories of many people alive in them today. Indeed, most nations in the world have had (or are now having) some form of catastrophic social experience that fractures the normal order of things and leaves their technological infrastructure either dysfunctional or unreliable. Yet, in the United States this same type of national-level disruption has not occurred since, perhaps, the Civil War near the middle of the nineteenth century.

It can be argued, of course, that the apparently heightened level of concern about Y2K in the United States came about because the United States has more to lose. Perhaps the United States is more dependent on its technological infrastructure than other nations, and therefore should be more anxious about its functioning properly. However, it seems more likely the case that United States society has come to equate social well-being with technological integrity, perhaps (at least) more than its industrialized counterparts around the globe where experiences of the past century have shown that people and nations survive catastrophic devastation of the "built" environment by turning to their social and cultural resources.

Implications of Y2K for the social amplification of risk framework

From the perspective of SARF, the Y2K case appears to be almost a pure example of how a relatively minor technical problem can expand through social amplification processes into a major issue of national and international concern. However, as much as the Y2K case speaks to the power of social amplification to influence how individuals and societies respond to events, it also reveals potentially more subtle aspects of the dynamic properties of social response to risk. A noticeable feature of the Y2K story is a strong and rapid orienting response toward the potential hazards of large-scale computer failures, prompted in large part by the media's reporting of Y2K, but also by actions taken by industry and government leaders to address what was perceived at the time as a national (and international) crisis. These responses were, in a sense, regenerative and lent additional credence and validity to concerns already being expressed in the media. Thus, like an amplifier that takes as one source of input its own output, the gain was enhanced, with a corresponding sharp rise in amplification.

However, also noticeable in the Y2K story is an interesting societal response over time marked by personal risk management strategies to deal with perceived consequences of not only computer failures, but also larger-scale social impacts. We speculate that these strategies are mechanisms by which individuals (and groups to some extent) adapt to situations or circumstances that pose threats (perceived or actual) to their well-being. These adaptive responses to the environment may, under some circumstances, act to *attenuate* risk, or at least to reduce the amount of risk amplification. In the case of Y2K, adaptation may have come in the form of specific plans or actions formulated by individuals with the intention of reducing the potential consequences to themselves of social disruption caused by Y2K, such as storing food, holding extra cash, or limiting travel during the turn of the year. The attenuating properties of these actions can be seen in the declining level of concern about Y2K as the 1999 calendar year progressed.

Another adaptive behavior applied by many people regarding Y2K was in the form of social interaction (e.g. meetings, conversations), by which Y2K issues were discussed, information was shared, and the meaning of Y2K was clarified and integrated into people's lives. Indeed, some of the attitudes people held about Y2K and behavioral intentions they expressed are examples of the complementary functions of assimilation and accommodation that are a part of adaptation. Many people assimilated Y2K by linking its features to other consistent attitudes or beliefs, thereby giving it a meaning in terms of pre-existing psychological and cultural concepts. For some, this included apocalyptic notions of (desirable) societal change on a grand scale. Extending the social amplification of risk framework to include adaptive mechanisms may help to understand better the dynamic properties of societal response to risk and risk management, and may also provide the basis for a predictive model of risk amplification.

11 The social dynamics of environmental risk perception: implications for risk communication research and practice

Tom Horlick-Jones, Jonathan Sime*, and Nick Pidgeon

Interest in risk communication has become increasingly widespread in recent years, attracting a global constituency of attention within government and industry alike. Starting, as it did, as an attempt to drive home the perceived wisdom of scientific risk assessments to unconvinced lay audiences, it has now diversified to encompass a number of wider objectives. As Baruch Fischhoff (1995, p. 138), in his recent review, concluded, whilst the starting-point of this shift may be parodied as "all we have to do is get the numbers right," the current position amounts to "all we have to do is make (lay publics) partners." Indeed, the emphasis on process issues: decision making, fairness, trust and "meaningful participation," and ideas about democracy, have come to play a central role in both the research and policy development agendas (e.g. Chess et al. 1995; Renn,

* **Jonathan D. Sime [1950–2001]**
On 16 January 2001, Jonathan Sime died suddenly, aged just 50. A significant contributor to the literature on risk and human behavior over a period of some twenty-five years, Jonathan combined the roles of scholar and consultant in the field of environmental psychology. His work on behavior in fires and other hazardous environments, associated aspects of risk communication, and the implications of this knowledge for design practice was especially important. Equally memorable was his passionate commitment to the practical application of social science knowledge in ways that appreciate human intelligence and creativity. At the time of his death he held a visiting chair at the University of Ulster, and he had just taken up a post at the University of Utah in the United States. He will be sadly missed.

We are particularly grateful to Peter Simmons, who helpfully provided detailed notes on our original manuscript. We also thank Mick Bloor, Graham Murdock, Judith Petts, Claire Marris, Lindsay Prior, Karen Henwood, and Miranda Green for a number of useful discussions on the topics we have addressed. We began this work with Barry Turner, who sadly did not live to see its completion; however his influence has stayed with us. The paper draws on research conducted as part of the European Commission's 4th Framework Programme (contract ENV4–CT96–0265), and we are pleased to acknowledge the collaboration of Ana Prades Lopez, Bruna De Marchi, and our other Spanish and Italian colleagues on that project. It also draws on work supported by the United Kingdom Economic and Social Research Council under its Risk and Human Behaviour program (awards L211252044 and L211272006) and the Leverhulme Trust as part of the Understanding Risk program.

Webler, and Wiedemann 1995; Stern and Fineberg, 1996; Shell United Kingdom 1998; Department of Health 1998; United Kingdom Interdepartmental Liaison Group on Risk Assessment 1998b; Bennett and Calman 1999; House of Lords 2000).

Underlying these changes, a number of interconnected social and political developments looms large. We are witnessing times of rapid change, economic re-structuring, and globalization, featuring a huge expansion of media and electronic communication, and significant cultural fragmentation. According to current wisdom, these changes, in combination, have produced a politicization of risk issues, the emergence of the active consumer and a new propensity for "moral panics" (Beck 1992; Giddens 1991; Thompson 1998).

Within the new risk communication agenda, the impact of social science research into risk perception has been significant, albeit in sometimes rather pragmatic forms. Despite ongoing debates in some quarters (Okrent and Pidgeon 1998), a recognition of the social and cultural dimensions of risk has now become part of the everyday talk of policy makers in government and industry on both sides of the Atlantic. Given the diversity of social science perspectives on risk, the promise of an integrated approach to risk communication that cuts across disciplinary and conceptual boundaries might be regarded as something of a policy maker's dream. Just such an approach is offered by advocates of the social amplification of risk framework, otherwise known as "SARF" (Kasperson, Renn, Slovic et al. 1988; Kasperson 1992; Renn 1992c; Pidgeon 1999).

SARF has proved influential in the academic risk literature, especially among North American scholars; however, serious criticisms have appeared. Rayner (1988), for example, has observed that in seeking to synthesize different conceptual approaches to understanding risk, SARF threatens to gloss over the tensions that exist between different paradigms. He also notes the possibility that the metaphors embedded within SARF may not be commensurate with the richness and complexity of human risk-related behavior.

Similar criticisms have recently been voiced in connection with the social impact of media coverage of risk issues. SARF, it is argued, fails to take full account of the diversity of the media and its dynamic role as a *symbolic* information system. Moreover, lay audiences are more than mere passive "receivers" or spectators (Petts, Horlick-Jones, and Murdock 2001; Murdock et al. this volume chapter 7); rather, their *active* voice and participation is critical to the sense-making dynamic.

The thrust of these critiques amounts to a caution that those features of SARF which make it most attractive to policy makers – its simplicity and its conceptualization in terms of an almost mechanical, engineering,

model of communication – are those very features that may create difficulties. As such, the adoption of SARF may be seen as part of a wider
tendency in which the incorporation of social science ideas into the policy
agenda has in practice amounted to a selection of those ideas that do not
appear to challenge the dominant positivist philosophical perspective of
natural science (Horlick-Jones 1998, 2000).

In this chapter we discuss some of the implications for, and possible challenges posed to, SARF by parallel, but distinct, work which has
developed over a similar period of time. Specifically, "interpretive" research into risk perception, which draws upon rather different intellectual roots; including constructionist and interactionist epistemologies,
and methodologies strongly influenced by ethnographic ideas (Macgill
1987; Zonabend 1993; Irwin, Dale, and Smith 1996; Walker et al. 1998;
Bickerstaff and Walker 2003). As noted above, an important feature of
interpretive research in risk perception is the recognition that lay publics
are able to engage in active processes of sense-making, and of the need
to appreciate the sometimes oblique and situationally specific logics entailed in the accomplishment of this task. As a result, one might argue
that, seen in this light, there has been a tendency, in much of the risk
communication research and development program, for recipients of
risk information to be regarded as passive entities: one might think of
them as "cognitive engines" or, as Garfinkel (1967) once put it, "cultural
dopes."

Here we examine some of these issues by drawing on a substantial
data set generated by our own research into community perceptions
of environmental risk issues associated with local industrial activities.
This was produced during 1996–98 by the PRISP project (Horlick-Jones
et al. 1998; De Marchi 2000), a European research consortium, which
attempted a cross-cultural understanding of the social dynamics of environmental risk perception. Although we illustrate our discussion using
United Kingdom data, the key findings were drawn from a cross-country
process of data analysis, and therefore, significantly, seem to indicate
certain robust features of risk perception processes that apply across contrasting geographical, cultural, regulatory, and political contexts.

The rise of interpretive risk perception research

Much of the voluminous social science literature on risk perception and
risk communication (for reviews see Pidgeon et al. 1992; Clarke and
Short 1993; Pidgeon and Beattie 1998) has been motivated by the not
infrequent mismatch between lay and expert risk assessments. Risk controversies are often associated with public "over-reaction" to officially

designated minimal risks, whilst, on the other hand, some hazards fail to motivate protective behavior despite government warnings. This disparity provided motivation for the work which led to the formulation of the SARF.

The two most influential strands of risk perception research have been the psychometric work associated with Paul Slovic and colleagues (Slovic, Fischhoff, and Lichtenstein 1980; Slovic 1987, 1992, 2000), and the "Cultural Theory" school of anthropologist Mary Douglas and her associates (Douglas and Wildavsky 1982; Douglas 1992). The former, rooted in psychological research, has focused on the measurement of subjective attributes of sources of risk. The latter has sought to understand risk perception and risk-related behavior in terms of the lifestyles of those doing the perceiving.

In recent years, however, both traditions have faced a number of theoretical challenges (discussed in Pidgeon et al. 1992; Pidgeon and Beattie 1998), while recent empirical attempts to explore the interface between cultural and psychological approaches have produced interesting, if mixed results (see e.g. Marris, Langford, and O'Riordan 1996, 1998; Sjöberg 1997; Slovic and Peters 1998). In methodological terms, it has become increasingly clear that questionnaire-based research alone does not capture the complexity of risk perception in specific hazard locations; suggesting that methods more sensitive to context are needed (Krimsky and Golding 1992). In addition, some researchers have begun to challenge the view that risk can be dealt with by separating out "hard" facts and "soft" values (Funtowicz and Ravetz 1985; Wynne 1992c; Clarke and Short 1993; Horlick-Jones 1998), thus leading to a problematization of the categories "expert" and "lay."

Accordingly, the last decade has seen a steady growth in studies which draw on hermeneutic and phenomenological traditions (e.g. Gadamer 1976; Schutz 1970); perspectives which recognize the central roles of meaning and interpretation in structuring social interactions and being. According to this approach, it might be anticipated that the concepts "risk" and "environment" could assume complex roles and multiple and symbolic meanings in lay discourse and action.

Such studies have utilized qualitative or mixed-method approaches, in order to obtain what Geertz (1973) described as a "thick description" of the circumstances in which given risk issues come to be identified and understood. In this way, researchers have attempted to understand the interpretive processes deployed by lay publics in making sense of risk issues, and in finding meaning in "risk objects" (Hilgartner 1992).

Within this approach are a number of strands of constructionist thinking, concerned with processes of social negotiation over what comes to be regarded as real and true: specifically, work on the sociology of knowledge (in particular, of scientific knowledge, Woolgar 1988); Berger and Luckman's (1967) reading of Schutzian phenomenology; the North American "social problems" literature (Spector and Kitsuse 1987); and analyses which see identity as arising from an open-ended interactional process (Shotter and Gergen 1989). Also relevant in this discussion is the literature concerned with the "public understanding of science" (Royal Society 1985). Here, as in risk communication studies, traditional views that regarded differences between experts and public perceptions as indicative of a "deficit" in public knowledge have come under sustained attacks that problematize these issues by setting them within their social and cultural contexts (Wynne 1995; Michael 1996; Irwin and Wynne 1996; Jasanoff 1998). The position adopted by a recent report by the United Kingdom House of Lords (2000) suggests that the authority of the traditional interpretation has now been seriously eroded.

The above insights have found practical expression in recent empirical studies of risk perception and risk communication which have been sensitive to the social generation of multiple meanings and the existence of multiple publics (Macgill 1987; Zonabend 1993; Irwin, Dale, and Smith, 1996; Walker et al. 1998; Howel et al. 2002). Similarly, the study by Fitchen et al. (1987) recognized the important role of community settings as arenas in which local risks are perceived and acted upon. Here, a range of key local influences bear upon the complex process of risk understandings, including: the perception of adverse health effects; the experience of nuisance; the presence of contaminants detectable by senses; lay familiarity with the contaminant; whether the contaminant is seen as originating within the community; whether "community leaders" are concerned about other risks (for example, local economic decline); and whether citizens trust local officials' competence in protecting their health and well being. Significantly, they note that such influences may be obscured in quantitative psychometric-style studies.

Within the interpretive studies literature, context, and situational-specificity have emerged as important features of the processes of sense making. Most people's sense of being continues to be predominantly local, and one's sense of self is closely related to ideas about place (Altman and Low 1992; Speller and Sime 1993; Urry 1995). Indeed, one's very ways of thinking, the logic of one's interpretive practices, may arguably be influenced in important ways by models of form and process, and sources of tacit knowledge, associated with local places of which one has experience (Thrift 1985; Schama 1995; Henwood and Pidgeon 2001).

In addition, there now exists a significant interpretive/interactive literature which has begun to shed light on the detail of risk-related practices in specific organizational and social settings. A number of examples serve to illustrate the range of this work: management of high-risk technologies (Perin 1995; Vaughan 1996) and of hospital hazards (Rayner 1986), regulatory practices (Hawkins 1984; Manning 1992; Short and Clarke 1992), HIV-related behavior (Bloor 1995), probation and psychiatric practice (Kemshall 1998; Horlick-Jones 2002) and policing (Brewer 1990; Horlick-Jones et al. 2001). The view that emerges from this work is one in which risk issues are embedded in a "tangle" of perceptions, associations and sometimes apparently unrelated agendas (see discussion in Horlick-Jones et al. 2001). In order to make sense of such issues people draw on shared interpretive resources: our taken-for-granted "stock of knowledge," as phenomenologists put it (Schutz 1970). Our understanding of risk issues, and our stance towards them, are talked into existence interactively, in ways that reflect and re-form values and power relations (cf. Molotch and Boden 1985).

Operationalizing an interpretive approach to environmental risk perception: the PRISP project

Here we consider a recent project in which we were involved which was established to investigate the influence of cultural, socio-economic, historical, regulatory, and other factors on public perceptions of certain industrial facilities. The project comprised a number of case studies of community perceptions of local industrial activity in three European countries – the United Kingdom, Spain, and Italy.

Drawing on a number of the theoretical and methodological considerations discussed above led us to conclude that in order to investigate the social dynamics of risk perception, we needed to surface people's subjective concerns and needs without constraining them into a pre-defined framework which defined which issues "should" be the pertinent ones. In this way, we sought to engage with the "messiness" of everyday practices of lay interpretation, rather than idealized conceptions of those practices, framed by the structure of a specific research method.

Our initial focus was on industrial sites (belonging to the chemical industry – broadly defined) where significant quantities of hazardous materials were stored. In Europe, such sites, which present major accident hazards, are subject to the provisions of the European Union Seveso Directive, now superseded by the Control of Major Accident Hazards (COMAH) Directive. The operators of the potentially more hazardous ("top-tier") Seveso/COMAH sites are required to undertake formal risk communication actions to inform local citizens about the nature of the possible off-site hazards that they pose. Very quickly, however, we recognized that in order to address our primary objectives, we needed to broaden the study into a wider examination of lay people's sense-making activities with regard to the impacts of local industry, and of the influence of political issues on these processes.

The communities we studied were selected in a coordinated way, so as to provide a spread of demographic and socio-economic settings, off-site impact (accident and pollution) of industrial facilities, and other contextual factors including past experiences of emergency and contamination incidents. In practice, the range of communities and associated industrial sites we chose to examine proved quite diverse; yet they also contained sufficient common aspects to present useful comparative dimensions.

In the real world, of course, industrial zones are often quite complex in nature (both physically and socially), combining multiple sites and activities, and formal and informal risk communication processes. This simple observation raises difficult questions about how best to carry out risk perception research that is applicable in such realistic settings. How can these "overlapping" effects best be investigated? Should researchers be examining sites or communities? Motivated by a wish to gain a quite general understanding of these processes, we selected a diverse range of sites and communities, including such complex zones, as the foci for our case studies, and, by necessity, these are some of the conceptual issues with which we grappled.

The methodological framework

We faced the challenge of designing a suitable methodological framework that would, in a relatively short period of time (two years), allow us to gain access to processes of lay social interaction within local communities. We took the view that questionnaire surveys, used alone, would almost certainly exclude those very features of social interaction that we sought to investigate. Accordingly, we developed a hybrid methodology by combining a portfolio of research tools: community profiles (this included semi-structured interviews with key local stakeholders, or "movers and shakers"), questionnaire survey, and focus groups. The theoretical basis of our methodology was rooted in the inductive approaches of *Grounded Theory* (Glaser and Strauss 1967; Henwood and Pidgeon 1992, 2003) and analytic induction (Silverman 1993), which led us to establish an iterative "learning process" of data gathering and analysis.

In the sections to follow we draw primarily upon the "community profile" and focus group data from the project. Our first stage of essentially ethnographic research, which we called "community profiles" drew on the tradition of community-based field-work *in situ*, insider accounts (including from interviews) and document analysis (Hammersley and Atkinson 1995). However, practical constraints on time and resources steered us away from a purely ethnographic approach for the remainder of the research, and towards a more speedy way of accessing data on how lay people made sense of risk issues. In common with a number of recent studies (e.g. Golding et al. 1992; Walker et al. 1998; Marris, Wynne, Simmons et al. 2001), we utilized focus groups as a means to subsequently elicit and observe lay talk about risk issues.

Focus groups are informal, facilitated discussion groups, typically involving lay participants. They are often used in commercial market research, but are also regarded as an important tool in academic research (Krueger 1994; Morgan 1997). Focus groups are not group interviews. The facilitator attempts to steer the group conversation in such a way as to ensure that certain topics are addressed. However, an equally important role is to encourage participants to air their views, to explore ideas and, where appropriate, to express disagreement. The resulting data can feature long runs of group conversation, often apparently rambling and featuring anecdotes and jokes.

It is important to note that the findings of focus group research are not "representative" in the manner of quantitative survey research. Rather, focus groups provide a powerful means to explore certain group norms and shared ways of conceptualizing and talking about things: arguably part of the very resources that allow intelligible conversation and meaningful social interaction to take place (Petts et al. 2001; Bloor et al. 2001). Focus groups allowed us to generate relatively unstructured conversations among small collections of people, hitherto unknown to each other, and specially recruited as participants. In this way, we used the device of staging "social microcosms" in order to produce talk about risk issues which drew on patterns of everyday understanding. We also wished to generate some comparative data with our parallel questionnaire survey results (which we do not report in detail here), so chose to identify a "pool" of potential focus group participants by inviting volunteers from those randomly sampled to receive the questionnaire.

Risk, interaction, and talk

The analysis of patterns of lay talk about risk has played a central role in interpretive research. Walker et al. (1998), for example, investigated "argumentation repertoires" deployed by people in their risk talk, for example, analogies and comparisons, allusions to consequences, moral arguments, trade-offs etc. Similarly, Petts et al. (2001) developed a method for the analysis of lay accounts of risk issues which drew upon both conceptual work on the analysis of arguments, and ideas from medical sociology concerned with the use of logics and categories in lay talk about health and illness.

Our own PRISP project found evidence that lay accounts drew upon "lexicons" of vocabulary, symbolic linkages, narratives, and imagery. In this way "standard" arguments and formulations concerning local risk issues re-appeared time and again during the initial interviews with "movers and shakers" and in local newspaper coverage. We also found evidence that the relative formality of completing a questionnaire often prompted rather different accounts from those in evidence in the informality of the focus group discussions (cf. findings reported in Marris et al. 2000). This use of language is reminiscent of the contrasting ways of talking about scientific practice that Gilbert and Mulkay (1984) found professionals adopted, according to context. Indeed, we feel that the concept of an "interpretive repertoire" that they introduced is a very useful one in trying to understand the variation in accounts which we found.

A further shared resource used in the construction of risk accounts was an apparent categorical distinction between risk as danger and risk as pollution. Our interview data displayed an engagement with either "danger" issues or "pollution" issues, but rarely with both. This demarcation was again reflected in local newspaper coverage, where simple counting procedures revealed an ebb and flow of danger or pollution themes within a roughly constant volume of risk stories about local industry during any given period.

In order to explore some of the richness of the perceptions of local lay publics within these settings, we present in the following sections material relating to a number of dimensions of sense-making processes. For the purposes of this chapter, we first set the scene by drawing on ethnographic data, and then illustrate our findings using extracts from the focus groups.

The context

Our two United Kingdom communities were, at first glance, very different: a horseshoe-shaped industrialized area in West Wales, arranged around a natural deep-water harbor and embedded in an area of outstanding natural beauty and farmland, and an urban industrial corridor adjacent to the River Thames in South-East London. However our initial ethnographic field-work revealed a number of interesting similarities as well as differences. We found, for example, widespread concern about the adverse health effects of local industry in both areas, with the frequency of asthma often being cited as an indicator of this perceived linkage. Indeed, on the whole, pollution issues associated with industry seemed to cause greater concern than the possibility of catastrophic explosions or toxic releases from Seveso/COMAH sites.

Pembrokeshire   The first community, which we label *Pembrokeshire*, has at its heart a huge natural harbor called the Milford Haven, which once possessed a large fishing fleet, and which attracted the oil industry during the 1960s. At that time a number of oil refineries were constructed in the "horseshoe," and the Haven began to be used by large oil tankers. A transformation from fishing port to oil port took place in just fifteen years (McKay 1989). During the period of our study, three oil industry facilities in the area were "top-tier" Seveso/COMAH sites; one of which, in the recent past, had been the site of a number of spectacular accidents with potentially serious off-site implications (HSE 1997). The Haven was also the site of a serious oil spill, from the *Sea Empress* tanker accident (MAIB 1997) a few months before we started our work.

In addition to the oil industry, a factory handling hazardous materials constituted a further Seveso/COMAH site within the horseshoe. During the period of our study, however, the politically most important local environmental risk issue was the proposal to burn Orimulsion (a bitumen slurry) in a local disused power station (Edwards 1996). This had generated an ongoing high-profile environmental controversy in the area. Towards the end of our work, the proposal was withdrawn by the developer, following the announcement by central Government of a Public Inquiry (in the United Kingdom this takes the form of a quasi-judicial procedure at which evidence is presented on the competing merits of some proposed development; for an example see O'Riordan et al. 1988).

The "horseshoe" area in Pembrokeshire has a relatively high unemployment rate compared to much of England and Wales, which also displays large seasonal variation. Those jobs that are available tend to provide low wages. There is significant migration out of the area by young people raised in the locality. The petrochemical industry in the area is in decline which, given its pivotal role as a local employer in this peripheral region, is the source of much local concern.

The recent proposal to burn Orimulsion at a local power station caused a great deal of controversy, primarily because of an alleged connection with air pollution and possible adverse health effects. Other objections included the possible environmental impact of accidents to tankers bringing this fuel into the Milford Haven waterway. We found that local newspapers played a significant role in providing high-profile coverage of the

Orimulsion controversy. We monitored these newspapers throughout the period of our research, searching for material concerning local industry, noting key themes, and recording the volume of coverage by means of simple counting procedures. Virtually the entire coverage, including news items, features, and letters pages, comprised forthright accounts, corresponding to a pro- or anti-Orimulsion position. News stories about the issue were often concerned with the statements of key protagonists, who sometimes attacked other prominent figures in the debate.

The main effect of this media intervention was to present a strongly polarized debate, splitting the community into two "camps" that were parodied as "jobs at any price" versus a coalition of people described variously as "cranks," "articulate middle class," and "outsiders." Such stereotype representations and associated "stories about risk" also featured strongly in our interviews with local people who were actively engaged – either professionally or politically – with this issue. The "stories," which occurred with almost predictable regularity, and which often drew on selective use of expert knowledge, for example scientific reports, were deployed as sources of authority to bolster positions or undermine the arguments used by opponents.

Bexley   The second community, which we label *Bexley*, comprises the riverside area of Belvedere and its immediate surroundings. This area is located within Greater London. It was transformed from a previously largely rural area during the second half of the nineteenth century, with the construction of riverside factories and associated working-class housing developments (Pritchard 1994; Barr-Hamilton and Reilly 1996). For much of the year Bexley has a much lower unemployment rate than does the Pembrokeshire community. Significantly, relatively few residents seem to find employment with local industry. Embedded, as it is, in Greater London, there exist many employment possibilities within relatively easy commuting distance. The existing industrial zone is located on reclaimed marshland, and combines heavy plant and factories. This zone includes one Seveso/COMAH site with toxic off-site hazard potential. A few years prior to our study, a proposal to site an incinerator in the area (Milne 1991) had prompted an environmental controversy that resulted in a Public Inquiry in 1992, which led to the proposal being blocked on technical grounds. At the time of our work, the level of political activity associated with this conflict had, it seemed, largely dissipated.

In comparison to the West Wales community, Bexley proved relatively quiet in terms of local environmental politics. Historical research revealed that the Seveso/COMAH site had been the subject of controversy in the mid 1980s. At that time, there had been extensive local newspaper coverage about the possible hazard posed by the site, and about the efficacy of the site's (pro-active) risk communication measures and the audibility if its emergency siren. Local politicians had become involved in the issue, as had a local environmental pressure group. At the time of our investigation, however, no one, other than those living in its immediate vicinity, seemed very interested in talking about this site and indeed, there seemed little awareness of its existence.

During the early 1990s, much more extensive and sustained local newspaper coverage was concerned with the proposal to site what was described as "Europe's largest waste-to-power incinerator" in the area. At this stage, there were similar patterns of polarization to coverage of the Orimulsion issue in West Wales. A vigorous conflict over the proposal took place at this time. One petition against the incinerator produced the signatures of over 27,000 people. A coalition of local pressure groups, local residents associations and the local authority in the area – Bexley Borough Council – all lined up against the developers, a major waste management company. The key arguments against the incinerator concerned the danger of air pollution, and a general objection about "becoming a dump for everyone else's waste." At the time the rhetorics deployed by environmental groups related these local concerns to wider issues concerning sustainable energy and waste policies. A formal application to construct the incinerator was made to central Government. This resulted in a public inquiry in 1992, which, as noted above, turned down the application on a technicality. However most people with whom we spoke seemed to think this defeat was a temporary setback for the scheme, and that the issue was far from over.

The two communities therefore presented complex tapestries of risk communication processes, as the impact of specific sites took place in the context of experiences with, and awareness of, other local industrial sites. Whilst formal risk communications to local people were required by law from the operators of the Seveso/COMAH sites, a host of informal communications complicated this picture with messages associated with, for example, local and national media, the activities of protest groups and community networks.

Focus groups

Details of specific features of the focus groups from which our data are drawn may be found in table 11.1. The focus group transcript extracts are identified by a letter (P for Pembrokeshire and B for Bexley) followed by the number of the group and of the extract. Each participant's contributions are labeled according to their gender (M or F) and their

Table 11.1 *Focus group details*

group	group size	location (date)	catchment area/comments
P1	6	Milford Haven (5 May 1998)	Milford Haven (largest community in area) and north-west of the Haven. Mix of socio-economic indicators and gender
P2	3	Milford Haven (6 May 1998)	As above, except all male, included close proximity to hazardous industry
P3	9	Neyland (7 May 1998)	north-east of the Haven. Bias towards higher socio-economic status, gender mix
P4	7	Pembroke Dock (9 May 1998)	Bias towards lower socio-economic status, gender mix, community with high unemployment
B1	5	Bexley (30 April 1998)	Belvedere – close to hazardous industry (up to 1 km), cheaper housing, gender mix
B2	7	Bexley (29 April 1998)	Includes industrial and shopping areas, outside 1 km zone but up to 2 km from hazardous industry, intermediate housing, gender mix
B3	5	Bexley (27 April 1998)	Outside 2 km zone, includes "leafy" suburbs, gender mix

(arbitrarily assigned) numbers. The group facilitator's contributions are labelled "R" (for "researcher") and reproduced in bold. On this occasion we have reproduced transcript material without detailed descriptions of the conversational dynamics of each extract.

Lay interpretations of expert accounts

First, we turn to similarities and differences between direct experiences of the impact of local industry and the (mediated) experience of hearing industry or "official" accounts of what is going on. In both Pembrokeshire and Bexley, focus group participants drew attention to personal experiences, for example noticing smells or observing plumes from chimneys, as important evidence in coming to some judgment about "the facts."

In the following extract, one focus group participant presented physical evidence she had brought with her in order to counter "scientific" facts in pronouncements by local industry. In the ensuing discussion, other participants offer similar, concrete, sources of evidence:

(P1.1,2)

F2 ... over the weekend by my bathroom window and tonight I went, I had the window open all day and I went out and on the white window ledge was all these black flecks so I got a bit of toilet paper and I brought that with me tonight. I've also brought my net curtain which shows evidence of the pollution that comes through our windows which is filtered through the net curtain. I was going to wash it but I thought no I won't get the chance again so I've brought it
...

M2 I could confirm what (F2) said to a degree but the thing is I wouldn't be too sure of where it came from. I recall coming to Dale first. Anything that was painted white would stay painted white for two or three years but now, and this is over the last few years, I find that if you paint either my boat or some door or something, an exterior door of the house, you do get these dark sooty streaks that run down the paint work, particularly after a long period of Easterlies which have become ...
...

F2 Well I can only answer that by saying if you have a look at the photos that I took from my bedroom window you can see the sort of thing that we have to put up with. And recently the dog's bowl goes outside the door when dog is out in the garden and I left her out one night and when I went to get it in the next morning there was oil floating on the top of the water because that's what had come over in the night

As the conversation continued, the participants wrestled with the problem of how to reconcile these contradictory accounts:

(P1.15,21)

F2 What I'm saying is right a scientist would have a parceled view of what it looks like and a housewife would have her own view of what it looks like. He will have the A plus B, whatever, and the housewife will have this is how it affects, this is where it sticks, this is what it affects, this is how it makes the dirt and things. But they will have a scientific explanation

F1 Yes

R And how would they differ?

F2 Say it goes on my windows, it affects my children's health, it makes dust, it makes us ill, it makes us sick whatever. And the scientist would say well yes ... goes out in the air and sulphur goes out in the air. But the housewife doesn't know about them sort of things, she only knows how it affects every single day
...

R So is there an authoritative source ... where you can find the information trustworthy in some way?

F2 I don't think so because, you see those two sheets –that you showed us just now, I see one as the scientist's and one as the housewife's

Here F2 refers to two advertisements which had recently appeared in a local newspaper (copies of which we had tabled at the focus group meeting). Both advertisements had professed to present "the facts" about

Orimulsion: one, "an industry view," and the other containing arguments associated with an "environmentalist" position.

Other researchers have found similar contrasts between lay and "official" accounts of local risk issues (e.g. Wynne 1992a, 1996; Michael 1996; Walker et al. 1998). Concrete lay experiences provide a powerful source of evidence for beliefs, and many of our participants felt that these experiences contradicted accounts of environmental performance voiced by local industry. They were far from passive recipients of "expert" communications. Rather, "scientific explanations" seemed to be denying what they could see and smell, with obvious implications for industry's credibility. Unsurprisingly, such tensions were particularly stark for those living in close proximity to industrial sites, and who regard themselves "on the front line" in the event of any incident.

Making sense of adverse industrial impacts

Here we look in a little more detail at some of the patterns of sense making processes about risk issues that were in evidence during the group discussions. Such processes reflect everyday concerns and local knowledge, issues of widespread relevance and meaning, and mediated knowledges. Importantly, these processes are dynamic, and draw upon shared resources, as people collectively talk their understandings and stances into existence.

The following sequence is concerned with the impact of industry in Bexley. Without exception, the focus group sessions included a great deal of discussion about smells from local industry, and this feature was used as a way of organizing and discussing shared experiences. Smell was the single most obvious impact of local industry, and was linked by most participants with local health problems:

(B1.1)
R what can you tell me about heavy industry in this area? . . . what's its character? how does it impact on local community? . . . Has it changed a lot over the years?
M1 getting more smelly
M2 yes, I agree with that
F1 yes it is
M1 it stinks . . . what with meat pies, chemicals at (factory) is it? . . . producing some sort of peculiar chemicals everywhere, choking sensation in our throat when you take the dogs for a run
F1 down on the river front especially.
M1 at the river front we get the chucking out of sewage from the water works, you get the perfume from the water works, it's quite a stinking area this place . . .

I don't think it's very healthy. In fact since I've been here, I've been in hospital twice, I've been sick about half a dozen times really ill ...

R you think that might have something to do with industry in the area?

M1 well I didn't think much of it at first, I thought it had just happened, but I've never been ill before in my life and suddenly coming down this area I start feeling unwell and my son's been unwell, and my grandson's been unwell and you've been unwell ...

Significantly, the focus group participants often displayed a critical perspective on the "common sense" of risk stories which featured in the media, and which also tended to form part of the rhetorical repertoires of the "movers and shakers." Take, for example, the case of asthma. At the time of the study, the British media had featured a number of stories about an increase in numbers of people receiving treatment for asthma. In the Pembrokeshire area, an alleged threat of increased asthma was an important rhetorical weapon deployed by those opposed to the burning of orimulsion in the local power station. Consider the following exchange, which illustrates a typically critical perspective:

(P3.5)

M1 you've only got to take a young child to the doctor's and say "there's a bit of a wheeze" and he is signed for a Ventolin pump.

R what do you think is going on though?

M1 it's a medical fashion.

M3 how can Ireland and New Zealand be worse on a list of cases for infant asthma than the United Kingdom? There's something else going on here

M1 yes

M4 they're keeping better records aren't they?

M1 well no, they don't bend the records

M4 keeping better records I said

M1 oh, sorry

M3 people are saying that where there is lead pollution, atmospheric pollution, that's going up, asthma is going up, there must a be connection. I don't buy it

A high frequency of asthma was also a concern among Bexley people; however, once again, focus group discussion displayed a critical perspective on the "standard" stories:

(B3.7)

R Were there always people who had problems breathing or something?

F3 well I think so

F1 oh yes they probably used to call it bronchitis then or something like that

This perspective tends to refute the simple amplification model of "process" that is found in SARF, in which passive audiences find themselves manipulated by the actions of "amplification stations." Lay publics are typically much more critical in their response to either "sources of authority" or positions advanced by "movers and shakers" irrespective of organizational or peer group affiliations. Importantly, the process of sense-making is a *collective* one, in which people cooperate in interrogating the claims of others.

Advantages and disadvantages of industrial activity

Official justification for the presence of local hazardous industry in the areas we studied is rationalized in terms of its "tolerability": striking a suitable balance between its associated advantages, perhaps in terms of jobs and wealth creation, and possible disadvantages presented by health or environmental risks (HSE 1992). Do people living in such communities think about local risk issues in these terms?

Consider the following sequences from the Pembrokeshire groups:

(P1.17)
F1 It's a jobs issue.
M1 Jobs.
F1 It has to be a jobs issue.
R Very, very simple – jobs.
M1 Jobs, jobs.
F1 There is nothing else in this area. The fishing industry has died, the oil industry is dying on its feet ... that's going to be the break-up of my family because he's going to have to go away to work ...

This first sequence illustrates the pervasive sense of gloom felt by many living in an area of high unemployment. Few argued that industry brought many advantages, but many were so desperate that they felt compromised about expressing concern about adverse environmental impacts; "hypocritical" as F1 went on to say. As illustrations of the advantages of local industry, participants in one group were only able to identify sponsorship of local community activities:

(P3.3)
F2 ... I can't really talk about anything else, but on the sports scene ... there is a tremendous support network for it, yes
M3 I think you've got to support (company X), (company Y) and (company Z) for the money that they have put in
F2 absolutely
M3 not just sport, but schools – (name)
F4 (name) Theatre
M3 So they have put a lot of money back
F2 Yes
M3 because they realize that they've come into an environmentally difficult area ... and they are going to make a lot of problem with the environment, which they have done, but they have put – not as much as they could have

done, with the amount of money they've been making – but every pound that comes into an area like this, you've got to accept and you've got to back them for that

The impact of heavy industry on other industrial activities presents a complicating factor to the notion of simple advantage/disadvantage balance:

(P3.2)
M1 ... You either have low employment and a beautiful environment or you have heavy industry, or big industry, big employer, affects the environment and you lose the tourists
R Do you all agree with that? Do you think it's a straight trade off?
F1 No I don't think so
M2 No
M3 It hasn't happened has it?
F1 I don't think it's quite as bad a scenario as that
R Why do you disagree?
M3 Because it hasn't happened. People still come to Pembrokeshire for the tourism, despite all the disasters

Here the first speaker presents a trade-off position between industry and environment; one that implies a potential incompatibility between heavy industry and tourism. The others are more pragmatic, suggesting that the situation is somewhat more complex than a simple matter of trading off costs and benefits.

In Bexley, views were clearly far more one-sided[1]: people recognized all the disadvantages of local industry but felt there existed few advantages, as the following exchanges testify:

(B3.14)
F2 yes I've lived here all my life and I don't know anyone that works locally now
M2 that's because industry has moved hasn't it?
M1 yes
F2 but it's still down there, but it's a different type isn't it
F1 we've still got it in Lower Belvedere haven't we, but I don't know anybody who works there now

(B1.5)
M1 ... lots of little firms making plastic bits and pieces and pallets and all sorts of odds and ends like that and they employ a sprinkling of people all the way through so I suppose they're not really a big employer now, I wouldn't say so, but they keep people in jobs which is a good thing.

---

[1] Responses from the quantitative questionnaire survey of the two communities clearly indicated a similar, large difference between the areas, with Bexley residents in particular reporting very few advantages to the community from local heavy industry.

F3 The only people I've seen...to be honest...going into the factories...is
   minibuses pull up with, it's full of (ethnic) people and they're the only people
   I ever see going round to that factory
   ...(discussion including a number of similar perceptions)
R Well basically they're bussed in, they're from somewhere else
F3 Yes, so they're not, they're obviously not local
F1 they're not local people

Few people in either community we studied seemed to feel confident
that heavy industry could be relied upon to provide sufficient jobs. Rather
than either a polarized stance or a calculated trade-off rationale, there was
a certain desperation about people's expressed views, apparently torn
between competing pressures and rather pessimistically hoping for better
times. There was little evidence that the concept of tolerability is at all
relevant to local sense making processes.

The symbolic politics of accounts

It is perhaps hardly surprising that people actively engaged in the politics
of environmental risk, whether campaigners or, for that matter, professionals, provide accounts that seek to persuade. Over twenty-five years
ago, Molotch and Lester (1975, p. 237) noted that "one dimension of
power can be construed as the ability to have one's account become the
perceived reality of others." Taking this observation one step further, we
suggest that it is important to recognize the (often tacit) political role of
all accounts when seeking to interpret risk perception data.

Despite their value as data, there are considerable dangers in taking
accounts at face value, and their analysis requires rigor and an awareness
of their nature (Brown and Sime 1981; Silverman 1985; Henwood and
Pidgeon 1995). This, of course, does not imply that respondents lie about
the matter in question. Rather, it reflects a recognition that none of us are
necessarily aware of all the influences on our thoughts, and that we are all
subject to post-hoc rationalization, romantic imagination, and selective
amnesia (Petts et al. 2001). Crucially, there may be important differences
between what people say they do, and what they do in practice; and
accounts can play both presentational (Goffman 1969; Eliasoph 1990)
and rhetorical functions (Radley and Billig 1996) within conversation.

According to this perspective, attending a focus group or completing
a questionnaire, as in the PRISP project, are never politically neutral
acts. In settings where the topic is a matter of local controversy, this
recognition seems likely to be even more important. Indeed, we found
clear evidence that accounts elicited by different research tools – the
questionnaire and focus groups – were somewhat different (we do not

report these differences in detail here), with this "anomaly" being more pronounced for the Pembrokeshire data. Clearly these claims raise quite profound methodological issues in that they pose serious questions about the status of findings from risk perception research that takes its data – whether qualitative or quantitative – simply at face value.

A further dimension of the politics of accounts is concerned with the establishment of linkages between risk issues and other agendas. We illustrate this phenomenon with some data from two of our Pembrokeshire focus groups. In the first extract, M1 identifies what he terms "environmental madness" with "foreigners" from England. When considering the "foreigner" remark, it is important to recall that Pembrokeshire is in Wales. Interestingly, however, this part of Wales has traditionally been regarded as having especially close ties with England ("little England beyond Wales"; Morton 1932), and the Welsh language continues to be spoken to a much lesser extent than in surrounding areas.

(P2.1,4b)

M2 ... I don't like to say it but there are too many foreigners coming down here telling us what to do. But there are certain organizations, I'm not going to name them which seem hell bent on turning this into a sterile country seat for people to come down here from England by decrying everything that will bring any industry into this area. Now having been on the environmental committee for all these years, and looking at some of the reports here today, there's nothing wrong with the atmosphere in this county. I mean, we've lost the Power Station, we've lost two refineries. There's only two refineries left and everybody seems hell bent on getting them closed. And I'm only looking after the interest of the people that I represent and I live with. To me Pembrokeshire is a great place. I was born here and my family roots are here. And I'm very disappointed about what's going on today, that they're environmental mad ...

...

M2 I'll tell you why because 40 percent of the people that live in Pembrokeshire at the moment are old age pensioners. And most of them have retired to Pembrokeshire, they couldn't care less. They're all on a pension and most of them are well off because they couldn't afford to come here and buy property otherwise. I mean it's not happening now at the moment but four or five years ago, people were selling up in the Midlands and in the South of England and they were getting an enormous price for their property, they were coming down here and buying a better place for half price and putting the money in the bank. And they've retired. They don't want industry around here ... they don't want anything around here because it might spoil their way of life

Running through these statements are concerns fashioned by the economic disparity between South Pembrokeshire, an area of high unemployment and low property prices, and parts of England. As noted above, South Pembrokeshire, with the possible exception of the "horseshoe" around the Haven, is also an area of outstanding natural beauty. The combination of these features has given birth to an important source of tension in the area: namely a not uncommon hostility to "outsiders": usually relatively well-off people from England who move to the area for retirement, as self-employed people, or as holiday home visitors.[2]

M1 seeks to establish his own Pembrokeshire and environmental credentials by citing his own family history and his long service on a local environmental liaison committee (associated with one of the industrial sites). He uses his association with the committee as a source of authority to deny suggestions that local industry presents a threat to local health, and to the local environment. He then claims that environmental protests are "really" about a quite different agenda, namely the removal of heavy industry from the area to make it a more acceptable "country seat" for people from England: an agenda he sees as inimical to the interests of Pembrokeshire people. He sees "certain organizations" (which he goes on to identify as environmental pressure groups) as colluding in this process of "foreigners coming here (and) telling us what to do."

Although, on the whole, the Pembrokeshire group discussions did not feature strongly polarized accounts, we did find evidence of related arguments being used by individuals who did not express anything like the same degree of political commitment as M1. Consider the following sequence:

(P4.2)
F1 Don't you think it was a lot, a lot of people against the orimulsion were retired people who had moved into the area
M2 that's right
F1 they weren't locals. They were quite happy with the environment as it was and they didn't want their pleasure spoilt
M2 that's right
F1 they couldn't care less about the locals, about the jobs, lack of jobs
M2 yes I think you've hit it on the head really
F1 yes that's what it was

In this way the politics of risk features such symbolic associations in which pre-existing political positions on ostensibly disparate issues can come to be associated with positions on a risk issue (Dalton 1959; Wynne 1982; Horlick-Jones 2000; Horlick-Jones et al. 2001). As noted above, the

---

[2] The question of who holds identities as "insiders" and "outsiders," as well as "who belongs" in the context of rural Wales today is far more complex than this simple caricature suggests. For example, in Pembrokeshire today those viewed as recent "incomers" may sometimes be Welsh themselves, typically relatively affluent migrants from urban Cardiff, as much as from England (see Cloke et al. 1997; Henwood and Pidgeon 2001).

existence of this phenomenon poses a serious methodological challenge for risk researchers, and reinforces the importance of the program of interpretive research into risk perception.

Conclusions

We have chosen to examine risk perception and communication research and development from a perspective that focuses on the relationship between risk, language, and knowledge. This stresses the central importance of the situated nature of accounts. We have drawn on a part of a substantial data set to illustrate some features of risk-related interpretive practices, and of ways in which risk issues can become embedded in the social fabric of language and action. A recognition of the need to take into consideration the situated nature of such accounts arguably necessitates a re-examination of much established work in the field. In our view, it also underlines the value of multi-method investigations as a means of eliciting rounded appreciations of these entities and processes.

Turning first to some policy implications of the findings of interpretive research, the recognition that there is no neutral way to talk about risk seems to raise profound difficulties, and may cause would-be risk communicators to give up all hope of achieving anything. We do not think that things are quite as hopeless as this. While it is not our intention to offer some programmatic statement for risk communication agencies here, a few ideas do present themselves, all of which require further elaboration:

- First, we underline the need for a design-based and user-centered approach to risk communication (also Murdock et al. this volume chapter 7). There is demonstrably a need for governments and businesses to gain a much better understanding of lay audiences, how they make sense of risk issues, and what they value.
- Any risk communication "agency" (whether government, business, or NGO) needs to monitor "global" and "local" discourses relating to the matter to be communicated. To support this at a local level, such communicators need devolved structures in order to both facilitate this local monitoring and enhance local visibility within communities.
- Local monitoring should include eliciting feedback on risk communication ideas from local people in informal, relatively unstructured and interactive fora e.g. focus groups or some variant of deliberative process (see O'Riordan et al. 1999; Renn, this volume chapter 16).
- Government agencies in particular must be unflinchingly even-handed, and above all *independent* in all their risk communication activities. That is, they should act (insofar as this is possible) as an "honest broker" for

information on all relevant risk issues. A commitment to providing a plurality of information and perspectives is preferable to the idea of a "single authoritative source."

- There is a need for reflection and self-awareness on the part of agency staff, and the specific risk communications functions need to be embedded into the nature (formal structure and informal functioning) of the agency.

Interpretive research into risk perception has also provided us with important insights into the social dynamics of risk perception. On the basis of evidence presented here, it appears to pose a number of challenges to certain fundamental aspects of the SARF. It does so in three main ways.

First, interpretive research reveals lay audiences to have the capacity and inclination to engage in active interrogation of risk-related information, which contrasts with the passive conception implicit in the SARF. Indeed, the classic formulation of SARF does not immediately suggest that the reception and interpretation of risk-related information is anything other than the mechanical arrival and "processing" of a "packet" of knowledge by individuals (although see Kasperson et al. this volume chapter 1). In contrast, interpretive research indicates that active work is required to make sense of risk issues, and that this work is collective, and draws upon stocks of shared interpretive resources. Moreover, we would suggest that assessing the potential for "amplification" necessitates an understanding of the nature of those shared resources.

Second, the SARF amplification mechanism envisages a central (and unproblematic) role for the rules "by which society and its subgroups should select, order and explain signals concerning the threats emanating from human activities" (Kasperson and Kasperson 1996, p. 96). In so doing it reinforces a passive, rule-following conception of lay audiences which is at variance with a recognition of the problematic nature of rules and social norms, the potential for slippage between rules and actions, and the capacity for rules to provide resources to account for actions (for example, Wittgenstein 1958; Bittner 1967; Garfinkel 1967).

Third, despite allusions to "symbolic connotations" in the original SARF paper (Kasperson et al. 1988), the Framework presents what appears to be an essentially instrumental conception of risk. It therefore does not appear to take into account the capacity of risk issues to become embedded in symbolic tangles (cf. Krimsky and Plough 1988), and in this way associated with other issues and agendas, resulting in risk controversies sometimes being "about" issues quite distinct from what is ostensibly the "risk object."

SARF was initially proposed as an integrative framework for a quite diverse range of risk perspectives. On the basis of the evidence presented here, we suspect that its underlying metaphoric structure does not have the capacity to respond fully to, and embody, all the challenges posed by the interpretive program of research into risk perception. In that sense, this chapter throws down a gauntlet to the advocates of SARF: a challenge with important implications for risk communication research and practice.

12   Understanding amplification of complex risk issues: the risk story model applied to the EMF case

Peter M. Wiedemann, Martin Clauberg, and
Holger Schütz

This chapter outlines a new concept for risk amplification: the risk story model. The starting-point is the well-known conflict situation of risk evaluation as seen by experts and laypersons. To address this conflict, a typology of risk issues can be developed, based on the different risk communication challenges. Laypersons may perceive each type of risk issue as a different risk story. In the second part of the chapter, the relationship between risk stories and social risk amplification is explored. Examples of radio frequency electromagnetic fields (RF EMF) issues are used to illustrate the approach to understanding risk perception and communication. Furthermore, empirical data are provided that support the basic assumption of a risk story model. Finally, the consequences for EMF issues and risk communication in general are discussed.

Experts and laypersons: two views on risks

Experts

Experts and laypersons perceive risks differently. Experts see risks as possible chains of cause-and-effect. They regard risks as indicators of hazard potentials. Risk assessment involves answering four questions: Is there a potential hazard and what is its nature? What dose will induce a harmful effect? Who is exposed to what dosage? How significant is the risk?

Figure 12.1 shows the challenges associated with assessing risks, and what – in the view of the experts – the assessment ought to take into account. For the experts, the crucial point is whether and with what degree of confidence the risk can be assessed. To meet these criteria, experts need scientific evidence that a harmful, that is toxic, effect exists. Without evidence, anything and everything could be suspected of causing a risk.

The expert is also interested in the details of the risk. Is it a low-dose, long-term exposure risk resulting from normal plant operations, or is it a

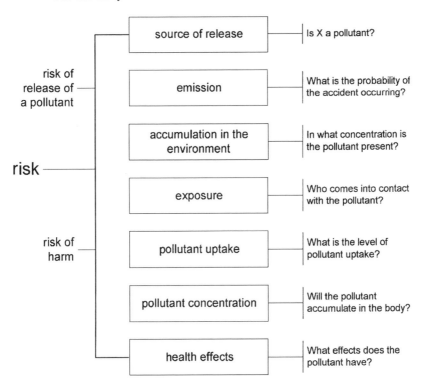

Figure 12.1 Risk problems from the perspective of experts.

short-term accidental release risk? If the latter, what is the frequency with which these accidental releases may occur? If it is the former, it will be necessary to determine the level of emissions and the pathways by which the pollutant reaches the receptors.

Experts consider whether the pollutant can accumulate in the environment and how long it retains its harmful effect. Next, exposure must be assessed. Who comes into contact with the pollutant, by which exposure routes does the pollutant enter the body, and can it accumulate within the body?

Finally, there is the question of the potential health effects and the toxicity of the pollutant. Taken all together, these specific characteristics allow experts to distinguish between certain categories of risk problems.

To the expert, it is equally important to identify the *types* of risk which are, or could be, associated with the situation at hand, such as constructing a new industrial plant. Five basic risk types can be distinguished in this context (figure 12.2).

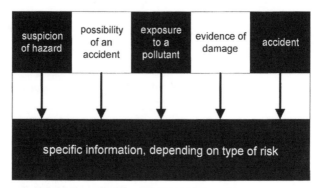

Figure 12.2 Types of risk from the perspective of experts.

Suspicion of hazard. In the case of the first risk type, "suspicion of hazard," it is assumed, but not proven, that a certain substance has harmful effects on human health or the environment. A case in point is the discussion about whether chemicals in the environment affect the hormonal balance, where it is assumed that even minute amounts can have a serious impact on gender-specific development (see Royal Society 2000). Such a suspicion can lead to even stronger public reactions than the possibility of an industrial plant accident.

Possibility of an accident. The possibility of an accident, for example in a chemical plant or waste incinerator, is the next risk type. Communication challenges for this type of risk may arise, for example, if a company is looking for a site for a new plant. The issue centers around how probable an accident is and what effects it might have. Different public reactions should be anticipated depending on the probability and the magnitude of the possible damage and the particular perspective on the risk. The primary question here is whether the risk is purely theoretical ("It could happen..."), or whether there are sufficient grounds for suspecting that a risk actually exists ("It's been shown that...").

Exposure to a pollutant. Exposure to, in other words, coming into contact with, a pollutant is another type of risk. One example would be the realization in 1978 that an old chemical dump under homes at Love Canal, New York State, was leaking (e.g. Levine 1982). In contrast to cases involving "suspicion of hazard," there is no doubt here that a potentially harmful contaminant is present. The crucial question is the exposure. There can only be a health risk if receptors, people or animals, come into contact with the contaminant. The risk also depends on the details of exposure, for example, how much of a pollutant was present, how often each individual was exposed to it, and by which route. The point here is to quantify the exposure and the associated risk. For this purpose it may be necessary to determine whether there is a threshold of exposure, below which it can be assumed that the contaminant in question does not constitute a hazard at all.

Evidence of damage. The situation is very different if there is observable damage. In this case there is an actual health problem, but the cause is unclear. One example would be "disease clusters" observed in the vicinity of an industrial plant; the issue here is whether the cause of the disease can be traced back to the industrial plant. Risk communication in this context must be aimed at clarifying the suspected causes. The goal is to obtain proof of the assumed cause/effect relationship and to try to explain it. This type of situation provides the greatest conflict potential for the company involved.

Occurrence of an accident. The occurrence of an accident is a further distinct type of problem. Examples would be the Three Mile Island nuclear accident in 1979; the catastrophic release of methyl isocyanate at Bhopal, India in 1984; the 1986 reactor meltdown in Chernobyl, Ukraine; a rash of oil tanker disasters in the 1990s; or the Concorde air disaster in Paris, France, in 2000. In some cases, the risk develops into a crisis. Quite apart from the acute damage that may arise from, for example, explosions or chemical poisoning, there is the additional problem of how to assess and clarify the longer-term risks associated with the emission of hazardous substances. Then there is always the question of blame: who or what caused the accident in the first place?

Laypersons

Laypersons approach questions of risk in ways rather different to experts. Of course, laypersons are also interested in the possible consequences. However, they perceive risks primarily in a social and relationship-oriented context. Risk statistics such as estimates of probability are less important or take on a different meaning. Laypersons transfer questions of risk into their framework of perception of the routine events of everyday life. This perspective is based on common patterns for interpreting events, which are heavily influenced by the media, such as scandal stories, investigative exposés, tragedies, and disaster reports. Such interpretive patterns, or stories, include (see Heath 1997; Palmlund 1992; Wiedemann, Carius, Henschel et al. 2000):

- casting the implicated persons in particular roles – preferably those of victim and perpetrator, hero or villain, etc. (characters involved);

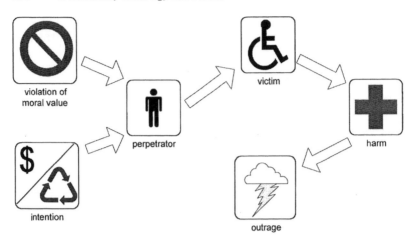

Figure 12.3 Interpreting lay views on risk.

- ascribing objectives and motives (intentions);
- exploring the conflict leading up to the event (dramatization), attributing a logic to the event;
- describing the consequences (harm done), and formulating a conclusion or lesson to be drawn (moral of the story);
- citing other "examples" which make the occurrence of the event or the moral of the story particularly clear (citing precedents).

Thus, laypersons look for, and frame risks in terms of, elements that typically play no part in a scientific risk assessment and would indeed be considered completely unsuitable for scientific discourse. Yet, from the layperson's perspective, these elements are of crucial importance in perceiving and understanding risks.

These story elements form the basic building blocks of the way laypersons view risk issues (figure 12.3). Assembled together, they form the typical patterns for interpreting and discussing risk issues from the layperson's perspective. Some of these outlooks are so widely held and established that they can be epitomized with popular phrases.

For example: "Things can happen sooner than you think," "Who is to say there isn't...?," "We are all victims already," "Don't let them get away with it!," "It was bound to happen sooner or later."

"Things can happen sooner than you think." The theme of this interpretive pattern focuses on the chance an accident could happen or on the possible harmful outcome, such as industrial plant or transportation accidents. This argumentation is loosely based on the logic of Murphy's law, or more

specifically on the idea of "What if..." Information on probabilities is interpreted in the context of this chain of logic.

Examples which are cited as a precedent are highly important. Emphasis is also placed on the traits of the characters involved such as reliability, prudence, sense of responsibility, "human error," etc. on the one hand, and blind trust, indifference, or fear and worry, on the other. If the basic type of risk involved is the "possibility of an incident," the following questions should be anticipated:

- What could happen?
- How bad would that be?
- Who are the potential victims?
- Is the potential harm tolerable?
- Are there lower-risk alternatives?
- Why is the risk tolerated and imposed on us? Are there good reasons for it?
- Is the risk offset by a benefit, and how is this benefit distributed?

"Who is to say there isn't...?" This argumentation pattern focuses on the assumption that there is a risk. Although there is no sound evidence, there are suspicions or indications that there could be a risk. "Couldn't Compound X be bad for you?" is a typical question. A current example of this pattern is the debate about the possible harmful effects of electromagnetic fields (EMF) on human health. The risk is presented in the form of a suggestive story with a corresponding event logic ("It could be..."), precedents ("It took ages for asbestos..."), suspicious circumstances and potentially incriminating factors ("Have you ever wondered why...?") and ulterior motives ("All they are after is a fast buck.") The suspicion of being exposed to a risk gives rise to diffuse worries and fears. Questions such as the following are often asked:

- What could happen? Can harm be positively ruled out?
- Why have no studies/investigations been carried out to find out whether people or the environment have already been harmed?
- Is information about the pollutant being withheld? If so, why? Is there a conspiracy between industry and the authorities?
- Who is standing up for our interests?

"We are all victims already." This pattern of interpretation assumes that a hazardous substance is already present in the environment and it is only a matter of time before it causes serious harm. An example of this pattern is the controversy about amalgam tooth fillings. It is assumed that the victims are exposed to a toxic substance. But the harm has not yet been recognized or will take some time to manifest itself. The logic behind this pattern is "perhaps not yet, but any time now." If there is a widespread assumption that the public has already been exposed to

contamination, a mixture of fears and outrage should be anticipated. Here a risk communicator might expect the following questions:

• Who has been exposed? What could happen?
• When was the pollution first discovered?
• How long has the company known about it?
• What has the company done since then? Why has it done nothing yet?
• What safeguards are needed?

   "Don't let them get away with it!" This interpretive pattern not only assumes that harm has been caused, but also claims to have identified the cause of the harm. This pattern typically takes the form of a scandal story. Although the cause of the harm is believed to have been known in advance by those with responsibility, nothing seems to have been done to stop it. Examples of this pattern are people who are hypersensitive to electricity and blame EMF for their problems, or Multiple Chemical Syndrome patients who regard chemical substances as the root cause of their complaints. Here moral attributes ("irresponsible," "inconsiderate," "acting against one's better knowledge," etc.) are used to characterize the players. Overall, this pattern is marked by outrage and appeals for action. If ailments and health conditions are attributed to a possible risk source, the following questions will have to be addressed:

• Why are they denying that the ailments originate from this risk source?
• Why are the experts we rely on not listened to?
• Why are the authorities doing nothing?
• Why are the affected people branded as "psychosomatic" cases?

   "It was bound to happen sooner or later." Typical of the response to a disaster, an accident, or some unfortunate outcome, this argumentation follows the event logic of a tragedy. That is to say, the circumstances are interpreted in a way that makes the catastrophe appear to have been inevitable. Attention is focused on describing the suffering of the victims as well as the motives of those who caused the tragedy, either knowingly and deliberately, or through their negligence. A textbook example of this perception pattern is the Chernobyl disaster. Following the occurrence of an accident or other such incident, the following questions are likely to be voiced:

• What has happened? Who has been harmed?
• How did it happen? Who is responsible?
• Who is to blame?
• Could the accident have been prevented? If so, why weren't safety measures in place?
• What secondary damage can we expect?
• Could the accident occur again?
• What is being done to prevent the accident repeating itself?

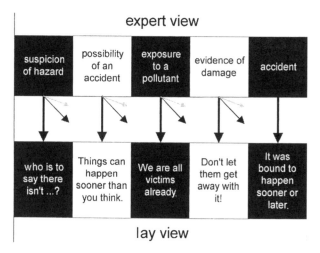

Figure 12.4 Juxtaposing risk perspectives of experts and laypersons.

Differences in perception can lead to social risk amplification

In an ideal world, each of the risk types from the view of the experts as depicted in figure 12.2 would correspond directly to a layperson's risk perspective (see bold arrows in figure 12.4). So, for example, the "possibility of an accident" type of risk might correspond to the interpretative pattern "Things can happen sooner than you think," and "Exposure to a pollutant" corresponds to "We are all victims already," etc. (see figure 12.4). However, we wish to argue in this chapter that the lay perspective, which emphasizes above all the social context of the risk, usually tends to *intensify* the magnitude of the perceived risk (light arrows in figure 12.4). This magnification of the perception of risk is one of the basic ideas behind the social amplification of risk framework (SARF).

The SARF (Kasperson 1992) states that risk perception and media reports on risks directly influence the scope and extent of social responses to a risk source. They modulate technical risk aspects, such as the number of persons exposed and the size of the region affected by the potential damaging event. According to Burns et al. (1993) the focus is above all on the signaling effects of the risk event; that is, the perception of future risks as well as the perception of management (in)competence (or "recreancy": see Freudenburg, this volume chapter 4).

The challenge of risk communication is all the more difficult (higher potential for amplification) if the public perceives the risk involved in a different risk story context. To give an example: the risk type "suspicion of hazard" may already be regarded by the public as proof of contaminant exposure and may trigger the "We are all victims already" or even the "It was bound to happen sooner or later" interpretive response pattern.

Clearly, the prevailing interpretive pattern of risk perception and the layperson's associated beliefs and attitudes, must be taken into account when comparing and contrasting the views of the experts and laypersons. The social amplification approach can be linked with the risk-story model described here, which can map both signaling effects and management characteristics, that is, the social aspects of risk.

Supporting evidence for the risk story model

Experimental evidence

We now report data from a series of experiments conducted to provide empirical evidence for the basic assumption of the risk story model (Wiedemann and Schütz 2000). The experiments were designed in the following way. First, a group of subjects (the "story writers") were asked to construct two risk stories focusing on the story type "It was bound to happen sooner or later." One story should arouse outrage, the other one leniency. The "story writers" were requested to use the identical risk information in both stories: that is, the same type of risk and severity of consequences. However, the subjects were instructed to vary the following features: company descriptions, cause of incident, possible motives behind the incident, knowledge and control of the incident.

The stories were then given to a second group of subjects for evaluation ($N = 174$). Among other criteria, these subjects had to rate the severity (badness) of the risks. The statistical analysis of these ratings reveals a significant effect (t-test: $t = -4.381$; $df = 172$; $p = 0.000$): in the outrage condition ($N = 87$), the risk ratings were higher than in the leniency condition ($N = 87$): $m_{(outrage)} = 6.92$, $m_{(leniency)} = 5.45$. In other words, although the "objective" risk information given in the stories was practically the same, the risks were judged rather differently (see figure 12.5). Obviously, the context provided by the story frame, influenced the risk judgments. In addition to rating the risks, the subjects were also asked to indicate which elements of the risk stories they used in making their risk judgment. The results confirmed that the most frequently chosen elements were related to the social context in which the risk arose, that is, the company's actions and motives before and during the incident, and not necessarily the magnitude or likelihood of damage, which are the risk characteristics usually considered as most relevant by experts.

These data support the basic premise that the social features of a risk story influence perception of risk.

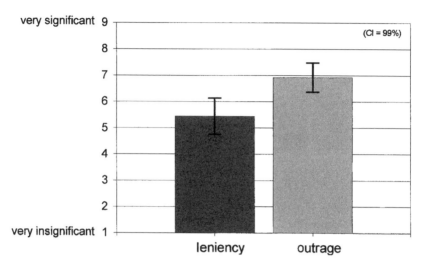

Figure 12.5 Amplification of perceived risk in a risk story context.

The case of electromagnetic fields: risk assessment and risk stories

Most scientists conclude that EMF risks, if they exist, seem to be rather small. Some critics assume that possible effects of radio frequency EMF on humans might occur even at very low doses (non-thermal effects). They refer to brain tumour promotion, changes in the brain metabolism, effects on blood pressure, and subjective well-being. On the one hand, a large scientific review conducted by the World Health Organization (Matthes et al. 1997) concluded that there is no convincing evidence that exposure to RF EMF shortens the life span of humans, induces or promotes cancer. On the other hand, the same review underlined that further research is needed to draw a more comprehensive picture of EMF health risks, especially about possible cancer risk from exposure to low levels of RF EMF.

As shown in the preceding section, risks are judged by laypersons through the use of risk stories. Three of the five risk stories described above are circulating among the general public with respect to RF EMF.

EMF story: who is to say there isn't. . .? This story is above all voiced by scientists who are regarded as critics of mobile phone technology. They refer to certain biological effects of EMF exposure (e.g. von Klitzing 1995) which are interpreted as potential hazards. This issue has formed the foundation for the "better safe than sorry" story.

Since the public typically lacks the knowledge to always differentiate between an effect and a harmful effect, something which is also a challenge for scientists, this risk story is highly plausible to laypeople.

EMF story: we are all victims already. This story is characterized by the conviction that we are all already victims of exposure to noxious electrosmog. In this context, it is argued that the harmful effects will only manifest themselves after years of delay, such as cancer, fertility disturbances, Alzheimer's, and other diseases. In this interpretative pattern, synergistic and cumulative effects are frequently referred to. The synergistic effects are illustrated in this context by the "cup model" according to which humans are previously damaged by various noxious substances so that even the smallest amounts may have great effects so as to make the cup overflow (Bürgerwelle 1998). This story, too, is plausible to the layperson since it relates to everyday convictions. Experts find it difficult to refute because it is impossible to disprove health disorders which may only occur after a thirty-year incubation period.

EMF story: don't let them get away with it! Electrosensitive persons attribute their complaints and health disorders to electrosmog. The range of complaints is large: lack of concentration, sensitivity to changes in the weather, impairment of learning faculties, impaired memory, inability to sleep, lack of drive, and allergies. The Association for the Electrosensitive in Germany estimates that approximately one to two million people are electrosensitive. This story is not only disseminated through the media. It is re-born spontaneously again and again. Following the realization that a base station has been built in the vicinity, any feelings of ill health are attributed to this station by the local residents. Given the public health assumption that 70 percent of the population temporarily suffer from ill health and considering the fact that about 60,000 radio transmitter stations have been licensed since the early 1990s, such a coincidence of the construction of a transmitter station and the onset of complaints is not infrequent. The plausibility of this story is convincing to many people, especially since epidemiologists cannot in principle disprove such individual claims.

Social amplification and EMF risk stories

Taking the risk story approach as a basis, the following hypotheses can be derived for social risk amplification in the field of RF EMF.

- *The existence of several risk stories can lead to mutual amplification and thus support the view on the risk.*

The example of EMF shows that possible risk issues may arise in several ways. Apart from inconclusive scientific studies (is an adverse effect involved?) and dissemination in the media, evidence of damage from the perspective of those affected plays a decisive role. This damage evidence may also be "corroborated" by referring to effects found by scientists in the laboratory. And this, in turn, creates the platform for the idea that others are already victims, too, and that damage has already occurred but only needs time to manifest itself.

A corollary to this concept is the possibility that mutual amplification due to differing risk stories leads to an increased public demand for scientific studies of the risk issue. However, since science cannot unambiguously disprove the existence of negative health impacts, efforts are focused on providing evidence – or lack of evidence – for a negative health impact. Just the idea of undertaking scientific investigations, sometimes regardless of the actual results, may be taken as evidence itself of risk and can then be integrated by the public into existing or new risk stories. Thus, a potentially self-propagating, amplification feedback loop exists between the laypersons' risk stories and the demand for scientific evidence.

- *The "Don't let them get away with it" story, which already assumes the occurrence of damage, leads to a dramatic amplification of the perception of a risk.*

A number of examples show that the existence of damaging events which are related to a potential risk source leads to outrage. Examples are the discussion about clusters of cancer in the vicinity of television transmitters (United States), the controversies about the Sellafield nuclear reprocessing plant in the United Kingdom or about the Krümmel nuclear power station in Germany. The Krümmel nuclear power plant received intense media coverage and increased public attention within the last couple of years because a leukemia cluster among children in the surrounding area has been blamed on radiation released from the plant.

Experimental studies on risk perception, in turn, show that outrage leads to a significant amplification of risk perception (Sandman et al. 1993; Wiedemann and Schütz 2000). Indeed, such outrage may negatively impact public health and lead to, at least partially, a negative placebo effect or a self-fulfilling prophecy.

- *Once a story is born, assumptions on the reasons and motives for causation play a decisive role. If the damaging event is attributed to internal corporate and intentional motives, a considerable degree of outrage must be expected.*

In the literature on crisis communication, great importance is attached to the assessment of causes for crises and damaging events (Coombs

1995). The focus is on the appraisal of a company's responsibility: was the case of damage to be foreseen, had it been recognized and condoned? Or was it an external event beyond control, an act of God?

Wiedemann and Schütz (2000), as well as Nerb et al. (1998), have demonstrated that the type of emotion triggered depends on the attribution of causes in the assessment of damage. If it is assumed that the originator intentionally caused the damaging event, that he has basic control over the event, and that the whole matter does not serve a higher purpose, outrage is triggered as the main emotion.

• *The dissemination of risk stories and their impact depends on general assumptions and convictions (supporting worldviews). Typically, the more negative the public's appraisal is of a risk generator (a company, for example, the mobile communication network provider), the more skeptically will the public appraise the statements of scientists, public administrators, and politicians. At the same time, the more strongly an esoteric worldview prevails among the public, the more probable the risk story will sound and the more it will meet with implicit approval.*

The role that "confidence" plays in public perception in regard to the assessment of risks is rated high in the literature (Renn and Levine 1991). Opinion polls have shown again and again that companies and the state do not enjoy much confidence. Moreover, scandals like the suppression of risk information in connection with the Bovine Spongiform Encephalopathy (BSE) incidents or falsifications by scientists have shaken the public's confidence in experts.

Earle and Cvetkovich (1993) have demonstrated that confidence depends on the worldview that dominates. A representative of the Green party places his confidence in different persons and processes compared to a committed strict supporter of the market economy or an advocate of the idea of law-and-order.

Figure 12.6 shows how the amplification factors described here could interact. Two paths are to be differentiated. On the one hand, there is the amplification of the evidence of risk stories by attitudes to companies, science, administration, and politics, as well as critical but also esoteric worldviews. These risk stories mutually support each other as evidence. According to Heath (1997) the focus is on narrative probability and fidelity:

Narrative probability is a judgement of the extent to which a story holds together, rings true and is free from internal contradiction. Narrative fidelity refers to the weight of values, good reasons, consideration of fact, consequence, consistency, and to the degree to which the story has a bearing on the relevant issues (Heath 1997, p. 319).

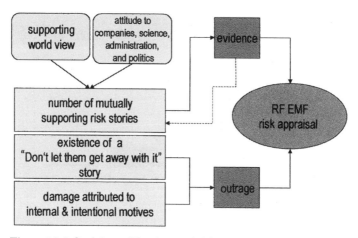

Figure 12.6 Social amplification and risk stories.

These risk stories are then drawn upon to support the belief in the existence of a risk.

The second path relates to the activation of emotions (especially outrage). In this case, reference to already existing damage plays a prominent role and if, moreover, the damage is attributed to internal and intentional motives of the risk generator, then amplified views on the risk are to be expected.

Conclusions and outlook: some reflections on risk stories and risk communication

Risk communication under conditions discussed here using the example of EMF risk issues is not easy. Risk stories effectively resist most of the counter-arguments because, on the one hand, they are mutually plausible and supported by existing conviction contexts, while, on the other hand, they can evoke high levels of emotion. Communicating the "facts" is clearly not sufficient.

The first potential strategy available to a risk communicator is a "risky" one: it focuses on finding an even more plausible counter-story which is compatible with existing convictions and attitudes. However, certain limits have to be acknowledged here. First, convinced supporters of the "Don't let them get away with it" story cannot be reached, unless a better explanation for their complaints and ailments is offered. Furthermore, and perhaps even more importantly, this approach could raise ethical questions (see Morgan and Lave 1990). Is it morally acceptable,

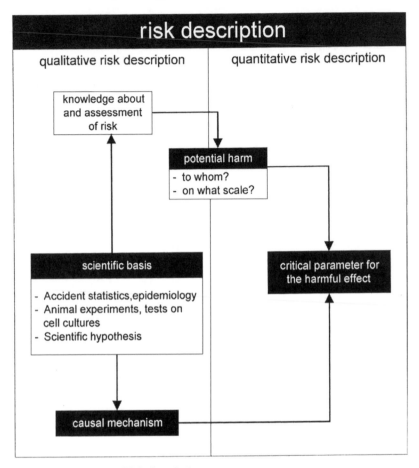

Figure 12.7 Risk description.

especially when there is no clear proof of the contrary, to manipulate people's opinions by this type of risk communication strategy?

An alternative, and perhaps "better," strategy is to aim at a qualitative risk description (see figure 12.7). For instance, a disagreement may exist as to whether there is a risk at all, for example where there is "suspicion of hazard." Yet the public widely assumes that exposure has taken place and they have "already become victims." In this case, information is required about the type of risk present and the evidence in support of this reasoning.

The aim here is to bring the prevailing risk perspective of the laypersons and the presumed type of risk judged by the experts into closer alignment.

As long as the risk perspective differs significantly from the type of risk identified by experts, it is pointless to try to communicate risk statistics, since they will not be given serious consideration.

There are a number of possible approaches that can be used for this second strategy. For the case of exposure to a contaminant, for example, the details of exposure routes or pathways leading to health impairment might be explained. Alternatively, the exposure dose needs to be identified: who is exposed and to what extent? In "suspicion of hazard" cases, the discussion about whether there is a risk or not should be conducted using the scientific principles of risk analysis.

The following questions give an idea of the topics that could be of significance in any qualitative risk description:

- How good are the scientific models on which the risk assessment is based?
- How good are the data on which the risk assessment is based?
- To what extent do unconnected studies agree? Do they arrive at different or the same conclusions?
- Can exposure be reliably detected?
- Is there a dose/response relationship, that is, does the risk grow proportionally larger with higher exposure?
- Can the influence of secondary risk factors be controlled?
- Can procedural and measurement errors be ruled out?
- What support does the risk assessment enjoy in the scientific community?
- What do the subject experts say?

The type of questions listed here clearly shows that assessment knowledge is needed. The task is to impart this knowledge in such a way that it takes the form of plausible stories. It may well be that a quantitative description of the risks is helpful only after agreement has been reached as to the actual type and nature of risk present (see figure 12.7).

Part IV

Risk ripples and stigma effects

13   Integrating politics with the social amplification of risk framework: insights from an exploration in the criminal justice context

M. V. Rajeev Gowda

Some risk-related incidents have far-reaching societal impacts while others gradually fade from public attention and memory. These societal impacts include direct policy responses such as stricter regulation of the relevant risk and also "significant indirect impacts such as liability, insurance costs, loss of confidence in institutions, stigmatization, or alienation from community affairs" (Kasperson 1992, p. 158). Paradoxically, the magnitude of such societal impacts often has little to do with the technically assessed magnitude of the actual risks involved. Attempts to explain this puzzle resulted in the development of the social amplification of risk framework (SARF) (Kasperson, Renn, Slovic et al. 1988).

The developers of the SARF have argued that amplification and attenuation depend on a complex set of behavioral, psychological, social, and cultural processes, rather than objective measures of risk. Factors affecting social amplification include public concern and fears about the risks and attention from the media and active opposition from key individuals and groups in society. While the SARF clearly makes a substantial contribution to our understanding of why the social amplification of risks occurs, it has not yet arrived at a clearly developed understanding of how some risk-related incidents get attenuated rather than amplified. The developers of the SARF clearly recognize this problem and are actively exploring different hypotheses to enhance our understanding of attenuation. For example, Kasperson has asked whether "individual components of social amplification processes have a 'necessary but not sufficient quality,' that multiple elements of social amplification must be present if the process is to 'take off' and to be sustained?" (Kasperson 1992, p. 174). Elaborating on this question, Kasperson and Kasperson have raised

This chapter was previously presented at the 1999 conference on the Social Amplification of Risk Framework, Cumberland Lodge, United Kingdom. Earlier versions were presented at research conferences of the Social Science Group on Risk, the Association of Public Policy and Management, and the Society for Risk Analysis. Comments from participants at these conferences, and from reviewers, especially Claire Marris, are gratefully acknowledged.

the question of whether attenuation results because the risks involved "occur in distant times, distant places, or [to] distant – that is, powerless or marginal – social groups?" (Kasperson and Kasperson 1996, p. 103) Clearly, much more work needs to be done to enhance the SARF and to make it a unifying and overarching explanatory framework for both the social amplification and attenuation of risks.

In this chapter, we aim to enhance the explanatory power of the SARF by starting from an explicit recognition that the SARF is fundamentally a *political* account of how people and societies deal with risks and risk-related incidents. Therefore, we argue that the SARF can be strengthened substantially through the integration of insights drawn from political analysis and studies of the policy process. Specifically, we draw on Kingdon's (1984) "agenda-setting model" to highlight how the various stages of the policy process affect whether or not societal reactions to risks get translated into tangible policy outcomes. Further, we pay special attention to the inherently political nature of policy solutions and how this affects the success or failure of efforts aimed at the social amplification of particular risk-related incidents.

In order to make our insights more compelling, we draw on empirical cases from a domain hitherto left alone by most risk analysts; that of criminal justice. While the SARF was developed in the context of health and environment conflicts, investigating its utility as an explanatory framework in the very different domain of criminal justice should yield new and useful insights to enhance its analytical power. Further, we may be able to generate useful insights from the traditional domains of risk analysis research – health and the environment – to improve the societal administration of criminal justice. Within the domain of criminal justice, we focus our attention on policy efforts to protect children from predators, particularly sex offenders who have served their terms in prison and have since moved back into the community. This domain has witnessed tremendous policy activity, across continents, over the last few years. It is to this policy context that we now turn.

Social amplification in the criminal justice domain: the case of Megan's Laws

On 29 July 1994, Megan Kanka, a seven-year-old New Jersey girl, was raped and murdered by a paroled child molester who lived across the street from her. Outraged by this tragedy, her parents, Richard and Maureen Kanka, lobbied state and federal officials to enact tougher laws that would prevent such tragic incidents. They argued that Megan could have been saved if they had known of their neighbor's criminal background and taken appropriate precautions. They therefore called for a law that would ensure that local law enforcement officials and parents would be informed when convicted child molesters and rapists moved into a community after their release (Bredlie 1996). This right-to-know approach to addressing people's concerns about the risks posed to their children by released sex offenders quickly attracted attention all over America. The publicity accorded to the Kankas' efforts and Megan's tragic death resulted in a wave of legislation across America whereby this right-to-know approach was implemented as the predominant policy response to managing the risks posed by released sex offenders. While the term "Megan's Law" applies specifically to the New Jersey state law, it has become synonymous with the broader policy approach generally. We shall therefore use the umbrella term "Megan's Laws" to describe legislation patterned wholly or partly on the original Megan's Law in New Jersey.

The phenomenal and quick passage of Megan's Laws around the United States suggests that these developments may be an interesting example of the social amplification of risk (Kasperson 1992; Kasperson et al. 1988). After all, it is particularly hard to pass new legislation in the United States, given the design of the democratic process in America and the competition among varied groups in the country's political economy. As a result only a small fraction of proposed legislation ever makes it to the statute books. Given this low base rate, the rapid passage of Megan's Laws may demonstrate social amplification in action. It may therefore be particularly insightful to analyze the political and risk-related processes that led to the proliferation of Megan's Laws.

Just as with other instances of social amplification, Megan's Laws are fundamentally driven by risk perceptions. They represent a policy response to people's concerns about recidivism, that is, that sex offenders are likely to repeat their crimes. However, in the case of sex offenders, there is no objective measure of the rate of recidivism. The evidence on the subject is controversial, with one study reporting that the probability of recidivism ranges from practically zero to more than 50 percent (Furby et al. 1989). More recently, Bredlie (1996) reports that the United States Department of Justice states that the recidivism rate for sex offenders who have not been given treatment is nearly 60 percent. Further, former Attorney General Janet Reno is reported to have asserted that "convicted child molesters have a recidivism rate as high as 40 to 75 percent" (Seper 1995, quoted in Bredlie 1996).

These numbers are open to question because some of the threat to children comes not from strangers but from family members themselves (Gillespie 2000), and the evidence on this aspect of the problem is probably underreported. Lotke (1996) emphasizes the significant problems associated with assessing the risks posed by sex offenders and argues that people are not aware of the fact that large numbers of sex offenders within families do not get caught. If caught, the majority can be treated and the threat of recidivism reduced.

Regardless of the fact that it is seeing only a part of the larger problem, given the absence of consensus on an objective assessment of the risks involved, it is quite possible that the general public may consider every released sex offender to be a definite candidate for recidivism. It is also understandable that people desire to ensure that their children are exposed to absolutely no risk from paedophiles. Thus, it follows that the public will support risk-reducing measures based on the notion that even one repeat offense by a released sex offender is one too many. The reactions that sexual attacks on children provoke may be similar to "dread" which has a significant effect on people's perceptions of risk in the health and environmental domains (Slovic 1992). Thus the nature of the response to the risk of repeat crimes by released sex offenders has many of the elements found in traditional social amplification of risk contexts and may indeed be more potent in the case of sex crimes against children. It is thus hardly surprising that there is tremendous public support for registration and notification laws aimed at informing citizens about sex offenders in their midst. Politicians have reacted quickly to tap this widespread political support by pushing for the passage of variants of Megan's Laws across the United States.

The first major statute to adopt the right-to-know approach was the Washington State Community Protection Act of 1990. This law was triggered by a brutal attack on a seven-year-old boy by Earl Shriner, a convicted child molester. It turned out that Shriner had been released even though authorities knew that he might still be dangerous. In response to this discovery, the state legislature passed this law in the belief that registration of sex offenders with the police coupled with community notification of the presence of offenders would reduce the probability of recurrence of such attacks. The Washington state legislature's actions were also influenced by media coverage of attacks on children by repeat offenders in other states (Bredlie 1996). At the federal level, contemporaneously with the New Jersey developments in 1994, the United States Congress passed the Jacob Wetterling Crimes Against Children and Sexually Violent Offender Registration Act modeled after the Washington statute.

New Jersey, which promulgated the actual Megan's Law, has among the more refined systems for dealing with released sex offenders. The New Jersey system is explicitly tied to the judged seriousness of the risk posed by the released offender. All released sex offenders must register with law enforcement authorities. There are then three levels of notification based on the law enforcement agency's assessment of the offender's chances of re-offense, which is to be based on a set of risk factors including the offender's criminal and psychological history (Bredlie 1996). For those offenders considered to pose low risks only law enforcement agencies that are likely to encounter them are to be notified. For those offenders considered moderate risks, notification is extended to community groups involved in caring for women and children who are likely to encounter them. For those offenders considered high risks, notification must be extended to members of the community who are likely to encounter the released sex offenders (Bredlie 1996).

In spite of the care with which the actual Megan's Law has been designed by New Jersey, the author of one of the few critical essays on Megan's Law argues that it is an example of legislation passed in an election year which has not considered all the potential consequences and constitutional issues fully (Crimaldi 1995). This criticism may be too strong in the case of New Jersey's law but is perhaps more appropriate in the context of a similar program in Louisiana and one in California. The Louisiana law requires sex offenders to notify communities themselves by publishing notices in local newspapers. These notices must include their names, addresses, and their crimes. Further, local parole boards have the discretionary authority to require other forms of identification including vehicle bumper stickers that state "Sex Offender On Board" (Bredlie 1996); this "Scarlet Letter" law is currently encountering legal challenges.

In California, the then state Attorney General, Dan Lungren, who was running (it turns out unsuccessfully) for election as governor, announced that the state would publish a CD-ROM containing information on upwards of 60,000 convicted sex offenders. The CD-ROM would be available to the public at their local police departments. An article in the *New York Times* (1 July 1997) pointed out that the information contained in the database was not accurate, comprehensive, or up-to-date; e.g. it included people who were convicted of same-sex consensual acts which have since been decriminalized. Thus, in California, some people whose names were found on the list ended up losing their jobs, even though their original crimes would no longer qualify them for the sex offender tag.

The same *New York Times* article referred to the public furor that often accompanied the discovery that a sex offender who has completed his term in prison was now living in the community. While such public concern is legitimate in the light of recidivism, it also hampers rehabilitation, and provides governments with an excuse not to consider other forms of treatment of sex offenders. Public hounding of sex offenders who have served their term clashes with values associated with the rule of law. An even larger danger is that of vigilante justice where individual citizens or groups attack released sex offenders even if they have not committed any crimes after their release; such actions would be in violation of the constitutionally guaranteed rights of released sex offenders. This should be cause for concern for civil rights organizations because convicted sex offenders are less likely to have defenders. However, even leading civil rights organizations such as the American Civil Liberties Union have chosen not to test the constitutionality of these laws, except in the narrow context of double jeopardy: that is, that released sex offenders were being unfairly punished again through the process of notification. However, commentators, such as Schopf (1995), have argued that Megan's Laws can survive constitutional challenges on many different fronts.

In considering the constitutionality of such laws, courts have ruled that the interests of the state and parents in protecting children outweigh any potential stigma effects or threats of vigilantism (Bredlie 1996). A 1998 decision by the United States Supreme Court not to review suits challenging lower courts' upholding of Megan's Laws has spurred the full implementation of such laws in virtually every state. These lower courts had ruled that Megan's Laws were not unconstitutional on the grounds that mere notification is not a significant punishment and therefore does not constitute double jeopardy. Therefore, how people behave in response to such notification will be key to the determination of the constitutionality of Megan's Laws.

Our reading of the literature from risk analysis and cognitive psychology would suggest that punitive untoward effects of notification are likely to occur in the course of time. One concern is the NIMBY (not in my back yard) phenomenon that may cause communities to reject the relocation of released offenders; some instances of this are already available (Nordheimer 1995). The end result of such reactions could mean that released offenders may not be able to locate anywhere in the country, and perforce lose their right to live in the location of their choice. It could also lead to more parole violations and the spreading of risks posed by released offenders if they are forced to move from place to place or to go underground beyond the reach of police monitoring. Vigilante attacks on released sex offenders are another cause for concern because such attacks imply that some citizens are willing to break the law in an attempt to alleviate their fears about the potential risks posed by released sex offenders. Further, the community at large may be willing to tolerate such illegal interventions. Such a development, ultimately, does not bode well for the rule of law. These developments indicate how difficult it will be to simultaneously empower citizens, prevent crimes, and protect the civil rights of re-leased offenders. That Megan's Laws have been enacted throughout the country is then a clear indication of the paramount importance American society places on the protection of children.

Political analysis and Megan's Laws

The central issue that forms the backdrop for Megan's Laws is the decline in people's trust in the American criminal justice system (Tyler and Boeckmann 1997). Throughout the 1980s and thereafter, conservative politicians have seized upon salient instances of perceived judicial fa-voritism toward criminals to argue that the legal system needs to be overhauled. Indeed, one of the key factors that led to the defeat of a liberal presidential candidate, Michael Dukakis, in 1988, was a political advertisement (the "Willie Horton" ad), which focused on the crimes committed by a criminal released under a parole program established by Dukakis, the then Governor of Massachusetts (Ansolabehere and Iyengar 1995). This decline in trust in the criminal justice system has led to pop-ular attempts to overhaul the system, for example, through referenda, in ways which reduce the flexibility available to judges, and which ultimately override legal authority. One such referendum in California resulted in a "three strikes and you're out" law which ensures that repeat criminal offenders are permanently incarcerated (Tyler and Boeckmann 1997).

Another manifestation of the decline in trust in the American legal sys-tem is people's increased willingness to tolerate the vigilante or extralegal actions of citizens, and their willingness to dispense with procedural pro-tections for criminal defendants (Tyler and Boeckmann 1997). A further development that has resulted from people's decline in trust in the judi-cial system is the victims' rights movement. The proponents of victims' rights argue that the American judicial system should balance its con-sideration for the civil rights of criminals with attention to the rights of victims. Megan's Laws arguably fit into this framework because they involve balancing the right to privacy of released sex offenders with the right of potential victims to be free from attack.

In working out how to determine this balance between civil rights and the rights of potential victims one may assume that lawmakers in a republican form of government would consider various policy options thoroughly. That is, they would weigh the constitutional implications and potential vigilante attacks against popular pressure to enact right-to-know laws in the case of sex offenders. Indeed Suedfeld and Tetlock (1992, p. 51) point out that people generally assume that good political deci-sion making is characterized by "extensive information, search, empathy for the positions of other participants, openness to disagreement, and the wish to find a mutually acceptable outcome." However, political decision making does not necessarily conform to this narrower and idealistic conception of rationality but focuses instead on a broader strategic rationality centered on elections and electability (Mayhew 1974). Politicians may care less about the fine balance between civil rights of released prisoners and the right of citizens to live in a crime-free environment; they may care more about what set of actions will return them to office. Thus, the widespread and quick enactment of Megan's Laws all over the United States can partly be attributed to politicians catching on to a strategically advantageous policy option that would allow them to demonstrate their toughness on crime. The only people fundamentally empowered by Megan's Laws may be politicians themselves!

We thus argue that one central reason why social amplification occurred in the Megan's Law case was because the policy solution offered by its proponents was easily enactable and electorally beneficial to the political players who propelled it forward. This insight enables us to bridge the SARF with a political framework of agenda setting and policy action (Kingdon 1984) to explain how amplification and attenuation can occur. Kingdon argues that public policy making involves a set of processes including : (1) the setting of the agenda, (2) the specification of alternatives from which a choice is to be made, (3) an authoritative choice among those specified alternatives, as in a legislative vote or a presidential decision, and (4) the implementation of the decision. Success in one process does not necessarily imply success in others (Kingdon 1984, p. 3). In a manner similar to that proposed by the SARF, Kingdon suggests that issues can get onto the agenda through salient events that generate media coverage, especially when promoted by policy entrepreneurs.

However, Kingdon (1984) points out, merely getting on the agenda need not guarantee success. Problems have to come together at propitious moments (policy windows) with policy solutions and with favorable political circumstances, if there is to be a likelihood of policy action. According to Kingdon, "the probability of an item rising on a decision agenda is dramatically increased if all three elements-problem, proposal, and political receptivity – are coupled in a single package" (Kingdon 1984, p. 204). Thus, in Kingdon's framework, advocates of policy initiatives must take advantage of policy windows that have opened due to perhaps a salient, newsworthy identification of a problem. They must then argue that their policy solution is the most appropriate to deal with this problem. And the political climate should be receptive to such arguments, perhaps because politicians see electoral advantage in responding to the problem through the adoption of the proposed solution.

In the Megan's Law case, we have a pressing problem (protecting children from the risks posed by released sex offenders) coupled with a policy solution (information provision) coupled with a political climate favorable to such action (because right-to-know laws are politically difficult to oppose and financially easy to implement in an anti-crime, anti-big-government era) which enabled the Kankas' public-spirited policy entrepreneurship to be amplified in the form of Megan's Laws around the country. Thus, the lesson for social amplification is that the Kingdon (1984) agenda setting model may help describe why some risk incidents get amplified and others attenuated. Attenuation may occur simply because the salient risk incidents which result in problem identification are not coupled with politically viable policy solutions that would result in significant policy action.

Extending the analysis

Megan's Laws in the United States provide an insightful illustration of the utility of combining Kingdon's (1984) agenda setting model of the policy process with the SARF. However, two other developments from the same domain of criminal justice can enable us to extend and strengthen our analysis even further. The first development involves the case of Polly Klaas in the United States and the second development involves the case of Sarah Payne in the United Kingdom. Both these cases involved tragic incidents similar to that of Megan Kanka, but in neither case did policy developments of the range and scope of Megan's Laws result. The Polly Klaas case predates the Megan Kanka tragedy and, from the perspective of the SARF, can be considered to be an example of social attenuation. The Sarah Payne case is contemporaneous to the writing of this chapter, but developments to date indicate that the policy community in the United Kingdom is handling the situation without extraordinarily significant changes in the management of risks from sex offenders. The addition of the United Kingdom context also provides a useful contrast to the United States experience in managing these risks.

In the Polly Klaas case, the victim was a pre-teen girl in the town of Petaluma, California who was found missing on 1 October 1993. Her body was found a few days later, and a vagrant, Richard Allen Davis, was ultimately convicted of her kidnapping and murder. Mark Klaas, Polly's father, responded to this tragedy by vowing to create conditions that would ensure the safety of children. His agenda involved generating collective action in communities, whereby towns formed committees to promote children's safety. His activities influenced the establishment of the Polly Klaas Foundation (http://www.pollyklaas.org) and the Klaas

Foundation for Children (http://www.klaaskids.org), both of which are lobbying entities and information providers in the policy arena pertaining to children's safety.

While the Polly Klaas tragedy was widely covered in the news media (problem identification) and occurred during an era favorable to tough action against criminals (politically propitious policy window), its overall impact may have been limited by the policy approach chosen by Mark Klaas; that of collective action. Collective action is particularly hard to bring about because of rational free-riding behavior (Olson 1965), and this will arguably be the case even in the face of threats to children. Further, collective action takes away the responsibility of responding to the problem from the government and places it in the hands of citizens and community groups, thus lessening the potential for large-scale policy response. Indeed, we can observe that Mark Klaas's efforts have resulted in tremendous publicity, sympathy and attention to the problem of children's safety, but his activities have gradually faded from active public consciousness and the policy agenda. His civil-society-oriented collective action approach did not trigger the large-scale policy changes as witnessed under Megan's Laws.

Thus we would argue that the availability of a potent policy solution – the right-to-know – was significantly responsible for the success of Megan's Laws when compared to other approaches like collective action in terms of protecting children from criminal predators. This insight from Kingdon's (1984) political process model of agenda setting and policy formation helps us to understand a crucial factor affecting the social attenuation of risk.

We next turn to the United Kingdom for a case which presents a contrast to the United States' experience and raises important insights for the SARF. In the Sarah Payne case, the victim was a nine-year-old girl who was abducted and killed on 1 July 2000. A British tabloid newspaper, *News of the World*, reacted to this tragic incident by announcing a campaign to pressurize the government to enact a United Kingdom version of Megan's Law, termed Sarah's Law. The newspaper also went ahead and published the names, photographs, and locations of forty-nine convicted sex offenders. It also announced plans to develop an online database of sex offenders that would be accessible to the public (Gillespie 2000). Simultaneously, the parents of the murdered girl launched a signature campaign that resulted in 700,000 citizens signing a petition urging the government to enact Sarah's Law (Dyer 2000). Overall, these developments had many of the hallmarks of social amplification in action. Interestingly enough, the policy solutions of choice had crossed national boundaries and even generated some support from United States nongovernmental organizations such as those led by Mark Klaas.

However, the reaction from the British government and various British interest groups concerned about children's safety was substantially different from what emerged in the United States. The government pointed out that it had the situation under control and had already passed a law – the Sexual Offenders Act of 1997 – that also included a Sex Offenders Register. The administration of this act was the responsibility of Public Protection Units within police constabularies, whose officers were expected to interact with and monitor released sex offenders. Under this act, the police were authorized to disclose the identity of a released sex offender to various sections of society, depending on the assessed threat and need. While the Register was not intended to be a publicly accessible document, there have been instances of some of the information in it being disclosed to communities that were potentially threatened by released sex offenders (Gillespie 2000). It was expected that this threat of disclosure would be sufficient to ensure that released sex offenders would not reoffend.

The reaction to the *News of the World* campaign from government and interest group circles hardened when it was seen that the campaign had led to vigilante attacks: for example, on a person who looked like one of the offenders whose picture had been published. Because the newspaper did not have a sterling reputation for accuracy, and was publishing details based on its own sources rather than obtained from an uncooperative government, the likelihood of more mistakes was a significant possibility. Finally, the newspaper called off its high-profile campaign after a mob attacked the home of a suspected paedophile (Gillespie 2000).

Strictly speaking, it is hard to assert that in the Sarah Payne case the potential social amplification has been attenuated instead, given that these issues are too contemporaneous for such a judgment. Still, given the comparative rapidity of the passage of Megan's Laws around the United States, the fact that no such policy change occurred rapidly in the United Kingdom allows us to conclude that social amplification of risk, especially in terms of policy-related consequences, did not actually result.

From the perspective of our integration of the Kingdon (1984) agenda-setting model with the SARF, it will be useful to consider why such amplification did not occur. Once again, we had a pressing problem (protecting children from the risks posed by released sex offenders) coupled with a policy solution (information provision) but the political climate favorable to such action did not transpire and instead actually worsened. Clearly, the evidence of attacks on innocent people strengthened the resolve of the government to continue to adhere to its existing procedures and not to yield to public pressure. In addition, the government's hand was strengthened by the fact that the *News of the World* campaign was strongly opposed by independent child protection charities who argued that publication would drive paedophiles underground and thereby increase the risk to society. The United Kingdom thus witnessed a more thorough consideration of the issues involved in the passage of a right-to-know law in this context than was seen in the United States, and this helped to prevent hasty action driven by tabloid-generated public frenzy.

Another feature that arguably affected the passage of Sarah's Law is the parliamentary system in the United Kingdom. This results in a very different policy process than in the United States. In the United Kingdom, there is more centralized party control over policy, and there are fewer opportunities for individual political entrepreneurs or even entities outside the formal policy process to push agendas that translate into policy changes. Elections are also typically held only at approximately five-year intervals and then national issues tend to dominate campaigns. Thus, the political context of the United Kingdom does not provide easy routes for policy entrepreneurs to translate their agendas into action, and this becomes a crucial barrier to the social amplification of risk.

The inherent political nature of the right-to-know

Given our attention to the political nature of policy processes and specifically of policy instruments themselves, it would be worth our while to consider the political potency of policy instruments such as information provision or the right-to-know. Information-related policy approaches have a long history and information has come to be regarded as a key factor that could lead to improved risk management (Hadden 1989; Magat and Viscusi 1992). For example, information has been used as a policy tool in public information campaigns where governments attempt to change people's behavior through one-way messages (Weiss and Tschirhart 1994). Another way in which information serves policy purposes is through product labeling and hazard warnings aimed at consumers and workers; here information is provided in particular formats and consumers and workers are expected to process it and arrive at risk management decisions (Magat and Viscusi 1992). Information is also a key component of risk communication efforts aimed at resolving risk-related conflicts; Leiss (1996) discusses the various phases of risk communication research and describes how risk communication practice has moved from one-way education efforts to inclusive, participatory, information sharing processes aimed at consensual risk reduction.

But risk analysts have not emphasized the political nature of these information-related tools. Their political nature is nowhere more relevant than in the context of the relatively recent information-oriented innovation: the recognition of the public's right-to-know. At first glance, it would seem odd to term this policy instrument as inherently political. After all, rather than trying to persuade citizens toward some behavioral response, the right-to-know approach would simply place information about risks in the public domain. This way people can respond to the information in any manner they choose, though the expectation is that citizens and other entities will make better-informed decisions, particularly about risk management and self-protective behavior. Various features involving citizen participation can also be integrated with right-to-know laws to improve risk management (Hadden 1989).

Political scientists such as Williams and Matheny (1995) are more explicit about the fact that right-to-know laws are inherently political. They consider right-to-know laws as empowering weapons in the hands of environmental activists and consumers against the powerful forces of industry. They would consider opposition to right-to-know laws as arising from industry's efforts to suppress popular challenges to risk management decisions. Overall, the right-to-know approach has been hailed as a democratizing feature of American risk regulation (Sunstein 1997) and its application in the context of hazardous waste policy recognized as a significant policy success.

In hazardous waste policy, the right-to-know is central to the Superfund Amendments and Reauthorization Act, Title III of which is called the Community Right to Know Act. That law requires companies to make available to the public information about their hazardous waste emissions, which are also recorded in a database called the Toxics Release Inventory. The success of this approach lies in the feature that companies have drastically reduced their waste emissions in response to the law, presumably for fear of adverse risk perceptions in their host communities. Indeed Portney (2000) predicts that programs utilizing the right-to-know technique will soon proliferate in other domains of environmental policy because of their success in the hazardous waste arena. He succinctly summarizes the scholarly consensus on right-to-know policies when he asserts that

experience has shown that when firms are required to make public their emissions, they feel pressure to reduce them, even when the levels of emission are perfectly legal . . . So long as citizens are able to make sense of this information, programs like this are not only democratic but also efficiency-enhancing. (Portney 2000, p. 201)

The first sentence of the quote above captures the essence of the right-to-know approach. Information provision can be a remarkably simple policy instrument. Rather than persuading citizens and firms toward some behavioral response, it merely mandates that information about risks be placed in the public domain. People and firms can then respond to this information in any manner they choose, though the expectation is that they will make better-informed decisions, particularly about risk management and self-protective behavior (Hadden 1989). Information provision corrects a market failure; that of incomplete information. Firms will choose the level of emissions that is acceptable to a concerned public, even if that level goes beyond that required by regulators. The attention to people's preferences actually makes the end result more completely efficiency-enhancing than even a perfectly tuned regulatory standard that only considers the technical risks involved. Fundamentally, enhancing the public's right-to-know is politically empowering while it achieves the desired policy outcomes.

But the key challenge to the effectiveness of right-to-know policies can be discerned in the second sentence in the Portney quote above. For such policies to be effective, it is important that people "make sense of this information" correctly. Whether this will indeed occur is the central question facing policy analysts. Policy analysts need to be alert to the implications of choosing a policy instrument such as the right-to-know, fundamentally to avoid the false negatives and false positives associated with policy choices (Hammond 1996). The false positive would be judging something as a true warning signal when in fact it is false, and the false negative would be ignoring a warning signal with disastrous consequences. We suggest that risk analysts and policy makers need to work with this powerful instrument in order to minimize false positives and false negatives in people's reactions. This will help prevent such progressive, empowering techniques as the right-to-know from becoming counterproductive and yet another addition to the dreary catalogue of regulatory paradoxes where good intentions have often resulted in less than stellar policy outcomes (Sunstein 1990).

From a political perspective, the growing popularity of information provision proposals arises from their strategic superiority to opposing arguments. Because information is simply provided, such proposals are seemingly innocuous, and this makes them easier to implement politically. Information-related policy developments are also gaining momentum because political actors reason that by calling for such laws they are demonstrating their commitment to public health and public empowerment goals. After all, such proponents seem to suggest, if risk-related information is available to producers, what is the harm in sharing it with those who may be affected by the risks? The implication is that risk producers who oppose such information provision have something to hide, and that their actions are anti-democratic in an open society. Further, because information provision typically does not entail the establishment of a large regulatory apparatus, it is attractive to policy makers on cost considerations. Also, given the hands-off nature of the information provision, any negative reactions on the part of the public are harder to pin directly to governmental actions.

Risk analysts also need to recognize that the debate over right-to-know laws is embedded in a political process, where the choice over balancing false positives and false negatives will be made by policy makers paying attention to the competing power of different groups (Hammond 1996). In such debates, particularly in the context of social amplification, it is far from clear that all aspects of a policy solution will be discussed thoroughly. The reason for this is that people, whether laypeople or policy makers, fundamentally behave as politicians, with a keen concern for reputation effects (Tetlock 1997). When risk-related incidents occur, the process of collective belief formation may be driven by "availability cascades" where a given belief becomes accepted as the general consensus because people endorse the belief based on what they hear from others and by even distorting their own views in order to ensure that they are socially acceptable (Kuran and Sunstein 1999).

Further, law makers may often be loath to even appear to question popularly acceptable developments such as Megan's Law for fear of their views being used against them in negative advertisements in future elections. Because party control over legislators is comparatively minimal in the United States, elections are held frequently, and political competition is substantially individual-centred, legislators are constantly attuned to how their actions will be perceived in an electoral arena where negative political advertisements and campaigning are a central feature. In such advertisements, candidates often resort to half-truths, misleading statistical inferences, and distortions to portray their opponents as deficient on some aspect of concern to the electorate. In recent years, one such aspect of concern has been candidates' views on crime, and candidates considered "soft" on crime have had a difficult time at the polls (Ansolabehere and Iyengar 1995). Further, "[p]osturing for their next campaigns, elected officials sometimes introduce legislation designed to embarrass the opposition" (Ansolabehere and Iyengar 1995, p. 149).

We can therefore surmise that if some elected officials were to advocate Megan's Laws, their opponents would be hard pressed to counsel a careful consideration of the issues because such moderation may be out of tune with the prevailing public sentiment and may well be used against them in future elections. Thus the process of social amplification may often involve a debate characterized by one dominant viewpoint, and this may prevent judicious insights from being integrated with the policy solution. Thus the political power of the combination of policy context and instrument may well come in the way of appropriate safeguards and modifications to the right-to-know.

Policy implications

Risk analysts can play a significant role in helping to inform and guide people's reactions to risk-related information, particularly in complex areas such as those involving environmental, health, and crime risks (Noll 1996). It is important that these insights be considered because, fundamentally, it is not clear how people are even expected to react to information about released sex offenders in their midst. Will people move out of their neighborhood? Will people drive the released sex offender from their community, even in violation of laws? Will people restrict their children's activities substantially in order to ensure their safety? We will find the answers to questions such as these over the course of time.

Risk analysis has two central insights for right-to-know laws. One insight derives from risk communication, which represents an understanding of the systematic ways in which people respond to risk-related information. The other insight derives from the study of the not-in-my-backyard (NIMBY) phenomenon characteristic of many risk-related disputes. Unfortunately, these insights seem to have generally escaped the purview of proponents of right-to-know legislation in recent years.

In the field of risk communication, a large body of literature and experience demonstrates that mere provision of information is not enough to ensure that people take appropriate risk-reducing and self-protective behavior. Problems in information processing can arise because of "source problems (who says it), message problems (what is said), channel problems (how it is said), and receiver problems (to whom it is said)" (Nordenstam and DiMento 1990, p. 346). While these points refer to actively delivered messages, they also suggest the need for research into how passively provided information may generate a variety of reactions, and for research into how different channels, including the Internet, may affect how people react to information provision.

Behavioral decision theory focuses on how people respond to risk-related information (Gowda 2002). Behavioral decision theory's findings show that people: (i) use shortcuts when processing information; and (ii) rely on inherent preferences that are significantly different from that assumed in expected utility or rational choice, the economic standard of behavior. Thus individuals deviate from the rational choice standard of rationality in ways that are "persistent and large" and "systematic rather than random" (Knetsch 1995, p. 75; see generally, Kahneman et al. 1982).

The use of shortcuts, or heuristics, is sometimes efficient in that they facilitate judgments without tremendous information-processing costs. Some heuristics can lead to inefficient or suboptimal outcomes that people would reject if confronted with a detailed analysis utilizing statistical arguments. When heuristics lead to suboptimal outcomes from the normative standpoint of economic rationality, they are termed biases (Camerer 1995). However, in the realm of choice, where people have to make decisions rather than arrive at judgments over probabilities, their preferences are significantly different from those considered strictly rational. This is made clear in Prospect Theory, a descriptive theory of choice advanced by Kahneman and Tversky (1979) that is a key component of behavioral decision theory.

Among the key deviations from rational choice in judgment, which affect how people respond to risk-related information, are the availability heuristic and the representativeness heuristic. The availability heuristic states that people "assess the frequency of a class or the probability of an event by the ease with which instances or occurrences can be brought to mind" (Tversky and Kahneman 1974, p. 1127). In other words, if people can readily think of examples of events, they will inflate their estimates of the likelihood of their occurrence. In the Megan's Law context people may base their estimates of the likelihood of encountering a released sex offender on media coverage, which may result in exaggerated risk perceptions. The representativeness heuristic focuses on people's difficulties with the working of probability, for example, by ignoring base rates, sample size, and regression to the mean (Tversky and Kahneman 1974; Tversky and Kahneman 1982). Working in tandem with the availability heuristic, the representativeness heuristic may lead people to make incorrect extrapolations from media coverage of particular risk-related issues. In the Megan's Law context, this heuristic may result in people's unwillingness to differentiate between sex offenders based on their likelihood of recidivism, even if that were determined in some objective manner.

Thus people rely on several important and systematic shortcuts when they make judgments about the probabilities of events. While such errors in judgment could theoretically be ameliorated through education, deviations from rationality in the realm of choice are caused by factors other than "rational laziness." People stand by "inferior" or "irrational" choices even after they are made aware of their mistakes. This is because when individuals make choices, their heuristics are derived more from intuition than from cognition, that is, they represent true preferences. While errors in judgment result from correctable mistakes in the thought process, errors in choice stem from fundamental violations of the assumptions of rationality (Tversky and Kahneman 1986). This has led scholars to search for dimensions of choice that are not traditionally included in rational models of decision making. Key dimensions relevant to our discussion of Megan's Law are the certainty effect and the zero risk bias.

The certainty effect states that people prefer small benefits that are certain to larger benefits that are uncertain (see Baron 1994, pp. 358–361 for a discussion; Plous 1993). For example, people tend to place a higher value on reducing the probability of a negative outcome from 5 percent to 0 percent than reducing the probability of another, perhaps more serious, danger from 30 percent to 20 percent. In the Megan's Law context, people will generally support any moves that promise to ensure that any threat to their children from released sex offenders will be eliminated, regardless of the financial and social costs of these measures. Politicians seem to understand the certainty effect well and often offer "certain" solutions such as eliminating all carcinogenic food additives (Gowda 1999), or three-strikes-and-you're-out laws. Voters, meanwhile, seem to expect clear and certain solutions, and politicians propagate the view (myth?) that they exist by continuing to promise them. While incorporating certainty is a worthy aspiration, it may be inefficient from an economic perspective and impossible in the real world.

The insights from behavioral decision theory discussed above seem to suggest that people react to risk-related information in a flawed manner. However, scholars working on risk perception argue that the public, far from being ignorant and irrational, seeks to improve risk regulation (Hadden 1991; Slovic 1987, 1992, 2000). Slovic (1987, p. 285) lucidly captures the essence of this argument: "Lay people sometimes lack certain information about hazards. However, their basic conceptualization of risk is much richer than that of the experts and reflects legitimate concerns that are typically omitted from expert risk assessments." The concerns affecting the public include qualitative factors such as voluntariness, catastrophic potential, and impact on future generations, which experts typically ignore by restricting their focus to only quantitative factors such as expected mortality and morbidity (see Slovic, 2000). As Leiss (1992) points out, the public's perceptions of risk have also been affected by its awareness of the historical record of risks being underestimated by governments and industries (see also Freudenburg, this volume chapter 4; Leiss 2001 and chapter 15 this volume).

Kunreuther and Slovic (1996) therefore advocate a "contextualist" view of risk, where quantitative, qualitative, and values aspects are all considered but with different emphases in different contexts. They then call for risk management strategies which involve "more public participation [in] both risk assessment and risk decision making to make the risk-decision process more democratic, improve the relevance and quality of technical analysis, and increase the legitimacy and public acceptance of the resulting decisions" (Kunreuther and Slovic 1996, p. 123). This is perhaps the way in which Megan's Laws should be considered; as efforts which in their own complex way attempt to help people protect themselves in as workable a manner as possible.

Such insights need to be integrated with Megan's Laws so that the information provided generates the *intended* self-protective outcome rather than a vigilante response that violates laws. Information providing entities, such as local law enforcement authorities needs to heed the lessons of risk communication research because "a demonstrated commitment to responsible risk communication by major organizational actors can put pressure on all players in risk management to act responsibly" (Leiss 1996, pp. 90–91). Indeed, if right-to-know laws do not involve responsible action aimed at careful risk management but are instead utilized for quick political gains, they would be laying the stage for a further diminution of trust in various societal institutions in the future.

The other major consideration from risk analysis relevant to Megan's Laws is the NIMBY phenomenon. NIMBY refers to a phenomenon that typically arose in the context of the siting of noxious facilities. Potential host communities often witnessed significant grassroots mobilization around the slogan of "Not In My Back Yard" that resulted in the rejection of siting proposals. In the Megan's Laws context, it is important to note that a NIMBY-type response may well be the consequence of risk-related information provision.

A NIMBY response arises for a variety of reasons. It is partly triggered by cognitive psychological features: people may misperceive the extent of the risks due to availability and representativeness, and may demand zero risk in their backyards due to the certainty effect and zero risk bias. It is partly triggered by value conflicts, for example between the rationales of siting proponents or law enforcement agencies against that of lay publics. Finally, it is triggered by rational self-interest, where communities would rather have the risk transferred to an alternative location.

Some commentators regard NIMBY-type reactions as failures of the democratic process. However, commentators drawn from the communitarian perspective, such as Williams and Matheny (1995) who are favorable to the NIMBY phenomenon, offer arguments that support the development of information provision-type laws. They argue that NIMBY is an example of empowerment at the local level which raises consciousness and impresses "upon nascent citizen-activists the connection between information about the risks they live with and, lacking access to that information, their powerlessness to affect those risks" (Williams and Matheny 1995, p. 169). Their response would be to address "the information problem by redrawing the boundaries among market, government, and community [by envisioning] information as a public right rather than a private or privileged commodity" (Williams and Matheny 1995, p. 170). Information provision laws draw significant political support from such arguments about the empowering aspects of information provision, which also embody a strongly optimistic view of how this information will be used by people, in contrast to our cautious treatment in this paper.

Other key results from risk analysis, and indeed from the social amplification literature, suggest that NIMBY concerns can be rational because they may stem from worries that a location will be tainted by stigma effects (Flynn, Slovic, and Kunreuther 2001). Stigma effects may result in a fall in property values and other economic losses, even in areas some distance removed from the risk-imposing facility (Kasperson 1992). In the Megan's Law context, stigma effects have only been discussed in the context of their impact on sex offenders. Sex offenders may be stigmatized by the public knowledge of their background and this may prevent them from ever reintegrating into the community. But there may be a more substantial stigma-related impact on communities as well. Once it becomes known that a community is host to released sex offenders, the whole community may be stigmatized as people "vote with their feet" and move out to avoid the risk. This potential impact has so far not been considered in the discussion surrounding Megan's Laws.

Finally, another central insight of risk communication research is that process equity matters (see also Gowda and Easterling 2000). That is, people do not care to be talked down to or to merely be the recipients of one-way messages from government agencies. Rather, people are willing to accept creative risk management solutions provided they are involved in the decision process and there is adequate public participation in the choice of risk management solution, before, during, and after a risk-related event (Leiss 1996). The New Jersey version of Megan's Law contains within it the possibility of heeding this lesson. If law enforcement agencies work together with communities by ensuring that local residents are kept informed and even somehow involved in the monitoring of high-risk sex offenders, then the trust generated by such interaction could prevent vigilante attacks while also ensuring the protection of the community. Law enforcement agencies in the United States are moving toward active involvement with communities through "community policing" efforts; such efforts could lead to more proactive, less legally violative risk management. The policy response in the United Kingdom already seems oriented toward active involvement with the community and that may have been a factor that affected people's willingness to accept the rejection of the Sarah's Law effort.

As we conclude, we reflect on the fact that the goals of right-to-know laws are noble, and actions that empower people truly demonstrate democratic statesmanship. However, if this innovative policy instrument – the right-to-know – is misused as a populist measure through the provision of inaccurate information or in ignorance of behavioral responses, the consequences for public policy and particular disadvantaged groups may be far from positive. This may ultimately result in the rejection of innovative policy tools like information provision and make for a less open, less deliberative democracy. Further, if the end results of empowering tools such as the right-to-know turn out to be vigilante attacks which are violative of the fundamental tenets of the rule of law, the end result for society could be a further erosion of trust in the legal system and its continued delegitimization, in contrast to the positive aspirations of the proponents of this policy approach.

14 Nuclear stigma

James Flynn

News reports about the accidents and events associated with modern science and technology have, in certain cases, stigmatized places, products, or technologies (Gregory et al. 1995). Our understanding of these results are informed by the conceptual model outlined in the Social Amplification of Risk Framework, and as modified subsequently (see chapter 1 this volume, figure 1.2) to highlight the stigma effects (Kasperson, Renn, Slovic et al. 1988; Kasperson 1992; Flynn, Slovic, and Kunreuther 2001). This chapter considers nuclear stigma in the United States with attention to how it came about. Understanding how nuclear stigma was created is basic to understanding what to do about it.

The danger of nuclear technology is exposure to radiation with potential consequences of death, cancer, and genetic mutations. The long-lasting hazards of many radioactive materials, even at low or moderate exposures, which may or may not prove fatal until years later, constitute dreaded threats to existing and future biological existence (Slovic 1987). During the last quarter of the twentieth century a history of repeated failures in nuclear management was revealed. Some of this history goes back to the Manhattan atomic bomb project and taken together it provides a basis for nuclear stigma. This paper summarizes a study of the United States nuclear experience. It focuses on the official and expert standards, values, and levels of management performance applied to nuclear technologies in contrast with the public's expectations.

The use of risk analysis to inform public decisions directs attention to issues of control. The decision maker who can specify risks is in a very

In addition to expressing appreciation for the support of the conference at Cumberland Lodge in September 1999, which is included in the documentation by the editors of this volume, I would like to acknowledge the support of work on the phenomena of public responses to nuclear science and technology by the following organizations and individuals: the Alfred P. Sloan Foundation for research on public perception of nuclear power in the United States and France, the Nevada Nuclear Waste Project for research on the socio-economic impacts of high-level radioactive waste, the National Science Foundation with grants numbered SBR 9321029, SBR 94122754, SBR-9631635, and SES9876581, and the United States Department of Energy, Low Dose Radiation Research Program, for research on risk communication and low dose radiation exposure.

different position from, and potentially in conflict with, those who will experience the outcomes but who lack control over decisions or their implementation. Public acceptance of this decision condition requires trust that outcomes are made in the public interest and with full consideration of those put at greatest risk. When trust is missing, social and political opposition, which ultimately threatens to scuttle official decisions entirely, becomes the final, viable means of citizen control.

The public's suspicions of nuclear decision makers have plentiful evidence of past faulty judgments and management failures. Such failures are an organizational risk added to the inherent dangers of the technologies. The high correlations between risk and distrust found in many social science studies should be considered as the public's intuitive estimate of organizational contributions to risk (Flynn, Burns, Mertz et al 1992). The idea that organizations are a risk factor is almost never examined in formal risk assessments. In part this is because proponent organizations prepare risk assessments and they lack the required motivation and levels of organizational self-awareness to conduct such self-examinations. As it is, organizational personnel who benefit from the decision processes and who have long since rationalized to themselves, and proclaimed to their audiences, their own good motives, intentions, capabilities, organizational structure, and decision procedures define risk variables (see Perrow 1984; Freudenburg 1993; Freudenburg and Youn 1993; Clark 1993). This study shows that the organizations managing nuclear technologies are a major source of risk and their performance over half a century has shaped the creation of nuclear stigma.

What stories initiate the social amplification of risk? The original definition was of "accidents and other events" (Kasperson et al. 1988). Some stories carry "signals" about the source of an accident or event and provide clues about the causes. Signals in this context are messages about what might happen in addition to being reports of what did happen. These signals implicate analogous places and conditions as potentially dangerous; the report of a nuclear power plant problem casts doubt on all other such plants.

The rise and fall of nuclear power involves potential dangers that resonate with deeply responsive social-cultural beliefs and myths, reinforced in the large number of stories about nuclear-related events (Weart 1988).

An overview of nuclear industrial development

A brief overview of the dominant sources for nuclear stories is shown in figure 14.1, which begins with the production of uranium fuel, the essential material for the United States weapons program and the civilian

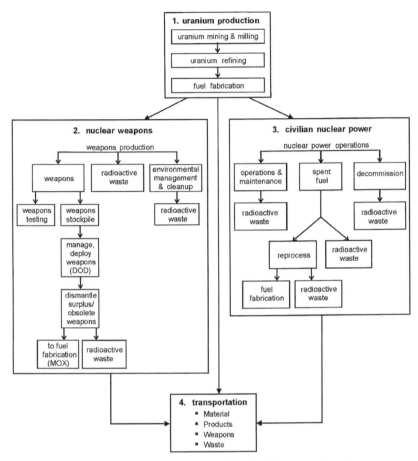

Figure 14.1 Major components of United States nuclear industrialization.

nuclear power industry. The final steps are disposal of radioactive residues, the "back-end" of nuclear cycles – reprocessing, decommissioning, and waste disposal.

Mining and milling

Originally uranium was imported into the United States from the Belgian Congo (now Zaire) and Canada. However, by 1948 the Atomic Energy Commission (AEC) had created a new United States uranium mining industry and the AEC was the sole consumer of the industry output for more than two decades (see Schurgin and Hollocher 1975). Once mined and milled, uranium went through two additional steps, enrichment and fuel fabrication.

Mining uranium was a dangerous occupation (see Walker 1992, chapter 10). Hundreds of miners died extracting uranium ore, many of them Navajo Indians. The AEC did not implement available mine safety systems (e.g. in use at American coal mines) that could have been put into place quickly and economically even when public health reports recommended such systems to save miners' lives. Then when legal suits were filed, the federal government fought for decades against accepting any responsibility for the results of their program (Ball 1986; Udall 1994). After years of mining and milling uranium ore, the nation was left with "about 50 contaminated ore processing sites and about 5,000 nearby properties in various states and on some Indian tribal lands" (United States General Accounting Office 1995). Eventually, Congress enacted the Uranium Mill Tailings Radiation Control Act of 1978 (PL 95-604), which assigned the remediation tasks to the United States Department of Energy (DOE) and mandated cleanup by March 1990, a deadline that has repeatedly been extended. DOE now estimates cleanup by 2014, probably an optimistic goal, with uncertain final costs greater than the original estimate of $2.3 billion (Hollocher and MacKenzie 1975). The problems are with residential areas as well as industrial waste sites. Waste materials were mixed into cement for sidewalks, basements, and other building components contaminating about 3,300 buildings in and around Grand Junction, Colorado, a total of 5,000 buildings in all of Colorado, and perhaps another 1,000–2,000 buildings elsewhere in the United States.

The nuclear weapons complex

The United States weapons program involved the most complex, long-standing, and inherently dangerous of all nuclear technologies. It is the original and most powerfully affective source of nuclear stigma. The bombing of Hiroshima and Nagasaki in August 1945 introduced the public to a new and massively destructive technology. This was followed by the Cold War rush to develop ever more powerful weapons and weapons delivery systems. Fear of sudden, surprise attack with nuclear weapons flooded public consciousness. The Cold War profoundly influenced development of civilian nuclear technology. When the federal government initiated its civilian nuclear programs in the 1950s, it consciously created a vast scientific and technical capability that would benefit weapons as well as civilian applications.

The dominant nuclear enterprise during the last half of the twentieth century was the vast Nuclear Weapons Complex, a tightly administered empire whose fourteen major facilities in thirteen states covered more than 3,350 square miles and in the year 1990 employed more than 100,000 people (Office of Technology Assessment 1991). Between the establishment of the Manhattan Engineering Project in 1942 and the termination of weapons production in 1992, this enterprise manufactured tens of thousands of nuclear warheads and detonated more than a thousand (see DOE 1995a; O'Neill 1998). Since 1951, United States nuclear weapons testing was done primarily at the Nevada Test Site, although various tests, some of them associated with attempts to develop civilian uses for nuclear explosions under the auspices of the Plowshares Program, also took place in Alaska, Colorado, Utah, and Mississippi. The largest single underground weapons explosion (five megatons) took place in 1970 at Amchita Island, Alaska, one of the Aleutian Islands. Only now are some key details of the weapons program becoming known (O'Neill 1994; St. Clair 1999). The overall effort involved radiation exposure to workers, the general public, and the environment. Within this history is a range of anecdotes ranging from tragic to comic.[1]

New information about the weapons complex appears at irregular intervals. One dramatic story revealed the December 1949 "green run" experiment conducted at Hanford, shortly after the August 1949 explosion of the Soviet Union's first nuclear bomb. The Hanford facility normally cooled fuel, from which weapons grade plutonium was extracted, for a period of 80–100 days. This allowed short-lived radioactive elements time to decay. The suspicion was that the Soviets used "green" reactor fuel (with shorter cooling periods) and released unfiltered radiation into the atmosphere in their haste to develop an atomic bomb. To better understand data about Soviet weapons production, AEC officials released the radiation from one ton of 16-day-old fuel.[2] The results were unexpected. The experiment released three times the anticipated amount of radioactivity and contaminated an area stretching from Hanford to Spokane, Washington (about 100 miles northeast) and Klamath Falls, Oregon (on the California/Oregon border, well over 200 miles south). This test and its results were classified as top secret, national security information.

---

[1] In some cases there is a mixture of the comic and tragic. For example, a United States General Accounting Office (1991) report, found that Westinghouse Hanford had estimated that one tank of highly radioactive waste had leaked about 5,000 gallons. The GAO audit found that it had leaked much more, perhaps 800,000 gallons but this had been kept secret. In response, a Westinghouse source said "it was following a long-standing practice at Hanford of not considering the water to be a pollutant after it came out of the tank, because at the time it went into the tank [to cool the wastes] it was clean." *New York Times*, "Leakage at N-plant Concealed," *Eugene* [Oregon] *Register-Guard* (20 September 1991): 5C.

[2] For a journalistic account, see: H. Murphey, "Blowing in the wind," *Pacific Northwest* (January 1991): 9–13.

The Green Run incident and numerous other releases became known with DOE declassification of 19,000 pages of documents in 1986 under pressure from the State of Washington. Even with these records available, Hanford officials denied that any health risk had resulted. It wasn't until 12 July 1990 that then Secretary of Energy, James Watkins, in a dramatic break with government policy, admitted that Hanford "released enough radiation in the 1940s to pose a serious health hazard to nearby residents." The earlier government practice was to classify all radiation data and information, to provide assurances of safety to the public and even to other governmental officials, and to deny problems of access to existing radiation data.[3] And despite the new public access to records of the nuclear weapons complex, much remains sequestered under the doctrine of national security and large amounts of important historical information is said to be unavailable or to have been destroyed (Adler 1994; National Research Council 1995).

Nevertheless, the release of formerly confidential government documents since the mid-1980s has greatly increased public information about the nuclear weapons complex. One result of these developments has been a number of class action suits against past and current managers at the weapons complex sites.[4] When weapons production stopped in 1992, the weapons complex sites became environmental management and cleanup problems. After fifty years of on-site temporary radioactive waste storage, the federal government is attempting permanent disposal.

Nuclear weapons testing

Atomic soldiers

Between 1946 and 1962 the United States conducted weapons tests that involved the exposure of military personnel to radioactive fallout. These tests began at Bikini in the south Pacific and after 1951 were mostly conducted at the Nevada Test Site. According to the Defense Nuclear Agency, about 225,000 military personnel were involved in nuclear blast tests after World War II, 57,000 as part of combat training exercises,

---

[3] Stenehjem (1990) provides a brief historical account of the period 1943 to the mid 1980s with a focus on the Columbia River and the Columbia Basin.

[4] M. Wald, "Energy dept. to pay $73 million to settle uranium case in Ohio," *New York Times* (1 July 1989). Associated Press, "Uranium-peril suit settled" *Eugene* [Oregon] *Register-Guard* (27 January 1995). Department of Energy, Office of Environment, Safety, and Health, "Richardson unveils health initiative for DOE workers," press release, <http://www.eh.doe.gov/portal/feature/071599pr.html>, 15 July 1995; Associated Press, "Uranium-peril suit settle," *Eugene* [Oregon] *Register-Guard* (27 January 1995). See also Flynn, Peters, Mertz et al. (1998).

where some soldiers experienced nuclear blasts from within two miles of ground zero (Makhijani and Schwartz 1998; Manning 1995). A 1995 Associated Press report quotes a 1951 memo from Rear Admiral W. K. Mendenhall on the military viewpoint: "The field commander is not interested in the science of measuring radiation. He merely wants to know, can the troops tolerate the radiation to which they are being subjected for five minutes or five days."[5]

The chances of getting a cancer from radiation exposure can take twenty to thirty years, depending upon the exposure and the individual. At that point it is almost impossible to demonstrate a causal relationship between a specific exposure and a resulting cancer. The burden of proof in the case of radiation exposure falls to the individual veteran, an almost impossible task as indicated by the fact that the Veterans' Administration recognized only one claim of the first 600 filed by atomic veterans. Records are often incomplete and files have been lost or destroyed. For example, official military records for more than 17 million veterans were destroyed in a 1973 fire at a St. Louis, Missouri federal storage building. After a long series of court cases and political action campaigns, Congress passed the Radiation-Exposed Veterans Compensation Act of 1988 (PL 100-321). This act listed thirteen cancers[6] as "presumptively service connected" and thereby compensable without a legally binding causal demonstration. Treatment and compensation for exposed military personnel required political action in lieu of scientific or medical assignment of causes for health claims. In 1994 Congress mandated (PL 103-446, section 508) an evaluation of whether or not it was feasible to study the genetic effects of radiation on children, grandchildren, and spouses of qualified veterans. The subsequent report from the Institute of Medicine concluded that the difficulties of conducting a scientific epidemiological study on this subject were "insurmountable" (Institute of Medicine 1995). The problems of civilian exposures are even more difficult in most cases.

Downwinders

The term "downwinders" applies to people who were exposed through the transport of radiation to their geographical location. Most of these

---

[5] Associated Press, "GIs placed near N-blasts to blunt fear of radiation," *Eugene* [Oregon] *Register-Guard* (2 June 1995), 11A.

[6] Leukemia, multiple myeloma, lymphoma except Hodgkin's disease, and cancers of the thyroid, breast, pharynx, esophagus, stomach, small intestine, pancreas, bile ducts, gall bladder, and liver. Subsequently, the Act was amended to add cancers of the salivary gland and urinary tract (PL 102-578).

exposures were the unintended consequence of nuclear weapons testing or the operations of nuclear facilities. More than 900 nuclear tests were conducted at the Nevada Test Site with atmospheric tests conducted from 1951 to 1963 and underground tests from 1963 to 1992 (Schwartz 1995). The Nevada tests concentrated exposure to downwind communities in Nevada, Arizona, and Utah, such as St. George, Utah. Regional "hotspots," some as distant as the upper Mid-west and even the Northeast, have subsequently been identified.

Opposition to programs producing fallout came from many sources including scientists, doctors, and other medical people. These public reactions forced the government to continually deal with demands to limit and stop fallout exposure. Federal officials assured the public that there was little or no danger from the nuclear weapons tests and mounted public relations programs to make their point. They denied all claims of damage in public and in court. When forced into litigation, the government employed every legal and political tactic to deny liability. In some cases they simply destroyed records. In these efforts, they relied heavily on claims of national security and federal sovereign immunity.[7] They opposed United States Public Health Studies even after the 1963 ban on atmospheric testing had reduced public concerns. The primary concerns were stated in a 1965 memo from the AEC general manager: "(a) adverse public reactions; (b) lawsuits; (c) jeopardizing the program at the Nevada Test Site" (Titus 1986, p. 104).

Despite federal government efforts, the basic outlines of the weapons testing program are known and in some cases, especially those that were litigated, there are plentiful details. Miller (1986) presents a history of the period with a set of appendices showing the fallout patterns from specific tests on national maps. Ball (1986) covers the same period but focuses more on the public health issues and the litigation over fallout. One case involved the revival of the Bulloch case.

In 1982 United States District Judge Sherman Christensen reviewed the Bulloch suit twenty-six years after it originally went to trial. The original suit claimed damages resulting from the exposure of sheep to radiation fallout from a specific test at the Nevada Test Site, a claim the government denied. Christensen had dismissed the case on the testimony and evidence presented by the government in court proceedings during 1955–56. Information about the case came up during a 1979 Congressional hearing in Salt Lake City where once-classified documents were

---

[7] Various accounts of the AEC and DOE responses to public concerns about radiation from weapons testing are widely available, including Titus (1986), Miller (1986), Ball (1986), and Udall (1994).

presented. This information put the case back into Judge Christensen's court. After a four-day hearing in 1982, Judge Christensen found that the government lawyers had intentionally deceived the original trial court by: "false and deceptive representations of government conduct," "improper but successful attempts to pressure witnesses," "a vital report intentionally withheld," "information in another report presented in a deceitful manner," "interrogatories deceptively answered," and "deliberate concealment of significant facts with reference to possible effects of radiation upon plaintiff's sheep" (Ball 1986, p. 209). A plaintive motion for a retrial was ordered but it was rescinded on government appeal to the Tenth Circuit Court, an outcome that Udall (1994) called "a grotesque episode of American jurisprudence."

Human radiation experiments

On 3 October 1995, President Clinton accepted the report from the National Advisory Committee on Human Radiation Experiments at a White House ceremony. The committee spent eighteen months and examined more than 800,000 pages of documentation, 4,000 radiation experiments, and the records of hundreds of radiation releases from government facilities covering the period 1944 to 1974 (DOE 1995b).[8] The questionable ethical standards used in these experiments were much noted as was the participation by government agencies and highly regarded medical research universities and institutions (see Gordon 1996; Welsom, 1999). If anything, these reports understated the actual extent of human experimentation, which may never be known. The federal agencies involved are those most likely to classify information and many records have been lost, misplaced, or destroyed.[9]

The Advisory Committee (DOE, 1995b) defended the need to understand the effects of radiation during the Cold War, arguing that: "Often non-beneficial experiments on unconsenting patients constituted only

[8] In addition to the departments of Energy (and its predecessor agencies, primarily the Atomic Energy Commission), Defense, Health and Human Services, and the Veterans' Administration, there was some involvement by the Central Intelligence Agency and National Aeronautics and Space Administration. Also involved were some of the nation's most highly regarded research centers such as those at the universities of Rochester, Cincinnati, Chicago, California, and Washington; Vanderbilt University, Harvard, MIT, the United States Naval Hospital at Bethesda, Maryland, Massachusetts General Hospital, and many more.

[9] GAO (General Accounting Office), "Status of federal efforts to disclose Cold War radiation experiments involving humans," testimony by Victor S. Rezendes, Director, Energy and Science Issues, Resources, Community, and Economic Development Division before the Committee on Governmental Affairs, United States Senate, GAO/T–RCED–95–40, 1 December 1994.

minor wrongs. Often there was little or no risk to patient-subjects and no inconvenience." The report does state that some experiments were "ethically troubling" such as those "conducted on institutionalized children, seriously ill and sometimes comatose patients, African-Americans, and prisoners." News media were more dramatic and descriptive.[10] The highlighted stories included accounts of mentally retarded teenagers at a state school in Waltham, Massachusetts who were fed radioactive milk in the 1940s and 1950s by a group of Harvard and MIT scientists who dubbed their experiment "The Science Club." Seven newborn infants were injected with radioactive iodine at the University of Tennessee in 1953. Vanderbilt University researchers gave 751 pregnant women radiation pills in the 1940s to determine the effects of radioactive iron on fetal development. The women thought they were taking normal iron pills. Six healthy patients were injected with uranium salts at the University of Rochester to determine how much it would take to damage their kidneys. From 1963 to 1971, researchers X-rayed the testicles of 131 prisoners at the Oregon State Prison and the Washington State Penitentiary to measure the effects of radiation on male fertility, an issue for workers at the weapons complex. Heavy doses of radiation, up to 250 rads (a 300-rad dose would be expected to kill half an exposed population), were administered to eighty-seven terminally ill patients in a Cincinnati experiment. The average IQ of these subjects was a subnormal 86; sixty-one of the subjects were Black, and twenty-five of the patients died within sixty days. Radium and thorium were fed to twenty elderly patients in an MIT experiment conducted during the early 1960s to estimate the resulting internal doses.

The ethical standards of medical research were not as well formulated or enforced during the 1950s as they are today. None the less, the principles were well known and clearly articulated. One scientist involved in early experiments (1945–47) where patients were injected with plutonium without their consent, warned the AEC that the research protocol had "a little of the Buchenwald touch," referring to the notorious Nazi medical experiments on concentration camp prisoners during World War II.[11]

Hilts reported that one major motive for restricting public information about these experiments was concern about lawsuits and unfavorable publicity.[12] The documents uncovered by the Advisory Committee

---

[10] K. D. Steele, "Radiation revelations: new administration brings the spotlight back to dubious experiments," *Spokesman-Review*, 9 January 1994.

[11] The phrase is contained in a 1950 memo from biologist Dr. Joseph Hamilton to his AEC supervisor. See, Steele ("Radiation revelations").

[12] P. Hilts, "Inquiry on radiation tests links United States secrecy to fear of lawsuits," *The New York Times*, 15 December 1994.

contain numerous memos discussing the problems that might result from public knowledge of the experimental activities. In one case, an Oak Ridge manager wrote that release of information on radiation releases might adversely affect "insurance claims...labor relations, and...public sentiment." As Hilts comments, these reasons may not be a legal basis for classifying medical research documents.

Nuclear power

During the height of the Cold War while great effort was made to build new weapons, scientists, engineers, industrialists, and political leaders strove to find and develop the industrial benefits of the atom. The vision of harnessing nuclear energy to fuel growing demand for electricity in the United States was especially attractive. After two decades of concentrated effort, the nuclear power industry was created and by 1975 more than 200 nuclear power reactors were built, under construction, or planned. Toward the end of the "great bandwagon period," in the early 1970s, the Atomic Energy Commission forecast that 60 percent of United States electric generation would be nuclear by the year 2000. The future of nuclear power looked bright.

But even as the most optimistic forecasts were being made, the downturn for nuclear power began. Between 1974 and 1979, fifty-one nuclear power plant orders were canceled. Nuclear power siting was being effectively opposed at the state and local levels (see e.g. Wellock 1998). In an implausible turn of events, the anti-nuclear film *The China Syndrome* was two weeks into its highly publicized release when the March 1979 accident at Three Mile Island (TMI) shocked the public. No new nuclear power reactor has been ordered since that event. It is presently unclear whether a revival of nuclear power in the United States will take place during the new millennium. In the short term at least nuclear power faces a gradual and relentless closing of existing plants. This is a remarkable outcome for the first nuclear era.

Public discontent with nuclear power has led to a number of attempts by opponents to close nuclear power plants through political means, such as by public referenda or by influencing legislative, judicial, or executive actions. Most of these efforts have failed. The larger public has demonstrated a pragmatic view; for the most part voters and office holders have resisted closing operating plants. However a few closures have taken place, the most dramatic being the Shoreham station on Long Island in New York, which was decommissioned just before it was scheduled to begin commercial operation. This was the abandonment of a $5.5 billion investment (McCaffrey 1991). An earlier case was the 1989 referendum vote that closed the Sacramento Municipal Utility District's Rancho Seco plant in California. A few years later, in 1993, owners of the Trojan nuclear power plant in Oregon closed the facility after fighting off four statewide referendum attempts. In this case, the utility maintained that the closure was for economic reasons and not as a response to the repeated political campaigns against the plant.

To better understand the role of public opinion in determining the differential success of nuclear power, Decision Research conducted an extensive survey in the United States and France during 1992. English and French versions of the same survey instrument were administered to more than 1,500 respondents in each country. French respondents were expected to record lower perceptions of risk from nuclear power than Americans, given the 75 percent dominance of electric production enjoyed by the French nuclear program. Surprisingly, nuclear power's risk ratings in France were almost identical to those in the United States. However, the survey data did provide responses that appear to be important in explaining the outcome differences for the two nuclear efforts (Slovic, Flynn, Mertz et al. 2000). Specifically, the French:

• Saw greater need for nuclear power and greater economic benefits from it.
• Had greater trust in scientists, industry, and government officials who design, build, operate, and regulate nuclear power plants.
• Were more likely to believe that decision making authority should reside with the experts and government authorities, rather than with lay people.

The French manage nuclear power with less public participation and more centralized control. Political scientists have argued that, in a climate of strong distrust, the French approach, in which policy formation and implementation is not as accessible to public intervention, is expedient (see Morone and Woodhouse 1989). Campbell (1988) agrees, arguing that United States democratic institutions providing political access to nuclear critics may be fundamentally incompatible with the commercial success of nuclear power. How well centralized decision making about nuclear power can be maintained in a period of rapidly expanding public communications and the rise of adversarial policy groups is an open question. In any case, public confidence in government management of nuclear power is clearly greater in France than in the United States.

These survey results indicate that public acceptance of nuclear power, if not active endorsement, requires positive judgments about (1) potential benefits, (2) management of the risks, and (3) necessity. An essential complicating factor is the contrast between the public's stigmatization of nuclear power, a widely held belief that certain nuclear technologies are inherently dangerous, unwise, unnatural, and even immoral, and the position of nuclear proponents who envision nuclear technologies as right, necessary, and inevitable because they are based on deep scientific and natural truths. Risk communication has been unable to bridge these gaps or even to fairly state the originating premises that are in conflict.

Radioactive wastes: management, storage, and disposal

The "back end" of the nuclear power industry requires management and disposal of radioactive wastes; at a minimum they should be safely stored. The federal government has established programs to deal with weapons complex wastes, civilian low-level radioactive wastes, and high-level wastes, mostly spent fuel. These programs envision the shipment of wastes to centralized facilities using the nation's rail and highway transportation systems. For example, the proposed high-level facility at Yucca Mountain, Nevada would require the transport of thousands of shipments through forty-three states and hundreds of communities over a period of thirty years or more. The decommissioning of existing facilities, cleanup, transportation, waste disposal site development, and permanent storage for all levels of radioactive wastes present federal, state, local, and industry personnel with difficult problems in addressing public concerns.

Low-level radioactive wastes (LLRW)

The low-level radioactive waste policy act of 1980 (Public Law 96-573) defines LLRW as: "radioactive waste not classified as high-level radioactive waste, transuranic waste, spent nuclear fuel, or byproduct material as defined in section 11(e) (2) of the Atomic Energy Act of 1954."[13]

"In 1990, 1.1 million cubic feet of LLW was sent to commercial disposal sites, with a total radioactivity of about 550,000 curies. Of this waste, nuclear power plants accounted for 56 percent by volume and 79 percent by radioactivity" (English 1992, p. 3). The LLRW resulting from weapons production is permanently stored at the Nevada Test Site, Hanford, Washington, Savannah, South Carolina, and at other facilities in the weapons complex often in a temporary status.

---

[13] The United States Nuclear Regulatory Commission recognized three classes of LLRW in its regulations of 26 January 1983 (10 CFR 61):44. Classes A, B, and C, depending upon the degree of radiation and the time during which exposure might adversely affect human health. Classes A and B require different packaging with Class B having the more stringent requirement and both classes of waste must decay to specified safe levels within 100 years. Class C wastes, mainly irradiated reactor parts, must meet a 500-year standard of protection with geological (deeper burial than Class A or B) and engineered (e.g. concrete vaults) barriers.

Congress passed the low-level waste policy act of 1980 (LLRWPA) after a determined effort by Washington, Nevada, and South Carolina to be removed as the three host states for civilian LLW. Other early sites for LLW disposal had experienced "casual" management, according to English (1992), with the result that facilities at West Valley, New York, Maxey Flats, Kentucky, and Sheffield, Illinois were closed due to serious environmental problems. The low-level waste disposal at these sites relied upon a shallow land-burial technique that did not perform well. This experience prompted several states to require more stringent engineered barriers for future LLW sites.

The LLRWPA created a unique program whereby the federal government turned the civilian low-level problem over to the states. This strategy sought to avoid conflict between federal agencies and the states or public groups over disposal sites and technologies (e.g. shallow land burial versus engineered barriers). The idea was to make the states responsible for locating and operating their own sites. They were subject to federal oversight and regulation but otherwise the states would be in charge of low-level waste facilities. The Act envisioned the waste sites as potential revenue sources for states and local communities, and attempted to consolidate waste disposal at the regional level by encouraging "compacts" or multi-state agreements to jointly develop sites.

Few policies that so obviously failed have lasted so long. In two decades the program has not produced one new low-level waste site despite dozens of extraordinary efforts by states and compacts (Weingart 2001). Meanwhile, the uncertainty about access to a disposal facility along with the steep increases in costs at the existing sites motivated waste producers to reduce the volume of wastes. These waste-reduction efforts have been so successful that it is now doubtful that the new sites envisioned under the 1980 federal LLW Act are needed. In 1995, 680 thousand cubic feet of wastes went to disposal sites, down from more than 2.6 million annually in 1984 and 1985 (United States Nuclear Regulatory Commission 1997).

Attempts to develop new sites have been stopped by public opposition despite expert opinion and the evidence of risk assessments that no significant danger exists at numerous places. Efforts to impose an expert-driven, top-down risk assessment process failed for one program after the other. This was replaced by attempts by some states and compacts to find an incentive approach and offer benefit sharing, especially economic development and support for public services. Local public officials who supported these efforts were quick to learn that these trade-offs were politically untenable. States and compacts abandoned their programs during the 1990s. Ward Valley in California, Boyd County in Nebraska, and Sierra Blanco in Texas were the last to go.

Meanwhile, a private firm, Envirocare, opened a remote Utah site in 1987. Between 1993 and 1998, fourteen million cubic feet of lightly radioactive wastes have been disposed of at this remote facility under contracts with DOE that amounted to as much as $250 million. Additional contracts for the next five years (1998 to 2003) are expected to provide $350 million. How did a private developer open a site when public authorities could not? Part of the answer came in 1998 when *The Washington Post* reported that Larry Anderson, a former director of the Utah Radiation Control Division, the state official responsible for issuing the Envirocare license and exercising operations oversight, sued Khosrow Semnani, the owner of the facility. Anderson apparently approached Semnani in 1986 with an offer to serve as a "consultant" for a payment of $100,000 and 5 percent of the profits. Semnani subsequently paid Anderson about $600,000 but discontinued payments when Anderson left his position with the Utah State office, which, in turn, prompted Anderson's suit. This, the *Washington Post* article, points out: "... raised questions about the validity of Envirocare's license and the adequacy of the state's response to the dump's history of safety violations – which include chunks of radioactive material literally falling from boxcars and top managers scoring a perfect zero on radiation competency tests."[14] While a federal grand jury investigated and various courts considered litigation, DOE negotiated a deal with Semnani allowing him to retain his 100 percent interest in Envirocare but giving up his management control to his long-time vice president as his successor. In turn, Envirocare could bid on DOE contracts. The agreement was quickly followed by new business from DOE contractors. Accounts of how the Envirocare site was licensed and operated along with DOE's special accommodations can hardly be expected to serve as a model for the siting of other low-level sites. Yet this is the only "successful" LLRW siting in recent decades.

Transuranic wastes

The waste isolation pilot project (WIPP) in southern New Mexico is designed to store transuranic wastes more than 2,000 feet underground.[15] These wastes come from nuclear weapons production and are stored at federal facilities in ten states. Work at the site began in 1975 and in 1980

---

[14] J. Warrick, "Waste dump paid Utah regulator," *Las Vegas Review Journal* (from *The Washington Post*), 6 April 1998.

[15] The Committee on the Waste Isolation Pilot Plant (National Research Council 1996) provide a short definition of transuranic waste and a more precise one at p. 155. The short definition is: "Transuranic waste – radioactive waste consisting of radionuclides with atomic numbers greater than 92 [uranium] in excess of agreed limits." The limits are provided for in DOE Order 5820.2A and the EPA regulation 40CFR191.

Congress authorized a "research and development facility for demonstrating safe disposal of radioactive waste from defense activities and program."[16] The designation of WIPP as a "defense facility" means it did not come under Nuclear Regulatory Commission oversight while the designation of the project as a pilot program for research and development minimized the immediate responsibilities to meet national and state environmental regulation. These congressional advantages were not entirely successful. Over the years, WIPP "evolved from a low-profile initiative to become highly disputed" (Jenkins-Smith 1991).

The social–political responses to siting radioactive waste facilities are complex. Originally, the Town of Carlsbad solicited and supported the WIPP program as an economic development and employment opportunity to replace an abrupt decline of potash mining in the area and over the decades the town has been a staunch supporter. The State of New Mexico was less enthusiastic and served as the focus of public sector opposition to WIPP. Citizen advocacy groups opposed the project. Thus, after its promising start, it took twenty-five years before the first, long-awaited shipments of waste began, and then only after years of negotiation between government agencies, Congress, and the State of New Mexico on a long list of items.

As the long political process at WIPP proceeded, a clear case of nuclear stigmatization was litigated and substantiated in the case of the *City of Santa Fe* v. *Komis*. One segment of the transportation route along the interstate highway system was planned to go through New Mexico's capital, Santa Fe, but this was avoided when the federal government agreed to construct a bypass for the waste transportation. One section of the bypass route required 43.4 acres of the property belonging to John and Lemonia Komis, leaving them the remaining 430 acres. The Komises refused to accept the city's offer because it did not provide compensation for the decline in the value of their remaining land due to stigma arising from public fears about the transportation of transuranic wastes on the bypass. The property was condemned in 1988 and went to a jury trial in 1991. In November 1991 the jury awarded the Komises $884,000, including $337,000 for the stigma damage claim. The city appealed to the New Mexico Supreme Court where the jury award was upheld in August 1992.[17] Subsequently, the New Mexico Department of Transportation settled a similar claim related to the WIPP route bypass at Roswell, New Mexico (see Mushkatel and Pijawka 1994). The Komis case is notable because it awarded compensation to a property owner based upon survey

---

[16] Department of Energy National Security and Military Applications of Nuclear Energy Authorization Act of 1980. Public Law 164. 96th Cong., 1st sess., 29 December 1979.

[17] "$337,000 WIPP road land award upheld," *Santa Fe Journal*, 27 August 1992.

interviews where respondents said they did not want to buy property or live near a radioactive transportation route.

High-level radioactive wastes

The management, storage, and disposal of high-level nuclear wastes (HLNW) from nuclear power plants is considered one of the keys to public acceptability of nuclear power in the United States. Although significant amounts of HLNW have been produced by the nation's nuclear weapons complex, the great majority of radioactivity requiring management and disposal comes from civilian power reactors in the form of irradiated or "spent" fuel.

At the present time most civilian HLNW is stored at reactor sites in cooling pools that require continuous supervision. As existing pool capacity fills, some utilities are providing storage in casks that are passively air-cooled and utilize a system of shielding. This "dry cask" technique, which works best with fuel rods that have had some years of aging to reduce the heat and radioactivity, has been certified by the United States Nuclear Regulatory Commission as a safe storage technique for at least a hundred years.[18] However, residents near nuclear power plants using dry-cask storage are not convinced the technology is safe. They question the potential effects of extended storage, the ability of utilities to correct problems that may occur, the design of specific cask types, and the security provisions at individual facilities (Sinclair, n.d.).

For four decades, the federal government's goal for HLNW and spent fuel has been permanent disposal, a solution that would "close the fuel cycle" and provide assurances that nuclear power could generate electricity and deal with the potential hazards of long-term radioactive wastes. Many sites have been suggested and abandoned thus bringing into question the government's ability to locate, study, license, construct, operate, and safely dispose of HLNW. After several years of negotiation with the many interested parties, Congress passed the Nuclear Waste Policy Act of 1982 (NWPA) (see Carter 1987).

The NWPA attempted to address some long-standing problems revealed in the early failures by establishing a set of democratic principles and ethical rules to guide the process of selecting a repository site.[19]

---

[18] United States Nuclear Regulatory Commission, 10 CFR Part 51, "Consideration of environmental impacts of temporary storage of spent fuel after cessation of reactor operations; and waste confidence decision review: final rules" *Federal Register* 55, no. 181 (18 September 1990).

[19] *Nuclear Waste Policy Act of 1982*, Public Law 425. 97th Cong., 2nd sess., 7 January 1983 (see also Easterling and Kunreuther, 1995; Flynn, Chalmers, Easterling et al. 1995).

Several principles were designed to produce an equitable outcome. The NWPA addressed geographic equity by mandating two repositories, one in the west, where DOE had already done some site studies, and one in the east, where most of the nuclear wastes are generated. The NWPA mandated that those who benefit from the repository pay for it and required fees charged on nuclear-generated energy to go into a Nuclear Waste Fund to finance repository development. Monetary compensation was authorized for those living near the repository. Other provisions of the NWPA were intended to ensure an equitable process of site selection. DOE was required to provide information about all of their activities associated with selecting and building the repository, including scientific data and analyses, to affected stakeholders such as state governments, Indian tribes, and the public. Program managers were to employ an objective selection process based on technical criteria. In addition, the decision process used to select or eliminate candidate sites was to be open to outside scrutiny, making it difficult to select a site on arbitrary or capricious grounds. DOE was to consult and cooperate with affected states and Indian tribes before making key decisions. (However, this provision did not give stakeholders authority to control the siting process.) Nuclear Waste Fund allocations were provided to affected states and Indian tribes to oversee DOE studies and conduct socioeconomic assessments. Importantly, the NWPA contained provisions to protect public health. It instructed the United States Environmental Protection Agency (EPA) to set radiation-exposure standards. DOE was to demonstrate how it would meet these standards, which would be used by the United States Nuclear Regulatory Commission (NRC) in deciding whether to grant a construction license. In addition, the NWPA permitted any state designated to host a repository to file a notice of disapproval – essentially a veto of the site. Although this provision exceeded previous state authority over the siting of a federal facility, it was still a weak power because Congress could vote to overturn a state veto.

The NWPA appeared to many observers as a reasonable political compromise, a good-faith effort to forge a successful siting process. The equity and public safety provisions were intended to ensure fairness in site selection and to make the eventual choice acceptable to those affected directly. And, indeed, NWPA appeared to have succeeded – at least to the extent of attracting, in 1982, the support of most congressional representatives from states then identified as potential repository host sites. The NWPA, which President Reagan signed into law on 7 January 1983, authorized the creation of the Office of Civilian Radioactive Waste Management (OCRWM) within DOE.

Once the program was put into effect, however, the NWPA's principles and goals began to unravel. Mandated schedules were missed and the expected dates for opening the repository slipped from 1998 to sometime in the second or third decade of the twenty-first century. Problems surfaced with DOE oversight of contractor work and data on sites were compromised (United States General Accounting Office 1987). As early as 1985, the NRC warned that the DOE quality-assurance plan did not meet regulatory requirements, an opinion reiterated in 1986 (United States General Accounting Office 1988a). Numerous requirements of the NWPA, such as the mandate that DOE negotiate cooperation and consultation agreements with potential host states, were not completed. DOE made a unilateral decision in 1986 to abandon the search for a second repository site in the east, claiming that the single western facility would meet the nation's needs. This came in the midst of a congressional election period and effected eastern states where public opposition was fierce. States and public-advocacy, community-based, and industry groups filed numerous suits against the program. In 1986 the United States General Accounting Office quarterly reports to Congress began to include a section on litigation; at one time more than twenty cases, some of which grouped plaintiffs, were active (United States General Accounting Office 1988b, Appendix 1). By 1987 it was clear that the program was failing (Carter 1987; Jacob 1990).

In the closing days of 1987, Congress passed amendments to the NWPA, and over the objections of Nevada, selected Yucca Mountain, Nevada as the only site to be studied. Over the following years Congress abandoned many of the original assurances to potential host states in attempts to salvage a failing program. In response the State of Nevada moved into open opposition to the repository program. This creates a serious problem for the federal government since states in the United States federal system have significant political power. Combined with the difficult scientific and technical problems the HLNW program faces, this means that the final outcome will remain in doubt for some time.[20]

Looking ahead: unresolved issues for the twenty-first century

The last half of the twentieth century saw the United States develop an awesome nuclear weapons system and the world's largest nuclear power industry. During the same time public attitudes toward nuclear

---

[20] The social problems are given significant attention in a recent report from the National Academy of Sciences (2001).

science and technology shifted from support to suspicion and then to significant opposition. This shift developed along with nuclear stigmatization to create a social context that led to the gradual decline of nuclear power, continuous public concerns about the cleanup of old weapons facilities and questions about new waste-management programs and sites.

In addition, three problem areas remain unresolved: reprocessing, decommissioning, and the transportation of radioactive wastes. These activities can be expected to become public concerns and issues early in the twenty-first century.

Reprocessing

In the past reprocessing was seen as a way to close the nuclear fuel cycle and "provide another source of fuel to a growing industry and also largely relieve owners of individual power plants of the burden of storing spent fuel" (Walker 1992, pp. 24–25; see also Carter 1987, chapter 3). It would use reprocessing techniques developed in the weapons' program to recover uranium and plutonium from spent nuclear fuel. These resources would be recycled to fabricate mixed oxide (uranium and plutonium – MOX) fuel rods, which would then be sent to reactors as a new fuel source. There was support from scientists for a breeder reactor, which in creating more fuel (plutonium) than it consumed as uranium thereby creates an endless supply of fuel (Cohen 1990).[21] Historically, many scientists and nuclear experts thought that uranium was a scarce resource and a breeder reactor as a source of future fuel would be an economic necessity. As it has turned out, now and for the foreseeable future, there will be an excess supply of uranium and plutonium (Carter 1987).

Also, there was the belief that the success of the weapons complex in reprocessing to produce plutonium for bombs could be transferred to the commercial fuel cycle. As Carter comments, "this was simply wrong." It was wrong for technical, economic, and political reasons. We know now that the weapons complex did not meet the minimum expectations of radioactive waste management although this was obscured for many years by the secrecy of "national security." As for the economics of reprocessing, weapons production was not budgeted in terms applicable to the conditions in the private sector, even under the regime of a semi-monopoly electric power industry. The direct and indirect costs

---

[21] For a more somber evaluation of past federal attempts to develop the breeder reactor with a focus on the Clinch River project see Cohen and Noll (1991, ch. 9), Carter (1987, pp. 117–118) and Marshall (1983).

absorbed by the federal government under conditions of the Cold War were beyond anything a civilian industry could do. Also, the political and public opinion issues of producing plutonium within a high-security weapons complex were quite different from producing plutonium within a commercial industry. Reprocessing faced another problem since the process produces plutonium that can, at least technically, be used to make nuclear weapons. The Carter administration canceled work on the breeder reactor program in the late 1970s at least in part because of concerns that nuclear weapons proliferation might result from a plutonium economy.

There were, however, three major attempts over almost two decades to establish a civilian reprocessing capability. They failed on a number of dimensions. The first attempt at West Valley, New York started operations in 1966 and was closed in 1972. Built at a cost of $35 million, it was designed to minimize capital investment. The history of West Valley problems and failures is long and bleak. Carter (1987) presents one anecdote, which is enlightening even if it is not typical. In early 1969 several fuel assemblies arrived from the Hanford N-reactor badly damaged, with some of the fuel rods ruptured along their entire length. When the rods were placed in the fuel storage pool, gross beta radiation in the pool shot up to more than sixty times what it should have been. The damaged fuel was hastily removed, put in scrap drums, and buried on site in a fifty-foot-deep hole, encased in concrete. This problem is part of the current cleanup effort. Nuclear Fuel Services exercised its legal rights to withdraw from the project in 1976 and turned over responsibility for the site and the wastes to the State of New York, which subsequently got Congress to assign the site to the United States Department of Energy in 1980 (the West Valley Demonstration Project Act, PL 96-368). West Valley was the only commercial reprocessing plant to operate in the United States; it quickly became a cleanup site and work there continues to the present.

Two other serious commercial reprocessing attempts were made. In the early 1970s, General Electric Company designed a new process and built a plant to reprocess 300 tons of spent fuel per year at Morris, Illinois. When a cold run test (with non-radioactive materials) was conducted in 1974, major problems were uncovered. A thorough corporate review found that the transfer of the process from the laboratory to industrial operations would result in inevitable failures and the effort was halted. As Carter (1987) remarks "General Electric and the State of Illinois were left with a white elephant, but at least it was not radioactive."

The final major reprocessing effort failed due to a lethal combination of technological, regulatory, and economic problems. Allied-General

Nuclear Fuel Services began the project at Barnwell, South Carolina in the early 1970s and it was abandoned in 1983 when a final attempt to put together a workable package of funding and government support failed.

The costs of reprocessed uranium and plutonium simply could not compete with other sources of uranium as a fuel in the world nuclear power market nor provide the assurances of fail-safe control in an international plutonium market.

While the United States civilian-reprocessing efforts floundered and collapsed, other sources of plutonium produced considerable results. Albright et al. (1997) estimate that worldwide there are 1,300 metric tons of plutonium and 1,750 metric tons of weapons grade uranium-equivalent, often called highly enriched uranium (HEU). The military stockpiles of all grades of plutonium are estimated at 250 metric tons, with about 1,750 metric tons of HEU. Separated civilian stocks of plutonium, mostly processed in the United Kingdom, France, Belgium, and Russia, amount to about 120 metric tons. The majority of the world's plutonium is in unreprocessed spent fuel. The potential problems with surplus plutonium and HEU have been the subject of extensive international negotiations about the best strategies for disposing of the stock of these materials (Bunn 1997; also Makhijani 1997).

As a result of weapons reduction agreements under the START II treaty between the United States and Russia, the United States in January, 1997 declared about fifty metric tons of plutonium as excess and announced a dual-track plan to dispose of this stock. This is only a start on the almost 2,000 metric tons of weapons grade plutonium and enriched uranium primarily held by the United States and Russia. The two tracks are: (1) blend the weapons grade plutonium with civilian uranium to create MOX fuel, which would then be burned in electric power reactors and disposed of as spent fuel; and (2) to mix the surplus plutonium with high-level wastes in a vitrification process and send the resulting combined waste product to disposal (Bunn 1997).

This program has engendered opposition from anti-nuclear activists who say that the program is designed to maintain the future options of fast breeder reactors and other forms of nuclear power, to subsidize the existing nuclear power industry by supplying MOX fuel at below cost, and to justify future reprocessing (Loeke et al. 1997; Greenpeace 1997). Other critics have focused on the proliferation issue and urged programs that will reduce any widespread use of plutonium in civilian reactors (Developi 1995). The mixing of civilian electric power and nuclear weapons materials would seem to provide another link for the deeper public concerns that link the risks of nuclear weapons and nuclear power.

Decommissioning nuclear power plants

The final task at any nuclear power facility is to decommission it and clean up the radioactive wastes and residuals from the equipment, buildings, and site. This is a formidable challenge, with a familiar litany of problems: funding, public acceptance, short and long-term site management, engineering and dismantling procedures, transportation of wastes and remains, cleanup standards, and regulation.

There appear to be three viable program options for decommissioning: (1) dismantle the facility promptly and remove the radioactive wastes; (2) provide interim on-site storage and management to allow radioactive decay and then remove the wastes; and (3) provide for long-term on-site storage such as entombment (Pollock 1986). In all cases, radioactive decontamination of the facility to some level is required. Entombment would maintain significant radioactive wastes on-site while the other two options require dismantlement and the transport of wastes to another site. About 115 commercial reactors will have to be decommissioned at some time in the future.

A number of commercial reactors have been taken out of service and designated for decommissioning. These plants divide into two classes, the early low-powered examples (such as Shippingport, Pennsylvania at 72 megawatts, Pathfinder, South Dakota at 62 megawatts, Fort St. Vrain, Colorado at 330 megawatts, and Peach Bottom I, Pennsylvania at 40 megawatts) and the later large plants (i.e. Rancho Seco, California, at 913 megawatts and Trojan, Oregon at 1,100 megawatts). The smaller plants have the advantage of being less contaminated and easier to take apart. For example, the Shippingport plant, which was decommissioned by the DOE for $91.3 million, was contaminated with about 30,000 curies of radioactivity. It also contained a relatively small reactor vessel (153 tons and about 25 feet high) that was removed in one piece to a burial site on the Hanford, Washington reservation. In contrast, the Rancho Seco plant was contaminated with more than 9,000,000 curies and the reactor vessel may weigh up to 1,000 tons (United States General Accounting Office 1990a). The General Accounting Office also looked at the lessons from Shippingport and concluded that other plants will be considerably more demanding (United States General Accounting Office 1990b).

Officials at the Sacramento Municipal Utility District, owners of the Rancho Seco facility, told the United States General Accounting Office in 1990 that it would cost at least ten times as much to decommission their plant as the amount DOE spent on Shippingport, that is, about $1 billion. The attempt at decommissioning Rancho Seco is scheduled to begin about 2008, almost thirty years after the plant was taken out of service. However, considerable attention has been given to decommissioning costs and other estimates have been substantially less for comparable power plants (see Pasqualetti and Rothwell 1991). It seems certain, however, that these costs will be substantial. For example, Commonwealth Edison operates the nation's largest nuclear power program with thirteen units. In 1997, the firm estimated that it would cost $4.6 billion to decommission these units (in 1997 dollars) and $1.6 billion for low-level waste processing and burial of the thirteen reactor units.[22]

In addition to the costs, the decommissioning of large reactors will increase the risk of worker and public exposure to radioactivity. This will be most acute for workers who must dismantle the large reactor vessels but the transportation of massive amounts of waste from the power-plant sites to appropriate waste-disposal sites will also present certain risks to the public. Pollock, for example, quotes a NRC estimate that it will take 1,363 truckloads of waste to remove 17,887 cubic meters of activated, contaminated, and radioactive wastes from a typical 1,100 megawatt pressurized water reactor (Pollock 1986).

Despite the engineering and economic analyses that have been applied to estimated decommissioning costs, the lack of experience with actually doing the work may conceal a number of costly factors that are not adequately accounted for in existing estimates. Robin Cantor (1991) points out some of the pitfalls and opportunities to learn from actual decommissioning experience. Strauss and Kelsey (1991) conducted a survey of operating nuclear power plants and obtained estimates of decommissioning costs. These cost estimates produced a mean value of $211 per KW (1989 dollars) and a standard deviation of $96/KW. At the extremes, four sites estimated costs of less than $100/KW and four sites estimated costs of more than $350/KW. Some of this difference is due to the various sizes and potential radioactive contamination of plants. Some is due to variations in what is included as decommissioning costs, such as whether costs of site remediation exceed the NRC trust-fund requirements. Future regulatory requirements can be expected to change over time with uncertain results for decommissioning costs. Projections of waste-transport and disposal costs are uncertain and may rise substantially. Cost estimates are an international problem; a study by the Organization for Economic Co-operation and Development (1991) laconically commented that costs could result from complex "political, institutional, technical, and economical factors."

---

[22] L. DelGeorge, Presentation to the National Research Council, Board on Radioactive Waste Management (17 July 1997).

In his review of past experience with decommissioning, Gene Fry (1991) found a large discrepancy between estimates to dismantle reactors and dismantlement experience. Fry concludes: "Either available experience is misleading, or there is a vast body of underestimated dismantlement costs." In terms of funding decommissioning costs, Fry suggests that unless dramatic cost savings are discovered "fund collection for most reactors is too small and future ratepayers, stockholders, and taxpayers will be left paying for today's errors." James Hewlett (1991) argues that because interest accrues exponentially, if a reactor is retired early a substantial shortage of decommissioning funds will result. If nuclear power plant owners are required to accept the costs of decommissioning and the regulatory agencies disallow transfer of those costs to ratepayers, then utilities may be encouraged to operate aging and troublesome plants simply to avoid serious economic losses. With increasing costs and fierce competition from other sources for electricity, Hewlett suggests the end result could be plants that are "too costly to run and simultaneously too costly to close . . . a situation to be avoided" (p. 290). There are several plants that are unlikely to operate for the thirty to forty years that was expected when they were built and licensed. These early retirement plants, such as Rancho Seco and Trojan, are seriously underfunded and may require substantial funds from other sources – ratepayers, stockholders, or taxpayers – to complete decommissioning. Even then, unless the problems with disposal are solved there will be no place for them to send their wastes and on-site storage may be the default choice.

The costs of decommissioning are important, of course, but Martin Pasqualetti has cautioned that we should not lose sight of the potential social issues that "will become more important to decommissioning policy just as they did in matters of nuclear power planning, design, siting, and operation. Nuclear programs throughout the world have been transformed by public opinion and ensuing policy changes stressing costs, risks, equity, and the like" (Pasqualetti 1991, p. 8).

Transportation of radioactive wastes

Shipments of nuclear materials, such as reactor fuel, weapons and weapons components, and isotopes for medical or research purposes, take place regularly with little public notice or concern. Transporting radioactive wastes is difficult, especially spent fuel, which is highly radioactive. These wastes require extraordinary precautions to maintain their containment under a wide range of possible conditions, including highway and rail accidents.

Transportation removes the wastes from the security provided at well-regulated facilities and puts them into contact with a wide range of potential social activities, over which the waste managers have only modest or even little control. These social activities include everything from careless driving along truck routes or at train crossings to fanatical attacks upon shipment casks by terrorists or revolutionaries. The 1996 return of spent fuel from a small research reactor in Colombia to the United States relied on air transport to a Colombian port rather than risk guerrilla attacks on trucks. Even the prospect of army escorts was considered problematic and thought to risk being a provocation to an attack rather than prevention (Munera et al. 1997). Certainly, transportation in the United States is not as risky as it is today in Colombia. Still, the rise of domestic and foreign terrorist activities in the United States over the past decade, and in particular events of September 11th 2001, highlights a problem area that cannot be dismissed (and see contributions to Anderson, ed., 2002).

The largest radioactive waste transportation program in the United States involves wastes, mostly spent fuel, from seventy-seven commercial nuclear power stations and six weapons-complex facilities. The shipping campaign would transport more than 85,000 metric tons of heavy metal (MTHM) over a period of about forty years. With maximum reliance on rail transport, about 10,000 shipments will be required with hundreds of truck shipments from reactors without rail access. If only trucks are used, over 40,000 truck shipments would be required (Bentz and Associates 1995). If high-level wastes were shipped to Yucca Mountain, Nevada by rail about 100 miles of new rail access would have to be built at a cost of $1 billion or more. Shipments would take place in more than forty states (Williams 1999), involving large numbers of interested parties – 199 state agencies with transportation authority, 140 state agencies concerned with emergency response to accidents or incidents, thirty-three state utility commissions, numerous public interest groups, and hundreds of cities, towns, and communities (Bentz and Associates 1995).

The case of HLNW transportation of this scope is expected to initiate public concern yet little is known about how people and communities will react. The Komis case in New Mexico signals the potential for impacts on property values, economic stability and growth, and quality of life. Such concerns may become powerful restraints on putting an efficient and acceptable HLNW program into effect (Slovic, Layman, Kraus et al. 1991; Slovic, Flynn, and Gregory, 1994). State and local efforts to control waste shipments can be expected with all the problems of route selection, emergency-response preparations, and direct public opposition to specific shipments.

The problems associated with reprocessing, decommissioning, and waste transportation are capable of casting a long shadow over nuclear power for decades into the twenty-first century. The issues from these residual problems are nationwide, especially in the case of transportation, and offer little in terms of immediate benefits while presenting risks that can quickly erupt into public opposition.

Closing comments

The problems confronting nuclear science and technology are clearly expressed in nuclear stigma, which functions as a composite evaluation of inherent hazards, the history of management, and the potential risks. The nuclear-stigma response runs wide and deep in American society. It is wide because concerns about nuclear facilities are shared across all segments of the population and for all forms of man-made radiation exposure. It is deep because there is a long history that supports public concerns. This history leads to an indictment of responsible organizations for failures to exercise good judgment, provide responsible administration, exercise fiduciary responsibility to public health and safety, and accept responsibility for adverse outcomes. The resulting public opposition undercuts expert and government prospects for future development of nuclear sciences and technologies. Yet the problems with management of nuclear programs and projects are not part of nuclear risk assessments and risk analysis except in the public's intuitive judgment, which underlies nuclear stigma.

New developments in communication technologies are transforming the roles of risk analysis and public decision making. News of events as understood in the social amplification of risk seems headed toward a broad-based public and interactive availability. Motivated advocates will gain more and earlier leverage. This has the potential to focus public attention ever more effectively on decision processes and to provide the means for new involvements in policy and program choices. Technological stigma and other ways of framing information, especially those approaches that provide quick, affective, and widely held guidelines, such as moral values, will become more important and influential. In addressing nuclear stigma, society must focus on organizational performance. Science and technology must be, and be seen as, the servant of human health and environmental preservation. Organizational goals must be recreated to these ends if management of inherently hazardous technologies is to achieve public acceptance and fulfill its potential contributions on behalf of mankind.

Part V

Policy and management

15 Searching for the public policy relevance of the risk amplification framework

William Leiss

The richness and indeed boldness of the concept of risk amplification has yielded to date both interesting theoretical discussions as well as applications to case materials. But as a concept it is sufficiently rich to encourage us to look further, to see what else it can yield: in particular, we should try to ascertain and extend the scope and possibilities for its relevance to risk management and in particular to public policy decision making.

Asking this in the context of a review of risk amplification is particularly appropriate. For this concept is premised on a very good core idea, namely, that risk issues – considered as a problematic for public policy and decision making – are an indissoluble unity of a hazard domain and a socially constructed process of concern about that domain.[1] This concept faithfully represents the reality that confronts public-sector risk managers on virtually every working day. The hazard and the concern almost always present themselves to managers in unison, not separately; moreover, even though such issues sometimes linger over long periods, the double-sided unity within them rarely decomposes.

The evolution of research in this area has singled out "managerial (in)competence" as a significant variable in determining the impact of risk events. This might be regarded as troubling, but it is actually good news, because, at least in theory, the level of managerial competence within organizations (including those charged with health and environmental risk issue management) ought to be amenable to improvement. From a public policy standpoint, therefore, this is the decisive question:

---

[1] I propose the use of a shorthand, hyphenated phrase, "hazard-plus-concern," to express this unity. It differs from the well-known "hazard *versus* outrage" in at least two ways: one, most risk issues evoke concern, whereas true outrage is a relatively rare phenomenon; two, "plus" is very different from "versus." To be sure, an emphasis on addressing concerns is to be found relatively early in the development of the field of risk communication. However, as that phase of risk communication began to be oriented to practitioners, it sometimes quickly degenerated into lessons on creating manipulative and soothing verbiage devoid of any substantive content; in other words, the need for a fair and balanced discourse about the hazard was forgotten. The most important thing is to preserve the unity of hazard-plus-concern.

what guidance does the risk amplification concept offer towards improving managerial competence for risk issue management?

Of course there is a sense in which public policy decision making appears to be inherently incompatible with any risk management approach. This is because policy urgently seeks a "yes/no" answer to public concerns, which further incorporates in Canada a resolve that the word "uncertainty" (much less its statistical expression) shall never pass the lips of a Minister of the Crown. It is doubtful that there is any more disastrous or expensive example of this futile and wrong-headed orientation than the politicians' line about British beef being "perfectly safe" during the run-up to the explosion of the BSE (or "Mad cow") crisis in 1996, but Canada and other countries have plenty of their own sins to confess in this regard.

The originators of the risk amplification concept framed it explicitly and broadly in a decision-making context about five years after it had originally appeared (Burns et al. 1993). Operating within this general context, my chapter takes as a starting point the idea of "providing tools for policy."[2] In particular, I want to take up the question posed there, as to whether "knowledge of the factors likely to lead to amplification effects, and the sociopolitical contexts in which they might operate, could possibly be used as a *screening device* for evaluating the potential for such effects" (Pidgeon 1999, p. 155).[3]

Pidgeon (1997) explicates this core idea in such a way as to suggest that there could be four potential outcomes[4] derived from the course of risk issues: appropriate or inappropriate intensification, on the one side, and appropriate or inappropriate attenuation, on the other.[5] It appears

---

[2] My personal motivation for taking this approach has much to do with the fact that, in addition to conducting academic exercises on risk management cases for the past ten years, I have been during the same period a close observer of, and sometime consultant for, the actual practice of health and environmental risk management by Canadian federal agencies. Issues in which I have had some such involvement include pesticides, toxic chemicals, tobacco, prescription drugs, nuclear waste, genetic engineering, radio-frequency fields, air pollution, and xenotransplantation.

[3] But I want to go further, and ask whether the guidance offered by the risk amplification concept can be even more useful, namely, in helping public-sector agencies to do much more effective risk issue management.

[4] The third ("appropriate attenuation") has no example specified or suggested.

[5] The risk amplification concept has been vexed from the outset by a possible misunderstanding, owing to the decision to have the term "amplification" represent (apparently somewhat paradoxically) the full range of the continuous spectrum from (signal) intensification to attenuation. The initial criticism by Rip (1988) pointed to a possible bias in the concept; namely, that it could be interpreted as implying that the most serious risk issues were all about exaggerated public fears. This has led to repeated "clarifications" (see especially Kasperson 1992, p. 161) which have not included, so far as I know, the relatively simple observation that "amplification" is an inherently relative term: that is, it alludes to a movement towards either higher or lower signal strength relative to a fixed starting point on a continuous scale.

that only two of the four possible placements of issues in the matrix will be of interest to risk managers and policy makers:

1. "Inappropriate intensification," because this can lead to wasting resources on unneeded risk reduction, setting improper priorities for institutional agendas, causing unnecessary public concerns, getting politicians upset or in trouble, and so on.
2. "Inappropriate attenuation," because this can lead to very real avoidable suffering (illness and death), avoidable economic costs imposed on various parties, and under-investment in risk reduction (relative to other risks) due to inadequate public support.

Indeed this may be a trivial point, because, considered from either a theoretical or a practical standpoint, the remaining two (appropriate intensification and attenuation) are both good things by definition.

In addition, for public-sector risk managers with broad mandates there is a "holding" category, filled with an indeterminate number of potential issues, some of which may lie dormant forever, others of which may erupt at unexpected times (the bureaucratic equivalent of dread risk). While they are in the holding pattern there is no *issue* to be managed, although risk assessments may be under way or completed, with respect to the particular risk factors related to the nature of the hazards. The absence of "issue" may be due to many reasons, perhaps even because, however unlikely it may seem, the expert risk construction and the public risk constructions are roughly in agreement, either by accident or design (for example, the existence of a healthy public risk dialogue). One question to be considered is whether or not there is a screening procedure that could be used to "scan" periodically at least the most volatile layers in the basket of hazards making up the holding category, in order to decide whether prophylactic measures are called for with respect to any of them.

Again, for public-sector risk managers this is the stuff of everyday life: a good deal of ongoing scientific review is mixed with some low-level issue management, but the organization never seems to know when something is going to erupt into a high-profile controversy. Can the risk amplification concept help risk managers at, say, Health Canada or the United Kingdom's Health and Safety Executive, and other such agencies, better meet their responsibilities?

The single most notable aspect of the risk amplification concept, without a doubt, is its attempt to synthesize otherwise fundamentally dichotomous aspects of risk issues, represented variously by the difference between (1) the (objective) hazard-risk characteristics of the "risk event" and (2) what may be called "the social construction of risk." This core idea has been put succinctly as follows (Renn, Burns, Kasperson et al. 1992, p. 140): "In the social amplification framework, risk is conceptualized partly as a social construct and partly as an objective property of a hazard or event."[6]

Public-sector agencies with risk management responsibilities are *ideal test-beds* for exploring the potential practical efficacy of the risk amplification concept! This is because they have no choice but to accept the twin responsibilities of doing both technical risk assessments, in the accepted sense, and also what I call "responsible risk issue management" (Leiss 2001), and some industrial firms, particularly in the chemical sector, have been moving in this direction as well. Responsible risk issue management is primarily an exercise in good risk communication practice, or what I call taking responsibility for the creation and maintenance of a "fair risk dialogue."

Risk management *versus* risk issue management

The history of modern health and environmental risk management, beginning around 1970 and continuing on the present day, has been bedeviled with seemingly intractable controversies. The word "controversy" here is used to indicate the presence of one or more of the following dimensions, among others: (1) confrontations between stakeholders, such as environmentalists and industry, over the fundamental values that should guide decision making; (2) technical disputes over what the risk assessments should say, based on inadequacies in available data, or differences in methodologies, or hidden assumptions; (3) differences in what uncertainties mean and how to act in the light of them; (4) dichotomies in the relevance of precautionary approaches, based on choices about type 1 and type 2 errors; (5) disputes over equity and the distribution of risks and benefits; (6) allegations of cover-ups, misrepresentations, improper denials of liability, and a host of other charges about alleged illegal, immoral, or reprehensible behavior.

Controversies involving these themes are documented in the case of literally dozens of hazards and risks, including notably pesticides (pentachlorophenol, 2,4–D, 2,4,5–T, the biological warfare substance known as "Agent Orange," alar); heavy metals (lead, mercury, manganese); minerals (asbestos, silicon); food and water-borne pathogens (prion diseases, salmonella, *E. coli*); chlorine chemistry (water disinfection byproducts,

---

[6] The language here runs counter to one of my mantras, drawn from Slovic (1998, p. 74) to the effect that "there is no such thing as real risk or objective risk." There is no really satisfactory short-hand terminology for the contrast; the closest I can come to one is "expert construction of risk" *versus* "intuitive construction of risk," although this is still unsatisfactory because it appears to deny the role of intuition in disciplined thought processes.

dioxins and furans, PCBs, endocrine disruptors); air pollutants (green-house gases, ozone, particulate matter, sulphur); electric and magnetic fields (power-line frequencies, radio-frequencies, UV radiation); tobacco; nuclear power; genetic engineering (foods, cloning, xenotransplantation).

Behind many public controversies over risks there is a significant public policy failure, and the source of that failure lies in the inability of some of those in government and industry to see the difference between risk management and risk issue management.[7] *Risk management* relies on scientific risk assessment to estimate the probable harm to persons and environments resulting from specific types of substances or activities. As such, even when risk managers seek honestly to take into account varying perceptions of the risk in question among different sectors of the public, they are necessarily and properly constrained by the scope and limitations of their scientific assessment in recommending specific courses of action. This is an inescapable part of their duty to protect public health to the best of their ability, taking into account the uncertainties that are always a factor in risk estimates. Mistakes can and will be made in this regard for a whole host of reasons; the public only has a right to expect that the risk management protocols will be sufficiently self-critical and iterative so that serious mistakes are discovered and corrected in the shortest possible time-frame.

Risk issue management is fundamentally different from risk management.[8] The most important difference is that risk issues, as they play out in society at large, are not primarily driven by the state of scientific risk assessments. Rather, such assessments are just one of a series of "contested" domains within the issue. Risk issues are configured by the competing attempts of various stakeholder interests to define or control the course of social action with respect to health and environmental hazards. Issue management refers to the relationship between an organization and its larger social "environment," where reigning public policy provides the basic "rules of the game"; and it is inherently governed by *strategic* considerations as developed by an organization or even a loose collection of individuals (see table 15.1). All those who wish to become skilled intervenors in risk controversies, such as (Environmental Non-Governmental Organizations (ENGOs), as well as those who will inevitably be caught up in them, namely industry and governments, become issue managers (by choice or default). To do so entails understanding the internal dynamics of risk controversies and seeking to influence them towards some

[7] It is derived from the approach taken in Heath (1997).
[8] It is important to specify at the outset what risk issue management is *not*: it is not seeking to control the information flow about an issue, which is what "issue management" has come to mean in some quarters.

Table 15.1 *Contrast between risk management and risk issue management*

	risk domain	risk controversy
type of responsibility	**risk management**	**risk issue management**
type of expertise required	**risk/benefit assessment**	**risk communication**
key activities	hazard characterization	science explanations
	exposure assessment	science/public interface
	benefits assessment	science/policy interface
	uncertainty analysis	explaining uncertainties
	options/decision analysis	stakeholder relations
orientation of activities	**"substantive"**	**strategic**
principal "language"	**technical/probabilistic**	**non-technical/graphics**

final resolution; in most cases this will be called the "public interest," although inevitably there will be diverse definitions of what this means in practice. These resolutions may be, for example, introducing a new substance or activity or banning an existing one; changing laws or the regulatory environment; adopting new principles, such as the precautionary approach; introducing changes in business practices; approving a new economic development project or creating wilderness preservation zones; and so forth.

To put the main point a bit differently: whereas risk management seeks to assess and control a *risk domain*, risk issue management responds to a *risk controversy*. A risk domain is a collection of risk factors associated with a specific activity or technology, such as smoking, biotechnology, or radio-frequency fields. The risk factors, as assessed or perceived by various parties over time, quantitatively and qualitatively, become the subject of risk management decision making, which may lead to risk reduction strategies or other action options. A risk controversy, on the other hand, is a risk domain which becomes the subject of a protracted battle among stakeholder interest groups, the outcome of which may or may not be consistent with any set of decision options preferred by the risk managers (in government or industry) who have "official" responsibility for the file in question. The evolution of a risk controversy is determined primarily by the competing strategies of whatever groups or organizations choose to, or are compelled to, enter into it; and as mentioned earlier, the objective of these strategies is to steer the outcome of the controversy towards some preferred risk management option. Since by definition a risk controversy is an area of competing visions about where an optimal resolution lies, competence in risk issue management should not be understood as seeking to "control" the outcome. Rather, it means in general being able to compete successfully with other influential stakeholders within the zone of controversy, *in a way that is appropriate to the specific positioning of an organization and its lines of accountability within the larger social matrix.* Industry, ENGOs, and governments all have quite diverse positionings in this regard. Governments' positioning is defined primarily by its responsibility to define and defend "the public interest" as such, for example, to seek to be as "inclusive" as possible in relation to the spectrum of social interests.

Risk assessment and management is strictly a subordinate activity within the field of risk issues: sometimes the scientific assessment is definitive for issue resolution and sometimes it is not; the outcome is often impossible to predict, and in any case depends primarily, in my view, on the specific pathway along which the issue evolves. It is possible that the former (i.e. where the scientific assessment is definitive) predominates, over the whole range of issues, although the most high-profile cases may be those that fall into the latter camp. Where broad stakeholder consensus emerges, as it has now with a group of chemicals called "persistent organic pollutants," the consensus is the product of a long and tortuous pathway filled with recriminations directed at some parties by others. In other cases (such as Alar and apples, or saccharin, for example) some of those affected directly by the outcome remain convinced, even years or decades later, that the wrong resolution occurred. In still others, such as BSE and British beef or health risks associated with radio-frequency fields, the weight of massive and irresolvable uncertainties about the scope of exposure and potential harm hangs like a dark cloud over both the issue and its resolution to date. In all such cases scientific assessment played or plays some role in issue evolution, but only as one factor among many. What issue managers most need to know is how scientific assessment will "play" at different times in the evolution of risk issues, especially those (like dioxin or now endocrine modulators) that have a very long life span.

The divide between risk management and risk issue management affects none more seriously than governments.[9] They must do both. Over the past thirty years, coincident with the rise of the modern specialized field of health and environmental risk management, many governments, including Canada's, have developed outstanding expertise in risk assessment. They are not as good by and large at risk management, mainly because they experience difficulties (just as citizens do) in integrating multiple decision inputs of qualitatively different sorts into a coherent framework within and across issue types (as such comparative risk management is a radically underdeveloped field of practice). And an

---

[9] Industry and governments have responsibilities for both types of management; here I will comment only on the situation of the latter.

unfamiliarity with how risk issue management differs from risk management has hampered the ability of governments to deal at all adequately with risk controversies.

Stages in risk issue development

Competence in risk issue management starts with an ability to understand that risk controversies have common structures and evolve over time in distinctive stages. The particular type of risk issue that becomes controversial is of fundamental importance to risk managers, because it determines which industrial sector and government agency is answerable to the public. But, although controversies originate with the products and processes of many different industrial technologies (chemicals, tobacco, nuclear energy, forestry, telecommunications, petroleum, food processing, to name but a few), the risk controversies themselves have many features in common.

The early stage   The early stage of every risk controversy has the following features. *First*, there is an incomplete hazard characterization, because scientific studies are inadequate, and sometimes scientists do not know at that point even what types of studies will clarify the concerns. At this stage it is not clear what is the range of adverse effects the public should be worried about, or sometimes whether anyone should be worried at all. These large unknowns are compounded by the propensity of spokespersons for industry, often seconded by their government counterparts, either to downplay or deny the scope of the hazards, to be reluctant to initiate adequate funding programs for the science that needs to be done, and to make soothing noises to dampen public concerns. *Second*, there is poor or non-existent exposure assessment: it is not clear who (if anyone) is at risk of harm from many of the suspected effects, nor is it readily apparent how to resolve this question. Providing an answer necessitates being able to separate out specific sets of factors from the entire gamut of the hundreds or indeed thousands of relevant risk factors impinging upon the lives of individuals in modern societies. Epidemiological studies that attempt to do this are notoriously hard to construct and carry out, and the results from such studies are fought over by specialists sometimes for decades. Compounding these intrinsic difficulties is the reluctance of industry and governments to provide early funding for these studies, which are often inconclusive and always expensive.

Third, in the early stage the industrial and government institutions which eventually will be answerable for the issue have a strong desire to avoid calling attention to it, in the hope that there will never be a major controversy. Their motto for this stage is: "Let sleeping dogs lie." Their fear is that, if they take the initiative to call attention to the newly suspected but poorly understood risk factors, they will raise alarms that might be unfounded and cause unnecessary worry in a population perhaps predisposed to worry needlessly about certain types of hazards. So typically little or no effort is made in risk communication, that is, explaining the nature of the hazards and the scientific studies being done to clarify them. *Fourth*, and following directly from the third, throughout the early stage there is the possibility of "issue capture" and "stigma." Issue capture refers to the process whereby one party seizes the initiative and succeeds in raising the profile of an issue, to the point where others can no longer pretend it is unimportant and are required to respond. Since there are tremendous advantages to be reaped by the party which succeeds in this endeavor, this is where the strategic competence of ENGOs is put to the test. And one of the most potent devices for issue capture is to find a way to brand the risk source with a stigma, that is, an image with strongly negative connotations and having dramatic power to call attention to a risk (Flynn, Slovic, and Kunreuther 2001); examples abound, in ranging from dioxins in the 1970s ("the deadliest chemical known to mankind") to today's "Frankenfood" label for genetically modified crops (also, Murdock et al. this volume chapter 7)

The early stage of a risk controversy can last for ten or fifteen years, as was the case with dioxins (*c.*1970–85); endocrine disruptors (*c.*1990–present), wireless telecommunications, global climate change, and food biotechnology are still in this formative period. It is possible to say for certain that many other applications of genetic engineering, especially as they apply to human health (xenotransplantation) and manipulations of the human genome (gene therapy, genetic screening, enhanced reproductive success) will generate significant risk controversies. In addition, there will be efforts to win support for the intensive engineering of plants and trees both for enhanced carbon sequestration (to offset greenhouse gas emissions) and to provide chemical feedstocks which promise far lower environmental impacts than conventional products have ("cleaner production"), and this too can be expected to be controversial.

The middle stage   The middle stage of every risk controversy has the following features. *First*, large-scale scientific research programs designed to produce a definitive hazard or risk characterization are well under way but remain incomplete, and early epidemiology studies (if they exist) are likely to be inconclusive as well. Typically, there is little, if any, effective communication to the public of the research program objectives, the reasons why certain programs and not others are under way, or how the results are expected to be applied to a surer understanding of the hazards. *Second*, there are initial risk assessments, giving some quantitative expression to the magnitude of the hazard (e.g. "excessive daily alcohol consumption (as defined) is estimated to represent an annual incremental risk of breast cancer on the order of 2×10^{-5} in the exposed population"). But often the uncertainties, which may or may not be specified clearly, remain rather large, or the initial estimates are challenged by subsequent findings. Typically, no effort is made to explain clearly to the public either the great complexities in the risk assessment exercises, or the strengths and weaknesses of competing assumptions and approaches. With respect to both the scientific programs and the risk assessments, the strongest inclination of industry and government, in most cases, is to continue to downplay concerns, to keep a low profile, and to pray that the issue just goes away of its own accord.

Third, the risk information vacuum usually subsisting in the second stage helps to keep an issue "in play," as it were, with various stakeholders jockeying for position and leverage during the ebb and flow of events such as the publication of key studies, calls for regulatory action, protests, closed-door negotiations, and lobbying. There is an inherent volatility in this stage which rules out reliable predictions about the future course of the issue agenda. For example, the release of a long-awaited major scientific study can generate competing efforts by opposed factions to provide the "spin" (interpretive context) that will define the public attitudes of the great majority of the population who will never see the study itself; for example, this happened a number of times during 1999 in the risk issue domain of radio-frequency fields used in wireless telecommunications. *Fourth*, and increasingly, an issue will be "bounced" around the globe as the contending parties (industry, governments, ENGOs, academics) find different venues in which to mount their campaigns in strategic issue management. Globalized business strategies mean that the same technologies are deployed around the world and, in reaction to this, many ENGOs have become highly adept at internationalizing their own operations and matching the capacities of multinational firms to operate on a world scale. Electronic mass communications and above all the Internet promote the increasingly sophisticated coordination of marketing campaigns for both products and issues.

Dioxins passed through the middle stage of controversy in the period 1985–99, as did the issues of risks associated with high-voltage transmission lines and household electricity supply (extremely low frequency electric and magnetic fields: ELF–EMF) during the 1990s. The intense international controversies over forestry practices, involving clear-cutting and the logging of old-growth forests, also seemed to enter this stage in the late 1990s.

The mature stage   The mature stage of every risk controversy has the following features. *First*, scientific research programs are scaled back to a "maintenance" state, although they never stop entirely for major risk domains, as the full hazard characterization is increasingly well understood. *Second*, exposure measures become more and more sophisticated, and therefore the quantitative risk assessments are correspondingly well defined and the uncertainties are reduced to acceptable levels. As a result, the public can expect few great surprises from the ongoing scientific programs in these areas, although essential new knowledge is gained all the time, some of which leads to important modifications in risk assessments even for relatively well-described risks. For example, both geological radon and food and water-borne pathogens appear to be more serious hazards than they were thought to be until quite recently.

Third, in most cases the longstanding inadequacies in risk communication typically are never repaired and therefore continue to take their toll, in that the framing of issues is frozen in time and cannot respond to changing circumstances. For example, there are those in Canada and elsewhere who now would like to see nuclear generation of electricity as a newly desirable option in an era of concern about lowering atmospheric greenhouse gas emissions; but there is an enormous weight of resistance to this option in public opinion to be dealt with, the legacy of decades of appallingly inadequate risk communication from the nuclear industry. *Fourth*, there is a shifting stakeholder interest profile in the mature stage, as businesses, governments, and NGOs make strategic choices about allocations of time and resources to a variety of risk issues.

Among major risk controversies reviewed in this and earlier volumes tobacco use and nuclear power probably entered the mature stage first (of course these two are among the oldest contemporary risk controversies), sometime in the 1980s. Asbestos risk – still an issue around the world and of great interest to Canada, as a large producer – also appeared to enter a mature phase of controversy in the 1990s, as did most aspects of pesticides use in agriculture. And it seems likely that both dioxins and most ELF–EMF issues have now entered this stage too.

In conclusion, the underlying common structure of risk controversies and their evolution through distinct stages has considerable significance for defining competence in risk issue management. At one time or another, intense and persistent risk controversies have affected, or are likely to affect, most major industrial sectors and many different government agencies. The "instinctive" response of managers within those organizations, when a brewing risk controversy first threatens to engulf them, is one of denial: denial, that the *issues* as represented by other interested parties are at all significant (and that those parties have any business meddling in such matters anyway); that the management of the risk factors in question is or should be open to dispute by those who are not "experts" in the relevant scientific disciplines; and that "the public" really needs to be involved in the intricacies of evaluating scientific research results, assessing the credibility of experts, figuring out exposures and uncertainties, doing quantitative risk estimates, and exploring risk-benefit trade-offs among the decision options for risk control. Certainly no sector could ever match the tobacco industry for turning its denial phase into the longest-running and most absurd charade ever staged, fully fifty years in duration extending from the 1950s until late 1999 when a major firm first explicitly recognized some elements of the truths about the risk factors associated with smoking conceded earlier by almost everyone else on the planet.

Countless case studies of risk controversies to date show, alas, that those instincts are unreliable guides to effective risk issue management. In all cases the opposite propositions are the better guides: namely, that public perceptions of risk are legitimate and must be treated as such; that risk management subsists in an inherently disputable zone; and that the public ought always to be involved (through good risk communication practices) in discussions about the nature of risk evaluation by scientists and risk managers.

A managerial approach derived from risk amplification

What are here called "risk controversies" all illustrate the process of risk amplification. What the perspective outlined above indicates, however, is *that risk controversies – and thus the process of risk amplification – are normal events in contemporary society.* In other words, risk controversies arise out of two independent sources: first, the inherent features of risk issues themselves, especially irreducible uncertainty; second, structural defects in risk management processes which have plagued risk managers in industry and government for a long time. Neither of these sources is about to dry up anytime soon. And in any case, only the latter is amenable to correction through improved practices in risk management and risk communication.

So far as I know, only two published pieces in the risk amplification literature (Renn et al. 1992; Burns et al. 1993) explicitly have raised the issue of managerial factors in this process, by identifying a variable

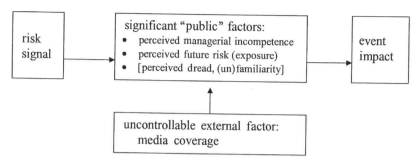

Figure 15.1 The risk amplification process.

called "perceived managerial incompetence"; the variable is defined as the "degree to which the public believes that a hazard implies that similar risks are being managed incompetently." The key finding is stated as follows (Burns et al. 1993, p. 621): "Perceptions of managerial incompetence influence the public's response to a hazard to a degree approaching the scale of the event."

Here is a finding, derived from risk amplification research, that is of direct relevance to the mission of public-sector risk managers. Should this be regarded as a plausible finding, it means quite simply that managers have a lever with which they can influence the outcomes of risk issues – so long as they are in a position to operate the lever. The critical question becomes then: how can the perception of managerial competence for risk issues be influenced?

Before suggesting a route towards an answer to this question I would like to expand on its description in the published study. This is where the perceived managerial incompetence variable seems to stand within the larger picture of the risk amplification concept:

"Future risk" is defined as the "degree to which other people are at risk of experiencing harm from future hazards of this type"; this variable is linked to the other and important key finding from this set of two studies (Renn et al. 1992, p. 151): "It was not the magnitude of a risk that was most influential in shaping the individual and social experience of risk, but the exposure to risk." It was further hypothesized that the two well-known factors elucidated in risk perception research, namely dread and familiarity, will combine with the "exposure" variable to influence public response (ibid., pp. 154–156).

Neither the perception factors of dread and familiarity, nor the perceived exposure variable, are directly amenable to managerial control during the active phases of a risk issue, certainly not in the short to medium term, which is the conventional horizon for decision making.

And the extent and type of media coverage, driven as it is largely by accidental circumstances, rests almost entirely outside of the managerial domain (see Freudenburg et al. 1996). Media coverage can be affected marginally by good risk communication practice, I believe, but pretty much has a life of its own, because journalists simply will not accept someone else's agenda for the development of a story line, especially if that person works for an organization which is caught up in the story.

This leaves "managerial competence" as a domain where improvement in risk issue management is or ought to be possible, at least in theory. My own conviction that such improvements are possible, and that the attempt to find a promising path to improvement ought to be made, stems in part from some fifteen years of involvement with personnel in Canadian federal government departments charged with environmental and health risk management over a broad range of hazards. It also stems in part from work on academic case studies of almost twenty major risk issues occurring in the period 1970–present (and ongoing), and a more casual acquaintance with a few dozen more.[10]

Managerial competence for risk issues

What are the prospects for improved managerial competence in risk management, especially where risk controversies are involved? I begin with a speculative diagnosis of the causes of perceived managerial incompetence here, because so far as I know it has not yet been presented in the literature.

I believe that at least some primary sources of this perception are to be found in a faulty self-assessment and self-representation, by the agencies charged with health and environmental risk management, of their basic mission. To put the point succinctly, they have conceived themselves (over a long period of time) as experts in hazard characterization, and to a lesser extent in risk assessment, whereas what is needed from them above all is expertise in risk issue management. Those agencies naturally also configured their professional staff complement in line with this conception. The commonest example of these faults can be found in the responses of such agencies over the years to public expressions of

---

[10] Over the last ten years I and my colleagues have collaborated on in-depth studies of the following risk issues: alar, pentachlorophenol and related fungicides, and electric and magnetic fields (power line frequencies), in Leiss and Chociolko (1994); bovine growth hormone, dioxins and chlorine, "hamburger disease," "mad cow" disease, PCBs, genetic engineering of food crops (environmental risks), and silicon breast implants, in Powell and Leiss (1997); MMT (manganese-based gasoline additive), tobacco, pulp and paper mill effluent, and radio-frequency fields (cellular telephone technologies), in Leiss (2001); climate change, endocrine disruptors (ongoing).

concern about hazards that fall under their mandates: all too often the representatives of those agencies addressed the hazard characterization (and did so quite fairly, on the whole), but not the concern.

What is needed above all is competence in addressing the unity of hazard-plus-concern. In terms of professional complement, this means that such agencies should be staffed primarily by specialists in risk issue management, who are assisted by risk assessors, and only secondarily by scientists who have been trained in specialized fields of chemistry, biology, toxicology, and so forth.[11]

The Golden Rule for risk managers is: always focus on the linked hazard-plus-concern. Their credo might be formed from the following propositions:

(1) With an awareness of the stations of risk amplification, anticipate the evolution of risk issue development;
(2) Use screening criteria on the holding issue basket to do forecasts and to set priorities for agency resource allocation;
(3) Ensure the existence of a healthy public risk dialogue (as the agency's primary mission);
(4) Clearly concede the existence of uncertainties and discuss the implications of this uncertainty for the individual's personal safety and well-being;
(5) Where final responsibility for risk management falls squarely on government, advocate strongly for the filling of key scientific knowledge gaps and the reduction of unacceptable levels of uncertainties;
(6) Assume responsibility for ensuring that some credible party is charged with periodic scientific review;[12]
(7) Promote clarity of public communication about the nature of the hazards and always address the specific concerns that are expressed.

Conclusion: application of the foregoing principles to a current risk controversy

In order to illustrate the possibilities of improved managerial competence, I offer here a précis of the still-emerging case of a global risk

---

[11] In the preceding generation Health Canada's Health Protection Branch, for example, had a large complement of outstanding scientists whose professional advancement was determined in part by success in publishing a stream of original research in peer-reviewed journals.

[12] In 1998 the Government of Canada commissioned an independent expert panel, through the Royal Society of Canada, to review and report on the state of scientific knowledge about the hazards associated with radio frequency (RF) fields. Their report, issued in May 1999, is available at <www.rsc.ca>; see also United Kingdom National Radiological Protection Board (2000).

controversy, about radio-frequency (RF) fields (wireless telecommunications technologies of different types, in particular cellular telephones).

RF fields lie in the range between 3 kHz and 300 GHz. The electromagnetic spectrum as a whole covers an extraordinary range of frequencies and includes, of course, two qualitatively different types (ionizing and non-ionizing). Thus the types of hazards vary quite considerably in qualitative terms. In addition, the hazard is a combined function of frequency and power, expressed in a measure known as the "power density of a field." Further, the hazard has the quite remarkable property of diminishing rapidly as a function of the distance from the source of the field (it diminishes according to the square of the distance). And there is more. Our bodies operate at the intra- and inter-cellular level on electrical fields of determinate frequencies, leading to the *possibility* that it is exposure to external fields of certain strength in those particular frequencies that *may* have biological "significance" (as yet undetermined), in the first instance; second, those fields *may* also have biological effects; and third, ultimately, some of those effects *may* turn out to be adverse effects entailing unacceptable levels of risk. On the other hand, fields of certain frequencies and strengths are known in medical science to have healing properties. All of the above, and other characteristics, make the nature of the risks a bit of a puzzle to many people, and quite reasonably so! Thus very good risk communication would be advisable (although precious little is in evidence so far).

In analyzing this issue I must first specify some arbitrarily chosen issue amplification criteria to be applied to this particular case.[13] The criteria are derived from a case study in progress, but they certainly appear in the same or related forms in many other cases as well:[14]

• Very wide *and increasing* exposure (practically universal at this point), and new types of exposure, due to a recent rapid expansion of the technology (including the use of many new frequencies);
• Exposure of both users (cellphones) and non-users (those living or working near antenna installations);
• Aspects of dread risk (radiation), including wide media coverage of brain cancer risk;
• Significant unfamiliarity with aspects of the hazard;

---

[13] Cases of inappropriate attenuation have a different structure and evolution. An exposition of this side of the matter must await another occasion.

[14] From a methodological standpoint, of course, this is not a predictive exercise, since the issue in this case has already "erupted" in the hazard-plus-concern mode. But it is still early enough in its development, I would contend, to be amenable to direction by competent risk issue management.

- Relatively poor scientific characterization of the full scope of the hazard profile, thus also entailing significant uncertainties that will not be reduced for some considerable time;
- Public disputes among some scientists, and between industry and credible scientists, over both the risk assessment and the quality of scientific research;
- A perception of evasiveness by risk managers about the full scope of the hazards;[15]
- Diffusion of responsibility for risk management (buck-passing) between governments which license the frequencies and industry, which installs, operates, and markets the technologies;
- Relatively poor or non-existent risk communication to date.

There are other interesting aspects, but this list will do. The list includes all of the more general ingredients that are common to significant environmental and health risk controversies: (1) a high degree of individual or group concern over health outcomes; (2) a complex technical description, including both scientific and statistical languages; (3) a long time frame and an extensive, sometimes daunting collection of pertinent documentation; (4) multiple and varied stakeholders; (5) possibly very large costs for remedial or precautionary measures to reduce risks or alleviate concerns; and (6) substantial elements of uncertainty about possible outcomes, even where the documentation is quite full. These general ingredients may or may not be adequate, at least as a starting-point, for working towards a set of screening criteria to apply to the holding basket of hazards. As a result of these characteristics attached to RF issues, there have been notable controversies of varying intensity in many different countries, including Canada, the United States, Britain, Ireland, Sweden, Austria, Australia, and others. When the above-listed characteristics are blended with the fact that these technological applications are still expanding (new frequencies and services), and that the attractiveness of wireless services to consumers is very strong (thus justifying large long-term capital investments in the required

---

[15] Until very recently, the public position of risk managers in the Canadian federal government, and in the wireless telecommunications industry as well, was to ignore a dimension of hazards, associated with RF fields, known as "biological" or "non-thermal" effects. Of course, both sets of risk managers knew that there is active, ongoing scientific research and discussion about such (possible) effects, but they appeared to believe that conceding this point, and providing useful communications about the scientific discussions, would merely confuse an all-too-easily confused public. However, one merely had to spend a little time surfing the Internet (which citizens began to do) in order to encounter very lively debates indeed about these effects! The net result was to encourage a belief among the concerned public that government and industry jointly had something to hide.

infrastructure), one has a promising recipe for intense, long-term risk controversy.[16]

What could be done by public-sector risk managers, to increase their perceived managerial competence sufficiently to make a noticeable difference in the quality of risk issue management for this case? Here is an example of a "program":

- State clearly that the national authority has the responsibility for risk management and will discharge that responsibility (because governments allocate the radio-frequency spectrum to industry);
- State unequivocally that the national authority will ensure that a scientific research program *adequate to the full range of the hazard characteristics* will be carried out at a pace that is responsive to public concerns;[17]
- Discuss clearly and thoroughly the implications of existing uncertainties in relation to some criterion of public safety;
- Assume responsibility for facilitating a credible, fair public risk dialogue for as long as the issue remains salient;
- Address the risk controversy aspects directly (for example, the fight between industry and scientists in the United States recently);[18]
- Always use independent, credible third parties to evaluate and adjudicate controversial points.[19]

In terms of program delivery, what to do for some of these activities is apparent, while others (especially the process for "fair risk dialogue")

---

[16] I have written up a case study report for at least some aspects of the controversy to date in Canada, in Leiss (2001). The title alludes to the use of Internet searches by concerned citizens looking for sources of information on these risks to supplement the meager fare offered by their federal government, which is the risk regulator, and the industry which has been too busy installing and marketing the technology so far to bother with providing anything in the way of credible risk communication.

[17] This will be expensive, although scientists in many different countries are being funded to do it at some level now, so the costs will continue to be distributed. Who should pay for it is an interesting question. For example, governments could, if they so wished, require the industry which is licensed to use the spectrum to do so, and could further specify that the research must be performed at arm's-length by independent scientists. The industry may counter that they already make license fee payments to governments (in Canada, about $150 million Cdn. annually), and that the research budget should be subtracted from such payments; both parties could agree to negotiate on this point.

[18] It is typical of practice to date that public-sector agencies will go about their risk assessment business, in the midst of intense, long-running risk controversies, as if other influential actors (such as prominent environmentalist groups) did not exist. This lends a distinct air of unreality to the proceedings.

[19] This is increasingly being done. The Royal Society (London) issued a short report on the very contentious issues about genetically modified foods in 1998. The Government of Canada requested an independent Expert Panel report on "The Future of Food Biotechnology" (2001). For an overview of the risk controversy see Leiss (2001), ch. 2.

obviously need to be explicated further. The particular list is far less important, however, than is the understanding of the "mission statement" which lies behind the entire set of them: namely, to improve the agency's standing with the public in terms of perceived managerial competence, *by demonstrating a commitment to, and competence in, risk issue management.* All the rest is details.

16   Social amplification of risk in participation: two case studies

Ortwin Renn

Inviting the public to be part of the decision making process in risk analysis and management has been a major objective in European and American risk policy arenas. The recent report by the National Academy of Sciences encourages risk professionals to foster citizen participation and public involvement in risk management (Stern and Fineberg 1996). The report emphasizes the need for a combination of assessment and dialogue which the authors have framed the "analytic-deliberative" approach. Unfortunately, early involvement of the public in deliberative processes may compromise, however, the objective of efficient and effective risk reduction or violate the principle of fairness (Okrent 1996).

The popularity associated with the concepts of two-way communication, trust-building, and citizen participation, however, obscures the challenge of how to put these noble goals into practice and how to ensure that risk management reflects competence, efficiency, and fair burden sharing. One of the major challenges in participation is the problem of putting risks in perspective. Experts and governmental regulatory bodies manage hazards based on numerical assessments of their potential risks, defined as magnitude times probability of a hazard event occurring (expected value). To the risk professionals, it has been hard to accept that the public judges the seriousness of risk according to a different set of characteristics and, as a consequence, places different priorities on where to reduce or manage risks first. Juxtaposing professional estimates of risks and public perceptions of risk has been a popular activity among risk researchers ever since the United States Environmental Protection Agency (EPA) published its *Unfinished Business* report (United States EPA 1987). Most of these studies have shown a discrepancy between the priority list of experts and the mean values of concerns among the general public. Obviously some risks are amplified in the public perception process, while others are attenuated (Kasperson, Renn, Slovic et al. 1988). The question here is: whether the amplification or attenuation processes that occur during participatory deliberations are indicators of an irrational or even erratic mental model for processing risk-related information or do they follow specific lines of reasoning? And if so, is the discursive procedure powerful enough to help participants reflect their patterns of risk amplification and attenuation and assist them in arriving at a rational, competent, and fair recommendation?

This paper examines the problem of how people in different participatory settings deal with amplification and attenuation tendencies in public discourse. Social amplification of risk is based on the thesis that events pertaining to hazards interact with psychological, social, institutional, and cultural processes in ways that can heighten or attenuate individual and social perceptions of risk and shape risk behavior (Kasperson et al. 1988; Renn 1991a). One way to cope with the effects and consequences of amplification or attenuation is to improve risk communication programs as a means to make people more aware of these implications. Another, probably more effective way is to include those people who are likely to be affected by risk decisions as participants in the decision making process, and to engage them in an analytic-deliberative process where amplification effects are explicitly included as an important element of discussion during the deliberations (Renn 1998c).

The first section of this chapter provides a brief review of the social amplification model as the author and other scholars have interpreted it in the past. The second and third sections describe two case studies: the first one with a high potential for amplification (siting of an incinerator) and the second one with a high potential for risk attenuation (policies for noise reduction). These cases illustrate some of the challenges posed by the practice of scientific risk assessments and its perception by participants of participatory processes. The emphasis of the empirical study is on the processes and mechanisms of how participants dealt with the experience of amplification and attenuation. The last section summarizes the findings and draws some conclusions for the appraisal of discursive methods in risk management.

The concept of social amplification of risk

Amplification as a metaphor for dynamic communication

The concept of social amplification of risk is based on the thesis that a combination of the direct physical consequences of the event and the interaction of psychological, social, institutional, and cultural processes determine the social and economic impacts of an adverse event. Kasperson et al. (1988) proposed it in the late 1980s with the aim of explaining the social responses to risk that were not adequately captured in competing concepts, such as the approaches of psychometric or cultural theory.

Amplification includes both intensifying and attenuating signals about risk. Thus, alleged overreactions of target audiences receive the same attention as alleged "down-playing."

The social amplification of risk framework presents a way of coping with uncertainties and ambiguities by examining the collective effect of multiple actors in a given scenario. Whereas traditional social science concepts of risk center on the individual, the social amplification approach places foremost attention on signals (Renn 1991a). Signals are created as a response to a risk event.

A cluster of meaningful signals pertaining to the same topic is called a message. Signals and messages may be created by individual actors or they may emerge from a group process (such as when a newspaper editorial board writes an editorial). In either case it is the content and ordering of the message that is of analytical interest. By comparing these properties of messages about a risk event in society, one can learn how actors selectively interpret (through social interaction) facts and anticipated consequences. This provides a basis for testing hypotheses (albeit only retrospectively, since there is not enough evidence to suggest generalization beyond the immediate case study) about how the privileging of information can influence the social construction of risk (Pidgeon 1999).

In the framework risk is conceptualized partly as a social construct and partly as an objective property of a hazard or event (Short 1989, p. 405). This avoids the problems of seeing risk in terms either of total relativism or of technological determinism. The experience of risk is not only an experience of physical harm, but also the result of a process by which individuals or groups learn to acquire or create interpretations of hazards.

The intuitive attractiveness of the metaphor "amplification" demonstrates the merits, but also the limitations of using a metaphor common to the description of electronic signal theory.

The function of electronic transmitters and the interrelatedness of message and messenger have been the two major arguments against the metaphor of amplification and the use of information theory for analyzing risk communication. In his review of the original paper introducing the concept of social amplification in *Risk Analysis*, Steve Rayner criticized the social amplification metaphor as a mechanistic understanding of social communication which cannot be characterized as a system in which messages and messenger are separate entities (Rayner 1988). The changes wrought in the signal bearers constantly transform the instrument, that is, society.

The proponents of the social amplification concept have responded to this criticism by stating explicitly that using signals as the basic unit of analysis does not imply that stations of signal processing are passive and mechanical transformation stations (Renn 1991a; Kasperson 1992). On the contrary: all actors participating in the communication process transform each message in accordance with their previous understanding of the issue, their application of values, worldviews, and personal or organizational norms, as well as their own strategic intentions and goals. The social amplification metaphor has evolved as an umbrella framework that provides ample space for social and cultural theories. It is not based on a theoretical concept other than the idea that social experiences of risk are only partially determined by the experience of harm or even expected harm.

Case study 1: siting of an incinerator

The controversy over solid waste management in Germany

The issue of waste management not only involves complicated technical issues but also touches upon the main concepts of fairness and equity. Dealing with waste management, at least in Germany, always means dealing with a difficult problem where no "easy" solutions can be found. The NIMBY-Syndrome (Not In My Back Yard) is only one obstacle (albeit an especially important one) in the siting process for any kind of waste treatment plant. Other problematic aspects, however, like uncertainties in waste prognoses, a range of complex technologies with multi-dimensional consequences for the surrounding area, and changes in the legal framework also need to be addressed.

In Germany, special administrative entities named "Gebietskörperschaften" (a county or a regional district) are responsible for waste collection, treatment, and disposal. But in a densely populated country like Germany it becomes more and more difficult to assign new sites for waste disposal. Together with increased efforts for recycling and other strategies for waste reduction, a law has been established defining specific standards for any material to be legally disposable after the year 2005. To comply with these requirements, all counties or cities have to upgrade their waste treatment system by the year 2005 such that the resulting material can meet these standards and therefore be disposed of legally. While the legal setting does not explicitly call for a certain technical option of waste treatment, in practice a priority for incineration is set, because at the moment the only practicable treatment technology to produce material meeting the official criteria for disposal would be incineration. But critics question the scientific validity of the criteria and doubt that the law itself will survive in the longer run. Both lines of criticism are discussed widely and this causes a great deal of uncertainty in the public debate on waste management planning.

Case history

The official process of waste management planning in the Northern Black Forest Region was a response to the legal position in Germany described above. After a history of separate planning efforts and different systems implemented in this field, in 1993 three rural counties and the City of Pforzheim formed a cooperation to seek a common solution on the regional level for their waste problems. For this task a special planning organization (PAN) was established and supported by the counties and the City. An engineering consultant was hired to provide the decision making committees with the necessary technical information. When PAN representatives learned about the experience of the Stuttgart Center of Technology Assessment (directed by the author) in conducting public participation in a structured way, they decided to incorporate such a program in the upcoming planning process and started a cooperation with the center (overviews in Renn, Schrimpf, Büttner et al. 1999; Schneider et al. 1998).

In the official process of decision making the task of developing the waste management concept was divided into three consecutive decision phases, each of them setting the necessary framework for the following phase. The first step consisted of a waste prediction for the planning horizon to the year 2005, setting the minimum and maximum benchmarks of the treatment capacity needed for the region. Based on this result, in the second phase the appropriate treatment technologies (type of facility) had to be selected in order to define the specific selection criteria for the third step, the siting of the selected facilities. The results of the participation program had to correspond with this time frame and the discussions had to proceed parallel to the topics of the official phases. Figure 16.1 illustrates the overall structure of the involvement scheme that was developed for the case, based on a conflict analysis prior to the start of the participation program (adopted from Schneider et al. 1998).

The decision making methodologies changed during the three phases. In phases II and III the organizers of the center applied the method of value tree and multi-attribute utility (MAU) decision analysis (Edwards 1977; Keeney et al. 1984, 1987; Renn, Kastenholz, Schild et al. 1998) for structuring the decision making process. The first phase (waste prognosis) did not call for such a formal procedure, as forecasting waste quantities is an evolutionary procedure.

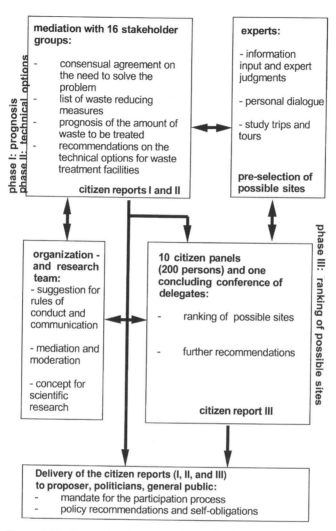

Figure 16.1 Overall involvement scheme for the waste project: (macro-structure).

In phases I and II stakeholder groups came together in a series of consensus conferences, first developing a waste prediction and then ranking possible technical options for waste treatment. After these tasks were completed and the political decision for a combination concept for the region made, the third phase of site selection was started. The task for participants here was to locate one central incinerator and two biomechanical

treatment plants in the region. Sixteen communities had been identified in a preliminary suitability study by the consultant as potential sites
for waste treatment plants, some of them being suitable for both basic
technologies.

In this third phase we applied a modified version of the concept of planning cells (Dienel 1989; Dienel and Renn 1995). A random selection of
around 200 inhabitants from the potential sites for waste treatment facilities in the region was conducted. The 200 randomly selected citizens were
assigned to one of ten parallel working citizen panels, each consisting of
the same number of representatives from each potential site community.
The panels were given the mandate to find the most suitable sites among
these sixteen. Four of the panels focused on the siting of the incinerator
and six groups developed criteria for siting the biomechanical treatment
plants. They developed site selection criteria and ranked all the sites,
considering social, political, ecological, and economic impacts as well as
equity issues including benefit-sharing packages. The team used again
value tree analysis and a modified MAU procedure to reach a consensus
among the participants. The decision making process included:

- construction of a value tree in one brainstorming and several discussion
  sessions, so that all members of the group could agree on the values
  and on their hierarchical structure;
- construction of a catalogue of criteria which could be used as benchmarks for collecting and processing information for each potential site
  on each criterion;
- weighting of the criteria;
- judging and ranking of the options relative to each other according to
  their performance profiles with regard to the different criteria;
- discussing the results and compiling a final document.

Each of the ten panels reached a unanimous conclusion with respect to
the ranking of potential sites. In the end, every group elected three delegates, who met in a conference with the specific objective of composing
one common suggestion for a combination incorporating both treatment
technologies in the best way. Finally, each panel was given the opportunity to comment on the result of the conference of delegates and all
suggestions were included in the citizens' report. Figure 16.2 shows the
applied set of methodologies used in each of the three phases (adopted
from Schneider et al. 1998).

One critical aspect was the handling of complex, uncertain and ambiguous information during an open planning process. Prior to the decision
making the moderators had to select and transmit all relevant information the participants wanted to obtain. This was an especially difficult

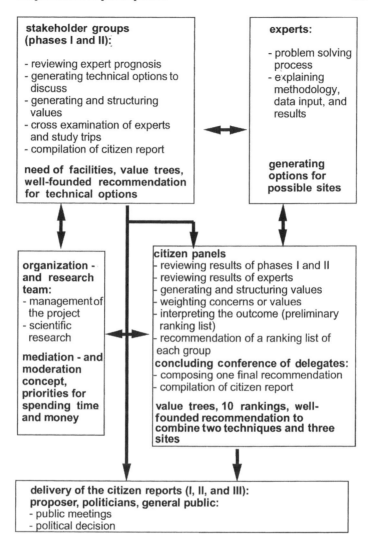

Figure 16.2 Applied methodologies adopted in the project: (micro-structure).

task in the third phase of the project asking citizens to evaluate sites for waste treatment facilities, in particular incinerators. It was crucial to maintain a neutral position on all issues but at the same time to make sure that participants were arguing on the basis of proven knowledge rather than prejudices or mere guesses. Participants were also challenged to acknowledge the remaining uncertainties and to understand the reasons for ambiguity in professional assessments and evaluations.

Social amplification of health risks due to incineration

The public concern about incineration   In the third phase of the participatory process, the randomly selected citizens were asked to find the best suitable site for an incinerator and two biochemical waste treatment plants. As incineration has become a major political issue in Germany on which different social groups strongly disagree we expected that the participants would be most worried about the risks of inciner-ation. Many observers of the public debate on incineration claim that the public is overly worried about the release of dioxin and other toxic chemicals. Experts have calculated that the total amount of dioxin re-leased from all German incinerators is less than one per thousand of the dioxin released from all motorcars in Germany. In addition, all modern incinerators are legally bound to meet the new technical requirements including a guarantee that combustion temperatures are continuously kept at a level that would prohibit the recombination of flue gases. Most professionals believe that the health risks as well as the environmental risks from solid waste incinerators are far below the routine risks of daily life.

Public concerns, however, have not decreased over the last decade. Many environmentalists and health activists have expressed great skep-ticism over the experts' assurance of low risks. Their main argument is that the same professionals or similar experts had been reassuring the public in the past that risks were minimal at a time when emissions were still high and worrisome. It was by political action only that standards for dioxins were promulgated and enforced. Most critics also fear that emissions may be worse in the case of an accident or where negligent behavior occurs. These arguments have left their mark on public opinion. A majority of the German population (54 percent) opposes the building of incinerators in general. That opposition is even stronger (78 percent) if the survey question includes the possibility that such a facility would be located near the respondent (Martens 1997).

The results of previous psychometric studies on risk would also sug-gest that people will be particularly worried about toxic emissions from incinerators. The potential damage is cancer, a very dreadful disease. Most people are unfamiliar with risks of incineration, have no immediate control over them, and depend on the "good will" of operators whom they may not trust. Based on the psychometric literature and studies on risk attitudes, the research team expected to face a series of amplification mechanisms, as follows:

- overestimation of the likelihood of negative health impacts from incinerators;
- a strong stigma effect related to dioxin and carcinogenic chemicals in the flue gas;
- request for scientific certainty and unanimity among experts;
- reluctance to make trade-offs between the different risks of waste disposal options;
- lack of trust in operators and regulators as well as skepticism about their capability to manage and control the risks associated with incineration.

These effects were indeed visible during the second and third phases in which the risks of incineration were discussed. The next section deals with the discourse among stakeholders, the following section with the discourse among the randomly selected citizens.

Social amplification among stakeholders   During the second phase, representatives of stakeholder groups were asked to evaluate the risks and potential benefits of different technologies for waste disposal. Four options were considered:

Option 1: all waste that could not be recycled or reduced was to be incinerated.

Option 2: all waste that could not be recycled or reduced was to be treated by biochemical facilities with no incineration.

Option 3: all waste that could not be recycled or reduced was to be treated first by biomechanical facilities and the remaining residues should be incinerated.

Option 4: all waste that could not be recycled or reduced should be treated first by biomechanical facilities, the remaining residues should be separated into two fractions according to their calorific value (low and high). The fraction with high calorific value should be incinerated, the other one directly disposed of in landfills.

The debate among the stakeholders was very intense since outspoken proponents and opponents of incineration were represented at the Round Table. These people were neither willing nor politically legitimated by their group to give up their preferred option of waste disposal. Although the less committed participants favored one of the two compromise solutions (such as option 3 or 4), the more radical groups insisted on either option 1 or 2. Polarized views and highly amplified and attenuated risk perceptions of the two major camps among the representatives characterized the situation.

In terms of information input, we provided all participants with the opportunity to hear and question experts from both sides, to study scientific material, to visit existing sites and to talk to people living near waste treatment facilities. In addition, we used consensus-building techniques for making people respond to the needs and assessments of the other side. In particular, we divided the whole group of thirty-four into small groups of five or four each and asked them to generate common criteria to evaluate the various options of waste disposal. The same small groups were given the task to evaluate each option on each criterion, again based on small group consensus.

The first task, generation of criteria, worked well and all thirty-four participants were able to find an agreement on the criteria that policy makers were advised to use when evaluating different waste disposal options. The second task was not completed. The two opposing factions were unable or unwilling to compromise on three major criteria: health impacts, eco-toxicological impacts, and incentive for further waste reduction. The proponents of incineration were convinced that the risks were minimal and that incineration would not compromise the national goal of further waste reduction. The opponents believed the opposite. It should be noted, however, that on all other criteria a consensus was established. The process was successful as far as it identified the crucial areas of dissent.

The process was also successful in producing a common document in which the potential risks and benefits of all four options were described. This document was signed by all participants and was later used as an important input to the political decision making body (County Parliaments and City Council of Pforzheim). It was certainly a proof of the willingness of all parties (even the most radical representatives) to accept a balancing procedure when making these decisions. They all agreed that each option had specific advantages and disadvantages and that it was legitimate to assign trade-offs between them. Fundamentalist positions were gradually phased out during the deliberation process. Purely strategic reasoning was replaced by an exchange of arguments, evaluations, and interpretations.

In terms of amplification and attenuation, it was clear from the beginning that certain groups had strong convictions, which were not changed during the deliberation process. The two camps were successful in mobilizing expertise that provided evidence in favor of their respective positions. There was neither a serious attempt to challenge critically each piece of evidence that provided support for one's view nor were participants willing to accept a group of "neutral" scientists to play the role of arbiters. It was interesting, however, to observe that those claims which were not confirmed by an expert nominated by one or the other group were not explicitly renounced but simply downplayed and later "forgotten" in the course of time. For example, the most vocal group against incineration had claimed that during accidents a concentration of at least ten times the permitted dose of dioxin would pollute the environment. When their "own" expert reported a multiplier of a maximum of two to three for accidental release in comparison to routine releases, the whole argument was dropped and removed from the written statement of this specific group. Rather than saying that they had to correct their initial assessment, they omitted the whole argument in a kind of face-saving effort. Similar processes took place with the representatives of other groups. Although the participants went along with the discourse structure of exchanging arguments, in order to remain credible they did not dare correct arguments that were obviously wrong. In this way, many arguments were removed from the list and only those survived where the respective proponents had sufficient evidence or back-up from experts to sustain their view. The discourse procedure had the effect of dissolving fundamentalist positions and created an atmosphere of tolerance of each other's point of view, a prerequisite for resolving conflicts. However, the participants were not willing to re-examine closely each argument under a set of commonly agreed criteria, as they did not want to risk an open process of examination that might result in a "defeat" for their original judgment.

Social amplification among citizens   In the third phase, the ten citizen panels of at least seventeen persons each were asked to evaluate different potential sites for up to three biochemical plants and one incinerator. Four of the ten groups were assigned the task of finding the appropriate host for the incinerator plant.

Before we assembled the panels we conducted a survey among the citizens asking them about their attitudes and risk perceptions as well as their expectations. Similar to the participatory experiences that our team made in Switzerland in 1992 (Renn et al. 1998), almost 80 percent of the citizens were convinced that their hometown was not suitable for any type of waste disposal facility (Vorwerk and Kämper 1997). More than 60 percent believed that incinerators were associated with high risks to human health and the environment, and 40 percent believed this was also true for the biochemical plants. One third of the citizens were very skeptical about the prospect of finding a common solution to the waste problem in the area, another 40 percent were rather skeptical, 20 percent were fairly optimistic and 6 percent very optimistic. Asked about the perceptions of risk with respect to the various waste disposal options, many of our hypotheses proved to be correct. People feared dreadful health impacts as a result of flue gas emissions; they had little confidence in regional regulatory agencies; they felt that many experts were bribed by industry or other powerful players; and they were thoroughly convinced that siting decisions were made by powerful political elites on the basis of strategic advantage rather than objective facts or criteria of fairness. In short, we faced a situation of risk amplification, almost like in a textbook case.

Again the deliberation process consisted of information input, small-group discussion, and a MAU decision making procedure based on a common value tree. To convey the necessary information, we had pre-pared a video with two experts who were pro and contra incineration (the advantages of using videotapes are described in Renn 1991b). The participants had asked us to invite a toxicologist (with a skeptical view on incineration) to report on the effects of flue gas emissions. We also invited a specialist on ash disposal and several experts on biomechanical technologies. The participants were given the opportunity to visit an in-cinerator as well as a biomechanical plant, talk to the operators as well as neighboring citizens (including the local opposition groups). We also prepared a booklet that explained the different technologies and provided a list of arguments pro and contra the different technologies of waste treatment. Lastly we had invited representatives of the second phase to explain to the citizens the reasons why they favored the respective option for which they had opted.

The results of this information input are difficult to evaluate. The sur-vey was repeated in the middle of the participation procedure (before making the final decision) and several months after the procedure. The survey results demonstrated that the participants gained confidence in the participation process (Vorwerk and Kämper 1997). Almost 65 percent were convinced that they could reach a consensual decision when they were asked in the mid-activity survey. They also showed more openness towards offering their hometown (40 percent still thought their town was not suitable, 42 percent thought it may be suitable, and 5 percent thought it was definitely suitable, the remaining 3 percent voiced no opinion). With respect to risk perception, the participants still considered the risks of incineration as being considerably high, but the same judgment also applied to the risk assessment of biomechanical plants. The perception of risk was at this point in time even higher than during the initial phase of responses.

A second indicator for changes can be found in looking at the value trees and the relative weights given to the different criteria. If one looks at the MAU tables of the four groups (Renn et al. 1999, p. 202) which were asked to evaluate locations for siting an incinerator, health impacts were given relative weights ranging from 14 to 21 percent. It is interesting to note that during the deliberations this aspect decreased in importance. In addition, aspects of transportation and odor, originally not seriously considered, became more important concerns. Risks of cancer were still part of the criteria list but not with a prominent relative weight.

The last indicator of a substantial change due to the deliberation process has been the resulting decisions. All ten groups reached a consensus on their final verdict. Nine groups provided a priority list for siting one of the planned waste disposal facilities. The four groups looking for a location to host an incinerator all agreed that the densely populated city of Pforzheim was the most suitable site. The reasons were:

• waste heat could be used for district heating;
• the solution was financially very attractive;
• the waste incineration plant was close to those people who generate the waste (fairness issue);
• the waste incineration plant would not impose risks on the local population that were higher than other risks to which they were already exposed;
• the waste incineration plant was close to the town hall and the city administration which would provide an additional assurance that the regulatory agencies within the administration would commit themselves to thorough inspections (since they would be the first victims if they failed to do so).

These explicitly articulated reasons provide sufficient evidence that the original fear of exaggerated risks was overcome during the process of deliberation. Similar to the Round Table in phase II all participants learned to refrain from fundamentalist positions and make decisions by assigning trade-offs and to reach a judgment by balancing pros and cons. In contrast to the representatives of phase II, the citizens were not committed beforehand and thus willing to change their previous beliefs and even attitudes. They had nothing to lose by examining each argument and decided on the basis of the evidence provided whether the argument was valid or invalid or whether it should be modified. Creating sufficient space between black and white provided the participants with ample opportunities to reach a consensus or at least a compromise.

It is interesting to note that the participants demanded to have a toxicologist invited with a clear negative attitude towards incineration. The video with a statement from each side was not seen as enough proof for making a balanced judgment. The toxicologist whom we invited has been known in the region for her public activities against incineration and a very persuasive style of argumentation. The audience, however, was not very impressed by her reasoning. Although we did not measure risk perceptions directly after her lecture, it became clear to the moderators that the participants felt that key aspects of evidence were deliberately omitted and that she did not respond to the questions in an "objective" manner. The reports of the moderators showed that some of the arguments against incineration were not taken as serious anymore after the presentation of the toxicologist. This is the more surprising as our random sample of participants included more than 16 percent voters of the Green Party and more than 45 percent who declared themselves supporters of environmental groups.

The team also offered all four groups the opportunity to have a toxicologist with a pro-incinerator position present his or her view or to invite a "neutral" expert. But all four groups independently declined our offer stating that their demand for information was satisfied and that they were now able to make a balanced judgment.

The effect of discourse on amplification   The database does not allow for measures of the direct effect of the deliberation process on social amplification and attenuation. The evidence collected here suggests that most participants learned through the deliberation process that their previous beliefs were partially based on either amplifying or attenuating risks and that they needed some corrections before reaching a responsible judgment. This learning process included the acknowledgment that each option poses specific risks and benefits and that some fears are based more on prejudices than on factual evidence. At the same time, they learned that even the most factual type of information incorporates some degree of uncertainty and ambiguity. This explains why different positions on the same issue are not only possible but also legitimate.

One of the crucial aims during the deliberations was to find ways to deal with uncertainty and ambiguity without breaching the limits of what appears to be scientifically reasonable and without assigning credibility according to peripheral attributes such as eloquence or alleged interests. Some of the survey results suggest we did indeed achieve this. More than 85 percent of the respondents were convinced that they had learned a lot during the deliberations. They emphasized that they found the procedure to be fair with respect to the different positions as well as to the populations of the different sites (Renn et al. 1999). They also recommended the procedure for similar controversies (74 percent). Although not directly asked, 6 percent of the respondents wrote in the open comment space: "we have changed our mind and we believe that the procedures used during the deliberation helped us to come up with a balanced view" (the wording was different each time, but the content was the same).

Second case study: noise reduction

The case history

The second case study refers to two communicative exercises that were organized to promote policies for noise reduction from traffic (Keck and Schene 1999; Keck 2001). The first exercise consisted of a Round Table discussion among stakeholders and interested citizens. The second exercise included the organization of focus groups in addition to a Round Table.

In the first exercise, the town of Vaihingen (a suburb of Stuttgart) was obliged to design a noise reduction plan as one major element of their overall town planning process. Such a reduction plan was considered necessary since the town has been in the process of constructing several bypass-roads around the center in order to keep city passing traffic out of town. The Center of Technology Assessment was asked to organize a Round Table with major stakeholder groups. The task of the participants was to design a plan for noise reduction and to draft recommendations for the City Council of both Vaihingen and Stuttgart. The Round Table included sixteen different groups or administrative units ranging from a representative of the largest German automobile association to the local chapter of the most popular environmentalist group in Germany. The meetings of the Round Table took place between November 1997 and March 1999. The Round Table drafted 142 recommendations of which 91 were accepted unanimously and 51 with modifications or minority amendments by one or more groups. The recommendations were printed in a report and handed over to the city government in June of 1999.

The second exercise took place in another town of the German State of Baden-Württemberg. The town of Ravensburg was selected by the Ministry of Environment to become a model town for experimenting with new economic measures for noise reduction. Such measures include special fees for motorists to use their cars or motorcycles on the town streets during night-time, increased parking fees, auctions for parking spaces, and others. As part of this experimental implementation of economic incentives, the Ministry had asked the Center of Technology Assessment to conduct a participatory program with the town's population. The approach of the Center in Ravensburg involved two different elements: a Round Table and two focus groups.

The first element was a Round Table similar to the exercise in Vaihingen. Members of the Round Table were representatives from the
town administration, including the city mayor, representatives of political parties, and organized stakeholder groups as well as experts from
various disciplines and institutional backgrounds. In addition, elected
spokespersons of the two focus groups were also regular participants in
the Round Table. In total twenty individuals participated in this exercise.
The members of the Round Table were given the task of evaluating the
different economic measures suggested by the research team, to select
those measures that were regarded acceptable, to facilitate implementation of these measures and to provide the guidelines for a communication
program to the public. The participants were encouraged to find consensual solutions, but if those were not acceptable to all members the
moderator collected all voices and opinions and reported them to the
City Council.

The Round Table had no formal authority to issue regulations, but
was asked to recommend regulatory actions to either the City Council or
the administration. The members of the Round Table met eight times in
the time period between October 1999 and May 2000. They handed the
final recommendations over to the City Council in August of 2000. The
City Council started to review the document with a view to finalizing its
decision in 2001. Some non-controversial measures such as identifying
detours for night traffic have already been implemented by the administration.

The second element consisted of two focus groups. We sent an invitation to participate to a random sample of all affected citizens in the
town. More than 10 percent of those who received an invitation agreed
to take part. The first focus group included thirteen participants, the
second fifteen. Each group selected one person as a representative to
the Round Table. The focus group sessions took place in July of 1999.
The organizers asked the following questions of each group:
• How do you feel about the noise situation in the location where you
  live?
• What impact does the noise have on your health and well-being?
• Is there a difference between day and night-time?
• What would you suggest the City should do in order to reduce the noise
  level in your home location?
• Is there anything that you personally could do to mitigate the situation?

The members of the focus groups did not receive the list of economic
measures suggested by the research team. The aim of this part was to let
the citizens suggest potential solutions and to identify their concerns and
worries. In addition, they were asked to specify their personal experiences

with noise and to rate the severity of the problem in relation to other economic or environmental problems.

Social attenuation of risk

Social attenuation among stakeholders   Although the focus of both Round Tables was noise reduction, it was obvious from the beginning of the deliberations, that most participants took the topic as a substitute or "placeholder" for allegedly larger and more important issues. The moderator of the Round Table in both Vaihingen and Ravensburg provided the participants with an information booklet that contained rather drastic results of risk assessments performed by various groups of epidemiologists and the German Environmental Protection Agency (UBA). The estimates drawn from these risk assessments range from 15,000 to 40,000 excess deaths due to noise exposure (Umweltbundesamt 1999; cf. comparable data from the United States in Miedema and Vos 1998). Hardly any environmental pollutant comes even close to such damage potential. In addition, a leading German specialist on the issue was invited to present his findings. He confirmed that the risks of noise exposure have been underestimated in the past and would need serious reconsideration. In addition, the State Environmental Ministry presented data from a representative survey. According to this survey, 57.1 percent of the State population feel seriously affected by noise pollution, while almost 60 percent suffer from traffic noise. More than half of the respondents attributed traffic as the main contributor to noise pollution. It was also rated as the most serious environmental problem for oneself compared to other problems such as air pollution or food additives (Zeus 2000).

None of the participants in both Round Tables challenged these risk data. There was no controversy about the methodological assumptions or the correct form of interpretation (as was the case with dioxin emissions). The information was acknowledged but, in the course of deliberation, most often ignored. The final report of the Vaihingen participants contained a total of three lines (Keck and Schene 1999). The participants in the Ravensburg Round Table did not even mention the health hazards connected with noise exposure in their final report (Keck 2001) but used the German equivalent of "nuisance or molestation" to describe the negative impacts of noise on the citizens. It should be noted, however, that none of the participants believed that the problem was insignificant or trivial but it was not associated with health impacts.

It is unfortunate for social researchers that participants of Round Tables find it unacceptable to be surveyed in the classical sense as each individual can easily be identified. We therefore asked for the permission to tape all interactions and use all written statements for a systematic content analysis. The participants agreed with this procedure under the condition that they are given the right to look at the results before they are published. This has been done for the Vaihingen group but not yet for the Ravensburg participants. Since the data processing is still incomplete, I can report only on some general trends that are clearly visible from the material.

Let me first turn to the Vaihingen deliberations. The issue of health risks from noise does not often appear in the transcripts there. Most of the times they are mentioned as one part of a larger list containing the negative impacts of vehicle traffic on human health and the environment. Negative health impacts are more frequently cited by environmental and citizen action groups than by city planners or pro-automobile lobbyists. If they were mentioned at all they were often combined with other (allegedly more serious) health risks from exhaust gases. One statement is typical for such a combined risk statement:

We have heard about the many people who suffer from noise. This number of additional dead bodies does not even include those who die from cancer or other diseases related to all the chemicals that come from the exhaust pipes. If we add these to the list, we end up with much higher numbers ...

The city planners were basically concerned about the noise reduction levels that are necessary to meet legal requirements. Again it was interesting to note that the arguments for noise reduction were not linked to health impacts but either to nuisance or legal standards. The following statement captures this view:

We know that noise reduction walls are expensive and we would prefer to have less traffic. But there is no legal ground to ban traffic just because some people feel discomforted by the noise level. So we go with the legal standards: if they can be met only on the condition that we construct noise reduction walls then we will do it ...

The automobile lobbyists did not deny the risks of noise but placed them in the context of the disadvantages of motorized mobility that society needs to tolerate if they want to allow its citizens the privilege of individual mobility. They were not opposed to noise reduction walls or any technical measure to reduce noise levels but were strictly against traffic regulations aimed at additional speed limits, road pricing or other form of restriction of traffic flow. They regarded noise as the price to pay for a mobile society.

Over the course of the deliberations, the seriousness of risks due to noise exposure was continuously attenuated. If the participants were searching for arguments that could support their claims or demands, noise was used as an introductory argument to open the debate rather than an argument for its own sake. The participants who favored stricter control measures to reduce traffic flow argued either with accident risks, in particular with respect to children playing on the streets, or with the more abstract notion of sustainable development. Traffic was seen as a symbol of non-sustainable lifestyle based on the consumption of non-renewable resources and the overuse of the environment as a sink for exhaust gases and waste. Although the scientific evidence on noise exposure provided a compelling reason for being more restrictive on traffic control, the proponents of such control did not take much advantage of this opportunity, almost as if they did not believe those figures themselves.

A similar picture emerged in the Ravensburg Round Table: health concerns were hardly picked up by any of the participants. The major point of discussion was the applicability of economic incentives and disincentives for noise reduction. Many participants favored strict governmental regulation, others opted for voluntary measures. This can be illustrated by the following two quotes:

A The main problem of environmental degradation is the continuous growth of the economy. And now we want to use the economy to improve the environment. That does not make sense to me . . . What we need is that the City tells the drivers what they can do and what they cannot do.

B If the government tells us what we should do, then we live in a totalitarian state. Is that what you want? We need our cars and we cannot live without them. If we all drove more carefully and thoughtfully, we would not have this problem. I think better driver education will do the job.

Most measures were aimed at reducing noise levels during night-time. Again the main reason for implementing these measures was to prevent citizens from being disturbed. A member of the local environmental protection group argued in this manner:

We all have heard that the citizens complain about loud noise during night-time. We all know how important a good sleep is, in particular for school children. We have a moral obligation to reduce noise during these precious times . . . We owe this to the next generation.

The two elected members of the focus groups reported about the complaints that the participants of the focus groups had voiced. But they did not mention health impacts although they were partially mentioned during the focus group discussions. The two members gave colorful descriptions of the noise sources and the exposure situations (such as young people riding motorcycles at night) but did not mention that several focus group participants had complained about headaches and other stress symptoms in connection with the same story. Potential health impacts were either regarded as obvious once the exposure story had been told or as too far fetched to be held credible in the presence of experts and administrators. The topic was clearly attenuated.

In the more than thirty hours of deliberation, I could detect only two instances in which health impacts were directly addressed (not counting the discussion period directly after the presentation of the UBA health study). The first instance referred to a situation in which one administrator accused one of the participants of dramatizing the effects of noise. He said:

Look X, we can go on like this and list all the evils of the world and attribute them to the automobile. This is not fair . . . Please stick with the subject and do not cover all what one can complain about.

x *responded* Did I get this right? Were you absent when Dr. U. presented us all the material about the impacts of traffic. I mean, those incredible numbers of fatal diseases and so on. I can't believe it. After so many meetings and you are still denying it. People die because of noise and traffic . . .

It is interesting to note that X used the figures of the introductory presentation, but was obviously not too confident that they could all be attributed to noise. He always added the abstract word "traffic" to his claim. So it appeared that accidents or toxic pollutants could cause the health impacts, too.

The second time health was mentioned occurred during the discussion on the final statement. One of the participants mentioned:

We need to say something about why we need all these measures. Some people still think that noise is only a trivial problem (a German idiom was used: *kavaliersdelikt*). It is not obvious that we have to do something to fight this problem. I mean, we should say something about those health effects and so on.

This reminder of the health impacts was not commented, let alone denied by anyone after it was voiced, but the statement was later forgotten when the final statement was drafted. As mentioned before, the final statement does not contain any explicit reference to negative health impacts.

Social attenuation among citizens   The focus groups sessions differed considerably from the Round Tables. First, the health data were not given to the focus groups at all. Rather, the participants were directly asked to express their concerns and complaints about noise without giving them information input. Secondly, the people were addressed as being the "victims" of noise not as the "managers" of noise reduction measures.

The participants were hence highly motivated to tell stories about their experiences with noise. Most people referred to incidents in which car drivers or motorcyclists had been negligent of the needs of the people living in the neighborhood.

Most of these stories had a moral component. People were particularly upset if noise exposure was associated with inconsiderate behavior. Some stories mentioned people speeding during night-time or during the afternoon when children return from school. Other stories blamed youngsters for circling the same streets over and over on their motorcycles. In addition to the general noise from cars, people complained about noise relating to street construction work, local fast food establishments (and the young motorists who parked there), and a planned 24-hour gas station. One person made the complaint that in particular foreigners were to blame for the increased noise level rather than the local German population. There was a heated debate afterwards about whether this claim was true or only a prejudice. The psychological finding that noise is taken as more serious and stressful if the situation in which the noise occurs is associated with negative feelings or emotions was frequently confirmed during the sessions.

As part of the story people also explained the effects of noise on their well being. One woman mentioned: "The noise is so bad. I feel the cars driving over my bed if I leave the windows open." Another woman commented: "I cannot sleep without earplugs any more." One man said that his wife moved out of their shared bedroom because of the noise (as one can expect the others joked about this). Several participants mentioned headache, stress, and being "railed" in the morning. The majority, however, referred to noise as nuisance. One woman explained her bad experiences:

This goes on – day after day. If you don't hear the noise, you think: there must be an accident or something else. I mean, we almost count on the noise. But it makes you tired and nervous. Not that I am sick or so, but it is not tolerable any more. Something has to be done

Nobody raised any serious health problems in connection with noise. Some people mentioned car accidents or car exhausts as the more serious health problems. When it came to instructing the elected spokesperson about his or her statement to the Round Table, all participants wanted them to tell those guys about their concerns and misgivings, but nobody explicitly mentioned health impacts as one could have expected from at least several stories. This pattern of not pursuing the route to health impacts was present in both focus groups and was also confirmed in the reports by the two spokespersons to the participants of the Round Table.

Common observations   In the two exercises we obtained similar results. The members of the focus groups mentioned and reported about negative health impacts, but they did not take the issue so seriously that they wanted this subject to be addressed during the sessions of the Round Table. The members of the Round Table used the health impacts that were presented to them in an introductory statement as strategic instruments for supporting their positions but were not keen on pursuing this problem for its own sake. Health was clearly a proxy for other environmental or social concerns.

What could be the reason for this obvious attenuation of health risks from noise? One hypothesis is that people have all experienced noise in their life and know other people who suffer from high noise levels. None of them have dropped dead due to the exposure to noise levels. Even if some of them experienced high blood pressure or other cardiovascular diseases, most physicians would give them alternative explanations such as high stress, lack of exercise, smoking, wear and tear, and so on, but would probably not mention exposure to noise. Most people's mental maps would also exclude a direct link between the nuisance of experiencing noise and serious somatic responses. Whereas most people can draw a direct connection between a dangerous chemical that one inhales and the development of a malicious tumor, it is more difficult to imagine a direct link between noise and heart failure. Most people associate nervousness and ear problems with high noise exposure but rarely more serious somatic reactions. Therefore none of the participants took the health risks from noise very seriously.

Conclusions

This chapter raised the question whether deliberative processes have the potential to make people aware of amplification or attenuation effects. Amplification and attenuation were conceptualized in this study as the conscious or subconscious processing of risk-related information (physical and communicative signals) resulting in particularly high or low risk evaluation. Whether such a resulting perception is justified in terms of scientific risk assessments is not the main concern of social scientists studying these phenomena. The main interest is to identify and, if possible, measure the factors that motivate people to amplify or attenuate their experience of risk. Previous studies on amplification have explored some of these factors, including the feeling of being exposed to a risk agent, the perception of a dreadful threat, or the belief that the risk receives ample media coverage (Renn, Burns, Kasperson et al. 1993; Kasperson 1992; Burns et al. 1996).

The case studies in this chapter confirmed the existence of risk amplification and attenuation among stakeholders as well as non-organized citizens. The main goal in this chapter was not, however, to understand the subjective reasons why participants in the two discourse activities demonstrated amplification effects. The main emphasis has been on the question of whether people could be made aware of these effects during the discourse procedures. Were these amplification processes discussed in the group, critically reviewed by the participants in the light of the evidence presented, and changed if deemed necessary? Although the two cases do not allow any major generalizations, the experience with amplification effects seems to suggest the following:

- Discursive procedures seem to dissolve fundamentalist moral viewpoints. It may be that people only agree to engage in such activities if they do not share fundamentalist viewpoints. The experience with the Round Table in the waste debate demonstrated, however, that even groups with strong moral convictions and beliefs accepted the general setting of mutual tolerance and respect. There was no debate during the discourse as to whether any of the positions forwarded by any of the participants was morally qualified or unqualified to be represented in the realm of arguments and worth being considered for further deliberation. The atmosphere of deliberation supports a relativist meta-position by which plural moral viewpoints are regarded as legitimate. In this sense deliberation can help to create a working atmosphere by which tolerance and respect for each other's viewpoint is enhanced. This was also true for the focus groups in the second case study. Although moral connotations dominated the stories by the participants, they refrained from moralizing other participants. The discourse setting facilitates an exchange of arguments and experiences rather than abstract positions.
- This respect for each other resulted also in a style of argumentation that differs considerably from the normal political debate. Whereas in political debates contestants make points by raising allegations, referring to external motives (for example driven by profits or motivated by leftist attitudes), or personalizing arguments, discourse procedures create an atmosphere of "moral politeness" as one German discourse analyst has phrased it (Bora and Epp 2000). The physical proximity and the emphasis on arguments lead even political enemies to refrain from the rhetoric of political "smearing" and engage in a sincere effort to understand the other side and convince the enemy that he or she is not right on the issue (but otherwise a respectable person). In addition, the absence of a stage with audience (such as in hearings) makes all attempts at political maneuvering useless and often counter-productive. There is

nothing to gain since the other participants can either ignore or simply dismiss such allegations.

- Regardless of whether an issue is highly polarized and proponents and opponents have each developed a clear and univocal position on this issue, discursive argumentation helps to create mutual understanding of each other's position and to facilitate a trade-off type of evaluation. Participants were willing to accept that even their preferred option had some disadvantages and the least preferred some advantages. This could also be observed in the noise context. Many participants had strong opinions on the type of management actions necessary to reduce noise levels. In spite of occasional heated exchanges during the debate, people at the end acknowledged the legitimacy of different policy actions and management alternatives without giving up their original preferences.

- In spite of the willingness to engage in mutual exchange of arguments and to assign trade-offs, most participants with a firm attitude on a subject and particularly stakeholders defending their group's position continued to assign the trade-offs in favor of their previously held position. They actively searched for signals from scientific or political authorities that supported their viewpoint. These signals were then highly amplified during the course of argumentation. Information that contradicted their position was either ignored or downplayed. This result is in line with most studies on the reduction of cognitive dissonance (cf. Festinger 1957). The learning that took place was more on the procedure of making prudent and fair judgments than on the subject itself. However, as discourse analysts have pointed out, the acknowledgment of other people's positions as legitimate and the willingness to assign trade-offs, is one of the major accomplishments of discursive procedures even if a consensus cannot be reached (Saretzki 1996; McDaniels 1998).

- Stakeholders and non-committed citizens do not differ in their mechanisms of processing risk information. Both groups show clear signs of amplifying or attenuating risks. However, non-committed citizens do not lose face when confronted with arguments that induce a change of attitude or position. Organized representatives of stakeholders, however, try to gather as much evidence as possible to support their position and do not attempt to find a fair balance between the pro and contra arguments. This was clearly demonstrated in the case studies presented here. In the first case study (incinerator) the stakeholders either amplified or attenuated the risks from incineration. Both sides referred to their respective scientists. Disagreement among scientists was seen either as bribery by industry (opponents' view) or as incompetence due to ideological reasoning (proponents' view). A constructive dialogue did not take place between the two camps although the representatives of each camp reassured each other in mutual understanding of their opponent's position. The citizen panelists, who had not committed themselves to one camp or the other, had far fewer problems in allowing themselves to be challenged by information that contradicted their previous views. Although the majority of the randomly selected citizens associated high risks with incineration at the beginning of the discourse, they deliberated the counter-evidence, invited additional experts to give testimony, and discussed each argument and counter-argument at some length. At the end, they were still convinced that incinerators pose risks to human health, but these risks were seen as much less dramatic than during the introductory sessions. The process of discourse did help to counteract or balance the original amplification process.

- If arguments do not fit with common sense experience or beliefs, learning processes are unlikely to occur. Here scientists trained to be skeptical about common sense reasoning may be more inclined to engage in learning exercises than stakeholder or members of the general public. The second, noise reduction, case study illustrated this problem of how a tendency to amplify or attenuate risks becomes immune to counter-attacks. Hardly anyone in the discourse, even those who depended on this argument to support their position of more traffic control, used the health impacts of noise as a genuine and serious argument for justifying government action against motorized traffic. The environmentalists as well as the representatives of affected neighborhood groups combined the noise issue with other (more credible) causes for detrimental health impacts such as exhaust gases or accidents. The hypothesis explaining this denial (or extreme case of attenuation) is that people feel so familiar with noise that they can hardly imagine that an exposure to such a normal thing as noise could result in serious health damage. Discourse procedures could not overcome these initial assessments of "direct obviousness." They did not challenge the expert's view on this (neither the proponents nor the opponents of stricter traffic control tried this route of argumentation). The health argument was either ignored, used only in the legal framework of noise standards, or seen as a substitute for other more serious problems (for example the alleged violation of sustainability).

- The focus groups in the second case study did mention health impacts as one element of their personal noise stories. Yet these impacts were presented as an illustration of the seriousness of the subject rather than an outcome to worry about. Some people even apologized for being so sensitive to noise. In the final statements of the two focus groups health effects were not included. Again the hypothesis is that noise is such a familiar experience that people tend to treat it as a normal circumstance of human existence. They feel bothered by noise and felt negatively affected but did not believe in long-term health implications connected with it. This basic belief seems to be so well positioned in "common sense" that even in the presence of respected scientific evidence, hardly any member of the Round Table dared to use this evidence to support his or her claims.

In essence, risk amplification and attenuation can be made a deliberate subject of discursive activities within participatory risk management procedures. The discourse helps people to realize that it is normal but also detrimental to prudent judgment if one selects and transmits only those pieces of information that one likes, if one amplifies signals that support one's own view and attenuates those that do not. The discourse, however, is no panacea to overcome these amplification mechanisms. If the participants have strong feelings about a risk source or if the risks appear as dramatic or trivial from the perspective of common sense, they will continue to amplify those signals that support their view. They would not refute expert knowledge or other forms of indirect experience but they would refrain from using this material for their own argumentation. The respective social context provides sufficient opportunities for some formal proof that will support the group's overall risk perception.

Is discourse therefore irrelevant or even dangerous for making decisions on risk? In my view this would mean throwing the baby out with the bathwater! First, amplification and attenuation will take place regardless of the type of risk management arrangement chosen. Even the most cautious risk professional will be selective when making judgments about risks (Dietz et al. 1989; Wynne 1989). Discourse may not eliminate these processes, but may provide a better opportunity than most other communicative instruments to make people aware of these processes.

Second, the discursive approach did accomplish a deviation from fundamentalist positions even among those who shared such positions before the discourse. It provides a platform for a mutual exchange of arguments and thus a learning experience for developing respect for other viewpoints and tolerance for other moral positions (cf. Charnley 2000). This is a prerequisite for the functioning of all modern, pluralist democratic countries. Providing this learning experience is in itself already a major step forward.

Third, participants who were not committed beforehand did use the opportunity of reflecting upon amplification processes, and corrected their beliefs if they felt this to be necessary. The possibility of uncommitted citizens using discourse as a means to resolve conflicts, and to come up with a common solution should encourage policy makers to make more use of these procedures and to increase efforts at integrating citizen participation into the legal decision making process.

Fourth, public involvement in risk management is motivated not only by the need for more competence but also, and even more pronounced, by the democratic goal of enhancing fairness and political transparency (Webler 1995; Fiorino 1989). This goal is independent of the capability of discursive procedures to facilitate the reflection and correction of underlying tendencies of risk amplification and attenuation. It is an end in itself.

Further research into the structure of discourse and dialogue is certainly necessary in order to find the appropriate rules and structural settings that help participants to become aware of their own patterns of risk amplification and attenuation. This self-awareness is a necessary step towards their mandate of drafting more competent recommendations that are in line with their preferences for the future. The ideal discourse is a process of group communication by which the participants are empowered to understand each other's viewpoint, reflect the potential consequences of different options for action, and to zoom in on the one course of action that seems most desirable or acceptable for all the people who must live with the consequences.

Bibliography

Adam, B. (2000) "The media time-scapes of BSE news" in S. Allan, B. Adam, and C. Carter (eds.) *Environmental Risks and the Media*. London: Routledge.

Adams, J. (1995) *Risk*. London: UCL Press.

Adams, W. (1992) "The role of media relations in risk communication." *Public Relations Quarterly*, Winter 1992–93: 28–32.

Adler, A. (1994) "Public access to nuclear energy and weapons information" in D. O'Very, C. Paine, and D. Reicher (eds.) *Controlling the Atom in the 21st Century*. Boulder, CO: Westview, pp. 73–106.

Aggleton, P. (1999) *HIV at the Crossroads: Reframing HIV Prevention*. London: National AIDS Trust.

Albright, D., Berkhout, P., and Walker, W. (1997) *Plutonium and Highly Enriched Uranium 1996 World Inventories, Capabilities and Policies*. New York: SIORI and Oxford University Press.

Alhakami, A. S. and Slovic, P. (1994) "A psychological study of the inverse relationship between perceived risk and perceived benefit." *Risk Analysis*, 14: 1085–1096.

Almond, G. A. and Verba, S. (eds.) (1980) *The Civic Culture Revisited*. Boston: Little, Brown and Company.

Altman, I. and Low, S. (1992) *Place Attachment*. New York: Plenum Press.

Anand, P. (ed.) (1997) "Symposium: economic and social consequences of BSE/CJD." *Risk Decision and Policy*, 2(1): 3–52.

Anderson, E. (ed.) (2002) Special edited collection on "Assessing the risks of terrorism," *Risk Analysis*, 22: 401–454.

Ansolabehere, S. and Iyengar, S. (1995) *Going Negative*. New York: Free Press.

Arlidge, J. (2000) "TV today: dumb and getting dumber." *The Observer*, 16 April: 5.

Arvai, J. L., Gregory, R., and McDaniels, T. L. (2001) "Testing a structured decision approach: value-focused thinking for deliberative risk communication." *Risk Analysis*, 21: 1065–1076.

Asch, S. E. (1951) "Effects of group pressure on the modification and distortion of judgements" in H. Geutzkow (ed.) *Groups, Leadership and Men*. Pittsburgh: Carnegie Press.

(1955) "Opinions and social pressure." *Scientific American*, 193: 31–35.

(1956) "Studies of independence and conformity: a minority of one against a unanimous majority." *Psychological Monographs*, 70: 416.

Aveni, A. (1989) *Empires of Time: Calendars, Clocks, and Cultures.* New York: Basic Books.

Baggot, R. (1995) "From confrontation to consultation? Pressure group relations from Thatcher to Major." *Parliamentary Affairs,* 48: 484–502.

Baird, B. N. R. (1986) "Tolerance for environmental health risks: the influence of knowledge, benefits, voluntariness, and environmental attitudes." *Risk Analysis,* 6(4): 425–435.

Ball, H. (1986) *Justice Downwind: America's Atomic Testing Program in the 1950s.* New York: Oxford University Press.

Banks, J. and Tankel, J. (1990) "Science as fiction: technology in prime time television." *Critical Studies in Mass Communication,* 24(36): 24–36.

Baram, M. (1997) "Shame, blame and liability: why safety management suffers organisational learning disabilities" in A. Hale, B. Wilpert, and M. Freitag (eds.) *After the Event: From Accident to Organisational Learning.* New York: Elsevier Science, pp. 161–178.

Barber, B. R. (1984) *Strong Democracy: Participatory Politics for a New Age.* Berkeley: University of California Press.

Barnes, M. (1999) "Researching public participation." *Local Government Studies,* 25: 60–75.

Barnett, A., Menighetti, J., and Prete, M. (1992) "The market response to the Sioux City DC-10 crash." *Risk Analysis,* 14: 45–52.

Baron, J. (1994) *Thinking and Deciding,* 2nd edition. New York: Cambridge University Press.

Barr-Hamilton, M. and Reilly, L. (1996) *From Country to Suburb: The Development of the Bexley Area from 1800 to the Present Day.* Bexley: London Borough of Bexley.

Barthes, R. (1973) *Mythologies.* London: Paladin Books.

Baum, A. (1987) "Toxins, technology, and natural disasters" in G. Vandebos, and B. Bryant (eds.) *Cataclysms, Crises and Catastrophes.* Washington, DC: American Psychological Association, pp. 5–53.

Beck, U. (1992) *Risk Society: Toward a New Modernity.* Translated by M. A. Ritter. London: Sage Publications.

(1995a) *Ecological Enlightenment: Essays on the Politics of the Risk Society.* Translated by M. A. Ritter. Atlantic Highlands, NJ: Humanities Press.

(1995b) *Ecological Politics in an Age of Risk.* London: Polity Press.

Beharrell, P. (1998) "News variations" in D. Miller, J. Kitzinger, K. Williams, and P. Beharrell (eds.) *The Circuit of Mass Communication.* London: Sage, pp. 46–67.

Behrens, E. G. (1983) "The Triangle Shirtwaist Company fire of 1911: a lesson in legislative manipulation." *Texas Law Review,* 62: 361–387.

Bennett, P. and Calman, K. (eds.) (1999) *Risk Communication and Public Health.* Oxford: Oxford University Press.

Bennett, R. M., Tranter, R. B., Mayfield, L. H., Jones, P. J., and Little, G. J. (1999) "Regional land use and employment impacts of bovine spongiform encephalopathy slaughter policy measures in England." *Geoforum,* 30: 159–169.

Bentz and Associates (1995) *Technical and Institutional Considerations Regarding Near-Term (1998) Spent Fuel Transportation to an Interim Storage Facility*, Report to the Nevada Nuclear Waste Project Office. Carson City: NWPO.

Berger, P. and Luckman, T. (1967) *The Social Construction of Reality*. Harmondsworth: Penguin.

Berlin, B. and Kay, P. (1969) *Basic Color Terms: Their Universality and Evolution*. Berkeley: University of California Press.

Berridge, V. (1996) *AIDS in the UK: The Making of Policy, 1981–1984*. Oxford: Oxford University Press.

Bickerstaff, K. and Walker, G. (2003) "The place(s) of matter: matter out of place. Public understandings of air pollution." *Progress in Human Geography*, 27(1): 45–67.

Bittner, E. (1967) "The police on skid row: a study of peace keeping." *American Sociological Review*, 32(5): 699–715.

Block, F. (1987) *Revising State Theory: Essays in Politics and Postindustrialism*. Philadelphia: Temple University Press.

Bloomgarden, R. (1983) *The Easy Guide to Chichen Itza*. Shawnee, KS: Forsythe Travel Library.

Bloor, M. (1995) *The Sociology of HIV Transmission*. London: Sage.

Bloor, M., Frankland, J., Thomas, M., and Robson, K. (2001) *Focus Groups in Social Research*. London: Sage.

Blumer, H. (1969) *Symbolic Interactionism: Perspectives and Method*. Englewood Cliffs, NJ: Prentice-Hall.

Bohölm, Å. (1998) "Visual images and risk messages: commemorating Chernobyl." *Risk Decision and Policy*, 3(2): 125–143.

Bora, A. and Epp, A. (2000) "Die imaginäre Einheit der Diskurse. Zur Funktion von 'Verfahrensgerechtigkeit'." *Kölner Zeitschrift für Soziologie und Sozialpsychologie*, 52(1): 1–35.

Bourdieu, P. (1984) *Distinction: A Social Critique of the Judgement of Taste*. London: Routledge and Kegan Paul.

Bourdieu, P. (1987) "What makes a social class? On the theoretical and practical existence of groups." *Berkeley Journal of Sociology*, 22: 1–17.

(1998) *On Television and Journalism*. London: Pluto Press.

Braxton, D., Wunderer, E., Campion, E., and Frewer, L. J. (1997) *Media Reporting of Risk in the UK. A Comparison of UK Media Reporting of the Chernobyl Accident and BSE*. Report to the European Commission. Norwich: Institute of Food Research.

Breakwell, G. M. (1994) "The echo of power: a framework for social psychological research." *The Psychologist*, 17: 65–72.

Breakwell, G. M. and Barnett, J. (2001) *The Impact of Social Amplification on Risk Communication*, Contract Research Report 322/2001. Sudbury: HSE books.

Breakwell, G. M., Millward, L. J., and Fife-Schaw, C. (1994) "Commitment to safer sex as a predictor of condom use among 16–20-year-olds." *Journal of Applied Social Psychology*, 24: 189–217.

Bredlie, K. R. (1996) "Keeping children out of double jeopardy: an assessment of punishment and Megan's Law in Doe v. Poritz." *Minnesota Law Review*, 81: 501–545.

Brewer, J. (1990) "Talking about danger: the RUC and the paramilitary threat." *Sociology*, 24(4): 657–674.

Breyer, S. (1993) *Breaking the Vicious Circle: Toward Effective Risk Regulation.* Cambridge, MA: Harvard University Press.

Brown, D. E. (1991) *Human Universals.* New York: McGraw-Hill.

Brown, J. and Sime, J. (1981) "A methodology for accounts" in M. Brenner (ed.) *Social Method and Social Life.* London: Academic Press, pp. 161–188.

Buber, M. (1957) *Pointing the Way: Collected Essays.* Translated by M. Friedman. Baltimore: Johns Hopkins University Press.

Bunn, M. (1997) "The case for a dual-track approach – and how to move forward from here" in *Nuclear Materials Monitor*, 1(5). Landsdowne, VA: Exchange Monitor Publications, pp. 1, 3.

Bürgerwelle (1998) www.buergerwelle.de

Burns, W. J., Slovic, P., Kasperson, R. E., Kasperson, J. X., Renn, O., and Emani, S. (1993) "Incorporating structural models into research on the social amplification of risk: implications for theory construction and decision making." *Risk Analysis*, 13(6): 611–624.

Buss, D. M., Craik, K. H., and Dake, K. M. (1986) "Contemporary worldviews and perception of the technological system" in V. T. Covello, J. Menkes, and J. Mumpower (eds.) *Risk Evaluation and Management.* New York: Plenum, pp. 93–130.

Cable, S., Shriver, T., and Hastings, D. W. (1999) "The silenced majority: quiescence and government social control on the Oak Ridge Nuclear Reservation." *Research in Social Problems and Public Policy*, 7: 59–81.

Camerer, C. (1995) "Individual decision making" in J. H. Kagel and A. E. Roth (eds.) *The Handbook of Experimental Economics.* Princeton: Princeton University Press, pp. 587–673.

Campbell, J. L. (1988) *Collapse of an Industry: Nuclear Power and the Contradictions of US Policy.* Ithaca, NY: Cornell University.

Cantor, R. (1991) "Applying construction lessons to decommissioning estimates." *The Energy Journal*, 12. Washington, DC: International Association for Energy Economics, pp. 105–117.

Carey, J. W. (1989) *Communication as Culture: Essays on Media and Society.* London: Unwin Hyman Ltd.

Carter, L. C. (1987) *Nuclear Imperatives and Public Trust: Dealing with Radioactive Waste.* Washington, DC: Resources for the Future.

Charnley, G. (2000) *Democratic Science. Enhancing the Role of Science in Stakeholder-Based Risk Management Decision-Making.* Report of Health Risk Strategies, Washington, DC.

Chateauraynaud, F. and Torny, D. (1999) *Les Sombres Précurseurs: une sociologie pragmatique de l'alerte et du risque.* Paris: Editions EHESS.

Chatterjee, A., Mandal, B. K., Roychowdhury, T., Samanta, G., and Chakraborti, D. (1995) "Arsenic in groundwater in six districts of West Bengal, India: the biggest calamity in the world, Part I: Arsenic species in drinking water and urine of affected people." *Analyst*, 120: 643–650.

Chess, C., Salomone, K., Hance, B., and Saville, A. (1995) "Results of a national symposium on risk communication: next steps for government agencies." *Risk Analysis*, 15(2): 115–125.

Chowdhury, U. K., Biswas, B. K., Roychowdhury, T., Samanta, G., Mandal, B. K., Basu, G. C., Chanda, C. R., Lodh, D., Saha, K. C., Mukherjee, S. K., Roy, S., Kabir, S., Quamruzzaman, Q., and Chakraborti, D. (2000) "Groundwater arsenic contamination in Bangladesh and West Bengal, India." *Environmental Health Perspectives*, 108(5): 393–397.

Clarke, L. B. (1993) "The disqualification heuristic: when do organizations misperceive risk?" *Research in Social Problems and Public Policy*, 5: 289–312.

   (1999) *Mission Improbable: Using Fantasy Documents to Tame Disaster*. Chicago: University of Chicago Press.

Clarke, L. B. and Short, J. (1993) "Social organization and risk: some current controversies." *Annual Review of Sociology*, 19: 375–399.

Cloke, P., Goodwin, M., and Milbourne, P. (1997) *Rural Wales: Community and Marginalisation*. Cardiff: University of Wales Press.

Cohen, B. (1990) *The Nuclear Energy Option: An Alternative for the 90s*. New York: Plenum.

Cohen, L. R. and Noll, R. G. (eds.) (1991) *The Technology Pork Barrel*. Washington, DC: The Brookings Institute.

Cohen, S. (1972) *Folk Devils and Moral Panics: The Creation of the Mods and Rockers*. London: MacGibbon and Kee Ltd.

Coleman, J. S. (1990). *Foundations of Social Theory*. Cambridge, MA: Bellknap Press.

Combs, B. and Slovic, P. (1978) "Newspaper coverage of causes of death." *Journalism Quarterly*, 56: 837–843, 849.

Coombs, W. T. (1995) "Choosing the right words." *Management Communication Quarterly*, 8: 44–47.

Cotgrove, S. (1982) *Catastrophe or Cornucopia: The Environment, Politics and the Future*. New York: Wiley.

Cottle, S. (2000) "TV news, lay voices and the visualisation of environmental risks" in S. Allen, B. Adam, and C. Carter (eds.) *Environmental Risks and the Media*. London: Routledge, pp. 29–54.

Couch, S. R. and Kroll-Smith, S. (1998) "Environmental movements and expert knowledge: evidence for a new populism." *International Journal of Contemporary Sociology*, 34: 1–28.

Countinho, L. and Banerjea, N. (2000) "Social production of blame: case study of OPV-related deaths in West Bengal." *Economic and Political Weekly*, 35(8 and 9): 19–26.

Cramer, P. (2000) "Defense mechanisms in psychology today. Further processes for adaptation." *American Psychologist*, 55(6): 637–646.

Crimaldi, K. (1995) "'Megan's Law': election-year politics and constitutional rights." *Rutgers Law Journal*, 27: 169–204.

Cvetkovich, G. and Earle, T. (eds.) (1991) "Risk and Culture." Special issue of *Journal of Cross-Cultural Psychology*, 22(1): 11–149.

Cvetkovich, G. and Löfstedt, R. E. (eds.) (1999) *Social Trust and the Management of Risk*. London: Earthscan.

Cvetkovich, G., Siegrist, M., Murray, R., and Tragesser, S. (2002) "New information and social trust: asymmetry and perseverance of attributions about hazard managers." *Risk Analysis*, 22: 359–369.

Dake, K. (1991) "Orienting dispositions in the perception of risk: an analysis of contemporary worldviews and cultural biases." *Journal of Cross-Cultural Psychology*, 22: 61–82.

Dalton, M. (1959) *Men who Manage: Fusions of Feeling and Theory in Administration*. New York: Wiley.

Das, D., Chatterjee, A., Samanta, G., Mandal, B. K., Roychowdhury, T., Chowdhury, P. P., Chanda, C., Basu, G., Lodh, D., Nandi, S., Chakraborty, T., Mandal, S., Bhattarcharya, S. M., and Chakraborti, D. (1994) "Arsenic contamination in groundwater in six districts of West Bengal, India: the biggest arsenic calamity in the world." *Analyst*, 119: 168N–170N.

Das, V. (1995) *Critical Events: An Anthropological Perspective on Contemporary India*. Delhi: Oxford University Press.

Davidson, D. and Freudenburg, W. R. (1996) "Gender and environmental risk concerns: an empirical re-examination." *Environment and Behavior*, 28(3): 302–339.

De Marchi, B. (2000) "Learning from citizens: a Venetian experience." *Journal of Hazardous Materials*, 78(1–3): 247–259.

Deal, T. E. and Kennedy, A. A. (1982) *Corporate Culture*. Reading, MA: Addison-Wesley.

Department of Health (1998) *Communicating About Risks to Public Health: Pointers to Good Practice*, revised edition. London: The Stationery Office.

Developi, A. (1995) "Fast finish to plutonium peril." *The Bulletin of the Atomic Scientists* (September/October 1995): 20–21.

Dienel, P. C. (1989) "Contributing to social decision methodology: citizen reports on technological projects" in C. Vlek and G. Cvetkovich (eds.) *Social Decision Methodology for Technological Projects*. Dordrecht: Kluwer Academic Press, pp. 133–150.

Dienel, P. C. and Renn, O. (1995) "Planning cells: a gate to 'fractal' mediation" in O. Renn, T. Webler, and P. Wiedemann (eds.) *Fairness and Competence in Citizen Participation. Evaluating New Models for Environmental Discourse*. Dordrecht: Kluwer Academic Press, pp. 117–140.

Dietz, T., Frey, S. S., and Rosa, E. A. (2002) "Risk, technology, and society" in R. E. Dunlap and W. Michelson (eds.) *Handbook of Environmental Sociology*. Westport, CT: Greenwood Press, pp. 562–629.

Dietz, T., Stern, P. C., and Rycroft, R. W. (1989) "Definitions of conflict and the legitimation of resources: the case of environmental risk." *Sociological Forum*, 4: 47–69.

DOE (Department of Energy) (1995a) *Estimating the Cold War Mortgage: The 1995 Baseline Environmental Management Report*. Springfield, VA: NTIS.

(1995b) *Report of the Advisory Committee on Human Radiation Experiments*. Washington, DC: GPO.

(1997) *Long-Term Stewardship of DOE Sites: Scope of Work and Considerations for Success*. Washington, DC: Department of Energy, Office of Strategic Planning and Analysis, Draft Report.

Douglas, M. (1992) *Risk and Blame: Essays in Cultural Theory*. London: Routledge.

(1997) "The depoliticization of risk" in R. J. Ellis and M. Thompson (eds.) *Culture Matters: Essays in Honor of Aaron Wildavsky.* Boulder, Colorado: Westview Press, pp. 121–132.

Douglas, M. and Wildavsky, A. (1982) *Risk and Culture: The Selection of Technological and Environmental Dangers.* Berkeley, CA: University of California Press.

Dunlap, R. E., Kraft, M. E., and Rosa, E. A. (eds.) (1993) *Public Reactions to Nuclear Waste: Citizens' Views of Repository Siting.* Durham, NC: Duke University Press.

Durant, J. and Lindsey, N. (1999) *The Great GM Food Debate: A Report to the House of Lords Select Committee on Science and Technology Sub-Committee on Science and Society.* London: The Science Museum.

Durkheim, E. (1933) *The Division of Labor in Society.* Translated by George Simpson. New York: Free Press.

Dyer, C. (2000) "Straw rejects 'Sarah's Law'." *The Guardian,* 16 September.

Eagly, A. H., and Chaiken, S. (1993) *The Psychology of Attitudes.* New York: Brace Jovanovich.

Eagly, A., Wood, W., and Chaiken, S. (1978) "Causal inferences about communicators and their effect on opinion change." *Journal of Personality and Social Psychology,* 36: 424–435.

Earle, T. C. and Cvetkovich, G. (1993) "Risk communication: the social construction of meaning and trust" in B. Brehmer and N. E. Sahlin (eds.) *Future Risks and Risk Management.* Dordrecht: Kluwer Academic Press, pp. 141–181.

(1995) *Social Trust: Toward a Cosmopolitan Society.* Westport, CT: Praeger.

Easterling, D. and Kunreuther, H. (1995) *The Dilemma of Siting a High-Level Nuclear Waste Repository.* Boston: Kluwer Academic Press.

Edelman, M. (1964) *The Symbolic Uses of Politics.* Urbana: University of Illinois Press.

Edelstein, M. R. (1987) "Toward a theory of environmental stigma" in J. Harvey and D. Denning (eds.) *Public Environments.* Ottawa: Environmental Design Research Association, pp. 21–25.

Edwards, R. (1996) "Greens attack plans to import 'dirty fuel'." *New Scientist,* 13 July: 9.

Edwards, W. (1977) "How to use multiattribute utility measurement for social decision-making." *IEEE Transactions on Systems, Man, and Cybernetics,* SMC-7: 326–340.

Edwards, W. and von Winterfeldt, D. (1987) "Public values in risk debates." *Risk Analysis,* 7: 141–158.

Eiser, J. R. (1994) *Attitudes, Chaos and the Connectionist Mind.* Oxford: Blackwell.

Ekman, P., Friesen, W. V., and Ellsworth, P. (1972) *Emotion in the Face.* New York: Pergamon Press.

Ekstrom, M. (2000) "Information, storytelling and attractions: TV journalism in three modes of communication." *Media, Culture and Society,* 22: 465–492.

Eldridge, J. (1993) "Whose illusion? Whose reality? Some problems of theory and method in mass media research" in J. Eldridge (ed.) *Getting the Message: News, Truth and Power.* London: Routledge, pp. 331–351.

Eliasoph, N. (1990) "Political culture and the presentation of a political self: a study of the public sphere in the spirit of Erving Goffman." *Theory and Society*, 19: 465–494.

English, M. (1992) *Siting Low-Level Radioactive Waste Disposal Facilities: The Public Policy Dilemma*. New York: Quorum.

Epstein, S. (1994) "Integration of the cognitive and the psychodynamic unconscious." *American Psychologist*, 49: 709–724.

Erikson, K. (1994) *A New Species of Trouble: The Human Experience of Modern Disasters*. New York: W. W. Norton.

Evers, A. and Nowotny, H. (1987) *Über der Umgang mit Unsicherheit die Entdeckung der Gestaltbarkeit von Gesellschaft*. Frankfurt am Main: Suhrkamp.

Expert Panel on the Future of Food Biotechnology (2001) *Elements of Precaution: Recommendations for the Regulation of Food Biotechnology in Canada*. Ottawa: Royal Society of Canada (www.rsc.ca).

Eyles, J., Taylor, S. M., Baxter, J., Sider, D., and Willms, D. (1993) "The social construction of risk in a rural community: responses of local residents to the 1990 Hagersville (Ontario) tire fire." *Risk Analysis*, 13: 281–290.

Farmer, P. (1992) *AIDS and Accusation: Haiti and the Geography of Blame*. Berkeley, CA: University of California Press.

Fazio, R. H. (1989) "On the power and functionality of attitudes: the role of attitude accessibility" in A. R. Pratkanis, S. J. Breckler, and A. G. Greenwald (eds.) *Attitude Structure and Function*. Hillsdale, New Jersey: Erlbaum, pp. 153–179.

Festinger, L. (1957) *A Theory of Cognitive Dissonance*. Stanford: Stanford University Press.

Fife-Schaw, C. R. and Rowe, G. (1996) *Monitoring and Modeling Consumer Perceptions of Food-Related Risks*. Guildford: University of Surrey SPERI.

Finucane, M. L., Alhakami, A. S., Slovic, P., and Johnson, S. M. (2000) "The affect heuristic in judgments of risks and benefits." *Journal of Behavioral Decision Making*, 13: 1–17.

Fiorino, D. J. (1989) "Technical and democratic values in risk analysis." *Risk Analysis*, 9(3): 293–299.

Fischhoff, B. (1989) "Appendix C: a guide to risk controversy" in National Research Council, *Improving Risk Communication*. Washington, DC: National Academy Press, pp. 211–308.

(1995) "Risk perception and risk communication unplugged: twenty years of process." *Risk Analysis*, 15(2): 137–145.

Fischhoff, B., Watson, S., and Hope, C. (1984) "Defining risk." *Policy Sciences*, 17: 123–139.

Fitchen, J. M., Heath, J. S., and Fessenden-Raden, J. (1987) "Risk perception in community context: a case study" in B. Johnson and V. Covello (eds.) *The Social and Cultural Construction of Risk*. Dordrecht: Reidel, pp. 31–54.

Flynn, J., Burns, W., Mertz, C. K., and Slovic, P. (1992) "Trust as a determinant of opposition to a high-level radioactive waste repository." *Risk Analysis*, 12: 417–429.

Flynn, J., Chalmers, J., Easterling, D., Kasperson, R. E., Kunreuther, H., Mertz, C. K., Mushkatel, A., Pijawka, K. D., and Slovic, P., with Dotto, L. (1995)

One Hundred Centuries of Solitude: Redirecting America's High-level Nuclear Waste Policy. Boulder, CO: Westview.

Flynn, J., Peters, E., Mertz, C. K., and Slovic, P. (1998) "Risk, media and stigma at Rocky Flats." *Risk Analysis,* 18: 715–727.

Flynn, J., Slovic, P., and Kunreuther, H. (eds.) (2001) *Risk, Media and Stigma: Understanding Public Challenges to Modern Science and Technology.* London: Earthscan.

Flynn, J., Slovic, P., and Mertz, C. K. (1993a) "The Nevada initiative: a risk communication fiasco." *Risk Analysis,* 13: 497–502.

(1993b) "Decidedly different: expert and public views of risks from a radioactive waste repository." *Risk Analysis,* 13: 643–648.

Flyvbjerg, B. (2001) *Making Social Science Matter: Why Social Inquiry Fails and How it Can Succeed Again.* Cambridge: Cambridge University Press.

Foster, K. R., Vecchia, P., and Repacholi, M. H. (2000) "Science and the precautionary principle." *Science,* 288: 979–981.

Freudenburg, W. R. (1988) "Perceived risk, real risk: social science and the art of probabilistic risk assessment." *Science,* 242: 44–49.

(1991) "A 'good business climate' as bad economic news?" *Society and Natural Resources,* 3: 313–331.

(1992) "Nothing recedes like success? Risk analysis and the organizational amplification of risks." *Risk: Issues in Health and Safety,* 3: 1–35.

(1993) "Risk and recreancy: Weber, the division of labor, and the rationality of risk perceptions." *Social Forces,* 71: 909–932.

Freudenburg, W. R., Coleman, C. L., Gonzales, J., and Hegeland, C. (1996) "Media coverage of hazard events – analyzing the assumptions." *Risk Analysis,* 16(1): 31–42.

Freudenburg, W. R., Frickel, S., and Dwyer, R. E. (1998) "Diversity and diversion: higher superstition and the dangers of insularity in science and technology studies." *International Journal of Sociology and Social Policy,* 18: 6–34.

Freudenburg, W. R. and Gramling, R. (1992) "Community impacts of technological change: toward a longitudinal perspective." *Social Forces,* 70(4): 937–955.

Freudenburg, W. R. and Pastor, S. K. (1992) "Public responses to technological risks – towards a sociological perspective." *Sociological Quarterly,* 33: 389–412.

Freudenburg, W. and Youn, T. (1993) "A new perspective on problems and policy." *Research in Social Problems and Public Policy,* 5: 1–20.

Frewer, L. J. (1999) *Demographic Differences in Risk Perceptions and Public Priorities for Risk Mitigation. Final Report.* Report submitted to MAFF/DoH. Norwich: Institute of Food Research.

Frewer, L. J., Howard, C., Campion, E., Miles, S., and Hunt, S. (1997) *Perceptions of Radiation Risk in the UK Before, During and After the 10th Anniversary of the Chernobyl Accident.* Report to the European Commission. Reading: Institute of Food Research.

Frewer, L. J., Howard, C., Hedderley, D., and Shepherd, R. (1996) "What determines trust in information about food-related risks? Underlying psychological constructs." *Risk Analysis,* 16: 473–486.

(1997) "The use of the elaboration likelihood model in developing effective food risk communication." *Risk Analysis*, 17: 269–281.

Frewer, L. J., Miles, S., and Marsh, R. (2002) "The GM foods controversy. A test of the social amplification of risk model." *Risk Analysis*, 22: 713–723.

Frewer, L. J., Raats, M., and Shepherd, R. (1993/94) "Modelling the media: the transmission of risk information in the British quality press." *Journal of the Institute of Mathematics and its Applications to Industry*, 5: 235–247.

Frewer, L. J., Rowe, G., and Sjöberg, L. (1999) *The 10th Anniversary of the Chernobyl Accident: The Impact of Media Reporting of Risk on Public Risk Perceptions in Five European Countries*. Report to the European Commission. Norwich: Institute of Food Research.

Friedman, S., Dunwoody, S., and Rogers, C. (eds.) (1986) *Scientists and Journalists: Reporting Science as News*. New York: Free Press.

Fry, G. (1991) "The cost of decommissioning US reactors: estimates and experience." *The Energy Journal*, 12. Washington, DC: International Association for Energy Economics, pp. 87–104.

Funtowicz, S. O. and Ravetz, J. R. (1985) "Three types of risk assessment: a methodological analysis" in C. Whipple and V. Covello (eds.) *Risk Analysis in the Private Sector*. New York: Plenum, pp. 217–232.

(1991) "A new scientific methodology for global environmental issues" in R. Costanza (ed.) *Ecological Economics: The Science and Management of Sustainability*. New York: Columbia University Press, pp. 137–152.

(1992) "Three types of risk assessment and the emergence of post-normal science" in S. Krimsky and D. Golding (eds.) *Social Theories of Risk*, Westport, CT: Praeger, pp. 251–274.

Furby, L., Weinrott, M. R., and Blackshaw, L. (1989) "Sex offender recidivism: a review." *Psychological Bulletin*, 105: 3–30.

Gadamer, H. (1976) *Philosophical Hermeneutics*. Berkeley: University of California Press.

Galanter, M. (1974) "Why the 'haves' come out ahead: speculations on the limits of legal change." *Law and Society Review*, 9: 95–160.

Garfinkel, H. (1967) *Studies in Ethnomethodology*. Englewood Cliffs NJ: Prentice-Hall.

Geertz, C. (1973) *The Interpretation of Cultures*. New York: Basic Books.

Gerber, M. S. (1992) *On the Home Front: The Cold War Legacy of the Hanford Nuclear Site*. Lincoln: University of Nebraska Press.

Gerlach, L. P. (1987) "Protest movements and the construction of risk" in B. B. Johnson and V. Covello (eds.) *The Social and Cultural Construction of Risk*. Dordrecht: Reidel, pp. 103–145.

Gibbs, L. M. (1982). *Love Canal: My Story*. Albany: State University of New York Press.

Giddens, A. (1976) *New Rules of Sociological Method*. London: Hutchinson.

(1984) *The Constitution of Society*. Cambridge: Polity Press.

(1990) *The Consequences of Modernity*. Stanford, CA: Stanford University Press.

(1991) *Modernity and Self-Identity*. Cambridge: Polity Press.

Gilbert, G. N. and Mulkay, M. (1984) *Opening Pandora's Box: A Sociological Analysis of Scientist's Discourse*. Cambridge: Cambridge University Press.

Gillespie, A. A. (2000) "UK perspective." *Jurist*, 24 July. http://jurist.law.pitt.edu/world/uk3.htm

Glaser, B. and Strauss, A. (1967) *The Discovery of Grounded Theory*. New York: Aldine de Gruyter.

Goffman, E. (1963) *Stigma: Notes on the Management of Spoiled Identity*. New York: Simon and Schuster.

(1969) *The Presentation of Self in Everyday Life*. New York: Doubleday Anchor Books.

Golding, D., Krimsky, S., and Plough, A. (1992) "Evaluating risk communication: narrative versus technical presentations of information about Radon." *Risk Analysis*, 12(1): 27–35.

Goodell, R. (1987) "The role of mass media in scientific controversy" in T. Engelhardt and A. Caplan (eds.) *Scientific Controversies: Case Studies in the Resolution and Closure of Disputes in Science and Technology*. Cambridge: Cambridge University Press, pp. 176–192.

Gordon, D. (1996) "The verdict: no harm, no foul." *The Bulletin of Atomic Scientists* (January–February 1996): 32–40.

Goudsblom, J. (1992) *Fire and Civilization*. London: Penguin Books.

Gouldner, A. W. (1960) "The norm of reciprocity: a preliminary statement." *American Sociological Review*, 25: 161–179.

Gowda, M. V. R. (1999) "Heuristics, biases, and the regulation of risk." *Policy Sciences*, 32(1): 59–78.

(2002) "Enhancing the effectiveness of innovative policy instruments: the implications of behavioral decision theory for right-to-know policies" in M. V. R. Gowda and J. C. Fox (eds.) *Judgments, Decisions, and Public Policy*. Cambridge: Cambridge University Press, pp. 243–264.

Gowda, M. V. R. and Easterling, D. (2000) "Voluntary siting and equity: the MRS facility experience in Native America." *Risk Analysis*, 20: 917–929.

Greenpeace (1997) *Save Our Seas: Plutonium Reprocessing and the Contamination of the Seas*, brochure. Amsterdam: Greenpeace.

Gregory, R., Flynn, J., and Slovic, P. (1995) "Technological stigma." *American Scientist*, 83: 220–223.

Groeneweg, J., Wagenaar, W. A., and Reason, J. T. (1994) "Promoting safety in the oil industry." *Ergonomics*, 37: 1999–2013.

Gunther, A. C. (1992) "Biased press or biased public: attitudes toward media coverage of social groups." *Public Opinion Quarterly*, 56: 147–167.

Gusterson, H. (1992) "Coming of age in a weapons lab: culture, tradition and change in the house of the bomb." *The Sciences*, May/June: 16–22.

Gutman, A. and Thompson, D. (1996) *Democracy and Disagreement*. Cambridge, MA: Harvard University Press.

Habermas, J. (1984) *The Theory of Communicative Action: Reason and Rationalisation of Society*, vol. 1. Cambridge: Polity Press.

(1989) *The Structural Transformation of the Public Sphere: An Inquiry into a Category of Bourgeois Society*. Cambridge, MA: The MIT Press.

Hadden, S. G. (1989) *A Citizen's Right to Know: Risk Communication and Public Policy*. Boulder, CO: Westview.

(1991) "Public perception of hazardous waste." *Risk Analysis*, 11: 47–58.

Hall, E. T. (1984) *The Dance of Life: The Other Dimension of Time*. New York: Anchor Books.

Hammersley, M. and Atkinson, P. (1995) *Ethnography: Principles in Practice*, 2nd edition. London: Routledge.

Hammond, K. R. (1996) *Human Judgment and Social Policy*. New York: Oxford University Press.

Handmer, J. and Penning-Rowsell, E. (1990) *Hazards and the Communication of Risk*. Aldershot: Gower.

Hansen, A. (1994) "Journalistic practices and science reporting in the British press." *Public Understanding of Science*, 3: 111–134.

(2000) "Claims-making and framing in British newspaper coverage of the 'Brent Spar' controversy" in S. Allen, B. Adam, and C. Carter (eds.) *Environmental Risks and the Media*. London: Routledge, pp. 55–72.

Hardert, R. (1993) "Public trust and governmental trustworthiness: nuclear deception at the Fernald, Ohio, weapons plant." *Research in Social Problems and Public Policy*, 5: 125–148.

Hargreaves, I. and Ferguson, G. (2000) *Who's Misunderstanding Whom? Bridging the Gulf of Understanding Between the Public, the Media and Science*. Swindon: Economic and Social Research Council. http://www.esre.ac.uk/whom/

Harris, P. and O'Shaughnessy, N. (1997) "BSE and marketing communication myopia: Daisy and the death of the sacred cow." *Risk, Decision and Policy*, 2(1): 29–39.

Harrison, J. (2000) *Terrestrial TV News in Britain: The Culture of Production*. Manchester: Manchester University Press.

Harvey, D. R. (2001). *What Lessons from Foot and Mouth? A Preliminary Economic Assessment of the 2001 Epidemic*. Working Paper No. 63. University of Newcastle upon Tyne: Centre for Rural Economy.

Hautin, N. (1999) "The three-step controversy map." Presentation at the Annual Conference of the Society for Risk Analysis, Arlington, VA, 5–8 December.

Hawkins, K. (1984) *Environment and Enforcement: Regulation and the Social Definition of Pollution*. Oxford: Clarendon Press.

Hayles, N. K. (1995) "Searching for common ground" in M. E. Soulé and G. Lease (eds.) *Reinventing Nature?: Responses to Postmodern Deconstruction*. Washington, DC: Island Press, pp. 47–63.

Health and Safety Executive (1992) *The Tolerability of Risk from Nuclear Power Stations*, revised edition. London: HMSO.

(1996) *Use of Risk Assessments in Government Departments*. London: HMSO.

(1997) *The Explosion and Fires at the Texaco Refinery, Milford Haven, 24 July 1994*. Sudbury: HSE Books.

Heath, R. L. (1997) *Strategic Issues Management: Organizations and Public Policy Challenges*. Thousand Oaks, CA: Sage Publications.

Hempel, C. and Oppenheim, P. (1948) "Studies in the logic of explanation." *Philosophy of Science*, 151: 35–175.

Henwood, K. L. and Pidgeon, N. F. (1992) "Qualitative research and psychological theorizing." *British Journal of Psychology*, 83: 97–111.

(1995) "Remaking the link: qualitative research and feminist standpoint theory." *Feminism and Psychology*, 5: 7–30.

(2001) "Talk about woods and trees: threat of urbanisation, stability and bio-diversity." *Journal of Environmental Psychology*, 21: 125–147.

(2003) "Grounded theory" in P. M. Camic, J. E. Rhodes, and L. Yardly (eds.) *Qualitative Research in Psychology*. Washington, DC: American Psychological Association Press, pp. 131–155.

Hersch, R., Probst, K., Wernstedt, K., and Maxurek, J. (1997) *Linking Land Use and Superfund Cleanup: Uncharted Territory*. Washington, DC: Resources for the Future.

Herzik, E. B. and Mushkatel, A. H. (eds.) (1993) *Problems and Prospects for Nuclear Waste Disposal Policy*. Westport, CT: Greenwood Press.

Hewlett, J. (1991) "Financial implications of early decommissioning." *The Energy Journal*, 12. Washington, DC: International Association for Energy Economics, pp. 270–291.

Hilgartner, S. (1992) "The social construction of risk objects" in J. Short and L. Clarke (eds.) *Organizations, Uncertainty and Risk*. Boulder: Westview, pp. 39–53.

Hill, A. (2001) "Media risks: the social amplification of risk and the media debate." *Journal of Risk Research*, 4: 209–226.

Hoggart, R. (1966) *The Uses of Literacy*. Harmondworth: Penguin Books.

Hollocher, T. and MacKenzie, J. (1975) "Radiation hazards associated with uranium mill operations" in The Union of Concerned Scientists (eds.) *The Nuclear Fuel Cycle: A Survey of the Public Health, Environmental, and National Security Effects of Nuclear Power*, revised edition. Cambridge, MA: MIT Press, pp. 41–69.

Holzheu, F. and Wiedemann, P. (1993) "Introduction: perspectives on risk perception" in B. Rück (ed.) *Risk is a Construct*. Munich: Knesebeck, pp. 9–20.

Horlick-Jones, T. (1995) "Modern disasters as outrage and betrayal." *International Journal of Mass Emergencies and Disasters*, 13: 305–315.

(1998) "Meaning and contextualisation in risk assessment." *Reliability Engineering and System Safety*, 59: 79–89.

(2000) "On taking the real world into account in risk research." Keynote paper delivered to the ESRC Risk and Human Behaviour Conference, London, 11–12 September.

(2002) "The language and technologies of risk" in N. Gray, J. Laing, and L. Noaks (eds.) *Criminal Justice, Mental Health and the Politics of Risk*. London: Cavendish Press, pp. 149–167.

Horlick-Jones, T., De Marchi, B., Prades Lopez, A., Pidgeon, N., et al. (1998) *The Social Dynamics of Environmental Risk Perception: A Cross-Cultural Study*. Final Report of the PRISP Project European Commission 4th Framework Research Programme Contract ENV4-CT96-0265.

Horlick-Jones, T., Rosenhead, J., Georgiou, I., Ravetz, J., and Löfstedt, R. (2001) "Decision support for organisational risk management by problem structuring." *Health, Risk and Society*, 3(2): 141–165.

House of Lords Select Committee on Science and Technology (2000) *Science and Society, 3rd Report*. London: The Stationery Office.

Howel, D., Moffatt, S., Prince, H., Bush, J., and Dunn, C. E. (2002) "Urban air quality in North-East England: exploring the influences on local views and perceptions." *Risk Analysis*, 22: 121–130.

Hughes, H. M. (1937) "Human interest stories and democracy." *The Public Opinion Quarterly*, April: 73–83.

Hunt, S., Frewer, L. J., and Shepherd, R. (1999) "Public trust in sources of information about radiation risks in the UK." *Journal of Risk Research*, 2(2): 167–180.

Inglehart, R. (1988) "The renaissance of political culture." *American Political Science Review*, 82: 1203–1230.

Institute of Medicine (1995) *Adverse Reproductive Outcomes in Families of Atomic Veterans: The Feasibility of Epidemiological Studies.* Washington, DC: National Academy.

Irwin, A., Dale, A., and Smith, D. (1996) "Science and Hell's kitchen: the local understanding of hazard issues" in A. Irwin and B. Wynne (eds.) *Misunderstanding Science? The Public Reconstruction of Science and Technology.* Cambridge: Cambridge University Press, pp. 47–64.

Irwin, A. and Wynne, B. (eds.) (1996) *Misunderstanding Science.* Cambridge: Cambridge University Press.

Jacob, G. (1990) *Site Unseen: The Politics of Siting a Nuclear Waste Repository.* Pittsburgh: University of Pittsburgh Press.

Jacobs, R. (1996) "Producing the news, producing the crisis: television and news work." *Media, Culture and Society*, 18(3): 373–397.

Jaeger, C., Renn, O., Rosa, E. A., and Webler, T. (2001) *Risk, Uncertainty and Rational Action.* London: Earthscan.

Janis, I. L. (1958) *Psychological Stress.* New York: Academic Press.

(1982) *Victims of Groupthink, 2nd edition.* Boston: Houghton Mifflin.

Janis, I. L. and Mann, L. (1977) *Decision Making: A Psychological Analysis of Conflict, Choice, and Commitment.* New York: Free Press.

Jasanoff, S. (1998) "The political science of risk perception." *Reliability Engineering and System Safety*, 59(1): 91–99.

Jasper, J. M. (1990) *Nuclear Politics: Energy and the State in the United States, Sweden, and France.* Princeton, NJ: Princeton University Press.

Jeffrey, R. (1997) "Advertising and Indian-language newspapers: how capitalism supports (certain) cultures and (some) States, 1947–1996." *Pacific Affairs*, 70(1): 57–84.

Jenkins-Smith, H. (1991) "Alternative theories of the policy process: reflections on research strategy for the study of nuclear waste policy." *Political Science and Politics*, 26: 157–166.

Jennings, A. B. and Leschine, T. (2000) "The Bikini Atoll experience: inherent fallibility of institutional controls and the virtues of 'defense in depth'" in National Research Council, *Long-Term Institutional Management of US Department of Energy Legacy Waste Sites.* Washington, DC: National Academy Press, pp. 54–55.

Johnson, B. B. (1999) "Exploring dimensionality in the origins of hazard-related trust." *Journal of Risk Research*, 2: 325–373.

Johnson, B. B. and Covello, V. S. (eds.) (1987) *The Social and Cultural Construction of Risk.* Dordrecht: Reidel.

Johnson, B. B. and Slovic, P. (1995) "Presenting uncertainty in health risk assessment: initial studies of its effects on risk perception and trust." *Risk Analysis*, 15: 485–494.

Jones, G. (1998) "Nuclear waste: management problems at the Department of Energy's Hanford spent fuel storage project." Statement before the Subcommittee on Oversight and Investigations, Committee on Commerce, US House of Representatives. Washington, DC: United States General Accounting Office.

Jones, L. (1985) "Reagan's religion." *Journal of American Culture*, 8: 59–70.

Jones, T. (1989) "FBI alleges cover-up at Rocky Flats: papers say energy department knew of illegal atom waste disposal." *Los Angeles Times*, 10 June: 1.

JRA Research (1999) *The National Health Survey*. Nottingham: Jones Rhodes Associates Ltd.

Kahneman, D., Slovic, P., and Tversky, A. (eds.) (1982) *Judgement Under Uncertainty: Heuristics and Biases*. Cambridge: Cambridge University Press.

Kahneman, D. and Tversky, A. (1979) "Prospect theory: an analysis of decision under risk." *Econometrica*, 47(2): 263–291.

Kasperson, J. X. and Kasperson, R. E. (1993) "Corporate culture and technology transfer" in H. S. Brown, P. Derr, O. Renn, and A. White (eds.) *Corporate Environmentalism in a Global Economy*. Westport, CT: Quorum Books, pp. 149–177.

(2001) "Transboundary risks and social amplification" in J. Linnerooth-Bayer and R. Löfstedt (eds.) *Cross-National Studies of Transboundary Risk Problems*. London: Earthscan, pp. 207–243.

Kasperson, J. X., Kasperson, R. E., Perkins, B. J., Renn, O., and White, A. L. (1992) *Information Content, Signals, and Sources Concerning the Proposed Repository at Yucca Mountain: An Analysis of Newspaper Coverage and Social Group Activity in Lincoln County, Nevada*. Final report to the City of Caliente and the Joint/County Impact Alleviation Committee. Worcester, MA: Center for Technology, Environment, and Development (CENTED), Clark University.

Kasperson, J. X., Kasperson, R. E., and Turner, B. L. (eds.) (1995) *Regions at Risk: Comparisons of Threatened Environments*. Tokyo: United Nations University.

Kasperson, R. E. (1992) "The social amplification of risk: progress in developing an integrative framework of risk" in S. Krimsky and D. Golding (eds.) *Social Theories of Risk*. Westport, CT: Praeger, pp. 153–178.

(forthcoming). "Process and institutional issues in siting hazardous facilities."

Kasperson, R. E., Golding, D., and Tuler, S. (1992) "Social distrust as a factor in siting hazardous facilities and communicating risks." *Journal of Social Issues*, 48(4): 161–187.

Kasperson, R. E., Jhaveri, N., and Kasperson, J. X. (2001) "Stigma, places, and the social amplification of risk: toward a framework of analysis" in J. Flynn, P. Slovic, and H. Kunreuther (eds.), *Risk, Media and Stigma: Understanding Public Challenges to Modern Science and Technology*. London: Earthscan, pp. 9–27.

Kasperson, R. E. and Kasperson, J. X. (1991) "Hidden hazards" in D. G. Mayo and R. D. Hollander (eds.) *Acceptable Evidence: Science and Values in Risk Management*. New York: Oxford University Press, pp. 9–28.

(1996) "The social amplification and attenuation of risk." *The Annals of the American Academy of Political and Social Science*, 545: 95–105.

Kasperson, R. E., Kasperson, J. X., and Turner, B. L. (1999) "Risk and criticality: trajectories of regional environmental degradation." *Ambio*, 28(6): 562–568.

Kasperson, R. E., Renn, O., Slovic, P., Brown, H. S., Emel, J., Goble, R., Kasperson, J. X., and Ratick, S. J. (1988) "The social amplification of risk: a conceptual framework." *Risk Analysis*, 8(2): 178–187.

Kasperson, R. E. and Stallen, P.-J. M. (eds.) (1991) *Communicating Risks to the Public: International Perspectives*. Dordrecht: Kluwer.

Kates, R. W. and Kasperson, J. X. (1983) "Comparative risk assessment of technological hazards." *Proceedings: National Academy of Sciences*, 80: 7027–7038.

Keck, G. (2001) "Öffentlichkeitsbeteiligung zur Lämreduzierung in der Ravensburger 'Bahnstadt.'" Working Report of the Center of Technology Assessment. CTA, Stuttgart.

Keck, G. and Schene, T. (1999) "Pilotprojeckt Läminderungsplan Stuttgart-Vaihingen. Emfehlungen des Runden Tisches zu Lärminderungsmaßnahmen: Ergebnisbericht." *Schriftenreihe des Amtes für Umweltschutz*, 3: 3–34.

Keeney, R. L., Renn, O., and von Winterfeldt, D. (1987) "Structuring West Germany's energy objectives." *Energy Policy*, 15(4): 352–362.

Keeney, R. L., Renn, O., von Winterfeldt, D., and Kotte, U. (1984) *Die Wertbaumanalyse HTV Edition*. Münich: Technik und Sozialer Wandel.

Kemshall, H. (1998) *Risk in Probation Practice*. Aldershot: Ashgate.

Kingdon, J. W. (1984) *Agendas, Alternatives, and Public Policies*. Boston: Little Brown.

Kitzinger, J. and Reilly, J. (1997) "The rise and fall of risk reporting: media coverage of human genetic research, 'False Memory Syndrome' and 'Mad Cow Disease.'" *European Journal of Communication*, 12(3): 319–350.

Knetsch, J. L. (1995) "Assumptions, behavioral findings, and policy analysis." *Journal of Policy Analysis and Management*, 14(1): 68–78.

Krannich, R. S. and Luloff, A. E. (1991) "Problems of resource dependency in US rural communities." *Progress in Rural Policy and Planning*, 1: 5–18.

Krimsky, S. and Golding, D. (eds.) (1992) *Social Theories of Risk*. Westport CT: Praeger.

Krimsky, S. and Plough, A. (1988) *Environmental Hazards: Communicating Risk as a Social Process*. Dover, MA: Auburn.

Krueger, R. (1994) *Focus Groups*, 2nd edition. Thousand Oaks: Sage.

Kunreuther, H., Fitzgerald, K., and Aarts, T. (1993) "Siting noxious facilities: a test of the facility siting credo." *Risk Analysis*, 13: 301–318.

Kunreuther, H. and Linneroth, J. (1982) *Risk Analysis and Decision Processes: The Siting of Liquefied Energy Gas Facilities in Four Countries*. Berlin: Springer Verlag.

Kunreuther, H. and Slovic, P. (1996) "Science, values and risk." *Annals of the American Academy of Political and Social Science*, 545: 116–125.

Kuran, T. and Sunstein, C. R. (1999) "Availability cascades and risk regulation." *Stanford Law Review*, 51: 683–768.

Langer, J. (1998) *Tabloid Television: Popular Journalism and the "Other" News*. London: Routledge.

Langford, I. L. (2002) "An existential approach to risk perception." *Risk Analysis*, 22: 101–120.

La Porte, T. R. (1996) "High reliability organizations: unlikely, demanding and at risk." *Journal of Contingencies and Crisis Management*, 4: 60–70.

Lawless, E. T. (1977) *Technology and Social Shock*. New Brunswick, NJ: Rutgers University Press.

Lawless, W. F. (1991) "A social psychological analysis of the practice of science: the problem of military nuclear waste management" in R. G. Post (ed.) *Waste Management '91*, vol. 2. Tucson: University of Arizona, pp. 91–96.

Le Bon, G. (1969) *The Crowd: A Study of the Popular Mind*. New York: Ballantine Books.

Leiss, W. (1992) "Assessing and managing risks." *Policy Sciences*, 25: 341–349.
  (1996) "Three phases in the evolution of risk communication practice." *Annals of the American Academy of Political and Social Science*, 545: 85–94.
  (2001) *In the Chamber of Risks: Understanding Risk Controversies*. Montréal: McGill-Queen's University Press.

Leiss, W. and Chociolko, C. (1994) *Risk and Responsibility*. Montréal: McGill-Queen's University Press.

Leventhal. H. (1970) "Findings and theory in the study of fear communication" in L. Berkowitz (ed.) *Advances in Experimental Social Psychology*, vol. 5. New York: Academic Press.

Levine, A. G. (1982) *Love Canal: Science, Politics, and People*. Lexington, MA: Lexington Books.

Lévy, A. (1998) "Us et abus de la notion de crise." *Revue Internationale de Psychosociologie*, 5(8).

Lichtenberg, J. and Maclean, D. (1991) "The role of the media in risk communication" in R. Kasperson and P. Stallen (eds.) *Communicating Risks to the Public*. London: Kluwer Academic Press, pp. 157–173.

Lodwick, D. G. (1993) "Rocky Flats and the evolution of distrust." *Research in Social Problems and Public Policy*, 5: 149–170.

Loeke, P., Joop, B., and Bannink, D. (1997) "The MOX myth: risks and dangers of the use of mixed oxide fuel." *WISE News Communiqué 469/470*. Amsterdam: WISE Amsterdam.

Löfstedt, R. E. and Horlick-Jones, T. (1999) "Environmental regulation in the UK: politics, institutional change and public trust" in G. Cvetkovich and R. E. Löfstedt (eds.) *Social Trust and the Management of Risk*. London: Earthscan, pp. 73–88.

Logan, J. R. and Molotch, H. L. (1987) *Urban Fortunes: The Political Economy of Place*. Berkeley, CA: University of California Press.

Lotke, E. (1996) *Sex Offenders: Does Treatment Work?* http://www.igc.org/ncia/sexo.html

Luhmann, N. (1979) *Trust and Power: Two Works by Niklas Luhmann*. Chichester: John Wiley and Sons.
  (1993) *Risk: A Sociological Theory*. New York: Aldine de Gruyter.

Lukes, S. (1974) *Power: A Radical View*. London: The Macmillan Press.

Maass, A. and Clark, R. D. (1983) "Internalization versus compliance: differential processes underlying minority influence and conformity." *European Journal of Social Psychology*, 13: 197–215.

MacGill, S. (1987) *The Politics of Anxiety: Sellafield's Cancer-Link Controversy*. London: Pion.

MacGregor, D. G. (1991) "Worry over technological activities and life concerns." *Risk Analysis*, 11: 315–324.

MacGregor, D. G., Slovic, P., Dreman, D., and Berry, M. (2000) "Imagery, affect, and financial judgment." *Journal of Psychology and Financial Markets*, 2: 104–110.

Machlis, G. E. and Rosa, E. A. (1990) "Desired risk: broadening the social amplification of risk framework." *Risk Analysis*, 10(1): 161–168.

Macintyre, S., Reilly, J., Miller, D., and Eldridge, J. (1998) "Food choice, food scares, and health: the role of the media" in A. Murcott (ed.) *The Nation's Diet: The Social Science of Food Choice*. London: Longman, pp. 228–249.

Magat, W. A. and Viscusi, W. K. (1992) *Informational Approaches to Regulation*. Cambridge, MA: MIT Press.

MAIB (1997) *Report of the Chief Inspector of Marine Accidents into the Grounding and Subsequent Salvage of the Tanker Sea Empress at Milford Haven between 15 and 21 February 1996*. Report to the Marine Accident Investigation Branch. London: The Stationery Office.

Makhijani, A. (1997) "Technical Aspects of the Use of Weapons Plutonium as a Reactor Fuel." *Science for Democratic Action*, 5(4): 1–7.

Makhijani, A. and Schwartz, S. (1998) "Building the bomb" in S. Schwartz (ed.) *Atomic Audit*. Washington, DC: Brookings Institute, pp. 54–56.

Malotki, E. (1983) *Hopi Time: A Linguistic Analysis of the Temporal Concepts in the Hopi Language*. Berlin: Mouton.

Manning, M. (1995) "Atomic vets battle time." *The Bulletin of the Atomic Scientists* (January–February 1995): 54–60.

Manning, P. (1992) "Managing risk: managing uncertainty in the British Nuclear Installations Inspectorate" in J. Short, and L. Clarke (eds.) *Organizations, Uncertainty and Risk*. Boulder: Westview Press, pp. 255–273.

Marris, C., Langford, I. H., and O'Riordan, T. (1996) *Integrating Sociological and Psychological Approaches to Public Perceptions of Environmental Risk: Detailed Results from a Questionnaire Study*. Centre for Social and Economic Research on the Global Environment (CSERGE) working paper GEC 96-07. Norwich: University of East Anglia.

(1998) "A quantitative test of the cultural theory of risk perceptions: comparisons with the psychometric paradigm." *Risk Analysis*, 18(5): 635–648.

(2000) "Methodological issues in the study of public perceptions of risk: individual or collective data?" Paper presented to the ESRC Risk and Human Behaviour Conference, London, 11–12 September.

Marris, C., Wynne, B., Simmons, P., and Weldon, S. (2001) *Public Perceptions of Agricultural Biotechnologies in Europe*. Final Report FAIR CT98-3844 (DG12 – SSMI) (with contributions also from J. Cárceres, B. De Marchi, A. Klinke, L. Lemkow, L. Pellizzoni, U. Pfenning, O. Renn, and R. Sentmarti). Brussels: Commission of the European Communities. http://www.pabe.net

Marshall, E. (1983) "Clinch River dies." *Science*, 222: 590–592.

Martens, D. (1997) *Einstellung der Bevölkerung zur Abfallproblematik*. Habilitation an der Universität Tübingen, Germany.

Matthes, R., Bernhardt, J., and Repacholi, M. H. (eds.) (1997) "Non-thermal effects of RF electromagnetic fields." Proceedings of ICNIRP Munich meeting, November.

Mayhew, D. (1974) *Congress: The Electoral Connection*. New Haven: Yale University Press.

Mays, C., Brenot, J., and Poumadère, M. (1999) "From 'hysteria' to 'enlightened input': five dimensions of risk managers' integration of public perceptions" in P. Hubert and C. Mays (eds.) *Risk Analysis: Opening the Process*. Fontenay-aux-Roses: IPSN, p. 1055.

Mays, C., Poumadère, M., Brenot, J., Bonnefous, S., and Pappo, R. (1997) *Grille de lecture des risques et acceptabilité (Phase II)*. Rapport 95198 au Ministère de l'Environnement-DGAD-SRAE. Note SEGR 97-101. Fontenay-aux-Roses: IPSN.

Mazur, A. (1981) *The Dynamics of Technical Controversy*. Washington, DC: Communications Press.

— (1984) "The journalist and technology: reporting about Love Canal and Three Mile Island." *Minerva*, 22: 45–66.

— (1990) "Nuclear power, chemical hazards, and the quantity of reporting." *Minerva*, 28: 294–323.

— (1991) *Global Social Problems*. Englewood Cliffs, NJ: Prentice-Hall.

— (1998) *A Hazardous Inquiry: The Rashomon Effect at Love Canal*. Cambridge, MA: Harvard University Press.

McCabe, A. S. and Fitzgerald, M. R. (1991) "Media images of environmental biotechnology: what does the public see?" in G. S. Sayler, R. Fox, and J. W. Blackburn (eds.) *Environmental Biotechnology for Waste Treatment*. New York: Plenum, pp. 15–24.

McCaffrey, D. (1991) *The Politics of Nuclear Power: A History of the Shoreham Nuclear Power Plant*. Dordrecht: Kluwer Academic Press.

McCombs, M. (1981) "The agenda-setting approach" in D. D. Nimmo and K. R. Sanders (eds.) *Handbook of Political Communication*. Beverly Hills, CA: Sage, pp. 121–140.

McCoy, C. (1989) "Broken promises: Alyeska record shows how big oil neglected Alaskan environment." *Wall Street Journal*, 6 July: A1, A4.

McDaniels, T. (1998) "Ten propositions for untangling descriptive and prescriptive lessons in risk perception findings." *Reliability Engineering and System Safety*, 59: 129–134.

McGuigan, J. (2000) "British identity and the 'People's Princess'." *The Sociological Review*, 48(1): 1–18.

McGuire, W. J. (1985) "Attitudes and attitude change" in G. Lindzey and E. Aronson (eds.) *The Handbook of Social Psychology*, 3rd edition, vol. 2. New York: Random House, pp. 233–346.

McKay, K. (1989) *A Vision of Greatness: The History of Milford 1790–1990*. Haverfordwest: Brace Harvatt Associates in association with Gulf Oil Great Britain Ltd.

Merton, R. (1976) "Social knowledge and social policy" in R. Merton (ed.) *Sociological Ambivalence*. New York: Free Press.

Metz, W. C. (1996) "Historical application of a social amplification of risk model: economic impact of risk events at a nuclear weapons facility." *Risk Analysis*, 16(2): 185–193.

Michael, M. (1996) *Constructing Identities*. London: Sage.

Miedema, H. M. E. and Vos, H. (1998) "Exposure–response relationships for transportation noise." *Journal of the Acoustical Society of America*, 104: 3432–3445.

Miles, S. and Frewer, L. J. (2000) *The Impact of Social Context and Informational Context on People's Reactions to Food Risk Communication*. Final report submitted to the UK Food Standards Agency. Norwich: Institute of Food Research.

—— (2001) "Investigating specific concerns about different food hazards – higher and lower order attributes." *Food Quality and Preference*, 12(1): 47–61.

Miller, D. (1999) "Risk, science and policy: definitional issues, information management, the media and BSE." *Social Science and Medicine*, 49: 1239–1255.

Miller, D. and Beharrell, P. (1998) "AIDS and television news" in D. Miller, J. Kitzinger, K. Williams, and P. Beharrell (eds.) *The Circuit of Mass Communication*. London: Sage, pp. 68–90.

Miller, D. and Reilly, J. (1994) *Food "Scares" in the Media*. Glasgow: Glasgow University Media Group.

—— (1995) "Making an issue of food safety: the media, pressure groups and the public sphere" in D. Maurer and J. Sobal (eds.) *Eating Agendas: Food and Nutrition as Social Problems*. New York: Aldine de Gruyter, pp. 305–336.

Miller, R. (1986) *Under the Cloud: The Decades of Nuclear Testing*. New York: The Free Press.

—— (1991) "Safeguards go up in smoke in rush to build incinerators." *New Scientist*, 3rd August: 11.

Ministry of Agriculture, Fisheries and Food (1998) *National Food Survey 1996*. London: HMSO.

Mitchell, R. C., Payne, B., and Dunlap, R. (1988) "Stigma and radioactive waste: theory, assessment, and some empirical findings from Hanford, WA" in R. G. Post (ed.) *Waste Management '88: Waste Processing, Transportation, Storage and Disposal, Technical Programs and Public Education*, vol. 2: *High-Level Waste and General Interest*. Tucson, AZ: University of Arizona, pp. 95–102.

Mojtabai, A. G. (1986) *Blessed Assurance: At Home with the Bomb in Amarillo, Texas*. Boston: Houghton Mifflin.

Molotch, H. (1976) "The city as a growth machine: toward a political economy of place." *American Journal of Sociology*, 82: 309–332.

Molotch, H. and Boden, D. (1985) "Talking social structure: discourse, domination and the Watergate hearings." *American Sociological Review*, 50: 272–288.

Molotch, H. and Lester, M. (1975) "Accidental news: the great oil spill as local occurrence and national event." *American Journal of Sociology*, 81(2): 235–260.

Moores, S. (1993) *Interpreting Audiences: The Ethnography of Media Consumption*. London: Sage Publications.

Morgan, D. (1997) *Focus Groups as Qualitative Research*, 2nd edition. Thousand Oaks: Sage.

Morgan, G. (1986) *Images of Organizations*. London: Sage.

Morgan, G., Fischhoff, B., Bostrom, A., and Atman, C. (2001) *Risk Communication: A Mental Models Approach*. Cambridge: Cambridge University Press.

Morgan, G. and Lave, L. (1990) "Ethical considerations in risk communication practice and research." *Risk Analysis*, 10: 355–358.

MORI (1999) *Public Attitudes to Risk*. Survey Commissioned by the Cabinet Office Better Regulation Unit Task Force. London: Market and Opinion Research International.

Morley, D. (1992) *Television Audiences and Cultural Studies*. London: Routledge.

Morone, J. F. and Woodhouse, E. J. (1989) *The Demise of Nuclear Energy? Lessons for a Democratic Control of Technology*. New Haven, CT: Yale University Press.

Morton, H. V. (1932) *In Search of Wales*, 3rd edition. London: Methuen and Co.

Moscovici, S. (1976) *La Psychanalyse, son image et son public* (2nd edition). Paris: Presses Universitaires de France.

(1985) "Innovation and minority influence" in S. Moscovici, G. Mugny and E. Van Avermaet (eds.) *Perspectives on Minority Influence*. Cambridge: Cambridge University Press, pp. 9–51.

Moscovici, S. and Hewstone, M. (1983) "Social representations and social explanations: from the 'naïve' to the 'amateur' scientist" in M. Hewstone (ed.) *Attribution Theory: Social and Functional Extensions*. Oxford: Basil Blackwell.

Moscovici, S. and Lage, E. (1976) "Studies in social influence III. Majority versus minority influence in a group." *European Journal of Social Psychology*, 6: 149–174.

Munera, H., Canal, M., and Munoz, M. (1997) "Risk associated with transportation of spent nuclear fuel under demanding security constraints: the Colombia experience." *Risk Analysis*, 17: 381–389.

Murdock, G. (1989) "Critical inquiry and audience activity" in B. Dervin, L. Grossberg et al. (eds.) *Rethinking Communication*, volume 2: *Paradigm Exemplars*. London: Sage Publications, pp. 226–249.

(1992) "Citizens, consumers and public culture" in M. Skovmand and K. C. Schroder (eds.) *Media Cultures: Reappraising Transnational Media*. London: Routledge, pp. 17–41.

Mushkatel, H. and Pijawka, K. D. (1994) *Nuclear Waste Transportation in Nevada: A Case for Stigma-Induced Economic Vulnerability*. Report no. MRDB/RP0149 to the Nevada Nuclear Waste Project Office. Carson City, NV: NWPO.

National Academy of Sciences (2001) Committee on Disposition of High-Level Radioactive Waste Through Geological Isolation, *Disposition of High-Level Waste and Spent Nuclear Fuel: The Continuing Societal and Technical Challenges*. Washington, DC: National Academy Press.

National Research Council (1983) *Risk Assessment in the Federal Government: Managing the Process*. Washington, DC: National Academy Press.

(1989) *Improving Risk Communication*. Washington, DC: National Academy Press.

(1995) Committee on Declassification of Information for the Department of Energy Environmental Remediation and Related Programs, *A Review of* the Department of Energy Classification Policy and Practice. Washington, DC: National Academy Press.

(1996) Committee on the Waste Isolation Pilot Plant, Board on Radioactive Waste Management, *The Waste Isolation Pilot Plant: A Potential Solution for the Disposal of Transuranic Waste*. Washington, DC: National Academy Press.

(2000) *Long-Term Institutional Management of US Department of Energy Legacy Waste Sites*. Washington, DC: National Academy Press.

National Science Foundation / USA Today (1999) *Gallup Y2K poll*. www.nsf.gov/od/lpa/events/fow/y2ktopline.htm.

Nerb, J., Spada, H. and Wahl, S. (1998) "Kognition und Emotion bei der Bewertung von Umweltschadensfällen: Modellierung und Empirie." *Zeitschrift für Experimentelle Psychologie*, 45: 251–269.

Noll, R. G. (1996) "Reforming risk regulation." *Annals of the American Academy of Political and Social Science*, 545: 166–175.

Nordenstam, B. J. and DiMento, J. (1990) "Right-to-know: implications of risk communication research for regulatory policy." *University of California, Davis Law Review*, 23: 333–374.

Nordheimer, J. (1995) " 'Vigilante' attack in New Jersey is linked to sex-offenders law." *New York Times*, 20 February: B1.

OED (1982) *The Compact Edition of the Oxford English Dictionary (OED)*. Oxford: Oxford University Press.

Office of Technology Assessment (1991) *Complex Cleanup: The Environmental Legacy of Nuclear Weapons Production*. Washington, DC: GPO.

Okrent, D. (1996) "Risk perception research program and applications: have they received enough peer review?" in C. Cacciabue and I. A. Papazoglou (eds.) *Probabilistic Safety Assessment and Management ESREL '96 – PSAM III*. Berlin: Springer, pp. 1255–1259.

Okrent, D. and Pidgeon, N. (eds.) (1998) "Risk perception versus risk analysis." Special issue of *Reliability Engineering and System Safety*, 59(1): 1–159.

Olson, M. (1965) *The Logic of Collective Action*. Cambridge, MA: Harvard University Press.

O'Neill, D. (1994) *The Firecracker Boys*. New York: St. Martin's Griffin.

(1998) "Building the bomb" in S. Schwartz (ed.) *Atomic Audit*. Washington, DC: Brookings Institute, pp. 33–104; see table 3.1, pp. 86–91.

Organisation for Economic Co-operation and Development (1991) Nuclear Energy Agency, *Decommissioning of Nuclear Facilities: An Analysis of the Variability of Decommissioning Cost Estimates*. Paris: OECD.

O'Riordan, T., Burgess, J., and Szerszynski, B. (1999) *Deliberative and Inclusionary Processes: A Report from Two Workshops*. Center for Social and Economic Research on the Global Environment, working paper 99–06. Norwich: University of East Anglia.

O'Riordan, T., Kemp, R., and Purdue, M. (1988) *Sizewell B: An Anatomy of the Inquiry*. Basingstoke: Macmillan.

Otway, H. (1992) "Public wisdom, expert fallibility: toward a contextual theory of risk" in S. Krimsky and D. Golding (eds.) *Social Theories of Risk*. Westport, CT: Praeger, pp. 211–228.

Otway, H., Haastrup, P., Cannell, W., Gianitsopoulos, G., and Paruccini, M. (1988) "Risk communication in Europe after Chernobyl: a media analysis of seven countries." *Industrial Crisis Quarterly*, 2: 3–15.

Palmer, C. G. S., Carlstrom, L. K., and Woodward, J. A. (2001) "Risk perception and ethnicity." *Risk Decision and Policy*, 6: 187–206.

Palmlund, I. (1992) "Social drama and risk evaluation" in S. Krimsky and D. Golding (eds.) *Social Theories of Risk*. Westport: Praeger, pp. 197–212.

Pasqualetti, M. (1991) "The place of economics in decommissioning policy." *The Energy Journal*, 12. Washington, DC: International Association for Energy Economics, pp. 3–12.

Pasqualetti, M. and Rothwell, G. (eds.) (1991) "Nuclear decommissioning economics: estimates, regulation, experience and uncertainty." Special issue of *The Energy Journal*, 12. Washington, DC: International Association for Energy Economics.

Pasternak, D. (1993) "The Department of Energy's informational black hole." *Research in Social Problems and Public Policy*, 5: 171–177.

Peach, J. D. (1988) "Ineffective management and oversight of DOE's P-reactor at Savannah River, S.C., raises safety concern." Statement before Committee on Governmental Affairs, US Senate Subcommittee on Environment, Energy, and Natural Resources. Washington, DC: United States General Accounting Office.

Pendergrass, J. (1996) "Use of institutional controls as part of a superfund remedy." *Environmental Law Reporter*, 26: 10109–10123.

Perin, C. (1995) "Organizations as contexts: implications for safety science and practice." *Industrial and Environmental Crisis Quarterly*, 9(2): 152–174.

Perrow, C. (1984/1999) *Normal Accidents: Living with High-Risk Technologies*. New York: Basic Books (2nd edition 1999, Princeton University Press).

Peters, E. and Slovic, P. (1996) "The role of affect and worldviews as orienting dispositions in the perception and acceptance of nuclear power." *Journal of Applied Social Psychology*, 26(16): 1427–1453.

Peters, H. P. (1995) "The interaction of journalists and scientific experts: co-operation and conflict between two professional cultures." *Media, Culture and Society*, 17: 31–48.

Petterson, J. S. (1988) "Perception vs. reality of radiological impact: the Goiânia model." *Nuclear News*, 31(14): 84–90.

Petts, J. (2001) "Evaluating the effectiveness of deliberative processes: waste management case studies." *Journal of Environmental Planning and Management*, 44(2): 207–226.

Petts, J., Horlick-Jones, T., and Murdock, G. (2001) *Social Amplification of Risk: The Media and the Public*. Health and Safety Executive Contract Research Report 329/2001. Sudbury: HSE Books.

Petty, R. E. and Cacioppo, J. T. (1984) "Source factors and the elaboration likelihood model of persuasion." *Advances in Consumer Research*, 11: 668–672.

(1986) *Communication and Persuasion: Central and Peripheral Routes to Attitude Change*. New York: Springer-Verlag.

Phillips, Lord, Bridgeman, J., and Ferguson-Smith, M. (2000) *The Report of the Inquiry into BSE and Variant CJD in the UK*. London: The Stationery Office (www.bseinquiry.gov.uk).

PHLS (2000) *AIDS/HIV Quarterly Surveillance Tables: UK Data to End September 1999*. PHLS, 44: 99/3.

Pidgeon, N. F. (1988) "Risk assessment and accident analysis." *Acta Psychologica*, 68: 355–368.

(1996) "Technocracy, democracy, secrecy and error" in C. Hood and D. Jones (eds.) *Accident and Design*. London: University College Press, pp. 164–171.

(1997) *Risk Communication and the Social Amplification of Risk – Phase 1 Scoping Study*. Report to the UK Health and Safety Executive (Risk Assessment and Policy Unit), RSU Ref 3625/R62.076. London: HSE books.

(1999) "Risk communication and the social amplification of risk: theory, evidence, and policy implications." *Risk, Decision and Policy*, 4(1): 1–15.

Pidgeon, N. F. and Beattie, J. (1998) "The psychology of risk and uncertainty" in P. Calow (ed.) *Handbook of Environmental Risk Assessment and Management*. Oxford: Blackwell Science, pp. 289–318.

Pidgeon, N. F., Henwood, K., and Maguire, B. (1999) "Public health communication and the social amplification of risks: present knowledge and future prospects" in P. Bennett and K. Calman (eds.) *Risk Communication and Public Health*. Oxford: Oxford University Press, pp. 65–77.

Pidgeon, N., Hood, C., Jones, D., Turner, B., and Gibson, R. (1992) "Risk perception" in The Royal Society Study Group, *Risk: Analysis, Perception and Management*. London: The Royal Society, pp. 89–134.

Pidgeon, N. F. and O'Leary, M. (1994) "Organizational safety culture: implications for aviation practice" in N. Johnston, N. McDonald, and R. Fuller (eds.) *Aviation Psychology in Practice*, Aldershot: Avebury Technical.

(2000) "Man-made disasters: why technology and organizations (sometimes) fail." *Safety Science*, 34: 15–30.

Pijawka, K. D., Blair, J., Guhathakurta, S., Lebiednik, S., and Ashur, S. (1999) "Environmental equity in central cities: socio-economic dimensions and planning strategies." *Journal of Planning Education and Research*, 18(2): 113–123.

Plous, S. (1993) *The Psychology of Judgment and Decision Making*. New York: McGraw Hill.

Pollock, C. (1986) *Decommissioning: Nuclear Power's Missing Link*, Worldwatch paper 69. Washington, DC: Worldwatch Institute.

Poortinga, W., Bickerstaff, K., Langford, I., Niewöhner, J., and Pidgeon, N. (2003) "The British 2001 foot and mouth crisis: a comparative study of public risk perceptions, trust and beliefs about government policy in two communities." *Journal of Risk Research*, in press.

Portney, P. R. (2000) "Environmental problems and policy: 2000–2050." *Journal of Economic Perspectives*, 14: 199–206.

Potter, J. and Wetherell, M. (1987) *Discourse and Social Psychology: Beyond Attitudes and Behaviour*. London: Sage.

Poumadère, M. (1991) "The credibility crisis" in B. Segerstahl (ed.) *Chernobyl: A Policy Response Study*. Berlin: Springer Verlag, pp. 149–171.

Poumadère, M., Mays, C., Slovic, P., and Mertz, C. K. (1996) "Diversity in meaning: risks compared in France and the USA" in O. Renn (ed.) *Risk Analysis and Management in a Global Economy*, vol. 2: *Risk Perception and*

Communication in Europe. Stuttgart: Center of Technology Assessment in Baden-Württemberg.

Powell, D. and Leiss, W. (1997) *Mad Cows and Mother's Milk: The Perils of Poor Risk Communication*. Montréal: McGill-Queen's University Press.

Powers, A. and Andsager, J. L. (1999) "How newspapers framed breast implants in the 1990s." *Journalism and Mass Communication Quarterly*, 76(3): 551–564.

President's Commission on Three Mile Island (1979) *The Need for Change: The Legacy of Three Mile Island*. Washington, DC: US Government Printing Office.

Priester, J. R. and Petty, R. E. (1995) "Source attributions and persuasion: perceived honesty as a determinant of message scrutiny." *Personality and Social Psychology Bulletin*, 21: 637–654.

Pritchard, J. (1994) *Belvedere and Bostall: A Brief History of Erith Part V*, 2nd edition. Bexley: London Borough of Bexley.

Putnam, R. D. (1993) *Making Democracy Work: Civic Traditions in Modern Italy*. Princeton, NJ: Princeton University Press.

—— (1995) "Tuning in, tuning out: the strange disappearance of social capital in America." *PS: Political Science and Politics*, 28(4): 664–683.

Radley, A. and Billig, M. (1996) "Accounts of health and illness: dilemmas and representations." *Sociology of Health and Illness*, 18(2): 220–240.

Random House (1987) *The Random House Dictionary of the English Language*, 2nd edition, unabridged. New York: Random House.

Rappaport, R. A. (1988) "Toward postmodern risk analysis." *Risk Analysis*, 8(2): 189–191.

Rawcliffe, P. (1998) *Environmental Pressure Groups in Transition*. Manchester: Manchester University Press.

Rayner, S. (1986) "Management of radiation hazards in hospitals." *Social Studies of Science*, 16: 573–591.

—— (1988) "Muddling through metaphors to maturity: a commentary on Kasperson et al. 'The Social Amplification of Risk'." *Risk Analysis*, 8(2): 201–204.

—— (1992) "Cultural theory and risk analysis" in S. Krimsky and D. Golding (eds.) *Social Theories of Risk*. Westport, CT: Praeger, pp. 83–115.

Reason, J. T. (1986) "The Chernobyl errors." *Bulletin of the British Psychological Society*, 40: 201–206.

Reilly, J. (1998) "Just another food scare? Changes in public understandings of BSE" in P. Philo (ed.) *Message Received*. London: Longman, pp. 81–95.

Renn, O. (1991a) "Risk communication and the social amplification of risk" in R. E. Kasperson and P.-J. M. Stallen (eds.) *Communicating Risks to the Public: International Perspectives*. Dordrecht: Kluwer Academic Press, pp. 287–324.

—— (1991b) "Premises of risk communication: results of two participatory experiments" in R. E. Kasperson and P.-J. M. Stallen (eds.) *Communicating Risks to the Public: International Perspectives*. Dordrecht: Kluwer Academic, pp. 457–481.

—— (1992a) "The social arena concept of risk debates" in S. Krimsky and D. Golding (eds.) *Social Theories of Risk*. Westport, CT: Praeger, pp. 179–196.

(1992b) "Risk communication: towards a rational discourse with the public." *Journal of Hazardous Materials*, 29: 465–519.

(1992c) "Concepts of risk: a classification" in S. Krimsky and D. Golding (eds.) *Social Theories of Risk*. Westport, CT: Praeger, pp. 53–79.

(1998a) "Three decades of risk research: accomplishments and new challenges." *Journal of Risk Research*, 1(1): 49–71.

(1998b) "The role of risk perception for risk management." *Reliability Engineering and System Safety*, 59: 49–62.

(1998c) "The role of risk communication and public dialogue for improving risk management." *Risk Decision and Policy*, 3(1): 5–30.

Renn, O., Burns, W. J., Kasperson, J. X., Kasperson, R. E., and Slovic, P. (1993) "The social amplification of risk: theoretical foundations and empirical applications." *Journal of Social Issues*, 48(4): 137–160.

Renn, O., Kastenholz, H., Schild, P., and Wilhelm, U. (eds.) (1998) *Abfallpolitik im Kooperativen Diskurs. Bürgerbeteiligung bei der Standortsuche für eine Deponie im Kanton Aargau*. Polyprojekt Risiko und Sicherheit der Eidgenössischen Technischen Hochschule Zürich. Dokumente Nr. 19. Zürich: Hochschulverlag AG an der ETH.

Renn, O. and Levine, D. (1991) "Credibility and trust in risk communication" in R. E. Kasperson and P.-J. M. Stallen (eds.) *Communicating Risks to the Public: International Perspectives*. Dordrecht: Kluwer Academic Press, pp. 157–218.

Renn, O. and Rohrmann, B. (2000) *Cross-Cultural Risk Perception: A Survey of Empirical Studies*. Amsterdam: Kluwer Academic Press.

Renn, O., Schrimpf, M., Büttner, T., Carius, R., Köberle, S., Oppermann, B., Schneider, E., and Zöller, K. (1999) *Abfallwirtschaft 2005. Bürger Planen ein Regionales Abfallkonzept*. Baden-Baden: Nomos.

Renn, O., Webler, T., and Wiedemann, P. (eds.) (1995) *Fairness and Competence in Citizen Participation: Evaluating Models for Environmental Discourse*. Dordrecht: Kluwer Academic Press.

Rip, A. (1988) "Should social amplification of risk be counteracted?" *Risk Analysis*, 8(2): 193–197.

Roberts, K. H. (1989) "New challenges in organizational research: high reliability organizations." *Industrial Crisis Quarterly*, 3(2): 111–125.

Robison, W. L., Bogen K. T., and Conrado, C. L. (1997) "An updated dose assessment for resettlement options at Bikini Atoll – a US nuclear test site." *Health Physics*, 73: 100–114.

Rosa, E. A. (1998a) "Metatheoretical foundations for post-normal risk." *Journal of Risk Research*, 1(1): 15–44.

(1998b) "Old-fashioned hypertext." *Journal of Risk Research*, 1: 111–115.

Rosa, E. A. and Clark, D. L., Jr. (1999) "Historical routes to technological gridlock: nuclear technology as prototypical vehicle." *Research in Social Problems and Public Policy*, 7: 21–57.

Rosa, E. A., Dunlap, R. E., and Kraft, M. E. (1993) "Prospects for public acceptance of a high-level nuclear waste repository in the United States: summary and implications" in R. E. Dunlap, M. E. Kraft, and E. A. Rosa (eds.) *Public Reactions to Nuclear Waste: Citizens' Views of Repository Siting*. Durham, NC: Duke University Press, pp. 291–324.

Ross, J. F. (1999) *The Polar Bear Strategy*. Reading, MA: Perseus Books.

Rothstein, H. (2003) "Neglected risk regulation: the institutional attenuation phenomenon." *Health, Risk and Society*, 5: 85–103.

Rowe, G. and Frewer, L. J. (2000) "Public participation methods: an evaluative review of the literature." *Science, Technology and Human Values*, 25: 3–29.

Royal Commission on Environmental Pollution (1998) *Setting Environmental Standards, 21st Report*. London: HMSO.

Royal Society (1985) *The Public Understanding of Science*. London: The Royal Society.

(1992) *Risk: Analysis, Perception and Management*. London: The Royal Society.

(1998) *Genetically Modified Plants for Food Use*. London: The Royal Society.

(2000) *Endocrine Disrupting Chemicals*. London: The Royal Society.

Royal Society of Canada (1999) *A Review of the Potential Health Risks of Radiofrequency Fields from Wireless Telecommunications Devices*. Ottawa, Canada: The Royal Society of Canada (www.rsc.ca).

Ruckelshaus, W. (1996) "Trust in government: a prescription for restoration." The Webb Lecture to the National Academy of Public Administration, 15 November.

Ryan, C. (1991) *Prime Time Activism: Media Strategies for Grassroots Organising*. Boston, MA: South End Press.

Salomone, K. L. and Sandman, P. M. (1991) *Newspaper Coverage of the Diamond Shamrock Dioxin Controversy: How Much Content is Alarming, Reassuring, or Intermediate?* New Brunswick, NJ: Rutgers University Environmental Communication Research Program.

Sandman, P. (1988) "Telling reporters about risk." *Civil Engineering*, 58: 36–38.

(1993) *Responding to Community Outrage: Strategies for Effective Risk Communication*. Fairfax, VA: American Industrial Hygiene Association.

Sandman, P. M., Miller, P. M., Johnson, B. B., and Weinstein, N. D. (1993) "Agency communication, community outrage, and perception of risk: three simulation experiments." *Risk Analysis*, 13(6): 585–598.

Saretzki, T. (1996) "Wie unterschieden sich Argumentieren und Verhandeln? Definitionsprobleme, funktionale Bezüge und astrukturelle Differenzen von zwei verschiedenen Kommunikationsmodi" in V. von Prittwitz (ed.) *Verhandeln und Argumentieren. Dialog, Interessen und Macht in der Umweltpolitik*. Opladen: Leske and Budrich, pp. 19–38.

Schama, S. (1995) *Landscape and Memory*. London: Harper Collins.

Schanne, M. and Meier, W. (1992) "Media coverage of risk: results from content analysis" in J. Durant (ed.) *Museums and the Public Understanding of Science*. London: Science Museum Publications.

Schneider, E., Oppermann, B., and Renn, O. (1998) "Experiences from Germany: application of a structured model of public participation in waste management planning." *Interact: Journal of Public Participation*, 4(1): 63–72.

Schnellnhuber, H.-J., Block, A., Cassel-Gintz, M., Kropp, J., Lammel, G., Lass, W., Lienenkamp, R., Loose, C., Lüdeke, M. K. B., Moldenhauer, O., Petschel-Held, G., Plöchl, M., and Reusswig, F. (1997) "Syndromes of global change." *GAIA*, 6(1): 19–34.

Schoenfeld, A., Meier, W., and Griffin, R. (1990) "Constructing a social problem: the press and the environment." *Social Problems*, 27(1): 38–61.

Schopf, S. (1995) " 'Megan's Law': community notification and the constitution." *Columbia Journal of Law and Social Problems*, 29: 117–146.

Schurgin, A. and Hollocher, T. (1975) "Radiation-induced lung cancers among uranium miners" in The Union of Concerned Scientists (eds.) *The Nuclear Fuel Cycle: A Survey of the Public Health, Environmental, and National Security Effects of Nuclear Power*, revised edition. Cambridge, MA: MIT Press, pp. 9–40.

Schutz, A. (1970) *Reflections on the Problem of Relevance*, edited by R. Zaner. New Haven: Yale University Press.

Schwartz, S. (1995) "Four trillion dollars and counting." *The Bulletin of the Atomic Scientists*, (November–December 1995): 32–52.

Searle, J. R. (1995) *The Construction of Social Reality*. New York: Free Press.
(1998) *Mind, Language, and Society: Philosophy in the Real World*. New York: Basic Books.

Seper, J. (1995) "Reno backs notification law." *Washington Times*, 10 February: A4.

Sheak, R. and Cianciolo, P. (1993) "Notes on nuclear weapons plants and their neighbors: the case of Fernald." *Research in Social Problems and Public Policy*, 5: 97–122.

Shell UK (1998) *Report to Society*. London: Shell UK Ltd.

Short, J. F., Jr. (1984) "The social fabric at risk: toward a social transformation of risk analysis." *American Sociological Review*, 49: 711–725.
(1989) "On defining, describing, and explaining elephants (and reactions to them). Hazards, disasters, and risk analysis." *International Journal of Mass Emergencies and Disasters*, 7: 397–418.
(1992) "Defining, explaining, and managing risk" in J. F. Short, Jr. and L. Clarke (eds.) *Organizations, Uncertainties, and Risk*. Boulder, CO: Westview Press, pp. 3–23.

Short, J. F., Jr. and Clarke, L. (eds.) (1992) *Organizations, Uncertainties and Risk*. Boulder, CO: Westview Press.

Shotter, J. and Gergen, K. (eds.) (1989) *Texts of Identity*. London: Sage.

Shrader-Frechette, K. S. (1991) *Risk and Rationality: Philosophical Foundations for Populist Reforms*. Berkeley and Los Angeles: University of California Press.
(1993) "Risk methodology and institutional bias." *Research in Social Problems and Public Policy*, 5: 207–223.

Siegrist, M. and Cvetkovich, G. (2000) "Perception of hazards: the role of social trust and knowledge." *Risk Analysis*, 20: 713–720.

Siegrist, M., Cvetkovich, G., and Roth, C. (2000) "Salient value similarity, social trust and risk/benefit perception." *Risk Analysis*, 20: 353–362.

Silverman, D. (1985) *Qualitative Methodology and Sociology*. Aldershot: Gower.
(1993) *Interpreting Qualitative Data: Methods for Analysing Talk, Text and Interaction*. London: Sage.

Simon, S. L. and Graham, J. C. (1997) "Findings of the first comprehensive radiological monitoring program of the Republic of the Marshall Islands." *Health Physics*, 73: 68–85.

Sinclair, M. (nd) "Dry cask fact sheets," mimeo. Midland, MI: Don't Waste Michigan.

Singer, E. and Endreny, P. M. (1993) *Reporting on Risk: How the Mass Media Portray Accidents, Diseases, Disasters, and other Hazards.* New York: Russell Sage Foundation.

Sjöberg, L. (1997) "Explaining risk perception: an empirical evaluation of cultural theory." *Risk Decision and Policy*, 2: 113–130.

—— (1999) "Risk perception in Western Europe." *Ambio*, 28: 555–568.

Sjöberg, L., Jansson, B., Brenot, J., Frewer, L. J., Prades, A., and Tonnessen, A. (1999) *Risk Perception in Commemoration of Chernobyl: A Cross-National Study*. Report submitted to the European Commission. Stockholm: Centre for Risk Research, Stockholm School of Economics.

Slovic, P. (1987) "Perception of risk." *Science*, 236: 280–285.

—— (1992) "Perception of risk: reflections on the psychometric paradigm" in S. Krimsky and D. Golding (eds.) *Social Theories of Risk*. Westport, CT: Praeger, pp. 117–152.

—— (1993) "Perceived risk, trust, and democracy: a systems perspective." *Risk Analysis*, 13(6): 675–682.

—— (1998) "The risk game." *Reliability Engineering and System Safety*, 59: 73–77.

—— (2000) *The Perception of Risk*. London: Earthscan.

—— (2002) "Terrorism as hazard: a new species of trouble." *Risk Analysis*, 22: 425–426.

Slovic, P., Finucane, M., Peters, E., and MacGregor, D. G. (2002) "The affect heuristic" in T. Gilovich, D. Griffin, and D. Kahneman (eds.) *Heuristics and Biases: The Psychology of Intuitive Judgment*. New York: Cambridge University Press, pp. 397–420.

Slovic, P., Fischhoff, B., and Lichtenstein, S. (1980) "Facts and fears: understanding perceived risk" in R. Schwing and W. Albers (eds.) *Societal Risk Assessment: How Safe is Safe Enough?* New York: Plenum Press, pp. 181–214.

Slovic, P., Flynn, J., and Gregory, R. (1994) "Stigma happens: social problems in the siting of nuclear waste facilities." *Risk Analysis*, 14(5): 773–777.

Slovic, P., Flynn, J., and Layman, M. (1991) "Perceived risk, trust, and the politics of nuclear waste." *Science*, 254: 1603–1607.

Slovic, P., Flynn, J., Mertz, C. K., Poumadère, M., and Mays, C. (2000) "Nuclear power and the public: a comparative study of risk perception in France and the United States" in O. Renn and B. Rohrmann (eds.) *Cross-Cultural Risk Perception: a Survey of Empirical Studies*. Amsterdam: Kluwer Academic Press, pp. 55–102.

Slovic, P., Layman, M., Kraus, N., Flynn, J., Chalmers, J., and Gesell, G. (1991) "Perceived risk, stigma, and potential economic impacts of a high-level nuclear waste repository in Nevada." *Risk Analysis*, 11: 683–696.

Slovic, P., Lichtenstein, S., and Fischhoff, B. (1984) "Modeling the societal impact of fatal accidents." *Management Science*, 30: 464–474.

Slovic, P. and MacGregor, D. (1994) *The Social Context of Risk Communication* (Report). Eugene, Oregon: Decision Research.

Slovic, P. and Peters, E. (1998) "The importance of worldviews in risk perception." *Risk Decision and Policy*, 3(2): 165–170.

Smith, A. (ed.) (1974) *British Broadcasting.* Newton Abbot: David and Charles.

Smith, D. and McCloskey, J. (1998) "Risk communication and the social amplification of public sector risk." *Public Money and Management*, 18: 41–45.

Smith, H. (1986) *The Religions of Man.* New York: Harper.

Southwood, R. (1989) *Report of the Working Party on Bovine Spongiform Encephalopathy.* London: HMSO.

Spector, M. and Kitsuse, J. (1987) *Constructing Social Problems.* New York: Aldine de Gruyter.

Speller, G. and Sime, J. (1993) "Anticipating environmental change: the relocation of a village and its psycho-social consequences." *People and Physical Environment Research: The Australian and New Zealand Journal of Person-Environment Studies*, 43: 1–18.

Stallen, P.-J. M. and Tomas, A. (1988) "Public concern about industrial hazards." *Risk Analysis*, 8: 237–245.

St. Clair, J. (1999) "The legacy of America's largest nuclear test." *In These Times* (8 August 1999): 21–23.

Stenehjem, M. (1990) "Indecent exposure." *Natural History* (September 1990): 6–22.

Stern, P. C. and Fineberg, H. V. (eds.) (1996) *Understanding Risk: Informing Decisions in a Democratic Society.* Report for National Research Council, Committee on Risk Characterization. Washington, DC: National Academy Press.

Stirling, A. (1999) *Science and Precaution in the Management of Technological Risk.* Final report of a project for the EC Forward Studies Unit. Brighton: University of Sussex, SPRU.

Stone, C. N. (1989) *Regime Politics: Governing Atlanta, 1946–1988.* Lawrence, Kansas: University Press of Kansas.

Strauss, P. and Kelsey, J. (1991) "State regulation of decommissioning." *The Energy Journal*, 12. Washington, DC: International Association for Energy Economics, pp. 55–72.

Suedfeld, P., and Tetlock, P. E. (1992) "Psychological advice about political decision making: heuristics, biases, and cognitive defects" in P. Suedfeld and P. E. Tetlock (eds.) *Psychology and Social Policy.* New York: Hemisphere, pp. 51–70.

Sunstein, C. R. (1990) "Paradoxes of the regulatory state." *University of Chicago Law Review*, 57(2): 407–441.

(1997) *Free Markets and Social Justice.* New York: Oxford University Press.

Svenson, O. (1988a) "Managing product hazards at Volvo Car Corporation" in R. E. Kasperson, J. X. Kasperson, C. Hohenemser, and R. W. Kates (eds.) *Corporate Management of Health and Safety Hazards: A Comparison of Current Practice.* Boulder, CO: Westview, pp. 57–78.

(1988b) "Mental models of risk communication and action: reflections on social amplification of risk." *Risk Analysis*, 8(2): 199–200.

Taggart, P. (2000) *Populism.* Milton Keynes: The Open University Press.

Tetlock, P. E. (1997) "An alternative metaphor in the study of judgment and choice: people as politicians" in W. Goldstein and R. Hogarth (eds.) *Research on Judgment and Decision Making: Currents, Connections and Controversies.* New York: Cambridge University Press, pp. 657–680.

Thompson, K. (1998) *Moral Panics.* London: Routledge.

Thrift, N. (1985) "Flies and germs: a geography of knowledge" in D. Gregory and J. Urry (eds.) *Social Relations and Spatial Structures.* Basingstoke: Macmillan, pp. 366–403.

Timmerman, P. (1986) "The risk puzzle: some thoughts." *Ethics and Energy,* 6: 1–2.

Titus, C. (1986) *Bombs in the Backyard: Atomic Testing and American Politics.* Reno: University of Nevada Press.

Toulmin, S. (1953) *The Philosophy of Science.* London: Hutchinson.

Trumbo, C. W. (1996) "Examining psychometrics and polarisation in a single-risk case study." *Risk Analysis,* 16: 429–438.

Turner, B. A. (1978) *Man-Made Disasters: The Failure of Foresight.* London: Wykeham.

(1994) "Causes of disaster: sloppy management." *British Journal of Management,* 5(3): 215–220.

Turner, B. A. and Pidgeon, N. F. (1997) *Man-Made Disasters,* 2nd edition. Oxford: Butterworth-Heinemann.

Turney, J. (1998) *Frankenstein's Footsteps: Science, Genetics and Popular Culture.* New Haven: Yale University Press.

Tversky, A. and Kahneman, D. (1974) "Judgement under uncertainty: heuristics and biases." *Science,* 185: 1124–1131.

(1982) "Judgments of and by representativeness" in D. Kahneman, P. Slovic, and A. Tversky (eds.) *Judgment Under Uncertainty: Heuristics and Biases.* Cambridge: Cambridge University Press, pp. 84–98.

(1986) "Rational choice and the framing of decisions." *Journal of Business,* 59: 251–278.

Tyler, T. R. and Boeckmann, R. J. (1997) "Three strikes and you're out, but why? The psychology of public support for punishing rule breakers." *Law and Society Review,* 31(2): 237–265.

Udall, S. (1994) *The Myths of August: A Personal Exploration of Our Tragic Cold War Affair with the Atom.* New York: Pantheon Books.

Umweltbundesamt (UBA) (1999) *Jahresbericht 1998.* Berlin: UBA.

UNAIDS (2000) *Report on the Global HIV/AIDS Epidemic.* New York: UNAIDS.

United Kingdom Cabinet Office (2002) *Risk: Improving Government's Capability to Handle Risk and Uncertainty.* London: Cabinet Office Strategy Unit.

United Kingdom Interdepartmental Liaison Group on Risk Assessment (1998a) *Risk Assessment and Risk Management: Improving Policy and Practice within Government Departments.* London: Health and Safety Executive.

United Kingdom Interdepartmental Liaison Group on Risk Assessment (1998b) *Risk Communication: A Guide to Regulatory Practice.* London: Health and Safety Executive.

United Kingdom National Radiological Protection Board (2000) Independent Expert Group on Mobile Phones *Mobile Phones and Health.* Chilton, Oxon: NRPB. (www.iegmp.org.uk/)

United States Environmental Protection Agency (1987) *Unfinished Business: A Comparative Assessment of Environmental Problems.* Washington, DC: EPA.

(1998) *Institutional Controls: A Reference Manual*. Washington, DC: EPA Draft Report.

United States General Accounting Office (1987) *Nuclear Waste: Status of DOE's Nuclear Waste Site Characterization Activities*, GAO/RCED-87-103FS. Washington, DC: GAO.

(1988a) *Nuclear Waste: Repository Work Should Not Proceed Until Quality Assurance is Adequate*, GAO/RCED-88-159. Washington, DC: GAO.

(1988b) *Nuclear Waste: Quarterly Report on DOE's Nuclear Waste Program as of September 30, 1987* GAO/RCED-88-56FS. Washington, DC: GAO.

(1989) *Nuclear Health and Safety: Savannah River's Unusual Occurrence Reporting Program Has Been Ineffective*. Washington, DC: GAO.

(1990a) *Shippingport Decommissioning – How Applicable Are the Lessons Learned?* GAO/RCED–90-208. Washington, DC: GAO.

(1990b) *Usefulness of Information from Shippingport Decommissioning for Rancho Seco*, GAO/RCED–90-171. Washington, DC: GAO.

(1991) *Hanford Single-Shell Tank Leaks Greater than Estimated*, GAO/RCED–91-1770. Washington, DC: GAO.

(1993) *Nuclear Waste: Hanford Tank Waste Program Needs Cost, Schedule, and Management Changes*. Washington, DC: GAO.

(1995) *Uranium Mill Tailings: Cleanup Continues, but Future Costs are Uncertain*, GAO/RCED–96-37. Washington, DC: GAO.

(1996) *Nuclear Waste: Management and Technical Problems Continue to Delay Characterizing Hanford's Tank Waste*. Washington, DC: GAO.

United States Nuclear Regulatory Commission (1997), *NRC Information Digest: 1997 Edition*, NUREG–1350, vol. 9. Washington, DC: US Nuclear Regulatory Commission.

United States Office of Technology Assessment (1991) *Complex Cleanup: The Environmental Legacy of Nuclear Weapons Production*. Washington, DC: US Government Printing Office.

Urry, J. (1995) *Consuming Places*. London: Routledge.

Vaughan, D. (1990) "Autonomy, interdependence, and social control: NASA and the space shuttle Challenger." *Administrative Science Quarterly*, 35: 225–257.

(1992) "Regulating risk: implications of the Challenger accident" in J. F. Short, Jr. and L. Clarke (eds.) *Organizations, Uncertainties, and Risk*. Boulder, CO: Westview, pp. 235–254.

(1996) *The Challenger Launch Decision: Risky Technology, Culture, and Deviance at NASA*. Chicago: University of Chicago Press.

Vaughan, E. (1995) "The significance of socioeconomic and ethnic diversity for the risk communication process." *Risk Analysis*, 15(2): 169–180.

Vaughan, E. and Seifert, M. (1992) "Variability in the framing of risk issues." *Journal of Social Issues*, 48(4): 119–135.

Vlek, C. J. H. and Stallen, P.-J. M. (1981) "Judging risk and benefit in the small and in the large." *Organizational Behavior and Human Performance*, 28: 235–271.

von Klitzing, L. (1995) "Low-frequency pulsed electromagnetic fields influence EEG of man." *Physica Medica*, 11: 77–78.

Vorwerk, V. and Kämper, E. (1997) *Evaluation der 3. Phase des Bürgerbete-iligungsverfahrens in der Region Nordschwarzwald. Akademie für Technikfolgen-abschätzung Working Report No. 70.* Stuttgart: Akademie für Technikfolgen-abschätzung.

Wåhlberg, A. (2001) "The theoretical features of some current approaches to risk perception." *Journal of Risk Research,* 4: 237–250.

Walker, G., Simmons, P., Wynne, B., and Irwin, A. (1998) *Public Perception of Risks Associated with Major Accident Hazards.* Sudbury: Health and Safety Executive Books.

Walker, H. A. and Cohen, B. P. (1985) "Scope statements: imperatives for eval-uating theory." *American Sociological Review,* 50: 288–301.

Walker, J. (1992) *Containing the Atom: Nuclear Regulation in a Changing Environ-ment 1963–1971.* Berkeley: University of California Press.

Ward, P. (1998) "Myths and misunderstanding" in J. Jones (ed.), *The Impact of New Treatments on HIV Prevention.* London: THT, pp. 36–45.

Weart, S. (1988) *Nuclear Fear: A History of Images.* Cambridge, MA: Harvard University Press.

Weber, M. (1946) "Science as a vocation" in H. H. Gerth and C. W. Mills (trans. and eds.) *From Max Weber: Essays in Sociology.* New York: Oxford University Press, pp. 129–156.

Webler, T. (1995) " 'Right' discourse in citizen participation. An evaluative yardstick" in O. Renn, T. Webler, and P. Wiedemann (eds.) *Fairness and Competence in Citizen Participation. Evaluating New Models for Environmental Discourse.* Dordrecht: Kluwer Academic Press, pp. 35–86.

Weick, K. E. (1987) "Organizational culture as a source of high reliability." *California Management Review,* 29(2): 112–127.

Weingart, J. (2001) *Waste is a Terrible Thing to Mind: Risk, Radiation, and Distrust of Government.* Princeton, NJ: Center for Analysis of Public Issues.

Weiss, J. A. and Tschirhart, M. (1994) "Public information campaigns as policy instruments." *Journal of Policy Analysis and Management,* 13(1): 82–119.

Wellings, K., Orton, S., and Samuels, J. (1988) *Evaluation of the HEA Public Education Campaign, February–June 1988.* London: HEA.

Wellock, T. R. (1998) *Critical Masses: Opposition to Nuclear Power in California, 1958–1978.* Madison: University of Wisconsin Press.

Welsom, E. (1999) *The Plutonium Files.* New York: The Dial Press.

Wiedemann, P. M., Carius, R., Henschel, C., Kastenholz, H., Nothdurft, W., Ruff, F., and Uth, H. J. (2000) *Risikokommunikation für Unternehmen – Man-ual.* Düsseldorf: VDI-Verlag.

Wiedemann, P. M. and Schütz, H. (2000) "Risk story and risk perception." Paper presented at the SRA Conference, December, Washington, DC.

Wilcox, D. F. (1900) "The American newspaper: a study in social psychology." *Annals of the American Academy of Political and Social Sciences,* 16 July: 56–92.

Wilkins, L. (1987) *Shared Vulnerability: The Media and the American Perspective on the Bhopal Disaster.* Westport, CT: Greenwood Press.

Wilkins, L. and Patterson, P. (1991) *Risky Business: Communication Issues of Science, Risk and Public Policy.* Westport, CT: Greenwood Press.

Williams, B. A. and Matheny, A. R. (1995) *Democracy, Dialogue, and Environmen-tal Disputes: The Contested Languages of Social Regulation.* New Haven, CT: Yale University Press.

Williams, J. (1999) "Nuclear Solutions." *Forum for Applied Research and Public Policy*, 14(2): 103–107.

Wilson, J. Q. (1980) "The politics of regulation" in J. Q. Wilson (ed.) *The Politics of Regulation*. New York: Basic Books, pp. 357–394.

Wilson, R. and Crouch, E. (1982) *Risk/Benefit Analysis*. Cambridge, MA: Ballinger Publishing Co.

Wittgenstein, L. (1958) *Philosophical Investigations*, 2nd edition. Oxford: Basil Blackwell.

Wojcik, D. (1997) *The End of the World as We Know It*. New York: University Press.

Woolgar, S. (1988) *Science: The Very Idea*. London: Ellis Horwood.

Worcester, R. M. (1999) "Seeking consensus on contentious scientific issues: science and democracy." Paper presented to the Foundation for Science and Technology, 12 July, The Royal Society, London.

Wynne, B. (1982) "Institutional mythologies and dual societies in the management of risk" in H. Kunreuther and E. Ley (eds.) *The Risk Analysis Controversy: an Institutional Perspective*. Berlin: Springer Verlag, pp. 127–143.

(1987) *Risk Management and Hazardous Wastes: Implementation and the Dialectics of Credibility*. Berlin: Springer Verlag.

(1989) "Sheepfarming after Chernobyl." *Environment*, 31: 11–15, 33–39.

(1992a) "Risk and social learning: reification to engagement" in S. Krimsky and D. Golding (eds.) *Social Theories of Risk*. Westport CT: Praeger, pp. 275–297.

(1992b) "Uncertainty and environmental learning. Reconceiving science and policy in the preventative paradigm." *Global Environment Change*, June: 111–127.

(1992c) "Misunderstood misunderstandings: social identities and public uptake of science." *Public Understanding of Science*, 1: 281–304.

(1995) "Public understanding of science" in S. Jasanoff, G. Markle, J. Petersen, and T. Pinch (eds.) *Handbook of Science and Technology Studies*. Thousand Oaks California: Sage, pp. 361–388.

(1996) "May the sheep safely graze? A reflexive view of the expert–lay knowledge divide" in S. Lash, B. Szerszynski, and B. Wynne (eds.) *Risk, Environment and Modernity: Towards a New Ecology*. London: Sage, pp. 44–83.

Zeus Institute for Applied Psychology, Environmental and Social Research, and IPSOS (2000) *Sozialwissenschaftliche Erhebung zur Lärmbelästigung der Bevölkerung in Baden-Württemberg*. Final Report to the Environmental Agency of the State Environmental Ministry of Baden-Württemberg. Project No. 1010/53478/33-90003913. Karlsruhe: LfU.

Zinberg, D. S. (1984) "Public participation in nuclear waste management policy: a brief historical overview" in W. R. Freudenburg and E. A. Rosa (eds.) *Public Reactions to Nuclear Power: Are There Critical Masses?* Boulder, CO: American Association for the Advancement of Sciences / Westview, pp. 233–253.

Zonabend, F. (1993) *The Nuclear Peninsula*. Cambridge: Editions de la Maison des Sciences de l'Homme / Cambridge University Press.

Index